# International Development

**David Stoesz**

*Virginia Commonwealth University*

**Charles Guzzetta**

*Hunter College of the City University of New York*

**Mark Lusk**

*The University of Montana*

**Allyn and Bacon**

Boston ■ London ■ Toronto ■ Sydney ■ Tokyo ■ Singapore

*To A. D. and Roy Stoesz, explorers both*    *D. S.*

*To J. Richmond Barbour and Mary Cunningham*    *C. G.*

*To Florene M. Lusk*    *M. L.*

**Series Editor, Social Work and Family Therapy:**   Judy Fifer
**Editor in Chief, Social Sciences:**   Karen Hanson
**Editorial Assistant:**   Jennifer Muroff
**Marketing Manager:**   Susan E. Ogar
**Editorial Production Service:**   Marbern House
**Manufacturing Buyer:**   David Repetto
**Cover Administrator:**   Jennifer Hart

Copyright © 1999 by Allyn & Bacon
A Viacom Company
160 Gould Street
Needham Heights, MA 02494

Internet: www.abacon.com

**Library of Congress Cataloging-in-Publication Data**
Stoesz, David
    International development / David Stoesz, Charles Guzzetta, Mark Lusk
        p.   cm.
    Includes bibliographical references and index.
    ISBN 0–205–26470–0
    1. Economic Development   I. Guzzetta, Charles.   II. Lusk, Mark
W., 1949–   .   III. Title
HD75.S785   1998
338.91–dc21                                        98-21668
                                                    CIP

**Photo Credits:** Page 173: James L. Stanfield/National Geographic Image Collection; 179: Superstock; 186, 189: Kevin Eilbeck, Natural Light Studio, Rapid City, SD; 205, 206: courtesy of the author; 210: courtesy of the Grameen Foundation, Washington, D.C.

Printed in the United States of America

10  9  8  7  6  5  4  3  2  1     03  02  01  00  99  98

# CONTENTS

# FOREWORD

**Katherine A. Kendall, Honorary President**

*International Association of Schools of Social Work*

On the cusp of a new millennium, it is timely and appropriate to take a comprehensive and critical look at international development. What has it accomplished in the twentieth century? What form should it take in the twenty-first? Answers abound in this text, which, going far beyond a new look, projects a new vision. David Stoesz, Charles Guzzetta, and Mark Lusk are scholars with deep knowledge of the subject, having had extensive field experience in Southeast Asia, sub-Saharan Africa, Eastern Europe, Latin America, and the former USSR. This combination of experience and erudition has produced a volume that may well be the most inclusive treatment of international development currently available. As a text or guide for all those in the various disciplines and professions involved in this field, it should prove invaluable.

International development is seen as one of the most pressing human welfare issues of the day. Despite the enormous strides that have been made since World War II in life expectancy, reduced infant mortality, nutrition, annual income, and education, the process of development has left untouched millions of people who live in absolute poverty. In a speech in May, 1997, James D. Wolfensohn, president of the World Bank, painted this stark picture: "[T]he fact is that today 3 billion of the 4.7 billion who live in the developing world live on less than $2 a day; 1.3 billion live on less than $1 a day; 1.3 billion do not have clean water; 150 million children do not go to school; 40,000 children die every day because of hunger-related diseases; and 50 million children are mentally or physically damaged because of improper or inadequate nutrition. This world, the world of 4.7 billion people, is not a world that we can turn our backs on."

International agencies, including the World Bank and the United Nations, frequently cite the reduction of poverty as a principal objective of international development. A concrete step in that direction was taken by the Organisation for Economic Cooperation and Development (OECD) in May, 1996, when it endorsed a report of its Development Assistance Committee (DAC) that outlined goals for twenty-first century. Central to these goals was a global effort to reduce by the year 2015 at least one-half the proportion of people living in extreme poverty. The goals also included universal primary education in all countries by 2015, assurance of gender equality in primary and secondary schools by 2005, stated reductions in infant, child, and maternal mortality rates by 2015, and ready access to safe and reliable methods of family planning by 2015. This is to be done through people-centered development.

People-centered development is the central message of *International Development*. It is not its purpose to disparage development, but to redefine it. What emerges is an amalgam of economic, social, and sustainable development with appropriate concern for growth with equity, basic human needs, human rights, and preservation of the planet for posterity. The limitations of the economic model; as typified by grand-scale, industrial infrastructure projects financed by international aid, are well-defined. The trickle-down policies of international aid have not had a positive effect on the quality of life of the millions of people who live in the absolute poverty described above. Nor have the benefits of the modern era—democracy, universal education, equality of the sexes, free markets, and constitutional government—reached a significant number of people.

The problems to be resolved are complex. Oligarchical regimes, closed markets, and reactionary governments remain realities to be taken into account in crafting new strategies. So, also, are underdeveloped social and physical infrastructure as a result of excess spending on the military. The environment has so recently come on to the development agenda that it will take decades to reverse the pattern of excess consumption of natural resources as the means of production.

However, rather than focusing on past and present problems in the management of international aid or on the protracted misery of the developing world, the text presents a hopeful outlook on the prospects of international development. As seen in the contents, the authors have adopted an all-inclusive approach that will enable readers to move along with them toward their vision of what is needed for the twenty-first century. They begin with a wealth of information about the developing world, continue with penetrating analyses of the strategies of development, offer case studies to illuminate problems and progress, and, finally, put forward their proposal for integrative development that incorporates economic and social components along with sustainability.

A journey through the text offers interesting and surprising insights. The chapter on "The Missionaries," for example, highlights the difference between effective and ineffective methods of working with people of other lands and other cultures. How an outsider becomes an insider who understands and respects "the others" is a lesson that everyone carrying out projects in the field of development should learn. The outsiders who learned the language, understood the culture, and identified with the aspirations of the people became the insiders who achieved the purposes of their mission.

Likewise, in looking historically at different strategies of development, the authors describe the social, philosophical, and political context of economic development, the relation of a basic-needs approach to social development and to many different forms of community development. They note the significance of nongovernmental organizations (NGOs) and what they call the *Third Sector* in defining how international development may proceed in the new millennium. In case studies of people-centered development in Latin America, Eastern Europe, Africa, and Asia, a picture emerges of a vast network of organizations (35,000 NGOs operate in the Third World) concerned with a wide range of social benefits related to health, education, housing, and anti-poverty programs.

Significant among the case illustrations is the incredible success of the Grameen Bank, which pioneered the microcredit movement in Bangladesh. This microeconomic strategy has erupted on the international development scene as one of the most interesting innovations now available in the struggle to eradicate poverty. The extension of small loans to the poorest families, particularly to women, has indeed helped many borrowers to become self-sufficient.

Converted to the benefit of grass-roots capitalization programs designed for the poor, the World Bank, USAID, and other governmental agencies have taken up the cause alongside NGOs and other private organizations. This has had a salutary effect on the status of women. As the major beneficiaries of the microcredit movement, women are empowered not only to generate income, but to see themselves as worthy of respect and on a parity with men as wage earners. They become aware of the value of education for their children, a more healthful diet, family planning, numerous other social benefits, and even political participation. With gender equity in development programs one of the questions that remains largely unaddressed in many parts of the world, it is helpful to find consideration of this issue carefully explored in a number of chapters.

The authors give full recognition to the shortcomings of even the most significant movements sponsored by the private sector. It is difficult to think of the long-range aspirations of micro-economic strategies as anything but modest. Opportunities of all kinds are still denied to large numbers of women, particularly in rural areas and in societies where religion rigidly orders women's lives. Even primary education is not available to girls in many parts of the world. In countries with little or no tradition of a civil society, local empowerment can lead to corruption instead of development. Nonprofits need latitude to operate, which can put them on a collision course with autocratic governments. And, of course, the sheer magnitude of the problems to be addressed almost defies comprehension.

Nevertheless, the authors present a reasoned optimism about the prospects of international development. They recognize its complexity as reflected in its successes, its failures, and its shortcomings. They note the significance of the globalization of democracy, markets, and culture and, at the same time, mark the uneven commitment to democratic principles, especially individual freedoms. While global capitalism may have improved the world's standard of living, there are still vast areas in the countries of the southern hemisphere that remain cut off from the modern world. Successful development may also have unforeseen and certainly unwanted consequences. UNICEF immunization and oral rehydration programs have saved the lives of millions of children, but the authors point out that the children saved may have lives worse than death because of famine, war, and exploitation.

In proposing an integrative model of development, the authors express their belief in what they describe as "a thoughtful, humane, and Earth-friendly process." They are optimistic that such a model can succeed, perhaps in part because of the extent to which certain social movements have been effective in influencing public policy. Increasing attention has been given to social development as a response to exclusive or excessive reliance on economic growth as the solution to problems of poverty. The basic-needs approach to development has also been widely accepted. This approach measures the success of development by the extent of its success in meeting such human needs as food, shelter, sanitation, clean water, basic education, and health. Environmentalists and their allies have raised public awareness of the need to curtail population growth and to carry out conservation measures to protect natural resources for the benefit of future generations.

The women's movement has called attention, with considerable success, to the failure of donor countries and international organizations to adequately integrate women into the development process. Until the U.N. Decade for Women (1976–1985), the economic contributions of women in the Third World were largely overlooked. Rural women in

Africa and parts of Asia do more work than men in agriculture and, as already noted, women are the major beneficiaries of the microcredit movement. Some progress has been made in addressing the crucial role of women in development projects. However, women still lose out because of the problems in making microcredit a truly global vehicle for development. The authors note, in their concluding chapter, how an opportunity to integrate microcredit institutions with the network of world capitalism was bypassed when the enormous bail-out packages of the International Monetary Fund to nations in Southeast Asia failed to include them.

We have seen in this informative account of international development how much has been achieved in the twentieth century and how very much more remains to be done in the twenty-first. The integrative model of development that emerges from the various chapters provides an excellent guide for progress in the approaching millennium. It includes the social as well as economic dimensions of development, with full attention to basic human needs, and serious consideration of the environment, women, and cultural minorities. More elaborate models may be proposed, but, as the authors conclude in their final paragraph, the ultimate purpose of development is "to enhance the human condition in a sustainable manner, respecting human rights and cultural practices. In the end, development is less arcane than it is a matter of simply embracing human dignity."

# PREFACE

Anticipating the twenty-first century is cause for reflection on the course of world development. The last decades of this century have witnessed profound changes in human relations around the globe. The end of the Cold War not only interred Communism as a viable political economy, it also coincided with the expansion of global capitalism. Eventually, the "new world order" would highlight the role of international organizations, particularly the United Nations and the International Monetary Fund, as the nations of the world struggled to contend with demands associated with poverty, ethnic strife, and corruption. As the visibility of international agencies increased, the role of the nation-state retreated. But leading international organizations evinced problems of their own—the highly bureaucratized UN and the poverty-exacerbating consequences of IMF debt restructuring policies being the most prominent. While attention was focused on UN and IMF efforts to resolve major disputes such as the so-called ethnic cleansing in Bosnia and the debt crisis affecting Latin America, Africa, and Southeast Asia, a constellation of NonGovernmental Organizations (NGOs) assumed more of the development burden.

Despite the expanded cast of actors in the drama of international development, questions remained about their capacity to address *old* problems that had plagued mankind for centuries, let alone *new* problems that followed industrialization. Unprecedented advances in technology have alleviated some problems (satellite weather mapping has helped minimize the results of natural disasters) at the same time it has aggravated others. For example, international currency transactions can destabilize a developing nation's economy within a matter of hours. Computer-assisted information systems have accelerated the evolution of industrialized nations into the post-industrial age, and the prospect of extensive genetic engineering is not far behind. Development per se has been preoccupied with issues that are earthbound. As the cover of the book suggests, the context of global issues, daunting as these may be, recedes in direct proportion to the geometric expansion of knowledge about the universe, the scale of which is often beyond comprehension.

These phenomena have immediate and profound implications for international development. Foremost, they challenge the imagination of development thinkers. Traditional categories for classifying the development of nations have collapsed under the weight of anomalies that have emerged during recent decades. The old scheme that featured a capitalist First World contending with a communist Second World over an emerging Third World is no more, even if the labels have not yet expired. Three decades after winning independence from imperial Europe, many nations of sub-Saharan Africa and Southeast Asia exhibit indicators that reveal *negative* development, that is, the current generation is worse off than those before. That a Fourth World of backward nations should appear and then continue to regress is nothing less than a betrayal of all that the human enterprise has accomplished in its relatively brief existence on Earth.

In recognition that development is neither uniform nor unilinear, development scholars have coined the term *distorted development*[1] to describe how nations elect paths that deny opportunities to people, suppress their aspirations, and sometimes even attempt to extinguish entire populations. Distorted development has a long, if tragic, history, evident in the genocide of the Holocaust, the killing fields of Cambodia, the mass executions of Burundi and Rwanda, the widespread pollution that accompanies industrialization in the former Soviet Union, and the deforestation that is rapidly consuming tropical forests around the world.

In contrast, development at its best has expanded the futures of people, inspired them to value and uplift one another, eventually constructing communities of collaboration. Fortunately, *transcendent development* also has a long history: the "green revolution" that saved millions of Asians from famine, the literacy and sanitation programs that have prevented the deaths of millions of children due to water-born parasites, and the rapid spread of microcredit that has offered poor women the prospect of economic security serve as illustrations. As the label suggests, *transcendent development* contributes directly to human prosperity and happiness, while it addresses the miseries associated with poverty and discrimination.

Developing nations choose between these two forms of development according to the policies they adopt. All too often, policies that result in distorted development crowd out those that might generate transcendent development. In May 1998, for example, India and Pakistan initiated an unprecedented arms-race within the Third World by exploding nuclear bombs. The prospects of nuclear warfare among these two nations are as frightening as the opportunities lost are dismaying. As this illustration attests, much of the development challenge is to avert the travesty of distorted development in order to pursue the virtues of transcendent development.

*International Development* is divided into four parts. The first gives an overview of the primary development regions: Asia, Latin America, Africa, and Eastern Europe. The second part provides a summary of the primary developmental approaches that have emerged over the decades, initially promoted by missionaries, later evolving into specific schools of thought focusing on economic development, community development, and sustainable development. In the third part, case studies of Nowa Huta, First Nations Development Institute, Habitat for Humanity, and the Grameen Development Bank illustrate actual development problems encountered in the field and the varying success of the efforts to solve them. In part four, the book concludes with a discussion of the relative development of the nations of the world as well as an integrated model of development.

As is the case with all projects as ambitious as this one, authorship is only the most visible indication of input. We want to thank colleagues who reviewed the manuscript and provided cogent suggestions: Richard J. Estes of the University of Pennsylvania, Mukunda Rao of West Virginia University, Satish Sharma of the University of Nevada at Las Vegas, and Robert P. Scheurell of the University of Wisconsin at Milwaukee. We owe a special thanks to Edgar Stoesz for his extensive connections and the Samuel Wurtzel Endowment, which contributed substantively to the project. In facilitating the manuscript through production, Judy Fifer proved an exemplary editor; Marjorie Payne and Sandy Kramer were patient and tactful in helping us tie-up what seemed to be an infinite number of loose ends.

Given the feed-back facilitated by information technology, we invite readers' comments and questions. Our e-mail addresses are

dstoesz@saturn.vcu.edu
cguzzett@shiva.hunter.cuny.edu
mlusk@selway.umt.edu

# Reference

1. James Midgley, *Social Development* (Thousand Oaks, CA: SAGE, 1997).

# 1 Asia: Awakening Giants

*It is monstrous in barbarians [Europeans] to attempt to improve the inhabitants of the Celestial [Chinese] Empire when they are so miserably deficient themselves. Thus, introducing a poisonous drug [opium] for their own benefit and to the injury of others, they are deficient in benevolence. Sending their fleets and armies to rob other nations, they can make no pretense at rectitude...How can they expect to renovate others? They allow the rich and noble to enter office without passing through the literary examinations, and do not open the road to advancement to the poorest and meanest in the land. From this it appears that foreigners are inferior to the Chinese and therefore must be unfit to instruct them.*

—G. W. Cooke, *Times* special correspondent to China, 1857–1858

No region presents greater paradoxes for international development than Asia. Half of the world's poor reside in Asia; yet, after the United States, the six next-largest economies are there (Brzezinski, 1997: 50). Asia's nascent economies could rival the present industrial powers of Europe and North America within a century if their present growth trajectories continue. Asia is the home of the world's largest democracy, India, as well as the world's largest Communist nation, the Peoples Republic of China. Both nations have baffled development experts, and for good reason.

Despite its origin with the United Nations, international development has been profoundly influenced by Western ideas that have arisen with industrialization. Few Westerners recognize that during the Dark Ages of pre-Enlightenment Europe, both India and China boasted of empires so advanced that the first European "discoverers" were dismissed as coarse, smelly, and ignorant primitives. Yet, within two centuries the dominance of Asian civilization over squalid Europe would be reversed; the glories of ancient India and China would vanish—casualties of internal conflict, population growth that outstripped agricultural production, and the insatiable appetite of predatory colonists for the riches of the East. Colonization on the part of European nations and Japan, compounded by the Second World War, and regional warfare have further retarded the development of continental Asia. Approaching the second millennium (another Western convention), prospects for Asian

2 CHAPTER 1

development are so disparate as to suggest the reassertion of its global hegemony at the same time hundreds of millions of Asians suffer from the most grinding poverty.

## Historical Background

The history of Asia is dominated by Indian and Chinese cultures that achieved unprecedented levels of prosperity and sophistication. Yet, Indian and Chinese cultures evolved independent of one another, largely as a result of the geographic barrier posed by the Himalayas. Until the colonial era, the influence of Europeans was negligible. Following the collapse of Imperial Rome, Europe regressed to the Dark Ages, while India and China rose to even higher levels of culture. Essentially self-sufficient, pre-colonial India and China had little reason to trade with the West until the British East India Company cajoled Indians, then forced the Chinese, into commercial relations.

Prehistoric civilizations of Asia evolved independently. Distinctively Indian culture can be traced to the Tigris-Euphrates River civilizations, which introduced irrigated agriculture, the first written texts, and metallurgy. By 3000 B.C., comparable civilizations had been established in the Indus River valley of present-day Pakistan as well as the Ganges River valley in India. From this origin, India boasts of the world's longest continuing culture. Neolithic Chinese culture, on the other hand, originates from northern Asia and has been dated to 8000 B.C. By 1500 B.C., the first literate, city-building, metalworking civilization was established as the Shang dynasty (Murphey, 1996: 6–16).

### India

Indus River civilization was built from the surplus wheat that was cultivated in the fertile flood plain. Cities were planned, wells strategically located, and most houses had piped water, bathrooms, and waste drains. The peaceful Indus culture was shaken by the invasion of Aryans from the North in about 2000 B.C., an event that introduced Sanskrit, the mother language to modern English, in addition to more male-oriented and aggressive deities to early Hinduism. The invasion of Alexander the Great in 326 B.C. introduced minor Greek influences into the culture as well as the population, as he encouraged his 10,000 soldiers to take Indian wives. Subsequent Maurya and Gupta dynasties, while largely unknown in the West, were characterized by remarkable accomplishments. By the sixth century A.D., Gupta mathematicians were facile enough at decile-based mathematics to be able to compute square and cube roots, solve quadratic equations, understand the values of zero and infinity, and figure pi to the ninth decimal, to say nothing of other methods that lay the foundation for trigonometry, three-dimensional geometry, and calculus. Early Indian astronomers understood that the Earth orbited the Sun. Gupta dynasty physicians contrived a vaccination against smallpox, successfully completed cesarean sections, and practiced plastic surgery. For leisure, early Indians invented chess (Murphey, 1996: 42). Europeans would not claim these accomplishments until centuries later, often observing them transmitted by Arabs during the Crusades.

Medieval India was buffeted by many forces. Circa 1000 A.D., Islamic forces under the command of the Mahmud of Ghazni, the "Sword of Islam," laid waste to northern India, ordered the deaths of thousands of Buddhist and Hindu monks, and caused the destruction of universities and monasteries. Subsequently, the Islamic sultans were vanquished by Mongol invaders led by Tamerlane, who ordered the slaughter of Delhi's inhabitants. Southern India rebuffed Islamic raids from Delhi and established a new Hindu kingdom in 1336, which prospered from extensive trading with peoples of Southeast Asia. Benefiting from the surpluses afforded by intensive rice cultivation, Southeast Asians prospered, eventually establishing their own civilizations—noted for monumental architecture, notably the cities of Angkor constructed by the Khmer in present-day Cambodia (National Gallery of Art, 1997).

From 1526 until 1858, India was governed by a series of Mughal emperors. Akbar (1483–1530) brought the divergent Rajputs under his rule, uniting much of modern-day India. A remarkably passionate man, despite being epileptic and illiterate, Akbar was a patron of the arts, accepted Hindus into his court, was well-versed in poetry and philosophy, and took particular delight in landscaping that integrated stone architecture with bubbling fountains. The failure of the Muhgal emperors to assure stable transfer of power contributed to palace intrigue and bloodletting. Akbar was poisoned by a son, Jahangir ("world seizer") whose son, Shah Jahan, put to death several rivals so that he might claim the throne. Shah Jahan enjoyed an ostentatious court, including some 5000 concubines, and was a great patron of the arts. Nonetheless, he expressed concern for the poor, twice a year participating in a ceremony in which he sat on a scale, his weight balanced by gold and jewels that were subsequently distributed to the destitute (Smithsonian, 1997). The death of Shah Jahan's wife, who had given birth to 14 children, left him so dejected that he memorialized her by constructing the Taj Mahal. Later, Shah Jahan's favorite son was beheaded by a younger brother, Aurangzeb, who imprisoned their father until his death. For fifty years Aurangzeb exterminated his opponents in a reign of terror—targeting the majority Hindus—that fractured a culture once unified by Akbar. By this time, Portuguese traders and Jesuit missionaries had established themselves on the Indian coast, the prelude to British colonization (Murphey, 1996: ch. 8).

Initially, British colonization of India was less an invasion and more a product of strategic trading concessions. Keen interest in Asia had been generated by Marco Polo's return from India and China in 1293, but the precocious explorer's reports were distorted to the point that few believed his claims of the advanced civilizations that lay to the East. By the sixteenth century, however, Portuguese traders had established ports, such as Bombay and Canton. In 1600, Queen Elizabeth authorized an East India Company for trade, a commercial group that excluded hereditary British aristocrats but was packed with commercial adventurers. Initial attempts to establish trade in the Spice Islands were repulsed by the Dutch, who had established a Dutch East India Company in 1602. More maneuverable British ships armed with superior cannon power soon put the Dutch and Portuguese on the defensive, however, affording the British the opportunity to establish "factories," or fortified trading sectors, in Madras, Calcutta, and Bombay. For a strife-ridden India that had degenerated into principalities often antagonistic to one another, not only were British offers of stability and prosperity attractive, but English fire-power against the Portuguese amply demonstrated that such overtures could not be spurned. By the mid-1700s, the British presence was secure enough that the English Parliament affirmed sovereignty through the India Act of 1784.

British–Indian relations were positive during the early colonial period. Indians were compensated from the export of tea, coffee, rubber, and what were regarded as the finest-woven cotton fabrics in the world; moreover the British introduced such technological innovations as the telegraph, a postal system, and railroad, which would leave India with "the most advanced political and administrative machinery in South Asia" by the end of the Second World War (Myrdal, 1968: 40). The British, for their part, found the exotic richness, the philosophical depth, and the social permissiveness of living in communities so far from London exhilarating. To be certain, British–Indian relations were hardly harmonious. An Indian revolt in 1857 was harshly suppressed by the British, who subsequently claimed military control of the subcontinent. Yet, the British East Indian Company, at least initially, governed with a degree of equanimity unlike most European colonial nations. "On a large view of the state of Indian legislation, and of the improvements possible in it," stated the Charter Act of India in 1833, "it is recognized as an indisputable principle that the interests of the native subjects are to be consulted in preference to those of Europeans whenever the two come in competition, and that therefore the laws ought to be adapted to the feelings and habits of the natives rather than to those of Europeans" (Murphey, 1996: 276). As upwardly mobile Indian families acclimated to British patterns, the groundwork for the prestigious Indian Civil Service was lain.

During India's preindustrial, mercantalist stage, India and Britain benefited from reciprocity in trade relations. The East India Company insisted that its agents learn at least one native language and be familiar with its respect for indigenous customs. Assignment in India was arduous for the British, who often fell ill to malaria, leading more affluent colonists to escape the heat and humidity of the monsoon at higher altitude "hill stations" farther inland (Crossette, 1997). The industrialization of India and her citizens' experience in two World Wars shattered the benign colonialism that the British cultivated. At the end of the First World War, Indian veterans grew restive under British occupation and began to demand self-rule through native organizations such as the Indian National Congress, which had been founded by an Englishman in 1885. As tensions rose, violence appeared inevitable, and in 1919 Indian troops under British command opened fire on a festival crowd at Amritsar, killing 400. Instrumental in the struggle for independence was Mahatma Gandhi, who had studied in the United Kingdom and introduced strategies of nonviolent protest while living in South Africa. By adopting the simple garments of peasant Indians and artful use of sacred Hindu texts, Gandhi compelled the British to comprehend the contradictions of their appreciation for freedom while denying Indians their liberties. Gandhi's philosophical craft was complemented by Jawaharlal Nehru's pragmatic leadership of the Congress Party, and the two guided India to independence from Britain at the end of 1947. To their great disappointment, however, Mohammad Ali Jinnah had advocated for a separate Muslim Pakistan, a "partition" that was granted upon independence. In the ensuing violence, ten million refugees were created and some one million died fleeing Hindu and Muslim mobs (Murphey, 1996: 412). Subsequently, East Pakistan declared itself an independent Bangladesh in 1971.

Post-independent India is rife with contradictions. Its commitment to democracy is firm despite, or possibly because of, the assassination of several leaders, including Gandhi, Nehru's daughter Indira Gandhi, and her son, Rajiv Gandhi. Despite a swelling population, India has become nutritionally self-sufficient, an accomplishment largely afforded by the development of high-yield grains of the "green revolution." Although half of the population is illiterate, by the mid-1980s a British-designed educational system led the world in producing scientists and technicians, second only to the United States and Russia. Despite the diversity of 950 million people speaking dozens of different languages, India is the largest English-speaking nation in the world. Celebrating a half-century of independence in 1997, India boasted a president whose family had once belonged to an untouchable caste, and a prime minister who had once been a penniless, partition refugee from Pakistan (Burns, 1997a). Despite substantial reductions in infant mortality and illiteracy, India continued to lag behind Pakistan, China, and Indonesia in per capita GNP (Burns, 1997b). India's progressive social agenda—which ranged from such initiatives as prohibiting widow self-immolation, *sati,* to establishing a quota for female representation in parliament—was retarded as economic progress dwindled (Cooper, 1997). Economic restructuring demanded by the World Bank resulted in liberalizations reinvigorating a lethargic Indian economy that expanded at desirable rates of 6 to 7 percent annually (World Bank, 1996). Regardless of how benevolent economic reform may have been for the national economy, the plight of the urban poor became increasingly desperate, contributing to ethnic violence that continued to wrack the nation and threatened to destabilize the polity (Kamdar, 1997).

## China

Ancient Chinese civilization evolved somewhat after that of India and followed a distinctively different path. The Shang dynasty, which evolved near the Yellow River about 1600 B.C., possessed writing, bronze metallurgy, and silk making. In 1050 B.C., a slave revolt of Chou serfs vanquished the Shang and introduced several enduring features of Chinese culture: the iron-tipped plow, extensive use of irrigation, and the tendency for Chinese dynasties to collapse in cycles of three centuries. Thus, in 771 B.C. the Chou were conquered by barbarians from the North, the Ch'in from which *China* is derived. During the Ch'in dynasty Confucius (551 B.C.–479 B.C.) developed a moral philosophy that emphasized learning and the value of merit in governance, an influence that served to cultivate and sustain leadership by the most capable. In addition, Ch'in leaders abolished slavery except in the case of household servants, introduced a universal code of law, and constructed the Great Wall. Recent archeological excavation of the tomb of Shih Huang Ti, the last Ch'in leader, revealed a terra cotta army of life-size soldiers that accompanied the king into the after-life.

About 200 B.C., Ch'in culture convulsed as a result of a depleted treasury, the desertion of army commanders, and defection of the educated class. The Han dynasty emerging from the chaos established the present-day parameters of China, promoted a blossoming of the arts, and constructed a leadership predicated on the learned gentry. Paralleling the height of the Roman Empire, Han culture was in many respects more advanced. Han development of paper and lacquerware are well known, but the Chinese of the period were also capable mariners who built multiple-masted ships with watertight compartments and used a compass for navigation, invented a chain pump for raising water and the suspension bridge in conjunction with irrigation, understood the circulation of blood, and mastered such processes as distillation and bellows-assisted metallurgy. The agricultural surplus generated through irrigation, the uniformity of rule facilitated by a learned gentry, and technological prowess all contributed to the unprecedented cultural development of the Han. The Han unifying philosophy was Confucianism, a system that "stressed the vital importance of self-cultivation and education as the only true assurance of morality," and also allowed the upward mobility of the most able. Indeed, observers of the rapid development of the "four dragons"—Hong Kong,

South Korea, Singapore, and Taiwan—might credit Confucius with their rapid development, more so than the typical paeans to capitalism (Murphey, 1996: 76–77).

Subsequent dynasties bloomed and faded, replaced by newer and more powerful leaders who added to Chinese culture. By 700 A.D., the T'ang perfected movable type, printing on wood, ceramics, and metal, and used it to popularize poetry and literature. The Sung dynasty unified China, modernized civil administration (requiring officials to move every three years to minimize corruption), and introduced paper promissory notes and government-printed currency to expand trade. It was the Sung dynasty that so marveled Marco Polo, whose Italian contemporary described Hangchou as "the first, the biggest, the richest, the most populous, and altogether the most marvelous city that exists on the face of the earth" (Murphey, 1996: 119).

Medieval Chinese culture was overrun by 1273 when Ghengis Khan's Mongols invaded from the north. Illiterate nomads, the Mongols failed to administer China successfully and were overthrown by the Ming almost a century later. The Ming were the first Chinese to encounter European culture, and the exposure was decidedly one-sided at the onset. By the fifteenth century, China boasted the largest ships afloat—400 feet long and capable of carrying 500 tons of freight—and had encountered Iberian traders in the Spice Islands. Economically self-sufficient, the Ming had little to gain from the Europeans, who were eager to expand Oriental trade. In addition to their disinterest in Europeans, the Ming had an arrogance at court that grated on many, particularly the British. Presented to the Son of Heaven, vassals were expected to prostrate themselves and *k'e t'ou* (or *kowtow*, banging one's head on the floor) as a sign of respect. Barbarians who failed to demonstrate suitable respect to the Emperor were dismissed and sometimes executed. Despite the humiliation of trading with the Ming, Portuguese and Spanish merchants soon mastered the customary requirements and were engaged in lucrative commerce. In exchange for corn, potatoes, chilies, and peanuts from the New World, the Chinese exported silk to the monarchies of Europe. Once the Chinese cultivated New World crops themselves, they insisted on the only scarce commodities that the Europeans could offer: gold and silver. Taking advantage of such commerce, Ming culture evolved into a level of artistic and technological sophistication that was unrivaled anywhere; the Chinese had added canal locks, porcelain, gunpowder, vaccination against smallpox, and a pharmacopeia of 10,000 drugs to their earlier inventions (Murphey, 1996: 179).

Needless of what the persistent Europeans offered through trade, the Chinese rejected their solicitations and isolated them in Canton. The Manchu dynasty, which succeeded the Ming, bordered on paranoiac with respect to European contact. Restricted to a six-month trading season in Canton where they were prohibited from bringing weapons and women, and from entering the city proper, Europeans chafed under Chinese restrictions. The British were unwilling to be as obsequious as the Iberian traders had been, and they lacked the precious metals to which the Chinese had become accustomed as exchange for goods. But the British did possess two resources that would open trade with the Chinese: faster, better-armed ships and opium. The opium trade had become big business for the British. "By 1780, the East India Company had become the exclusive seller of the drug, producing it in its own factories, which purified it, shaped it into three-pound balls, wrapped it in poppy petals, and packed it into distinctive chests, weighing about a hundred and forty pounds each" (Theroux, 1997: 55). With steam-powered battleships, the British had vanquished competitors from the Asian coast. The British East India Company also wanted to export some of the 280 tons of Indian opium it produced annually to China, but this had been outlawed by the Emperor. In 1839, the Chinese Imperial Commission destroyed 20,283 chests of British opium in Canton. The British responded with gunboats to back up their contention that "free trade" allowed them to traffic in opium (the origin of the term "gunboat diplomacy"). By 1860, after two "opium wars," the British had forced upon the Chinese the import of opium and obtained Hong Kong and Kowloon in addition, in the process earning the lasting hatred of the Chinese (Theroux, 1997).

British incursions in China further weakened a Ch'ing dynasty now burdened by population growth that outpaced agricultural production, resulting in rural famine, corruption on the part of the highest Chinese officials, and a xenophobia about Westerners that continued to intensify. In desperation, peasants rebelled against central authorities; in the Taiping rebellion some 40 million died. In early 1900, thousands of Christian missionaries and their converts were slaughtered during the "Boxer Rebellion" that was condoned by the Empress. As China dissembled, foreigners forced their entry into other ports; by 1910 more than 100 "treaty ports" had been established for trade. Unable to contend with internal divisiveness and external threats, the Ch'ing dynasty disintegrated in 1911, and China descended into twelve years of anarchy. Out of this chaos, Chiang Kai-shek emerged as a moderate adherent to Communist ideals advanced by the Kuomintang, a revolutionary political party. A challenge to Chiang by a radical sect led by Mao Zedong, a library assistant at Peking University, provoked him to attempt to annihilate his competitors; but they escaped. In what became known as "the long march" of the mid-1930s, Mao and his comrades used the months of retreat from Chiang's forces through rural China as an opportunity to radicalize the peasantry (Murphey, 1996).

Japan, in the meantime, had industrialized and developed imperial ambitions for the East. In pursuit of regional hegemony, Japan controlled Manchuria and by 1931 had begun to harass Chinese troops to the south. By 1937, Japanese troops were fighting skirmishes with Chinese troops in Peking and assaulted Shanghai in their endeavor to capture Nanking, the capital of the Kuomintang. In December 1937, the Japanese set upon Nanking, unleashing violence that claimed the lives of 400,000 innocents, including women and children, some of whom were butchered and burned to death. Japanese adventures in the East, of course, culminated in their attack on Pearl Harbor, which plunged the industrial nations into the Second World War. In 1945, a humiliated Japan relinquished control of China to the internal powers that had evolved before the War: the Kuomintang that controlled most of China and the smaller Communist Party led by Mao. In 1947, full-scale civil war erupted between them, and in 1949 the Communists emerged victorious. Chiang and the remnants of the Kuomintang fled to Taiwan (Murphey, 1996).

In modernizing China, Mao imitated the Russian model, which reorganized society around communes. With populations of 15,000 to 25,000, communes were to specialize on specific activities for the benefit of the Chinese people. In 1958, Mao proposed that China could overtake Britain in production if all communes cooperated in "the Great Leap Forward." Running counter to traditional notions of rural property rights and agricultural production, the Great Leap Forward was a dismal failure, contributing to a famine the following year that claimed 30 million Chinese. Still enthralled with national initiatives, Mao proposed a Great Proletarian Cultural Revolution from 1966 to 1976, that would restructure China in a manner that would benefit the rural peasantry. The Cultural Revolution disrupted what little coordination and industrialization had emerged in China, further retarding China's development. All universities were closed for several years in order to reduce the educated elite; Red Guards patrolled cities and the countryside with authority to root out officials who represented the reviled status quo, intimidating many and executing some in the process. One China scholar referred to the Cultural Revolution as "the greatest cataclysm in world history, measured by the hundred of millions of people involved in mass persecution and suffering" (Murphey, 1996: 373). The Cultural Revolution shook China to its fragile foundation until 1976, when it expired with Chairman Mao.

Contemporary China has been governed by hard-line pragmatists who have steered away from Mao's excesses. While attempting to modernize an archaic and inadequate industrial base, the leadership has insisted on control of the political economy. This strategy poses contradictions, particularly in light of the Western assumption that a command political economy is inconsistent with democratic capitalism, the optimal foundation for development. Yet, the most prominent leader of post-Mao China, Deng Xiaoping, was adept with such inconsistencies, once remarking, "I don't care if a cat is red [communist] or white [capitalist] as long as it catches mice" (Murphey, 1996: 377). Such facility notwithstanding, the old guard was unprepared for the pro-democracy demonstrations in Peking's Tienanmen Square in the spring of 1989. Thousands of students jammed the square, transmitting demands for democratic elections worldwide by fax then galvanizing public attention by the construction of a "Goddess of Liberty" modeled after the Statue of Liberty. On June 4, the leadership cracked down, dispelling the students and killing perhaps a thousand. On another front, Deng was more successful. The British had agreed to return Hong Kong to China in the fall of 1997, an agreement that generated anxiety among residents as the date approached (*World Press Review,* 1997). In anticipation of reversion, the British hurriedly held elections introducing democratic government for the first time. Although Deng died before Hong Kong was returned, his policy of tolerance toward the democratic-capitalist former colony seemed to be honored by its new Chief Executive, Tung Chee-hwa (Richburg, 1997; Ching, 1997).

China made remarkable progress during the eighteen years of Deng's leadership. Population growth slowed as a result of a strict one-child per family policy, and the number of rural poor declined from 260 million (33 percent) to 65 million (5.3 percent). Consumer products, such as telephones, washing machines, and televisions, became commonplace; and the amount of living space doubled for rural as well as urban residents. Education was reasserted as a priority; the number of graduate students increased fourfold, and the number of students studying in the United States increased from 28 to 45,280. Foreign aid flooded into China in search of footing in an emerging market of enormous proportion; for 1995, $37.7 billion was invested by foreigners, far more than in any other developing Asian country (Mufson, 1997a). The China economy grew at or above 10 percent annually during the mid-1990s, yet inflation that had approached 25 percent in 1994 was only 2.8 percent by May 1997 (Mufson, 1997b). However, China's experiment with "market socialism" was not without its problems, pauperizing large segments of the population (Maitra, 1997). Although absolute poverty has diminished, relative poverty has been exacerbated so that the Chinese population is bifurcated between officials who benefit from market economics and the common people who struggle to eke out a living (Spence and Chin, 1997).

Millions have illegally abandoned the countryside in search of opportunities in already congested cities. As Western influences extend deeper into Chinese culture, incipient voices for democratic government, muffled at Tienanmen Square, are heard once again (Spence, 1997). How these difficulties will be negotiated by the first post-Mao generation of Chinese leaders will determine the promise of modern China.

## Southeast Asia

As the British dominated India and China, so the Dutch eventually colonized much of the rest of monsoon Asia. Initially Southeast Asia was explored by the Portuguese, who had a strong presence established by the mid-1500s, but their ships and weapons were inferior to those of the Dutch, who defeated them in a sea battle in 1601. In 1602 the Dutch East India Company was authorized with extensive powers, including making war, establishing forts and colonies, and coining money. In the face of British competition, the Dutch were ruthless, executing a band of Englishmen who had begun to trade for spices in the Maluccas in 1623. Subsequently, British intrusion into Southeast Asia was confined to Burma, which was adjacent to India, and to isolated trading ports, such as Singapore. France coveted a role in colonizing the Orient, as well. In 1862, using the persecution of French missionaries as a pretext, French troops defeated Chinese forces who had held Cambodia, Laos, and Vietnam as tributary states. Under French colonial control, these nations became known as Indochina. The Philippines, claimed for Spain by Magellan during his global circumnavigation in 1521, remained a colonial backwater until American intervention several centuries later. In all this, only Thailand escaped colonization. Adept Thai rulers maintained the nation as an independent buffer between British and French interests in the region.

The Dutch were particularly interested in commodities that could be produced in large quantities through the plantation system. They introduced coffee to Java in the late 1600s, and a century later it was the colony's largest export to Europe. Successful with coffee, the Dutch soon branched out into sugar and indigo, forcing natives to manual labor. Soon plantations were established for the production and refining of a variety of commodities, such as rubber, palm and coconut oil, tea, and sugar. As a consequence of industrialization, the West had a seemingly insatiable appetite for such goods, and their production generated revenues that were reverted to European colonial nations. Later industrialization, which featured mass production of commodities, particularly automobiles, increased demand for rubber, petroleum, and metals mined in the region. They provided the raw resources and cheap labor, but the indigenous populations of Southeast Asia realized little of the benefits that flowed to Europe. As had been the case of the British in India, however, many Europeans were captivated by Asian cultures of the monsoon region, finding life as expatriates exotic—if also risky because of the diseases, such as malaria. As a result of exposure to Europeans, a small number of more prosperous indigenous families elected to send their male children abroad for a colonial education. Virtually all of the native leaders for the independence of Southeast Asian nations would be educated, at least in part, in Europe.

Freedom from colonial control was postponed by the introduction of the Second World War. After the attack on Pearl Harbor in December 1941, the Japanese stormed through Southeast Asia, conquering Malaya, Burma, Indonesia, and the Philippines. Already in control of Manchuria and Taiwan, the Japanese referred to their sphere of "Greater East Asian

Co-Prosperity" and promised reciprocity in its development. The harshness, and in many cases brutality, of Japanese occupation won few converts, however. The defeat of the Japanese in 1945 marked the end of the colonial era as well, although the Dutch tried unsuccessfully to retain control of Indonesia until finally conceding defeat in 1949 (James, 1996), and the French engaged in a protracted war with Communist Vietnamese insurgents before surrendering in 1954 (Murphey, 1996).

Independence was an inauspicious and elusive event for several Southeast Asian nations, however. Vietnam, then Cambodia, succumbed to internal strife that continued for several decades, subverting their developmental potential. A 1954 Geneva Conference partitioned Vietnam and called for nationwide elections. Fearing that Communists led by Ho Chih Minh would win, Ngo Dinh Diem overthrew the leader of South Vietnam and established a separate government. In response, the North Vietnamese established the National Liberation Front to gain control of the South. An ambiguous incident in the Gulf of Tonkin provided pretext for the United States to send troops to South Vietnam, and the American Central Intelligence Agency was implicated in the assassination of Diem. Confrontations escalated, and by 1965 over a half-million U.S. troops were in South Vietnam to prop up an ineffective South Vietnamese government. The North Vietnamese countered superior American firepower with withering guerilla warfare in the countryside. By the time the Americans quit South Vietnam in 1975, the United States had lost 58,000 soldiers in the conflict, while the Vietnamese counted far worse casualties, two million dead. Upon the American withdrawal, South Vietnam fell to Communist forces; the country was finally unified after three decades of warfare against colonial forces (Murphey, 1996: 396–97).

Cambodia was a tragic postscript to the Vietnam War. Willing to use extraordinary means to combat the North Vietnamese, the Nixon administration engaged in tactics in Cambodia that were prohibited by international law. In 1970, American and South Vietnamese forces invaded Cambodia to thwart North Vietnamese forces that were using the border for sanctuary. Unable to dislodge Communist forces, the United States resorted to "carpet bombing," the systematic destruction of infrastructure on the ground by high-altitude bombing. In eight months during 1973, the United States dropped twice the bomb tonnage on Cambodia that had been unleashed on Japan during the Second World War, but to little effect. Within two years, Communist insurgents under the name Khmer Rouge took over a Cambodia that was in shambles; their leader was a 32-year-old schoolteacher, Pol Pot. The Khmer Rouge attempted a fundamental restructuring of Cambodia, consigning educated citizens to hard labor in order to rid the population of elite influences. Under harsh conditions and capricious authority, perhaps two million, over a quarter of the Cambodian population, perished. In 1979, the horror of Pol Pot's leadership was attenuated by the invasion of North Vietnamese troops, which put in place a puppet state, the People's Republic of Kampuchea. Unrelenting foes of the North Vietnamese, the United States assumed a perverse position, joining China and Thailand in support of the Khmer Rouge. During the 1980s, Cambodia succumbed to intermittent warfare involving the resistance to the Khmer Rouge, led by Norodom Ranariddh, remaining Khmer Rouge forces led by Hun Sen, and the Chinese, who tried unsuccessfully to evict the North Vietnamese from Cambodia. In 1990 the principal parties agreed to a United Nations peace-keeping plan that included national elections, but the Khmer Rouge boycotted the election, which was won by Norodom Ranariddh (Richburg and Smith, 1997). In a desperate attempt to avoid renewed conflict, Norodom Ranariddh agreed to share governance with Hun Sen (Baker, 1997). The peace negotiated by the UN proved too fragile, however. Provoked by the capture of renegade Pol Pot, Hun Sen mobilized remaining Khmer Rouge fighters and ousted Norodom Ranariddh (Thayer, 1997). Leaving behind a failed peace effort that cost $3 billion and involved 22,000 foreign troops, Norodom Ranariddh fled Cambodia (Smith, 1997). After two decades of relentless civil war, Cambodia remains prostrate, convulsed in internecine violence that claims the lives of thousands of citizens while the prospects of development recede even farther into the distance.

Burma achieved independence from Britain in 1948, shortly after conservatives had assassinated political leader Aung San. A charismatic Buddhist, U Nu, led the government, but was overthrown by a military coup maneuvered by Ne Win, who suspended the constitution and imposed marshal law in 1962. U Nu fled to exile, leaving Burma to inept military rule that did little to modernize the nation, save changing its name to Myanmar. In May 1990, national elections were won by the National League for Democracy, a left-wing party led by Aung San's daughter, Suu Kyi, who had been placed under house arrest the year before. Immediately, the junta voided the election, instituting autocratic rule through the State Law and Order Restoration Council ("Suu Kyi's," 1996). For the next six years, Aung San Suu Kyi mounted a public relations offensive against the military, deploring the denial of civil liberties, the deaths of thousands by military tyranny, and a failing economy, leading to her receipt of the Nobel Peace Prize (Chatterjee, 1997). The military grudgingly freed Suu Kyi from house arrest, but prohibited her from making negative statements about military leadership. Promptly, she announced plans for an international boycott of investment, an initiative that could prove fatal to Burma's already fragile economy (Blustein, 1997).

While Burma lagged, another former British colony, Malaysia, prospered, propelled forward by Singapore. A long-standing dispute between Malays and Chinese was settled by partitioning the colony between Malay-governed Malaysia and a largely Chinese city-state, Singapore. Since that time, Malaysia has prospered by embracing a laissez-faire capitalism while abridging democratic process and civil rights through autocratic rule (Field, 1995). The growth rate from 1980 to 1990 increased at an enviable 5.2 percent per year, and between 1990 and 1995, it shot upward at 8.7 percent annually, among the highest in the developing world (*World Development Indicators,* 1997: 131). Much of this economic expansion is attributable to investments in human capital, particularly education. With more than 93 percent of children in primary school and over half continuing on to the secondary level, Malaysia has an educated workforce. This has allowed a relatively smooth transition from an economy dominated by primary exports (rubber and tin), to one diversifying into industry and high technology (Todaro, 1994: 392–94). Within three decades Malaysia had made such impressive strides in literacy, nutrition, and life expectancy that it was classified as one of the "high" ranking nations in human development (*Human Development Index,* 1996).

Indonesia, consisting of 3000 islands and a diverse population speaking more than 600 languages, is the largest Islamic nation in the world (James, 1996). Although Achmed Sukarno declared Indonesia independent from the Dutch immediately after the Japanese surrender in 1945, the Dutch persisted in an aborted attempt to retain the colony. In 1949, the Dutch conceded and Sukarno began the difficult task of nation building. In the absence of technical capacity and economic assistance, Sukarno's leadership faltered, and the military assumed power. As proof of his keen political instincts, Sukarno resurfaced as Indonesia's leader two years later, maneuvering an unlikely group of bedfellows consisting of the army and the Communist party. Yet, Sukarno's triumph was brief. In 1965, an army coup by junior officers murdered six generals, attributing the bloodbath to the Communist party. Amid extensive rioting and relentless efforts to crush left-wing influences in Indonesia, General Suharto rose to power, driving Sukarno into retirement. Until 1998 when he resigned after massive demonstrations, Suharto had been reelected as president in rigged elections that legitimized a police state. During this period, Suharto's regime produced modest growth: Per capita GNP exceeded that of India and China, illiteracy was low, and the number of technical graduates was high (Burns, 1997b). Despite such indicators, Indonesia suffers from a skewed population distribution, most of the population having resided in Java. To correct this, officials have begun an ambitious effort to redistribute six million Indonesians from Java to less-populated islands (Mydans, 1996). From 1990 to 1995, Indonesia's economy has grown at a relatively high rate of 7.6 annually, making it one of the most prosperous Third World nations. Indeed, Indonesia was ranked fourth by the World Bank (behind India, China, and Brazil, but ahead of Russia) as one of the "emerging giants of the developing world" (*World Development Indicators,* 1997: 129, 131).

Along with Malaysia and Indonesia, Thailand has shown remarkable development among Southeast Asian nations. Confounded by political instability—18 coups since the end of the monarchy in 1932—Thailand has been buffeted by foreign influences (Field, 1995: 153). British and French colonial interests were finessed during the nineteenth century, preserving a monarchy that eventually collapsed as Communist influences destabilized the region. The Vietnam War further confounded national development, and the military intervened, effectively repressing dissent. Throughout the turmoil, Thailand imitated the industrial policy that had catalyzed economic expansion in Taiwan and South Korea: Domestic production for export was protected by tariffs, nurturing a nascent economy that eventually took off (Todaro, 1994: 556–58). Between 1980 and 1990, the Thai economy expanded at an annual rate of 7.6 percent; subsequently it grew at an even higher annual rate of 8.4 percent between 1990 and 1995 (*World Development Indicators,* 1997: 132). Social indicators showed significant improvements corresponding with economic progress: Absolute poverty and illiteracy were virtually erased, population growth slowed, and women became more prevalent in the labor force (*World Bank Atlas,* 1997: 17; *Human Development Index,* 1996). By the mid-1990s, the World Bank included Thailand's modest economy as one of the ten "emerging giants of the developing world" (*World Development Indicators,* 1997: 129). The soundness of Thailand's development was brought into question in the spring of 1997, however, when currency speculators drove down the bhat, causing the government to take protective measures that made investors skittish (Sugawara, 1997a). As reverberations were felt throughout Southeast Asia, a shadow was cast on the future of development in the region.

In contradistinction with the more vibrant economies of Southeast Asia, the Philippines failed to bring into convergence the vectors necessary for development. This is paradoxical since the Philippines was among the first discoveries by Europeans as well as the least diverted by competing cultures from India and China. For over three centuries, the Philippines was a colony of Spain, then controlled by the United States. Despite major military investments concomitant with the Second World War, the resources that poured into the nation were squandered by corrupt officials, typified by Ferdinand and Imelda Marcos, who were more interested in personal aggrandizement than national development. The Marcos dictatorship not only stifled political opposition, but it also committed the nation to imperial development projects that drove the nation into debt, further impeding more populist development initiatives (Todaro, 1994: 560–61). In 1986, the Marcos regime was overthrown by a "power to the people" movement that grew out of the assassination of Benigno Aquino at the Manila airport three years earlier. By this time, however, critical time and resources had been lost, and development progressed glacially. During the 1980s, growth sputtered along at 1 percent annually; increasing to only 2.3 percent annually between 1990 and 1995 (*World Development Indicators,* 1997: 131). Social indicators reflected a dispirited population: Twenty-eight percent survived on less than one U.S. dollar per day; 30 percent of children under age five were malnourished; the portion of the population with access to safe water, health services, and sanitation lagged behind the more prosperous nations of Southeast Asia (*World Bank Atlas,* 1997: 17; *Human Development Index,* 1996: 144). By the mid-1990s, the Philippines was less mirroring the nations that had kicked-off the "Asian miracle" and more resembled the Third World nations of Southeast Asia and South America that had become developmental backwaters.

# Paths to Development

Approaching the second millennium, Asian nations are confronted with three patterns of development: the authoritarian capitalism of the "four tigers," the market socialism upon which China has embarked, and the welfare state capitalism being attempted by India. The extent to which each of these experiments in development succeeds is open to speculation, of course. Regardless of the strategy chosen, however, many observers of Asia believe that the region is poised for significant growth. According to the World Bank, most of the emerging Third World economies are located in Asia; as a result, private investment capital is flooding the region in anticipation of burgeoning markets (*World Development Indicators,* 1997).

## The Four Tigers

By the mid-1980s, four formerly colonial nations had demonstrated sufficient economic growth to attract international attention: Hong Kong, Singapore, Taiwan, and South Korea. Through a combination of government-directed industrial policy, a disciplined workforce, and strategically established tariffs, the "four tigers" achieved levels of development that differentiated them from other developing nations. While the OECD nations experienced per capita GDP growth of 2.1 percent between 1965 and 1995, the four tigers grew 6.6 percent; specifically, Hong Kong expanded 5.6 percent, Korea 7.2 percent, Singapore 7.2 percent, and Taiwan 6.2 percent (Radelet and Sachs, 1997: 52). Expansion of the Asian tigers at a rate three times that of the industrialized nations represented investment opportunities that were simply irresistible (*World Development Indicators,* 1997: 130–32). Much of the capital that fueled these expanding economies came from Japan, a nation whose considerable balance of trade surpluses could be put to use furthering hemispheric interests that had been crushed by defeat during the Second World War. Following Japan's lead, the four tigers adopted an export strategy for development: "The idea behind an export platform is to create an enclave economy hospitable to foreign investment and integrated into the global economy, without the problems of infrastructure, security, rule of law, and trade policies that plague the rest of the economy," observed Steven Radelet and Jeffrey Sachs of Harvard's Institute for International Development. In Japan, and subsequently with the Asian tigers, "The export strategy began with textiles and apparel but really took off with electronics" (1997: 52–53).

Having developed so quickly, the four tigers were emulated by other nations in the region. Soon, Malaysia, Thailand, and Indonesia had adopted their fivefold developmental formula:

- Following Confucian philosophy, heavy investments in education were made, particularly in skills necessary for the high-tech, postindustrial sector;
- rigorously encouraging savings, to the point that savings ratios exceeded 30 percent;
- deliberately deciding which industries to favor through an aggressive industrial policy that subsidized exports and protected them by high tariffs;
- by taking advantage of low-wage labor, export prices remained favorable, thus boosting nationally produced commodities in relation to imports;
- looking to the Japanese for capital, industrial guidance, and protection from other regional trade syndicates (Kennedy, 1993: 196–200).

The sudden prosperity of the four tigers was not attained painlessly, however. For Western observers (as well as many Western-educated natives), design of industrial policy by Eastern strategists evolved too often at the expense of democratic political values and modern sensibilities toward civil rights. Under the autocratic rule of Lee Kuan Yew, a British-educated Chinese, Singapore's economy shot upward, mirroring the dramatic gains of Hong Kong. Yew understood postcolonial prosperity to be a function of a strategically regulated capitalism coupled with suppression of civil liberties. Justifying this contortion of Western ideals as necessary to conform civil rights to Eastern requirements, Yew's orientation was adopted by Tung Chee Hwa, Hong Kong's new chief executive. This dispute between Western understandings of "human rights" and "Asian values" degenerated into a brouhaha that extended beyond the immediate confines of the former British colonies. Indeed, the economic success of Singapore, and to a degree Malaysia, was attributed by some as a necessary abridgment of civil liberties in order to accelerate capitalist expansion. In rebuttal, philosophers such as Amartya Sen have contended that classic Asian texts have celebrated personal achievement, political freedom, and civil rights as significantly as have the more frequently intoned texts from the West. "The case for liberty and political rights turns ultimately on their basic importance and on their instrumental role," noted Sen, "And this case is as strong in Asia as it is elsewhere" (Sen, 1997).

While the debate over "Asian values" heated up during the Summer of 1997 as China resumed control of Hong Kong, its regional resonance was muted by a dramatic economic downturn that shook the region. In retrospect, the "Asian miracle" had produced remarkable achievements: In three decades the per capita GDP increased by multiple factors—Hong Kong's from $4,843 to $26,334, Singapore's from $2,678 to $23,350, Malaysia's from $2,271 to $9,458, and Thailand's from $1,570 to $6,723 (Hiatt, 1997: A17). Perhaps inevitably, such prodigious growth invited speculative consumption and political corruption, factors that distorted economic performance. On July 2, 1997, the Thai government floated the bhat, which had been pegged to the dollar, and it promptly fell 20 percent. Fearing economic collapse, Southeast Asian governments, vulnerable because of rapid expansion, diverted billions to support their failing currencies (WuDunn, 1997). In response to perceived market failure, Western investors promptly withdrew $2 billion, further eroding the Southeast Asian economy (WuDunn, 1997). The prospects of Southeast Asia, once of buoyed optimism, suddenly darkened, and observers were divided over the likely outcome. Economist Robert Samuelson (1997) suggested that the formula for development, using foreign technology to generate exports, had become "stale" and that newer strategies were necessary. Journalist Fred Hiatt (1997) suspected that the culprit was "Asian values" insofar as the suppression of civil liberties, allegedly necessary to prompt economic growth, also depress civil institutions—particularly the electronic and print media—that serve as necessary correctives to government and corporate excesses. In the absence of a viable and critical media, "corrupt and authoritarian regimes" use "Asian values" as a "smokescreen" to evade oversight by journalists.

## India

Since the inception of development studies, India had commanded the attention of scholars, including such luminaries as J. S. Mill, Thomas Malthus, David Ricardo, and John Maynard Keynes (Cowen and Shenton, 1996). After attaining independence, India adopted a socialist path for development, assuming that industrialization would generate a surplus that could be diverted to a welfare state that would ameliorate the nation's chronic poverty. This "inward looking" strategy attempted to exclude imports from industrialized nations in order to promote markets for indigenous producers (Todaro, 1994). High tariffs on imports, relatively high wages for native workers in sectors targeted for modernization, and the nationalization of major industries owned by foreigners were characteristic of an "import-substitution" template for development. For several reasons, import-substitution seemed a desirable developmental strategy: It favored national industries and more skilled workers; it kept cheaper imports from industrial nations at bay; and it enhanced the treasury, particularly when foreign firms were confiscated. In the long run, however, import-substitution contained multiple disadvantages. Import barriers through high tariffs artificially shielded producers from competition; similarly, wages of workers in protected industries benefited from de facto subsidies; capturing foreign production facilities obviously antagonized foreign corporations. Despite these negative considerations, import-substitution proved a durable prescription for development for one compelling reason: National elites that owned production units were the primary beneficiaries of the strategy, and they used their influence in the national government to continue policies that worked to their short-run advantage. To the extent that elites controlled the national government, import-substitution was invariably beneficial for *their* development, even though its long-term consequences to the nation would prove disadvantageous (Thurow, 1996: 58–59).

The Indian legacy of import-substitution was uneven and flagging development. The socialist path of development brought India heavy industry in the production of steel, machine tools, automobiles, ships, weapons, and computers. Yet, this did little to improve the plight of the typical Indian villager who eked by on a few hundred dollars per year. From 1950 to 1970, the average income increased less than 2 percent. Whereas in 1955 India was the world's tenth largest industrial power, two decades later it had dropped to twentieth. Economically, the nation's ranking compared to other more successful developing countries was cause for reflection. In 1965, India's exports of manufactured goods were 8 times that of South Korea; by 1986, South Korea's exports were 4.5 times that of India (Kennedy, 1993: 174). During the 1980s, India slid further behind the four tigers; while India reported annual growth of 5.8 percent, it lagged behind Hong Kong's 6.9 percent, South Korea's 9.4 percent, and Singapore's 6.4 percent. What was more worrisome, China's growth of 10.2 percent outpaced them all, and China's economy promised to become so enormous that it was soaking up billions in foreign investment (*World Development Indicators,* 1997: 130–32). Comparatively poor economic performance further disadvantaged India, a nation with high levels of intractable poverty.

In light of such disappointing performance, India agreed to economic restructuring in the late 1980s. Such reforms were intended to diminish government influence in the economy, liberalize economic relations, and open trade to foreign countries (Todaro, 1994: 465–67). While India had not succumbed to the massive borrowing in which many developing nations had indulged as a result of the oil shocks of the 1970s, its debt was still at 24.9 percent of GDP (*World Development Indicators,* 1997: 187). The economic reforms introduced in 1990 generated increased economic growth of 5 percent from 1992–1994, 6 percent in 1994, and 7 percent in 1995. But economic performance had negligible benefit for the nation's poorest citizens. India ranks second only to Bangladesh in capability poverty (the prevalence of underweight children, births unattended by health care personnel, and female illiteracy) at 61.5 percent (*Human Development Index,* 1996: 27). Thus, a half-century following independence, India's development was showing improvement economically, yet its social progress was minimal. If industrialization was to introduce an advanced, socialist welfare state, that prospect was not yet in the foreseeable future.

## China

Unique among developing nations, China poses a fundamental contradiction: The enormity of its prospective market(s) attracts billions of dollars of overseas investment, yet it remains the final bastion of international Communism. Taking the lead of Soviet planners, Mao plunged China into massive undertakings—the Great Leap Forward and the Cultural Revolution—that resulted in massive economic and social dislocation, further retarding development (Kennedy, 1993: 175). It was not until Mao's leadership had ebbed that Chinese leaders began to distance themselves from "market Stalinism." China's subsequent flirtation with capitalism was more than a discreet event, since it had implications for other Communist nations of Southeast Asia, particularly North Korea and Vietnam. China "shed the trappings of Maoism and embarked on a pragmatic course of economic development and global trade," noted two veteran China watchers, in order to reaffirm "its conception of itself as a center of global civilization, and...to redeem centuries of humiliating weakness" (Bernstein and Munro, 1997: 22, 19).

China's subsequent economic progress was as astonishing as it was disputable. Chinese growth in real per capita income relative to other development categories is shown in Table 1.1. Despite admonitions that such data may be inflated (Murphey, 1994; Thurow, 1996), China's reversal of developmental fortune is a remarkable transformation.

**TABLE 1.1    Average Annual Growth in Real Per Capita Income**

| Country or Group | 1960–1970 | 1970–1980 | 1980–1993 |
|---|---|---|---|
| High human development | 4.3 | 2.8 | 1.5 |
| Excluding industrial countries | 3.9 | 3.7 | 2.5 |
| Medium human development (excluding China) | 2.5 | 4.1 | 1.1 |
| China | 1.8 | 9.1 | 8.1 |
| Low human development (excluding India) | 1.5 | 0.7 | 0.2 |
| India | 1.6 | 0.8 | 3.1 |
| World | 2.6 | 2.8 | 2.9 |

*Source:* From *Human Development Report,* 1996 by United Nations Dvelopment Program. Copyright © 1996 by the United Nations Development Programme. Used by permission of Oxford University Press, Inc.

China's propulsion to the front of the pack of developing nations is due to features that suggest a path to development that is different than that adopted by the four tigers and India. Lester Thurow attributes China's success to four factors: (1) a high domestic savings rate that provides capital for reinvestment independent of foreign investment, (2) a strong central government that has the authority to determine and coordinate development policy, (3) a cohort of overseas Chinese managers who are adept at international capitalism and willing to apply their skills, as well as their access to capital, for the benefit of China, and (4) a relatively small commitment to large state-run enterprises and rural communes that require dismantling in order to facilitate the emergence of a market economy (1996: 53–57). The result has been "a socialist commodity system influenced by market mechanisms" (Todaro, 1994: 217), a model that may prove as idiosyncratic as China itself.

The reversion of Hong Kong contributed to this protean brew. Although Westerners anticipated Hong Kong's repatriation to the mainland with considerable consternation, Chinese leaders moved adeptly by installing a transitional leader, initiating a quasi-democratic representational process, and assuring the protection of basic civil rights. Several months after reversion, Hong Kong not only continued to develop economically, but also respected Western freedoms. By the Fall of 1997, Hong Kong had become pivotal in the expanding economies of Southeast Asia, and, as if to reassure Western investors, hosted the annual meeting of the World Bank and International Monetary Fund (Sugawara, 1997b). Yet, Chinese leaders seemed eager to go beyond their assurance to the British that Hong Kong would remain a free, capitalist society for at least 50 years (Pomfret, 1997). Expanding the economic success of Hong Kong, China relaxed social and economic restrictions for neighboring Shenzhen in Quangdong province. Similar changes in Shanghai propelled that city's economy forward. China invested heavily in infrastructure, constructing a 95-story skyscraper, an 11-line subway system, an elevated highway system, and two bridges. Westerners invested $7 billion in Shanghai in 1996, alone, and committed to investing an additional $12 billion in the city. Approaching the end of the century, Shanghai was reemerging as an international hub of commerce and culture, reclaiming a stature last seen in the 1920s (Mufson, 1997c). Rather than becoming a troublesome impediment to national economic planning, Hong Kong had become a template for metropolitan development in other regions of China.

## Prospects for Development

More than any other region of the developing world, Asia brings into bold relief the significance of demography. Rapid population growth under conditions of intractable rural poverty drives large numbers of people into shantytowns skirting large cities. Congested cities become increasingly polluted as inefficient industries struggle to produce goods of even marginal value, while fossil fuels used for heating and cooking generate a suffocating, blue haze that pollutes the metropolitan area. At any given time, much of the urban population consists of squatters who are refugees, or people who have fled from political or economic hazards, and all too often both (Mayotte, 1992). Even under circumstances of relative prosperity, an increasingly marginal population of urban peasants poses threats to political stability, and the response by central authorities is often repressive. Thus, modest progress can exacerbate urban poverty, raising fundamental questions about the benefit of traditional strategies of development.

By the year 2000, the current world population of 5.5 billion will increase to 6.3 billion; 25 years later it will balloon to 8.5 billion. Over 60 percent of the population gain will reside in Asia (Todaro, 1994: 178, 183). As shown in Table 1.2, a substantial portion of the increase in the world's population will be poor. Such growth in the number of poor places enormous pressure on developing economies. At 1990 growth rates, China and India alone add 14 million and 17 million people annually to the world's population (Todaro, 1994:

**TABLE 1.2    Population Living on Less Than $1 a Day in Developing Economies**

| | Millions | | % of Population | |
|---|---|---|---|---|
| Region | *1987* | *1993* | *1987* | *1993* |
| East Asia and the Pacific | 464.0 | 445.8 | 28.8 | 26.0 |
| Europe and Central Asia | 2.2 | 14.5 | 0.6 | 3.5 |
| Latin America and the Caribbean | 91.2 | 109.6 | 22.0 | 23.5 |
| Middle East and North Africa | 10.3 | 10.7 | 4.7 | 4.1 |
| South Asia | 479.9 | 514.7 | 45.4 | 43.1 |
| Sub-Saharan Africa | 179.6 | 218.6 | 38.5 | 39.1 |
| **Total** | **1,227.1** | **1,313.9** | **30.1** | **29.4** |

*Source:* World Bank (1996) *Poverty Reduction and the World Bank: Progress and Challenges in the 1990s* (Washington, D.C.)

184), yet China has one-half the cultivatable land of the United States and India has even less (Murphey, 1996: 437).

Traditional methods of population reduction that have relied on public health strategies, such as birth control, may be less effective than more draconian methods, such as disease, famine, and war. In the absence of modern opportunities for upward mobility and income security, traditional societies, which tend to be most fertile, continue to have high birth rates in order for parents to be assured of sustenance in old age. That being the case, "one way to induce families to desire fewer children is to raise the price of child rearing by, say, providing greater educational opportunities and a wider range of higher-paying jobs for young women" (Todaro, 1994: 200). Thus, demonstrations such the Grameen Development Bank that enhance the opportunities of peasant women not only increase the assets of their families but also reduce the number of children that women are willing to bear (see Chapter 14).

Cities are perceived as opportunities for the poor of the Third World and they become magnets of upward mobility to rural immigrants. Until 2010, when rural population growth is expected to stabilize (Todaro, 1996: 344), cities in developing nations will continue to swell. By 2000, of the twenty megacities with populations of 11 million or more, seventeen will be in developing nations. Among the largest will be Mexico City with a population of 24.4 million, Sao Paulo with 23.6 million, Calcutta with 16 million, Bombay with 15.4 million, and Shanghai with 14.7 million (Kennedy, 1993: 26). By 2015, six of the ten largest cities with populations exceeding 10 million will be in Asian developing countries (*World Development Indicators,* 1997: 117). Delhi, a moderately sized city, absorbs 150,000 rural peasants each year. Attempts to reduce urbanization have been most aggressive in China, but internal immigration policies have not contained the rapidly expanding metropolitan areas. More than one million Chinese had become illegal residents of Shanghai by the mid-1990s (Murphey, 1996: 439).

Retarded opportunities in the midst of rapid population growth place enormous stress on the environment. This registers in two somewhat distinct ways. First, the immediate environment in developing locales is despoiled to a considerable extent. One need only step off an airplane in the typical Asian city to be suffocated by the "yellow dragon" of bluish, sulfurous smoke and haze from burning soft coal and two-cycle engines that pollutes the air (Murphey, 1996: 438). Second, the effects of environmental degradation spread around the Earth, posing problems for other nations. In 1987, for example, China and India ranked fourth and fifth in discharge of "greenhouse gas" emissions, pumping 380,000 and 230,000 metric tons, respectively, into the environment (Kennedy, 1993: 117). Water and sanitation are particularly inadequate. About one billion people do not have access to potable water, and another 1.7 billion lack basic sanitation. "Between 1970 and 1988, the number of urban households in the Third World without adequate sanitation rose by 247 percent and those without safe water increased by 56 percent" (Todaro, 1996: 348). Lack of sanitation degrades water supplies, and this contributes to waterborne diseases that contribute to the deaths of tens of thousands of infants annually. In order to purify water, poor women consume supplies of wood (contributing to deforestation) to boil it, often at considerable cost. The annual cost of simply boiling water in Jakarta, for example, is $50 million (Todaro, 1996: 349). But cooking fuel was the least of the pollution factors to bedevil Indonesia. In September 1997, forest fires intentionally set to clear land ran out of control, spreading through Sumatra and Borneo. The fires were among the worst "man-made disasters" in the region, denuding 1.3 million acres of forest and forcing the shutting of schools and businesses; they were also implicated in the collision of two freighters, resulting in the sinking of one and the loss of 29 crew members (Maniam, 1997).

Much of the downside of traditional development can be attributed to strategies that favored industrialization and encouraged poor peasants to flock to metropolitan areas in search of opportunity. The counterpoint to industrialization has been a recent emphasis on sustainable development, and a focus on more modest and rural-oriented strategies (Todaro, 1996). An exemplar is the Indian state of Kerala. With a population of 29 million, Kerala is typical of many areas striving to modernize: The per capita income is between $298 and $350 per year, chronic unemployment plagues an economy that runs continuous deficits, and there is little hope for a prompt economic rebound. Yet, Kerala defies classification as a Third World backwater: Life expectancy is 70 years; 100 percent of the population is literate; and the birth rate parallels that of the First World. Kerala's score on the physical quality of life index (ranking jurisdictions from 0 to 100) was 82 in 1981, comparing favorably with South Korea (85) and Taiwan (87). By 1989, Kerala's score had risen to 88. Such development without massive industrialization and rapid economic expansion suggests a low-consumption, sustainable path to development. In the words of environmental author, Bill McKibben, "Kerala demonstrates that a low-level economy can create a decent life, abundant in the things—health, education, community—that are most necessary for us all" (1996: 111). It remains to be seen if Kerala's example will become an alternative to the paths of development already elected by China, India, and the tiger economies of Southeast Asia.

# REFERENCES

Baker, Mark. (1997). "Cambodia's Tough Guy," *World Press Review* (September).

Bernstein, Richard, and Ross Munro. (1997). "The Coming Conflict with America," *Foreign Affairs* (March/April).

Blustein, Paul. (1997). "Burma Campaign Has Business Fighting Trend Toward Sanctions," *Washington Post* (March 4).

Brzezinski, Zbigniew. (1997). "A Geostrategy for Eurasia," *Foreign Affairs* (September/October 1997).

Burns, John. (1997a). "In Prime Minister's Life, a Parable of His Country," *New York Times* (August 14).

Burns, John. (1997b). "India's 5 Decades of Progress and Pain," *New York Times* (August 14).

Chatterjee, Sumana. (1997). "In Burma, It's Past Time for the U.S. to Impose Sanctions," *Washington Post* (March 2).

Ching, Frank. (1997). "Misreading Hong Kong," *Foreign Affairs* (May/June).

Cooper, Kenneth. (1997). "Free But Bound by Their Pasts," *Washington Post* (August 14).

Cowen, M. P., and R. W. Shenton. (1996). *Doctrines of Development* (London: Routledge).

Crossette, Barbara. (1997). "Summering, Colonial Style," *New York Times* (August 10).

Field, Graham. (1995). *Economic Growth and Political Change in Asia* (New York: St. Martin's).

Hiatt, Fred. (1997). "Tigers Declawed," *Washington Post* (September 8).

*Human Development Index.* (1996). (New York: United Nations).

James, Jamie. (1996). "The Indonesiad," *New Yorker* (May 27).

Kamdar, Mira. (1997). "Bombay/ Mumbai," *World Policy Journal* (Summer).

Kennedy, Paul. (1993). *Preparing for the Twenty-First Century* (New York: Vintage).

Maitra, Priyatosh. (1997). "The Globalization of Capitalism and Economic Transition in China," *Regional Development Dialogue* (Spring).

Maniam, Hari. (1997). "Two Ships Collide Off Malaysia," *Washington Post* (September 28).

Mayotte, Judy. (1992). *Disposable People* (Maryknoll, NY: Orbis).

McKibben, Bill. (1996) "The Enigma of Kerala," *Utne Reader* (March-April).

Mufson, Steven. (1997a). "China's Deng Xiaoping Is Dead at 92," *Washington Post* (February 20).

Mufson, Steven. (1997b). "China's 'Greenspan' Ends Perilous Economic Slide," *Washington Post* (August 21).

Mufson, Steven. (1997c). "Giving Hong Kong a Run for Its Money," *Washington Post Weekly* (June 30).

Murphey, Rhoads. (1996). *A History of Asia* (New York: HarperCollins).

Mydans, Seth. (1996). "Huge Exodus Succeeds, Fails," *Richmond Times-Dispatch* (August 26).

Myrdal, Gunnar. (1968). *Asian Drama* (New York: Twentieth Century Fund).

National Gallery of Art. (1997). "Sculpture of Angkor and Ancient Cambodia" (Washington, DC: National Gallery of Art).

Pomfret, John. (1997). "Hong Kong Fears China's New Leaders May Tinker with Takeover Agreement," *Washington Post* (February 21).

Radelet, Steven, and Jeffrey Sachs. (1997). "Asia's Reemergence," *Foreign Affairs* (November/December).

Richburg, Keith. (1997). "'Business as Usual' in Hong Kong," *Washington Post* (August 28), p. A28.

Richburg, Keith, and R. Jeffrey Smith. (1997). "What Went Wrong in Cambodia?" *Washington Post Weekly* (July 28), p. 14.

Samuelson, Robert. (1997). "End of the 'Asian Miracle'," *Washington Post Weekly* (September 15).

Sen, Amartya. (1997). "Human Rights and Asian Values," *New Republic* (July 14 & 21).

Smith, R. Jeffrey. (1997). "$3 Billion Effort Fails to Pacify Cambodia," *Washington Post* (June 14).

Smithsonian Institution. (1997). "King of the World" (Washington, DC: Sackler Gallery).

Spence, Jonathan. (1997). "Devotion and Hostility," *New Republic* (July 7).

Spence, Jonathan, and Annping Chin. (1997). "Deng's Heirs," *New Yorker* (March 10).

Sugawara, Sandra. (1997a). "Teetering on the Brink in Thailand," *Washington Post Weekly* (July 7).

Sugawara, Sandra. (1997b). "It's China's Shop Now, But Bulls Still Run in Hong Kong Markets," *Washington Post* (September 23).

"Suu Kyi's Steely Calm Stymies the Generals." (1996). *World Press Review* (September).

Thayer, Nate. (1997). "In Cambodia, a Truce That Almost Was," *Washington Post Weekly* (August 25).

Theroux, Paul. (1997). "Ghost Stories," *New Yorker* (May 12).

Thurow, Lester. (1996). *The Future of Capitalism* (New York: Penguin).

Todaro, Michael. (1994). *Economic Development* (New York: Longman).

World Bank (1996) *India: Five Years of Stabilization and Reform and the Challenges Ahead* (Washington, DC: World Bank).

*World Bank Atlas.* (1997). (Washington, DC: World Bank).

*World Development Indicators,* (1997) (Washington, D.C.: World Bank).

*World Press Review.* (1997). "The Dragon's Breath: Hong Kong Braces for Chinese Rule," (April).

WuDunn, Sheryl. (1997). "Asian Economies, Once a Miracle, Now Muddled," *New York Times* (August 31).

# 2 Latin America: Five Hundred Years of Purgatory

*As soon as we are strong, under the auspices of a liberal nation which lends us its protection, the world will see us cultivate with a single accord the virtues and talents which lead to glorious accomplishment; then we shall move majestically forward toward the great prosperity and development for which our Southern America is destined.*

—Simon Bolivar, 1815 (Crow, 1992: 444)

Latin America is a region of rich cultural history despoiled by massive corruption, of sublime art mirrored by savage barbarity, of untrammeled expanse set off by choking urban sprawl. Its disappointing record of development is matched only by its enormous potential. In scale it is larger than Europe. Its mineral resources alone were of sufficient magnitude to vault a lethargic Europe out of the Dark Ages into the modern era. Yet despite a Eurocentric culture, Latin America has failed to keep pace with the development of its Anglo neighbor to the north, let alone its colonial ancestors across the Atlantic. Unlike any developing region, Latin America has squandered the most propitious circumstances for development. Internecine squabbling has disrupted the evolution of sound political institutions; the church has vacillated from underwriting the excesses of national aristocracies to empowering the masses with "liberation theology"; corporations have been the scourge of progress when they are owned by foreigners, yet inaugurated as institutions of economic salvation when appropriated by national governments. Political instability, cultural upheaval, and corporate profiteering have become a trademark for Latin America, chronic symptoms of the region's antidevelopment syndrome. Despite decades of effort and billions of dollars for investment, Latin America registers only slightly better than the regions most lagging in development: Southeast Asia and sub-Saharan Africa (*World Bank Atlas,* 1997).

The Latin penchant for institutional instability could have been dismissed as a long-term residue of colonial exploitation had it not been for the debt crisis of the late 1980s and early 1990s. The oil shocks of the 1970s destabilized economies that, despite shaky foundations, had generated economic growth. Unwilling to curtail government spending and refusing to limit a level of consumption to which they had become accustomed, national aristocracies that controlled state-owned corporations and federal legislatures proceeded to borrow massively in order to keep their economies from foundering (Castaneda, 1993). A decade later, the borrowing strategy had reduced Latin American economies to chaos; currency was printed and devalued, inflation skyrocketed, subverting growth, and capital fled overseas. International financial organizations imposed reforms that, in the absence of radical redistribution of wealth, meant severe reductions in government spending for education, health, and welfare programs. By the end of the 1990s, economies of Latin American nations were on more solid footing, yet the well-being of most Latin Americans was ever more precarious. For all practical purposes the 1980s had become a lost decade. In retrospect, it seemed that Latin America, once raped by European colonists, had ravaged itself. Development on a par with the United States and Europe seemed even more remote. If there was a New World Order, it offered precious little for this region of the New World.

## Historical Background

Prior to the modern era, three prehistoric populations dominated the Americas: the Maya of Central America, the Inca of Peru, and the Toltec-Aztec of Central Mexico. These civilizations flourished as a result of a salubrious climate and the cultivation of New World crops, particularly corn. Each of these cultures erected massive monuments of stone that have endured to the present, but beyond those, the pre-Columbian cultures of America have distinct features. The Maya, for example, had developed a sophisticated 365-day calendar that called for inserting an extra day every fourth year and 25 extra days every 104 years, making it more accurate than any European calendar until 1582. Such a calendar required a mathematics with which the Maya were quite adept, developing a system based on units of twenty and incorporating zero. Maya cultural history was recorded by an elaborate system of hieroglyphs, which remains largely undeciphered. Despite advances in mathematics and astronomy, the Maya possessed only a rudimentary pictographic written form and failed to use devices such as the wheel and the arch. From its formative phase in 600 B.C., the Maya blossomed to a Classic Period from A.D. 300 to A.D. 900, and a post-Classic Period from A.D. 900 to 1441, when the civilization rapidly declined, succumbing to the Yucatan rainforest.

The Inca settled the inhospitable Peruvian highlands, prospering from an elaborate system of aqueducts that allowed the cultivation of maize and potatoes. Their theocracy was highly regimented yet incorporated a division of labor that assured the well-being of the commoner. Most agricultural land belonged to the people in the form of a commons, or *ejido,* and all able-bodied farmers worked for benefit of the community. "First the lands belonging to the Sun were cultivated; then those of the widows and orphans, the old and the infirm; next the land of the people in general was worked, and last all that of the Inca (chief)." Graft was not tolerated. A regional chief who diverted labor from lands set aside for welfare to that of a relative was hung on gallows erected at the scene of the crime (Crow, 1992: 28–29). The very regimentation that prevented starvation in a harsh climate also impeded social mobility; Inca civilization was based on a caste system that predestined work and opportunity at birth. It would also foretell their defeat by the Spanish. In pursuit of gold and silver in the Andes, a ruthless Pizarro had only to murder the Inca, and the whole population knelt before him.

Aztec civilization was arguably the most ill-fated in human history. In about 1200, the Aztec people moved to an expansive valley now occupied by Mexico City. Fertile lands produced abundant crops of corn, nearby mountains provided deer, and a large lake yielded fish. In a short time, the warrior-like Aztecs had subdued nearby native populations, brought fresh mountain water to the valley through aqueducts, and erected colossal stone structures for worship, sport, and human sacrifice. Their civilization was as monumental as it was fierce. Aztec cities were on a parallel with those of medieval Europe, and their subjugation of adjoining peoples notably relentless, as evident in the sacrifice of thousands of prisoners to various Aztec deities. Among these was Quetzalcoatl, who prophesied the arrival of blond men from across the sea in winged ships sometime around the landing of Cortes at Vera Cruz in 1519. So humbled before the conquistadors, the Aztec empire soon crumbled before a combine of Spanish and Indian forces assembled by Cortes in his relentless quest for gold (Crow, 1993).

The conquest of the New World on the part of Iberian explorers was in pursuit of "gold, glory, and God" in roughly that order. The intrigue surrounding the monarchies of fifteenth-century Spain and Portugal are substance for a contemporary soap opera. Ineptitude, corruption, and salacious living drove the kingdoms of Iberia toward bankruptcy, from which the most immediate salvation was a massive infusion of revenue. The most likely source of quick profit lay to the East, where Marco Polo had reported unparalleled wealth in spices, silk, and gold. Overland commerce in these commodities had already gilded the city-state of Venice; if a sea route could be established, the riches of the Orient could be claimed by Spain and Portugal because of their superior navies. In this pursuit, Isabel and Ferdinand dispatched several explorations to the East—among the least profitable, one captained by Christopher Columbus (Cristobal Colon).

What Columbus, a raffish fellow, lacked in integrity, he more than made up for with grit. Of the four trips Columbus undertook to cross the Ocean Sea in search of Cipango (Japan), it was not until the last that he declared having discovered a new continent. Other than naming prominent features to a handful of smaller Caribbean islands and Cuba, which he left intentionally ambiguous in order to confound explorers he feared would retrace his voyages, the discoveries of Columbus are most notable for their insignificance. (The exception seems to have been his spectacular ineptitude as a colonial governor.) During the first voyage, after the *Santa Maria* had sunk from running aground on a coral reef, Columbus left a colony—*La Navidad*—a fortress constructed with the help of the Taino, a Caribbean tribe. Columbus had encountered the Taino, the first "Indians" of the Orient, and found them quite helpful: "They are the best people in the world and above all the gentlest," he recorded in 1492. "They became so much our friends that it was a marvel…They traded and gave everything they had, with good will" (Sale, 1990: 99–100).

As Admiral of the Ocean Sea, Columbus soon returned to the Caribbean with 17 ships and between 1,200 to 1,500 colonists. On November 28, 1493, the Admiral set anchor near *La Navidad* and went ashore to find all the Spanish *colon*-ists slaughtered, evidently after taking liberties with Taino women. This incident served as sufficient pretext for the beginning of the slave trade in the New World; in 1495 Columbus rounded up 1,600 Tainos from the interior of Espanola, from which 550 were placed in chains for shipment to Spain, a trip that resulted in the death of 200 (Sale, 1990: 138–39). More barbarous was the tribute system that Columbus instituted in 1495 as governor. Every three months, each male Taino over age 14 had to produce a hawk's bell (about a thimble) of gold or 25 pounds of cotton in gold-deficient areas or risk the punishment of having his hands cut off. Such cruelty more than decimated the native population of the Caribbean, of course. If the pre-Columbian Taino population of Espanola once exceeded several million, by 1542 only 200 remained. And whatever the original number of Taino, by the end of the century, the tribe was extinct (Sale, 1990: 155–61).

Although the treasures from the Orient that Columbus promised the Spanish monarchy were more rhetorical than real, a sea route for trade with the East made his discoveries of great interest. In order to resolve Spanish and Portugese claims on the New World, an edict from Pope Alexander VI of 1493 and the Treaty of Tordesillas of 1494 set a line 370 leagues (approximately 1,100 miles) West of the Azores, and declared that those to the west belonged to Spain, those to the east, Portugal. Later, when the Latin American colonies drifted from the orbit of Europe, settlers of the Portugese colony, Brazil, would violate the treaty and claim lands to the east of the meridian. But the likelihood of settling a New World was largely dismissed; the real benefit of lands to the east of the Azores was for the establishment of ports for provisioning sea trade with the Orient (Crow, 1992).

That the colonies of Columbus would be little more than ports of call for ships shuttling from Europe to the Orient was immediately dispelled with the discovery of gold. The brash exploits of Cortes, who conquered the Aztec in 1519, the victory of illiterate Pizarro over the Inca in 1532–1553, and the successful campaign of Jimenez de Quesada over the natives of Colombia of the 1530s brought news of unexpected riches that the Spanish pursued with unremitting greed. In order to extract precious metals, the Spanish introduced the *encomienda* system, which gave the title owner of land the right to exact tribute and demand services from inhabitants. In virgin lands that lacked manual labor and beasts of burden, the Spanish used tribute to virtually enslave the Indians—who became indispensable in agriculture and mining. Tribute was required of males between ages 18 and 50 and consisted of two or three pesos annually. The avarice of Spanish landlords, many of whom had been *conquestadores,* quickly led to abuses. Indians were required to purchase clothing and tools from the *encomenderos,* often at inflated prices, and in some cases were provided credit that left them in permanent indenture. Native families were reduced to peonage since parental debt was inherited by children. In Chile, women and children were not exempt from having to pay tribute, and "each [Indian] had one foot cut off a little above the toe joints in order to make them incapable of flight" (Crow, 1992: 154–56). By 1556, $8 million in tribute was being shipped to Spain annually, of which the crown retained its "royal fifth" (Sale, 1990: 158). Between 1492 and 1800, as much as $6 billion in gold and silver was sent from the New World to Spain (Crow, 1992: 216).

The brutality of Spanish rule in the New World was so severe that it tarred the early colonial era as *La Leyenda Negra,* The Black Legacy. When a descendent of the Incas, Tupac Amaru II, objected to the *encomienda* system—and the resulting forced labor of Indians—only to find his voice ignored, he ambushed and hung the provincial governor. After he was hunted down and captured with his family, a death sentence was passed on the entire group. First, Tupac Amaru was to witness the execution of his wife, a son, an uncle, a brother-in-law, and his lieutenants, two of which would have their tongues cut out. Then Tupac Amaru would have his tongue cut out, his limbs tied to four horses that would pull him apart, and he would be beheaded. The sentence was carried out May 18, 1781, more than two centuries after the Spanish seized control of the Andes (Crow, 1992: 407).

For some colonists, such as Bartolome de Las Casas, who had been an *encomendero* before taking his religious vows, policies such as the *encomienda* were intolerable, and they worked to educate and care for the Indians (Sale, 1990: 156–58). Jesuit missionaries were particularly committed to uplifting the natives while protecting them from the predations of fellow colonists. In several sites, Jesuits established successful missions, essentially self-sufficient religious communes in which Indians were educated in religious liturgy, provided separate quarters for men and women prior to marriage, and taught a trade. The Jesuits did all this and made the necessary payments to the crown, but their success was their undoing. Because the Spanish were fearful of such extensive enterprise with the Indians, the Jesuits were expelled from the New World in 1851 (Crow, 1992: 628).

By the mid-nineteenth century, liberty had been won by the New World Spanish colonies and Brazil. The United States contributed to Latin American independence in two ways: The Constitution was a philosophical construct, if not a literal document, from which the fight for Latin freedom was waged, and an American president minimized European meddling in New World affairs by announcing the Monroe Doctrine in 1823. Beyond these not-insignificant contributions, victory over the Spanish was a product of the brilliance and stamina of Simon Bolivar, Jose de San Martin, and their commanders, who had overcome vast distances, penetrated impregnable wilderness, and suffered severe hardship.

Tragically, independence failed to germinate democratic institutions in Latin America. A residual caste system in which the *criollos* (Creoles), direct descendants of Spain and Portugal, lorded over mixed-race *mestizos,* leaving Indians and former African slaves as virtual nonentities, subverted the emergence of an open society as would be reflected in a market economy and democratic polity. Instead of elected officials who oversaw open civil institutions, *caudillos* exerted control over the political economy, pushing opponents aside, if not eliminating them altogether. The poverty and ignorance of South Americans, a result of the looting of the region by Iberia and the colonial failure to educate the masses, contributed to an era of *caudillo* rule. Often former revolutionaries whose families controlled vast ranches, *caudillos* brooked no quarter with those who preferred the niceties of civil society. The rule of Mariano Melgarejo, a licentious drunkard who ran Bolivia from 1864 to 1871 is a case in point. Confronting the Bolivian dictator, Belzu, in the presidential palace, Melgarejo drew a pistol and shot his rival dead. He strode to a window and shouted to a large crowd that had gathered, "Belzu is dead. Now who are you shouting for?" The crowd cheered heartily, "Long live Melgarejo!" (Crow, 1992: 625).

Latin America's industrialization was contorted by the dominant role of Creole families who retained hegemony in national affairs. The Iberian tradition of *mayorazgo,* through which estates were inherited intact by the oldest son, not only assured landed families of immense holdings, but it served to perpetuate a subordinate caste of manual laborers, the social process maintained by mixed-race *mestizos.* As an extension of colonial custom, the Creole aristocracy held political influence far beyond its small numbers, insulated itself from the masses by exclusive education of its youth and socialization of adults, and negotiated business deals that defined the national economy. Given the extensive natural resources of many Latin nations, the aristocracy frequently cut deals with foreign firms for the extraction of minerals and production of agricultural commodities. Consequently, the nations of Latin America, despite recent efforts to diversify, are still associated with traditional exports of the industrial era: Cuba for sugar, Chile for copper and nitrates, Venezuela for oil, Honduras for bananas, Argentina and Uruguay for beef and grains, and Bolivia for tin (Crow, 1992: 717). Reliance on single exports solved some of the problems for aristocratic rule by reducing the tax exposure of wealthy families, and it facilitated integration with more developed markets; but, it posed another problem because the national economy would be dependent on fluctuations on only one or, at best, a few, commodities.

Eventually, export dependence became associated with a skewed political economy. Critics from the Latin Left formulated "dependency theory" to explain the invidious relationship between aristocratic families that pulled the political and economic levers of a nation and the foreign corporations that benefited from cheap resources. According to dependency theorists, the brunt of the continual exploitation of Latin America's resources was borne by the unorganized masses, whose ignorance kept them passive. The absence of education, health, and welfare benefits for the masses was mandated by wealthy Creole families that functioned as *de facto* intermediaries for foreign corporations. Under conditions of deprivation and exploitation, dependecy theory resonates with the poor, and it became the template for revolutionary movements in Latin America from Castro's overthrow of Batista in Cuba in 1959 to the Sandanista revolution against Samoza in Nicaragua half a century later (Castaneda, 1993: 70–1).

Beyond these dramatic events, dependency theory provided little more than polemic. Many more insurrections mounted under the banner of dependency theory disintegrated into internecine squabbling than overthrew the Creole capitalist aristocracy; those isolated revolutionary successes soon evidenced structural failures on the economic or political front, and eventually both. In other instances, attempts at structural reform were simply canceled by putsches maneuvered by national cabals in collusion with foreign entities, such as the Central Intelligence Agency, as occurred in Guatemala in 1954 (Schlesinger and Kinzer, 1983) or Chile in 1973 (Crow, 1992). As a theory of development, dependency theory would probably have sputtered out because of its lack of an affirmative orientation for progress had it not been for the militarization of Central America following the Nicaraguan revolution. Previously, U.S. corporate interests had been able to rely on national militias to control dissident movements that threatened the rule of aristocratic Creoles. Immediately after the overthrow of Samoza, Sandanistas made indiscreet pronouncements favorable to Cuba as a revolutionary mentor and toward other insurgencies in Central America. This rattled a reactionary Reagan administration which dispatched, through means legal and otherwise, U.S. troops to equip and train "contra" counter revolutionaries. This overt militarization of what had previously been covert aid was the critical factor in the invocation of "*neo*dependency theory" (LaFeber, 1983: 18).

For all its rhetoric, the radical Latin Left was far from free of contradictions regarding matters political and economic. In his masterful review of the region's politics, Jorge Casteneda (1993) tells the story of the $70 million ransom secured by the Montoneros, a left-wing insurgency in Argentina, after a successful kidnapping. Because the Montoneros lacked the capacity to use such a large sum, it was deposited first in European banks, then, because of a dispute about fiduciary control, in American banks. Continued conflict among Montonero factions about the funds threatened further fragmentation, during which a Montonero financier disappeared—and possibly died in a plane accident—with some of the money. Subsequently, the balance was deposited in the National Bank of Cuba. By this time, the Montoneros were being decimated by the Argentine military, and their claim on the funds diminished as stronger insurrection movements in Latin America clamored for financial assistance. In 1981, the remaining Montonero leadership authorized the release of only $1 million to other leftist guerilla groups, leaving the balance in cash-starved Cuba. By 1991, the Argentine prosecutor of the kidnapping case had located the funds and filed an injunction freezing the deposit in Cuba. In response, Castro promised to return the monies to the remaining Montonero factions, pending the agreement of their leaders—a problematic prospect, at best (1993: 9–15). Thus, the final beneficiary of this comic adventure in revolutionary high finance was Castro, among the most conservative leaders in Latin America.

## Development through Import Substitution

More moderate strategies for national development focused on "import substitution industrialization" (ISI). The economic logic behind ISI was reasonable enough: High tariffs against imports from more advanced industrial nations would protect nascent national industry, which would eventually meet the consumer demands and expand, in the process providing jobs for workers and revenues for the state treasury. As Jorge Castaneda noted, "Protected, import-substitution industrialization, a large state-owned sector of the economy, across-the-board subsidies, and the pretense of a social safety net were all salient features of postwar economic development" (1993: 245). ISI, in other words, presumed that "national industry requires breathing space to catch up with foreign competitors" (Radelet and Sachs, 1997: 51). Thus formulated, ISI promised gradual industrialization, a less radical route to modernization. Despite its economic plausibility, ISI failed to vault Latin American nations into the ranks of the First World. If it had not succumbed to its economic contradictions, ISI would have foundered on the shoals of Latin American politics. As had been the case in other developing regions, ISI proved disappointing as a strategy for economic development.

> Infant industry protection often becomes senile industry protection: domestic firms in small markets never attain the scale at which they could overcome foreign cost advantages, and protection leaves enterprises lazy, dependent on state handouts, and behind in adopting technology. (Radelet and Sachs, 1997: 51)

In a perverse manner, however, the inadequacy of ISI reinforced the political status quo. National industries were controlled by the Creole aristocracy either outright or as proxies of international corporations, and ISI offered them even greater wealth. The worsening of an already skewed distribution of wealth fueled opposition parties that moved to increase taxes on personal and corporate income, the revenues of which would be invested in education, health, and welfare programs for the masses. In the face of increased taxes, Creole aristocrats sent capital to overseas accounts, depleting national savings. Populist politicians attempted to halt the hemorrhaging of capital by nationalizing industries, particularly those owned or proxied by Creole capitalists. While this generated much-needed revenues, governments have a poor reputation of corporate management, a manifestation of which was high levels of corruption in nationalized industries. With diminishing revenues coming in from nationalized industries, governments tended to meet mass demands for education, health, and welfare programs by printing money, in the process setting off skyrocketing inflation. The resulting economic instability would prove untenable, and correction could come voluntarily, usually by a populist government returning the reins of power to aristocratic capitalists, or involuntarily in the form of a military takeover (Castaneda, 1993). This scenario was repeated so often that it became a caricature of the Latin American political economy and would have continued indefinitely had it not been pushed over the abyss by the debt crisis.

For all its flaws, ISI did generate economic growth among the developing nations of Latin America. Between 1967 and 1974, for example, developing nations grew at annual rates of 6.6 percent, with Latin America exceeding that. The oil shocks of the 1970s, however, required developing nations to increase borrowing significantly. Reluctant to negotiate loans from international agencies that might demand economic reforms, developing nations resorted to commercial sources. When economic growth failed to reach levels that would cover increased borrowing, wealthy families sent capital abroad to protect assets from inflation, further aggravating the national shortage in capital. As Table 2.1 shows, Latin American nations were pulled into a downward economic spiral.

Debt of such magnitude contributed to inflation, as Latin American nations attempted to right their listing economies by printing currency. Annually, inflation increased 187 percent, further retarding economic growth (Crow, 1992: 879). But skyrocketing inflation was not the worst consequence of the debt crisis. The perniciousness of such massive debt is perhaps best related by the fact that "by 1984 the developing nations were paying back $10.2 billion *more* to the commercial banks than they were receiving in new loans" (Todaro, 1994: 464). As a result of the enormous burden of debt service, the flow of capital was reversed; developing nations were actually shifting more capital to the developed nations than they received.

In desperate financial straights, developing nations with severe debt approached international lending agencies, such as the International Monetary Fund (IMF), seeking to renegotiate their loans. In exchange for assistance, the IMF demanded economic reforms in which restraints on government spending featured prominently. In developing nations,

**TABLE 2.1   Debt and Growth of Selected Indebted Countries, 1990**

| Country | Debt in $Billions | Debt Service $Billions | Debt-to GNP Ratio | Annual GNP Growth* | Annual per capita consumption* |
|---|---|---|---|---|---|
| Argentina | 61.1 | 5.1 | 61.7 | 0.0 | −1.1 |
| Bolivia | 4.3 | 0.4 | 101.0 | 1.0 | −1.7 |
| Brazil | 116.2 | 7.4 | 22.8 | 2.5 | 0.5 |
| Ecuador | 12.1 | 1.1 | 120.6 | 2.0 | −0.5 |
| Mexico | 96.8 | 12.1 | 42.1 | 1.6 | −1.1 |
| Venezuela | 33.3 | 4.3 | 71.0 | 1.1 | −1.2 |

*Percentage from 1982–1990

Adapted from M. Todaro, *Economic Development in the Third World*, 5th Edition. © 1994 by Michael P. Todaro.

including those of Latin America, government spending is the primary vehicle for provision of education, health, and welfare benefits to the poor, so IMF economic concessions hit the impoverished masses hardest. Despite such adjustments, IMF loan restructuring did not necessarily result in across-the-board economic growth, however.

> Between 1982 and 1988, the IMF strategy was tested in 28 of the 32 nations of Latin America and the Caribbean. It was clearly not working. During that period, Latin America financed $145 billion in debt repayments but at a cost of economic stagnation, rising unemployment, and a decline in per capita income of 7 percent. These countries "adjusted" but did not grow. By 1988, only two were barely able to make their payments. (Todaro, 1994: 467)

The social and political implications of such "reforms" were not lost on proponents of a lapsed dependency theory, who alleged that IMF demands were no less than blackmail designed to induce "international peonage" on the ignorant masses of developing nations (Payer, 1974).

Eventually, it became evident that the rejection of ISI and resultant economic restructuring were imposing a significant penalty on economic performance. As Table 2.2 shows, of Latin American nations, only Chile maintained the level of annual growth—6 percent—that the region had enjoyed between 1965 and 1980. Not only had Latin American economic development slowed, but it lagged behind the more vital developing economies of Asia. Worse, at an annual rate of 3.1 percent, the economic growth of Latin America fell behind the level needed to reduce poverty, 3.4 percent annually. If economic restructuring was a solution to the flaws of ISI, it was not to the advantage of Latin America in relation to other developing regions, which sped past in pursuit of international markets.

## Prospects for Development

Economic reforms worsened the already ravaged societies of Latin America. Having lost government income supports, many of the poor were driven into the informal economy

**TABLE 2.2   Latin American GDP Growth**

| Country | 1991 | 1992 | 1993 | 1994 | 1995 | 1996 |
|---------|------|------|------|------|------|------|
| Argentina | 8.9 | 8.6 | 6.0 | 7.4 | −4.6 | 3.2 |
| Brazil | 0.4 | −1.2 | 5.3 | 5.8 | 4.1 | 3.1 |
| Chile | 7.3 | 11.0 | 6.3 | 4.2 | 8.5 | 6.8 |
| Colombia | 2.0 | 4.0 | 5.2 | 5.7 | 5.3 | 3.1 |
| Ecuador | 5.0 | 3.6 | 2.0 | 4.3 | 3.2 | 2.9 |
| Mexico | 3.6 | 2.9 | 0.7 | 3.5 | −6.2 | 4.2 |
| Peru | 2.9 | −1.8 | 6.4 | 13.1 | 7.0 | 2.0 |
| Venezuela | 0.7 | 6.1 | 0.3 | −2.8 | 2.2 | −1.1 |

*Source:* Edwards, Sebastian: "Latin America's Underperformance." Reprinted by permission of *Foreign Affairs,* Vol. 76, No. 2, 1997. Copyright 1997 by the Council on Foreign Relations, Inc.

that expanded dramatically (de Soto, 1989). Mobile workers pursued more viable economic opportunities, often emigrating to the United States, posing an enormous problem for elected officials there, particularly in California (Stoesz, 1996). For many of the rural poor, the income from cocoa production for the illicit drug trade became necessary for survival, fueling clandestine trafficking in narcotics that up-ended the normal political process in Colombia (Marquez, 1997) and aggravating border problems between Mexico and the United States (Branigin and Anderson, 1997). When landless Brazilians attempted to convert Amazonian rainforest to cultivatable land, they burned virgin stands of timber, destroying one-tenth of the two-million-square-mile jungle, and raising the concern of environmentalists around the world (Astor, 1997). Contrasted with the developmental problems historically associated with Latin America, these seemed to be of a different order entirely, posing even greater challenges for advocates of modernization.

The structural reforms endorsed by international aid organizations were part of an outward-looking export strategy that promised integration with the global economy. Nations that suppressed and delayed demands for expenditures for social programs would eventually gain ground lost to discredited ISI policies. The Asian tigers were testament to the logic; under the guise of "Asian values," domestic liberties were attenuated in the name of economic growth. For those nations of Southeast Asia in which autocratic leadership evolved, this had seemed to be the case. That it could be transferred to Latin America was another matter. Riven with divisive—on occasion revolutionary—politics, Latin America seemed more likely to fragment under the strain of economic restructuring instead of girding in anticipation of more scarcity. This bodes ill for reformist governments in the region: "This dynamic suggests that unless growth accelerates, real wages increase, and unemployment declines, political support for Latin American reformist governments will erode" (Edwards, 1997: 94).

Latin Americans would not tolerate indefinite belt-tightening without registering their objections. Mexico was a case in point. Among the Latin nations most eager to integrate with international markets, Mexico had restructured its once-nationalist economy, in the process reducing government expenditures for social development. How this would affect low-income Latin Americans is evident in their lost purchasing power. A hypothetical market basket consisting of one dozen eggs, one quart of milk, and one pound each of beans, rice, bread, and meat, required the following amount of labor to purchase: for U.S. workers, 1.50 hours; Argentine workers, 3.10 hours; Chilean workers, 4.60 hours; Brazilian workers, 4.90 hours, and Mexican workers, 8.00 hours (Crow, 1992: 706). Under such stringent circumstances, many Latin Americans, especially the poorest, found stringent economic reforms impinging not just on their lifestyle, but on their very survival. The result was a nasty rebellion in Chiapas, a southern state populated largely by marginalized Indians. Similarly, government cuts in expenditures roiled the indigent poor, flaming insurrection in Colombia and Peru. Rather than prepare Latin America for integration with global markets, economic restructuring appeared more likely to result in political destabilization.

Without a clear path for progress, Latin American prospects for development have diminished. To be sure, Latin America is somewhat more advantaged compared to other developing regions. In 1987, Latin America and the Caribbean accounted for 7 percent of the world's poor; by 1993, the region's 110 million in poverty accounted for 9 percent. More detailed comparison is provided in Table 2.3. Thus, in absolute numbers, the

TABLE 2.3   Human Poverty in Developing Countries (millions)

| Region | Illiterate Adults 1995 | People Lacking Access to Health Services 1990–95 | People Lacking Access to Safe Water 1990–96 | Malnourished Children Under Five 1990–96 | Maternal Mortality Rate (per 100,000 live births) 1990 | People Not Expected to Survive to Age 40 1990s |
|---|---|---|---|---|---|---|
| All developing nations | 842 | 766 | 1,213 | 158 | 471 | 507 |
| Least developing nations | 143 | 241 | 218 | 34 | 1,030 | 123 |
| Arab states | 59 | 29 | 54 | 5 | 380 | 26 |
| East Asia | 167 | 144 | 398 | 17 | 95 | 81 |
| Latin America* | 42 | 55 | 109 | 5 | 190 | 36 |
| South Asia | 407 | 264 | 230 | 82 | 554 | 184 |
| Southeast Asia** | 38 | 69 | 162 | 20 | 447 | 52 |
| Sub-Saharan Africa | 122 | 205 | 249 | 98 | 971 | 124 |

*Includes the Caribbean

**Includes the Pacific

*Source:* From Human Development Report, 1997. Copyright © 1997 by the United Nations Development Programme. Used by permission of Oxford University Press, Inc.

incidence of several factors relative to poverty in Latin America is substantially less than in other developing regions. Ominously, between 1987 and 1993 only two developing regions showed increasing rates of poverty: sub-Saharan Africa and Latin America (*Human Development Report,* 1997: 26). In 1987, Latin America and the Caribbean contained 22.0 percent of the world's population subsisting on less than $1 a day; by 1993, the region accounted for 23.5 percent of the world's most desperate poor. In the two decades following 1975, the per capita GNP of Latin America and the Caribbean improved negligibly, above the GNP losses experienced by sub-Saharan Africa, North Africa, and the Middle East, but far behind the rapid increases experienced by South Asia, East Asia, and the Pacific (*World Development Indicators,* 1997: 31, 24).

On the other hand, Latin America falls far behind the industrialized nations. By standards of development associated with North America and Europe, Latin America and the Caribbean lag significantly. Latin America exceeds the former with respect to the number of people not expected to reach age 40 by a factor of three, the number of children reaching the fifth grade by a factor of nine, the income of the poorest 20 percent of the population by a factor of five, the maternal mortality rate by a factor of 14, and the number of children dying before age one by a factor of 14 (*Human Development Report,* 1997: 56, 60). These last two indicators are particularly disturbing, since they are most directly related to the status of women.

# Strategies for Development

Post-ISI development of Latin America must acknowledge the significant diversity of the region. The geography of Latin America runs from the desert of northern Mexico, through the jungles of Central America and the Amazon, to the extraordinary wilderness of Patagonia. Aside from the dominant Creoles, its peoples vary from the Indians of Guatemala, to former African slaves in Brazil, to European refugees in Chile. The politics of Latin America are notorious for their instability, marked by revolutions of independence from Spain, intermittent revolutions against capitalist Creole control, and protracted guerilla insurgencies, to say nothing of the 60 or so military interventions of the United States (Crow, 1992: 687). As counterpoint to political instability in general and the militarization of Central America in particular, Costa Rica persisted in developing a democratic polity without an army, becoming a beacon in an otherwise clouded landscape. Economic progress has been similarly irregular. The discovery of oil in Venezuela, Mexico, and Ecuador has stimulated otherwise lethargic economic growth. The productive capacity of Brazil promises to vault it into the First World sometime in the next century, unless the enormous debt under which its people labor proves its undoing. Other nations, such as Chile and Argentina, are diversifying their exports in order to better integrate themselves with expanding global markets. Perversely, the prime export of Colombia—cocaine—has thoroughly corrupted that nation's political economy.

The unevenness of development is evident in the primary indicators comprising the UN human development index, as evident in Table 2.4.

The region's most dynamic economies are those of Brazil, Mexico, and Argentina. Brazil is larger than the continental United States and has abundant natural resources that are just being discovered. Mexico is advantaged by extensive oil reserves, an expanding tourist industry, and a rapidly elaborating string of assembly plants along the U.S. border—*maquiladoras*—that employ 500,000 Mexicans (Crow, 1992: 745). Argentina's expansive plains—the *pampas*—have attained an international reputation for production of livestock and grain. By the mid-1990s, the World Bank included all three nations among the "emerging giants of the developing world." In 1995, the GNP in "purchasing power parity" of Brazil was $585 billion, Mexico $305 billion, and Argentina $288 billion (*World Development Indicators,* 1997: 129).

Yet, Latin America's economic development was not as rapid as other regions, particularly East Asia and the Pacific. For 1985, Latin America and the Caribbean accounted for $55.0 billion in imports from the advanced nations, or 4.4 percent, an amount that increased to $162.4 billion, or 5.2 percent, in 1995. East Asia and the Pacific, however, recorded 1985 imports of $57.5 billion, or 4.6 percent, and a whopping $237.1 billion, or 7.7 percent, in 1995. Trade going the other direction showed similar disparities. In 1985 Latin American and Caribbean exports were $84.0 billion, or 6.2 percent, rising to $163.9 billion, 5.4 percent, in 1995. Meanwhile, East Asia and the Pacific reported exports of $78.5 billion, or 5.8 percent, in 1985 increasing to $306.3 billion, 10.1 percent, in 1995 (*World Development Indicators,* 1997: 296–97). In the mad scramble for increasing shares of international markets, these figures are disturbing. While Latin American and Caribbean imports from the industrialized nations increased during the decade, exports to the industrialized nations, as a percent of total imports by industrialized nations, actually

TABLE 2.4 Development of Latin American Nations, 1994

| Country | Human Development Index Ranking | Life Expectancy at Birth, Years | Adult Literacy, % | Combined Gross Enrollment Ratio, % | Adjusted per capita GDP, $ |
|---|---|---|---|---|---|
| Chile | 30 | 75.1 | 95.0 | 72 | 5,590 |
| Costa Rica | 33 | 76.6 | 94.7 | 68 | 5,919 |
| Argentina | 36 | 72.4 | 96.0 | 77 | 5,946 |
| Uruguay | 37 | 72.6 | 97.1 | 75 | 5,895 |
| Venezuela | 47 | 72.1 | 91.0 | 68 | 5,930 |
| Mexico | 50 | 72.0 | 89.2 | 66 | 5,913 |
| Colombia | 51 | 70.1 | 91.1 | 70 | 5,868 |
| Brazil | 68 | 66.4 | 82.7 | 72 | 5,362 |
| Ecuador | 72 | 69.3 | 89.6 | 72 | 4,626 |
| Cuba | 86 | 75.5 | 95.4 | 63 | 3,000 |
| Paraguay | 94 | 68.8 | 91.9 | 62 | 3,531 |
| El Salvador | 112 | 69.3 | 70.9 | 55 | 2,417 |
| Bolivia | 113 | 60.1 | 82.5 | 66 | 2,598 |
| Honduras | 116 | 68.8 | 72.0 | 60 | 2,050 |
| Guatemala | 117 | 65.6 | 55.7 | 46 | 3,208 |
| Nicaragua | 127 | 67.3 | 65.3 | 62 | 1,580 |

*Source:* From *Human Development Report,* 1997. Copyright © 1997 by the United Nations Development Programme. Used by permission of Oxford University Press, Inc.

declined. Uninhibited by political instability, inadequate investments in human capital, and crushing debt, East Asia and the Pacific galloped ahead of Latin America and the Caribbean in the race to integrate with international markets.

Compounding Latin America's loss of world trade to the developing nations of East Asia is the nature of those exports. Compared to the Asian nations, which have rapidly expanded into light manufacturing and computer technology, Latin American continues to produce low value-added commodities for export. "Almost a decade after the initiation of market-oriented reforms, most Latin American countries continue to export mostly resource-based products with low value added," commented Sebastian Edwards. "This situation contrasts sharply with that of China and India, which have rapidly upgraded their export mix and captured a growing share of the light manufactured export market" (1997: 96). In its export of low value-added goods, Latin American continues in its role as a subordinate supplier of an industrial world that is rapidly converting to a network of global markets served by postindustrial technologies. Under these conditions, Latin American trade with the industrialized nations will continue to ebb, until the region is able to make the quite considerable investments in education, infrastructure, and capital enhancements required by the new economic order.

The strategy adopted to accelerate Latin American economic performance has been one of regional trade pacts. Regional trade among developing nations was a strategy that addressed the tendency of individual developing nations to be disadvantaged in trade relations with those nations of the First World, forever incurring trade deficits and vulnerable to price swings of dominant exports. If developing nations could form their own pacts, they could evolve regional trade networks buffered from the predations of the industrialized world. Unfortunately, theory is more easily pronounced than executed. Between 1970 and 1987, regional trade syndicates, such as the Latin America Free Trade Area and the Andean Group, generated erratic increases in trade, while the Central American Common Market lost more than half its value (Todaro, 1994: 513). Undaunted, nations of the "southern cone" formed Mercosur in 1995, forging a trade pact including Brazil, Argentina, Uruguay, and Paraguay. Mexico became part of the North American Free Trade Agreement with Canada and the United States in 1996. Given such recent developments, it is too soon to know the extent to which regional economic integration will supercede ISI as the developmental paradigm for Latin America (Castaneda, 1993: 313–14).

Symptomatic of economic stagnation, various problems have swept from Latin America into the First World, posing serious threats. Specifically, the immigration of desperate workers from Latin America into the United States, the trafficking of narcotics into North America and Europe, and the environmental consequences of deforestation of the Amazon have all refocused the attention of the industrialized nations to the plight of Latin America. Simply put, international "drugs and immigration, global warming and ozone depletion, biodiversity conservation and sustainable development," were issues that were becoming unavoidable problems for the industrialized nations (Castaneda, 1993: 425).

Of these, the environmental issue is among the most compelling vis-á-vis the developed nations. The significance of the South American jungle for global environmental balance is profound.

> The amazon and its tributaries contain more species of fish than the Atlantic Ocean, and in the Amazon rain forest live more than one half of all known species of flora and fauna in the world. This vast forest replenishes one half of the earth's oxygen, and its great river basin is the source of one fifth of the earth's fresh water. (Crow, 1992: 877)

Despite its environmental import, the Amazon is, for purposes of many Brazilians, little more than a wilderness yet to be subdued. Eager to harness the potential of cheap land, landless peasants have moved to the Amazon and converted rainforest to cultivable land through extensive burning. By the mid-1990s, between 12 and 15 percent of the Amazon rainforest had already been destroyed, and burning denuded 5800 square miles each year. Despite efforts by international organizations to convince Brazil to restrain the practice, deforestation has increased 34 percent since 1991 (Schemo, 1997).

In 1992, the Rio de Janeiro Earth Summit focused the world's attention on environmental degradation. Portraying the Earth as a global commons, environmentalists convinced 34 nations of the North and the South to sign a treaty protecting biological resources and taking specific actions to implement sustainable development policies (Castaneda, 1993: 444). Already, NGOs had pioneered the idea of "debt-for-nature swaps," allowing developing nations to write off their debt to international lenders by setting aside virgin tracts of land and protecting them against exploitation. Such innovative strategies amounted to $98 million in debt relief and environmental protection in 1991 (Todaro, 1994: 356). For all the rhetoric, reversing the consequences of industrialization was easier said than done. At the Rio Summit, nations had agreed to reduce greenhouse gas emissions to 1990 levels by 2000, but only a handful seemed likely to meet that goal by the next meeting in Kyoto. Among the laggards was the United States, which had succumbed to the pressure of energy interests ("Can We Turn Down the Heat?" 1997: 6–7). Meanwhile, media from developing nations made light of the issue: A Chinese meteorologist argued that global warming would enhance agricultural productivity in his country; a Brazilian scientist contended the carbon created by burning would be quickly absorbed by the soil ("Degrees of Difference in a Heat Wave," 1997: 10). Such myopia revisits "the tragedy of the commons," the inability of multiple users of free resources to collectively decide how to ration them, thereby leading to their destruction.

Trafficking in illegal drugs is another international issue related to development. Driving the illicit drug trade are complementary dislocations—a spiritual deprivation among First World addicts, and an economic deprivation among Third World producers. "We have not yet come to understand the resolute, determined, amoral nature of the major traffickers or their enormous power," wrote Sidney Cohen, former director of the division of Narcotic Addiction and Drug Abuse of the U.S. National Institute of Mental Health.

> Perhaps we do not even recognize that, for tens of hundreds of thousands of field workers, collecting coca leaves or opium gum is a matter of survival. At the other end of the pipeline is the swarm of sellers who could not possibly earn a fraction of their current income from legitimate pursuits. (1987: 1–3)

In the mid-1990s, one kilo (2.2 pounds) of cocaine produced in Latin America for $2,000 would fetch $15,000 in San Diego and $31,500 in Washington, D.C. (Branigin and Anderson, 1997: A17). With such extraordinary profits, the earnings of drug barons in the developing world soon eclipsed those of more reputable businessmen. Cocaine generated $3 billion in annual revenues for Colombia, surpassing exports for coffee and oil (Crow, 1992: 804). Similar profiteering in Mexico and Peru destabilized governments of those nations. Assassinations of police, elected officials, and judges became commonplace in Colombia (Hammer, 1997) and Mexico (Reding, 1997); in Peru an indigenous insurrection—*Sendero Luminoso,* the Shining Path—spread death throughout the countryside (Castaneda, 1993: 122–8).

Using the abandonment of the masses by the national government as pretext, leaders of the drug mafia generated public support by defying official authority at the same time they made generous contributions to civic projects. The Medellin cartel contributed millions for recreation facilities for children as well as food and clothing for the poor (Crow, 1992: 806). A Mexican drug lord contributed $100,000 for recovery efforts after the 1985 earthquake (Moore, 1997). That the Latin America drug mafia could liquidate government officials while subsidizing the economic and civic needs of the poor shook the very foundations of government. Quickly the United States urged South American governments to collaborate in a "war on drugs" that would erase the production of cocaine in Latin America, offering incentives in the hundreds of millions of dollars. The resultant quandary revisited the worst in U.S.–Latin American relations: the specter of (c)overt U.S. military action with the tacit acceptance by acquiescent national governments.

Immigration is the third international factor influencing development. While the immigration of Central Americans to the United States predominated during the 1980s when the Reagan administration militarized the region in reaction to insurgency movements, most illegal immigration on the part of Mexicans is for economic reasons. A Mexican *dicho,* attributed to Mexican President Porfirio Diaz, runs: *Pobre Mexico, tan lejos de Dios, tan cerca de los Estados Unidos* (Poor Mexico, so far from God, so close to the United States). The *dicho* has a cogence that is far too real for many Mexicans:

> As long as the wage differential between the United States and Mexico…averaged eight to one, enterprising Mexicans of all social strata were going to continue their trek north. In 1990 the Mexican minimum wage was 55 cents an hour, whereas its counterpart in California, where fully half of all undocumented Mexican immigrants make their home, was $4.75 an hour. (Castaneda, 1993: 303)

Undocumented immigration from Mexico into the United States presents two problems. First, the large number of Mexican males who spend considerable time north of the border do so at considerable cost to the communities they leave behind (Conover, 1987). Second, in those metropolitan areas in the United States where large numbers of immigrants settle, they appear to take low-wage, unskilled jobs traditionally held by African Americans (Howell and Mueller, 1997). Unfortunately, the U.S. approach to the problem has been to emphasize interception and security, to the extent of building an impregnable fence on the border between San Diego and Tijuana, further antagonizing relations with Mexico.

Jorge Castaneda has proposed that the new issues of development—the environment, drugs, and immigration—serve as the catalyst for a "grand bargain for the millennium"—a pact for progress negotiated between the First and Third Worlds of the western hemisphere. The interdependence of North and South America, so evident in environmental degradation, international drug mafias, and economic immigration, can be used to forge agreements among involved nations: The industrial nations of North America agree to renegotiate Latin American debt, if the nations of Central and South America take parallel steps to halt exploitation of the Amazon, agree to deport drug lords, and restrain emigration. From this platform, a pathway to progress emerges; "The road to the region's modernity must lead to a special government–business relationship and social compensation for the ravages of the market." Such industrial policy would have three distinct objectives:

> first, the establishment of an authentic Latin American welfare state that extends its protection to a majority of the population; second, funding this goal through profound tax reform, massive debt relief, and major cuts in military spending; finally, laying the basis for the long-term viability of the first two objectives through a nationally devised strategy for export-led, environmentally sustainable industrial growth. (Castaneda, 1993: 446, 451)

So formatted, Castaneda combines the outward-looking, export-based industrialization model adopted by Japan with the inward-looking, corporate-oriented industrial policy of Germany to suggest a hybrid for Latin American industrialization.

The value of such a scenario rests as much on the necessity of avoiding the continual tumult and savagery that have typified Latin America over the centuries as it does with any inherent plausibility. Yet, recent events are cause for optimism. Although economic restructuring has imposed substantial sacrifices that have been borne disproportionately by the masses, enhanced economic performance appears likely. In retrospect, it seems that Latin America has had little choice but to select austerity; the failure to do so would have placed the region, already marginalized in global markets, further behind the Asian developing nations in global economic integration. With national governments having diminished opportunities to the masses for purposes of economic advancement, it remains to be seen if these national governments, historically controlled by aristocratic families, will open the political process to accommodate the interests of rural peasants and the urban poor through organized political opposition. The failure to allow such representation has been the Achilles heel of the Latin American political economy; in the absence of formal participation by parties representing the dispossessed, they have resorted to insurrection, and the aristocracy has sought support of the military to reassert civil control (Atwood, 1997). Democratic elections in general, and the formation of new political parties in particular, have been the source of recent reform movements in several Latin American nations (Dominguez, 1997). News from the political front, in other words, is encouraging.

This democratic interregnum is only viable to the extent that benefits are restored to the masses, however. "Trickle-down economics doesn't seem to work very well in Latin American societies," wrote Peruvian journalist Gustavo Gorriti. "And the failure of trickle-down policies is likely to exacerbate social tensions, to widen income disparity, to fuel new forms of violence" (1994: 37). The challenge to advocates of development is to craft strategies that supercede the traditional paradigm typified by grand-scale, industrial infrastructure projects financed by international aid with a new generation of grass roots initiatives that are low-technology, environmentally friendly, and democratic, while regardful of local customs. But this is insufficient. If such ventures are to be more than isolated experiments in progress, they must be connected to national and international markets. In so doing, development specialists would have not only elevated Latin America from centuries of disruption but also crafted a model for other developing regions around the world.

# REFERENCES

Astor, Michael. (1997). "Drought Speeds Amazon Blazes," *Richmond Times-Dispatch* (October 29).

Atwood, Robert. (1997). "Creeping Coup," *The New Republic* (October 6).

Branigin, William, and John Anderson. (1997). "Drug Corruption Heading North," *Washington Post* (November 3).

"Can We Turn Down the Heat?" (1997). *World Press Review* (December).

Castaneda, Jorge. (1993). *Utopia Unarmed* (New York: Knopf).

Cohen, Sidney. (1987). "The Drug-Free America Act of 1986," *Drug Abuse and Alcoholism Newsletter* (San Diego, CA: Vista Hill Foundation).

Conover, Ted. (1987). *Coyotes* (New York: Vintage).

Crow, John. (1992). *The Epic of Latin America,* 4th ed. (Berkeley, University of California Press).

"Degrees of Difference in a Heat Wave." (1997). *World Press Review* (December).

de Soto, Hernando. (1989). *The Other Path* (New York: Harper & Row).

Dominguez, Jorge. (1997). "Latin America's Crisis of Representation," *Foreign Affairs* (January/February).

Edwards, Sebastian. (1997). "Latin America's Underperformance," *Foreign Affairs* (March/April).

Gorriti, Gustavo. (1994). "Battle Scars," *The New Republic* (May 9).

Hammer, Joshua. (1997). "Running Scared," *The New Republic* (November 10).

Howell, David, and Elizabeth Mueller. (1997). "The Effects of Immigrants on African-American Earnings" (New York: New School for Social Research).

*Human Development Report.* (1997). (New York: Oxford University Press).

LaFeber, Walter. (1983). *Inevitable Revolutions* (New York: Norton).

Marquez, Gabriel. (1997). *News of a Kidnaping* (New York: Knopf).

Moore, Molly. (1997). "Mexican Priest Lauds Drug Lords' Charity," *Washington Post* (September 23).

Payer, Cheryl. (1974). *The Debt Trap* (New York: Monthly Review).

Radelet, Steven, and Jeffrey Sachs. (1997). "Asia's Reemergence," *Foreign Affairs* (November/December).

Reding, Andrew. (1997). "Aztec Sun Rising," *World Policy Journal* (Fall).

Sale, Kirkpatrick. (1990). *The Conquest of Paradise* (New York: Plume).

Schemo, Diana. (1997). "Rising Fires Renew Threat to Amazon," *New York Times* (November 2).

Schlesinger, Stephen, and Stephen Kinzer. (1983). *Bitter Fruit* (New York: Anchor).

Stoesz, David. (1996). *Small Change: Domestic Policy under the Clinton Administration* (New York: Longman).

Todaro, Michael. (1994). *Economic Development,* 5th ed. (New York: Longman).

*World Bank Atlas.* (1997). (Washington, DC: World Bank).

*World Development Indicators.* (1997). (Washington, DC: World Bank).

# 3

# Africa: The Fourth World

*We were wanderers on a prehistoric earth, on an earth that wore the aspect of an unknown planet. We could have fancied ourselves the first of men taking possession of an accursed inheritance, to be subdued at the cost of profound anguish and of excessive toil. But suddenly, as we struggled round a bend, there would be a glimpse of rush walls, of peaked grass-roofs, a burst of yells, a whirl of black limbs, a mass of hands clapping, of feet stamping, of bodies swaying, of eyes rolling, under the droop of heavy and motionless foliage. The steamer toiled along slowly on the edge of a black and incomprehensible frenzy. The prehistoric man was cursing us, praying to us, welcoming us—who could tell? We were cut off from the comprehension of our surroundings; we glided past like phantoms wondering and secretly appalled, as sane men would be before an enthusiastic outbreak in a madhouse. We could not understand because we were too far and could not remember because were traveling in the night of first ages, of those ages that are gone, leaving hardly a sign—and no memories.*

—Joseph Conrad *Heart of Darkness*

Cradle of man, caldron of violence, Africa poses challenges to development that are as unique as they are unfathomable. For eons, Pharaohs ruled civilizations north of the sands that divide Africa, ruling a culture that was infinitely more advanced compared to the stone and wattle huts that typified the prehistoric peoples who inhabited what is now Europe. Today, the majority of people of sub-Saharan Africa eke out a marginal existence, living in conditions that more accurately resemble Europe during the Dark Ages than they do postindustrial societies of the First World. Most confounding, however, has been the continent's resistance to strategies of modernization. Despite persistent efforts on the part of the nations of the West, international development agencies, and NGOs, the Africa of today often reflects an infrastructure in ruins, urban peoples living in squalor, rural populations unacquainted with basic education and health care, and the political leader with a predilection to be the Big Man. These are the factors that breed violence, a consequence that has metastacized into genocide all too frequently, as the massacre of Hutus and Tutsis in Central Africa tragically illustrates. By most indicators of development, the conditions of sub-Saharan Africa have worsened in the decades since nations gained independence during the 1960s.

## Overview

With an area of 11.7 million square miles, Africa is, after Asia, the world's largest continent. Populated by 2000 ethnic or tribal groups it is arguably the globe's most diverse. The population of sub-Saharan Africa is largely rural and is maintained by hand cultivation of small plots. Although the soil of many parts of Africa is quite rich, a scattered population and primitive agricultural methods produce yields far below those of more modern nations (Lamb, 1987: xiii-xiv, 6). In 1993, the population of sub-Saharan Africa totaled 522 million, a number expected to increase to 637 million by 2000. Driven by the highest fertility rate among the inhabited continents, sub-Saharan Africa's population growth is the highest, despite a 1993 life expectancy of 51 years and infant mortality rate of 97 per 1000 live births. The diet of 61 percent of Africans is below caloric requirements (Todaro, 1994: 44). More than 22 million children are malnourished, and more than 4 million die before reaching age 5. Only 57 percent of sub-Saharan Africans have access to health services, 45 percent to potable water, and 37 percent to sanitation. Some 13.3 million sub-Saharan Africans are HIV positive, 60 percent of the world's total (Richburg, 1997: 123). While 54 percent of children attend primary school, only 18 percent are enrolled in secondary school. Little over half of the population is literate (*Human Development Report,* 1996).

By many standards, Africa is the poorest of developing regions. Almost 40 percent of the population survives on less than $1 per day (*World Bank Atlas,* 1997: 11). The per capita GNP for sub-Saharan Africa is $555 (per capita GDP is $1,385). Two-thirds of workers are employed in agriculture, and only 9 percent in industry (*Human Development Report,* 1996: table 47). In comparison with other developing regions, Africa has lost ground economically, despite modest growth. For example, between 1985 and 1995, exports from OECD nations to sub-Saharan Africa increased from $27.9 billion to $40.3 billion, but related to total OECD exports sub-Saharan Africa's percentage dropped from 2.2 percent to 1.3 percent. Imports from sub-Saharan Africa to OECD nations show a worsening of the balance of trade. From 1985 to 1995, OECD imports from sub-Saharan Africa increased from $40.4 billion to $44.5 billion; yet, because of more rapid global economic growth, the percentage share dropped by half, from 3.0 percent to 1.5 percent (*World Development Indicators,* 1997: chart 6.2). Sub-Saharan Africa, in other words, was not only poor, but it was failing to keep pace with a growing global economy, a problem that further retards progress. This loss of competitive position has not been for want of assistance. Per capita assistance to sub-Saharan Africa exceeds $30, far beyond any other developing region, further confounding development strategies (*World Bank Atlas,* 1997: 35).

Development indicators, unfortunately, tend to fragment the nature of sub-Saharan poverty. Aggregating multiple indicators, Richard Estes has calculated that between 1970 and 1990, the Index of Social Progress for Africa dropped from 19.8 to 19.5, while that of Asia increased from 35.7 to 43.7, Latin America from 48.8 to 57, and the OECD nations from about 79 to 91 (Estes, 1998). Statistics fail to capture the oppressiveness of such destitution, however. The torpor of Africa is better reflected in the burned-out ruins of the New

Africa Hotel in downtown Nyeri, Kenya, and the heaps of old clothing and worn shoes being resold in the market in Lilongwe, Malawi. In its latent form it simply suffocates hope, as in V. S. Naipaul's description of stumbling upon the ruins of an abandoned village: "You felt like a ghost, not from the past, but from the future. You felt that your life and ambition had already been lived out for you and you were looking at the relics of that life. You were in a place where the future had come and gone" (1989: 27).

At its most malevolent, the poverty metastacizes into mass violence, as Keith Richburg chronicled. "They don't count the bodies in Africa," Richburg recalled of his coverage of the Rwanda genocide, "because death is anonymous in Africa, even mass death." At Rusumo Falls, where the Kagera River flows from Rwanda into Tanzania, he begins a macabre inventory:

> Here I check my watch. One minute goes by. And a corpse. Another minute, another body. Two more minutes, another, and on it goes like that. A body every minute or two...They were bloated now, horribly discolored. Most were naked, or stripped down to their underpants. Sometimes the hands and feet were bound together. Some were clearly missing some limbs. And as they went over the falls, a few got stuck together on a little crag, and stayed there flapping against the current, as though they were trying to break free. I couldn't take my eyes off one of them, the body of a little baby.... And I stand there for an hour, counting, watching, and waiting. Thirty bodies an hour, they tell me. Seven hundred each day. And it has been this way for several days. (1997: ix, 102–103)

The horrors of the Hutu and Tutsi massacres eclipsed the more organized butchery of Idi Amin in Uganda during the early 1980s, recalling the savagery that marked the development of nations now secure in their status within the First World: the Spanish Inquisition, the annihilation of Native Americans in the New World, to say nothing of the Holocaust.

## Historical Background

Although modern Africa dates with the arrival of traders and missionaries from Europe, these visitors encountered prehistoric peoples that were in many ways as advanced as those of literate civilizations (Franklin, 1980). As early as 500 b.c., the Nok of Nigeria were smelting iron and kiln-drying pottery that was as intricate as that found anywhere. The Songhai Empire influenced an expanse from Nigeria to Mali, and its cities were described by explorers as rivaling those found in the capitals of Europe. Contemporaries of Christopher Columbus reported African stone carving, textiles, and bronze casts that were in some cases superior to those produced in Europe. Yet, without a written tradition, those cultures that had not already succumbed to marauding African tribes were crushed by European settlement. Only Ethiopia with a written language and a dynasty traced directly to the Biblical era was able to resist the incursion by the white man (Lamb, 1987: 7–9).

The Portuguese were the first Europeans to exploit Africa, and they introduced two institutions that continue to shape the continent: slavery and the church. During their explorations of coastal East Africa, Portuguese navigators encountered the dominions of the Sultan of Zanzibar, whose people had established a slave trade with the Yao tribe that spanned central sub-Saharan Africa. The Arab-Yao collaboration in slaving was expanded by the Portuguese, who had a demand for labor in the New World and the ships to transport human chattel (Pike, 1968: 58). During the late eighteenth century, slaving expanded as the Yao collaborated with other tribes to capture other Africans, march them to Goree Island off Senegal, and transport them to the Caribbean, the Spanish and Portuguese colonies in South America, and the British Colonies to the north. At the peak of the slave trade, 1790, some 70,000 Africans were shipped to the New World each year. Estimates on the total number of Africans enslaved and transported to the Americas vary from between 10 and 15 million (Lamb, 1987) to 20 million (Richburg, 1996), but regardless, the consequences of the commerce in human cargo were considerable. Not only were African societies stripped of generations of their youngest and healthiest members, but a deep rage simmered among Africans toward whites who had decimated their peoples (Wills, 1985). This resentment would later reject western ideas of development associated with European colonists, in favor of collectivist, nativist strategies which, following independence, isolated African nations from the global institutions of democratic capitalism.

Missionaries were arguably the most influential of European colonists, introducing written and electronic communication from the industrial world, education and health services, and most significantly the Christian church. For all their enthusiasm, the early missionaries were ill-prepared for the harshness of Africa. Half the Baptist missionaries dispatched to the Belgian Congo between 1878 and 1888 died from disease; almost one-fourth of Methodist missionaries sent to British West Africa met a similar demise (Lamb, 1987: 263). The naivete of certain sects is simply astonishing:

> The Likoma missionaries [of Nyasaland, now Malawi] to convince the Africans of their good faith, elected to live in the same manner as primitive tribesmen, in small grass huts and eating the same diet. For nearly a decade they persisted in this mode of living and disease and death took a heavy toll. The death rate for the years 1885–1904 was 33 per 100, and in some years over 60 per 100, and many more were invalided home. This self-sacrifice was complete folly, impracticable and unrealistic, for it defeated the whole object of their existence in Africa (Pike: 1968: 79).

Among the missionaries, David Livingstone was singularly influential, not only for his respect and treatment of indigenous Africans, but also for his opposition to the slave trade. Between 1858 and 1863, Livingstone made several trips to the African interior (one resulting in the celebrated discovery of Livingstone by the journalist/explorer Henry Stanley) in search of the origin of the Nile. Upon periodic returns to England, Livingstone spoke passionately about the evils of slavery, fueling missionary interest in sub-Saharan Africa. Toward the end of his journeys, mistakenly believing he had located the headwaters of that great African river, Livingstone died during prayer. Adhering to his instructions, Livingstone's servants cut out his heart and buried it at the site, preserved his body with salt and sun-drying, then, in a nine-month trek, carried it to the coast where it was shipped to England for burial in Westminster Abbey (Gates, 1997: 19).

In addition to combating slavery, missionaries established schools and health clinics. Albert Schweitzer, a talented physician and musician, demurred from the opportunities awaiting him in Europe, and followed instead his Protestant impulses and moved to Africa, establishing a bush hospital in 1913 in what is now called Gabon. In 1952, Schweitzer was awarded the Nobel Peace Prize, an award he invested in furthering health care for rural Africans. Upon his death in 1965, Schweitzer was buried in a grassy plot behind the hospital (Lamb, 1987: 142).

The relationship between missionaries and Africans was by no means perfectly harmonious. The first uprising against colonial rule was organized in 1915 by John Chilembwe, an African theologian educated in the United States. Chilembwe, a Yao, became a follower of apocalyptic Christian Joseph Booth. Having taught himself to read and write, Chilembwe became the caretaker of Booth's children as well as the patriarch's companion and interpreter. When Booth left Africa for England and the United States in 1887, Chilembwe accompanied him, eventually attending a Baptist seminary in Lynchburg, Virginia, where he became influenced by the radical thinking of American abolitionists who surely introduced him to the martyrdom of John Brown. Repatriated to Africa, Chilembwe assumed the responsibility for an African congregation to which he ministered with typical Victorian restraint; however, his composure was constantly shaken by the racial injustices of colonial Africa. Confronted with chronic cruelty toward African laborers by a European landlord, W. J. Livingstone (son-in-law to David Livingstone)—for which the authorities remained indifferent—Chilembwe organized a raid on a local armory and the estates of several landlords. Chilembwe's raiders decapitated Livingstone in front of his family and presented his head to Chilembwe, who used it in a bizarre church service. While Livingstone's family was escorted to safety, Chilembwe's insurgents attacked other white settlements. But these were quickly organized, and vigilantes soon found Chilembwe, and killed him. Chilembwe's followers were tried and either executed or given long jail terms, serving as an example to other Africans who held reservations about colonial rule (Pike, 1968: 97–101).

Subsequent to European exploration, Africa was divided into colonies according to the whims of colonists and their host countries. The curious exception was Liberia, a nation of former slaves who had been returned to Africa. The origins of Liberia can be traced to the white American Colonization Society chartered by Congress in 1816. With a $100,000 appropriation, the society began organizing passage for freed slaves who wished to return to Africa. In 1822, the first shipload of American former slaves was denied permission to land in the British colony of Sierra Leone, so the captain deposited his passengers near the Mesurado River. At gunpoint and with $300 in gifts, a navy lieutenant convinced the local chiefs to allow the emancipated slaves to settle. Eventually 45,000 former slaves returned to Africa and settled in Liberia, establishing Monrovia as its capital (in honor of President Monroe) replete with an American-style government, and becoming the continent's first independent nation in 1847 (Lamb, 1987:124). What followed was 130 years of political tranquility during which the indigenous population was oppressed by the descendants of American slaves, an autocracy that was overthrown by a 28-year-old army sergeant, Samuel Doe. Thereafter, the government of Liberia exhibited the pattern of corruption, coup, and counter-coup that typified many African nations (Richburg, 1997: 135–36).

The European scramble for Africa was codified into the configuration of nation states that endures today. In 1884, delegates from 14 European nations met in a Conference of Great Powers, and the following year they signed the General Act of the Berlin Conference, formalizing the partitioning of sub-Saharan Africa. The Berlin Treaty chopped Africa up into parcels according to the interests of Europeans, completely disregarding the ecological and social features that had defined the continent for centuries. During colonization, Europeans influenced Africa in two major ways. Economically, colonists exploited cash crops that were of value to Europe and North America. As a result, the economies of African colonies were dependent on a few crops and their value abroad; industrialization and diversification were given little consideration, if at all. Secondly, Europeans instituted a colonial administration that was ruled by whites, but one in which certain tribes were selected for mediation with the African population. Consequently, few Africans were to acquire even a rudimentary knowledge of how to govern a modern nation-state. Compounding matters, colonial preference for certain tribes over others aggravated tribal jealousies (Lamb, 1987: 104, 135–170).

Within a decade of the end of World War II, Africans had begun speaking out against colonial abuses and in favor of independence. Aside from the Mau Mau rebellion in Kenya and guerrilla warfare in Angola and Mozambique, African independence avoided the armed revolutions that freed nations during the eighteenth and nineteenth centuries. Most African patriots were either ignored or incarcerated if their rhetoric provoked anxiety on the part of colonial powers. The diminishing demand for raw resources from Africa meant that several colonies were not as valuable as they had once been, and European nations began to deliberate granting independence. Britain granted Ghana independence in 1957. In 1960, a wave of liberation swept the continent when 17 new nations, including 198 million Africans, became free—among them Cameroon, the Central African Republic, Chad, the Congo, the Ivory Coast, Nigeria, Senegal, Somalia, and Zaire (now the Democratic Republic of the Congo). Within the next five years Kenya, Malawi, Tanzania, Uganda, and Zambia had gained independence. The 1960s were a euphoric period for sub-Saharan Africa. Having shed the oppressive and exploitive colonial governments, African nations produced leaders—Kwame Nkrumah of Ghana, Jomo Kenyatta of Kenya, Patrice Lumumba of Zaire, Julius Nyerere of Tanzania—who stepped confidently onto the world political stage.

Independence would prove problematic to the first generation of African leaders, however. Many European colonial regimes had neglected to plan for independence by training Africans to replace retiring white administrators.

> The Congo had but a single senior African civil servant. Mozambique had an illiteracy rate of 90 percent. Zaire, a country as large as the United States west of the Mississippi, had only a dozen university graduates among its 25 million people. Several countries, such as Guinea-Bissau and Cape Verde, had not one African doctor, lawyer or accountant. (Lamb, 1987: 139)

Confronted with an economy dependent on European consumption that was waning and a nonexistent civil service, the first African leaders often resorted to nativist solutions to the quite considerable development problems before them. Because the colonial governments had used capitalism to exploit African colonies, many leaders flirted with socialism, even communism, in order to define a strategy that avoided exploitive markets, yet promised social cohesion.

While some nations, such as Nigeria, fared relatively well after colonial rule, others faltered. Dwindling markets for exports depleted treasuries; tribal antagonism destablized democracies; natural disasters underscored the inadequacy of national governments. These were precisely the conditions that threw many nations into a whirlpool of economic failure, political corruption, and insurgency. In nation after nation, popular enthusiasm for an independence leader collapsed, giving way to a cynical opportunism that seduced military leaders into coups. Often coup leaders were buoyed by support from the West in a misdirected attempt to counter imagined Soviet influences in the Third World. Unaccountable neither to civic influences internally nor to foreign influences externally, many African nations came under the influence of "the Big Man." The charismatic leaders who had brought independence were followed or overthrown by opportunists and autocrats; Ghana's Nkrumah was succeeded by a cast of military rulers, most recently Jerry Rawlings; Kenyatta was followed by Daniel arap Moi in Kenya; in Uganda, Nyerere was succeeded by Idi Amin; Mobutu Sese Seko gained power after the assassination of Lumumba in Zaire. Ali Solih, mimicked the role of the Big Man when he said to the people of the tiny Comoros, "I am your god and teacher. I am the divine way, the torch that lights the dark. There is no god but Ali Solih" (Lamb, 1987: 108).

As the Big Man reigned and pocketed what remained of the wealth of Africa, white farmers and civil servants fled the continent, further depleting civic infrastructure. Many nations devolved into kleptocracies (states by theft) where heads of government raided the treasury, spent lavishly on themselves and members of extensive entourages, and invested in opulent villas abroad. During the 1980s, oil-rich Nigeria lost $10 billion in capital flight (Todaro, 1994: 452). Three decades of rule by Mobutu Sese Seko deprived Zaire of an estimated $4 to 5 billion, much of it invested in castles, palaces, and townhouses in Europe (Rupert and Ottaway, 1997: A21). The decades of theft experienced by many African nations contributed to the deterioration of physical infrastructure—disrepair of roads, crumbling bridges, decaying hospitals—just as it exacerbated tribal tensions—the Ibo fought the Yoruba in Nigeria in a failed attempt to establish Biafra; intertribal warfare in Somalia compounded by famine resulted in a problematic international relief operation; Kikuyu and Masai peoples often resorted to arms to settle disputes in Kenya's Great Rift Valley; chronic tensions between the Hutus and Tutsis in Rwanda resulted in massacres that paralleled the evils of Pol Pot and Nazi Germany. Political anarchy and social destabilization accelerated capital flight, further dampening the interest of foreign investors in Africa. By the late 1990s, the United Nations reported that foreign investment in Africa had dropped 27 percent in 1996 alone to only $2.1 billion, less than what China received in two months (Buckley, 1997: 8).

An oppressive and deteriorating political economy is not propitious for the rise of a civically minded middle class, particularly when intertribal tranquility is abraded. All too frequently, the result is the Big Man resorting to what Keith Richburg termed the "Big Lie"—rhetorical gestures to an open, democratic, capitalistic political economy when persecution, corruption, and imprisonment are the rule (1997: 140). The tragic fate of Ken Saro-Wiwa in Nigeria is a case in point. Increasingly dependent on oil extraction to prop up a collapsing economy and kleptocratic military rule, General Sani Abacha reduced revenues from oil companies that had been earmarked to local government. Coupled with environmental degradation resulting from unregulated oil pumping, the Ogoni people found their lands increasingly polluted, but there were few funds to repair the damage or purchase other land. Saro-Wiwa, an Oxford-educated Ogoni who was a poet and scriptwriter, spoke on behalf of the besieged Ogoni people, in the process forming MOSOP, the Movement for the Salvation of the Ogoni People. MOSOP agitated for restrictions on drilling and reparations from Shell Oil Company, which generated 90 percent of Nigeria's foreign exchange. After a demonstration involving MOSOP in which several deaths occurred, Saro-Wiwa was arrested, tried in secret, and sentenced to death along with eight other MOSOP members. Because of his international reputation, Saro-Wiwa's imprisonment ignited a firestorm of outrage in the international literary community. Despite the opposition, General Abacha was unmoved, and on November 10, 1995 Saro-Wiwa was hung with eight other members of MOSOP. The execution was an unusually grisly affair as a result of a stuck trapdoor and mistied nooses; on the gallows, Saro-Wiwa is reported to have exclaimed, "Why are you people doing this to me? What kind of nation is this?"—words that were muffled as he suffocated for 20 minutes as a result of an inept hangman (Rieff, 1997: 33–41).

The execution of Ken Saro-Wiwa for protesting environmental degradation and the displacement of his people represented a nadir in African authoritarian rule. Not content with expropriating a nation's wealth, aggravating intertribal tensions, and harassing the media, General Abacha was willing to use the instrument of government to eliminate the most educated among a small middle class. The Nigeria military was devouring the nation's educational elite. As much as the incident revealed the ruthlessness to which Abacha would go to rid Nigeria of opposition, it also illuminated Saro-Wiwa's dismay at the bloodletting that had become pandemic in Africa. This was expressed eloquently in a poem:

To Sarogua, Rain Maker

*We have returned*
*With empty hands*
*And hollow minds*
*From the thunderstorm*
*Raining blood*
*Oh mighty one*
*Whose wink brings rain.*

*We did not pray for war*
*Wash the stain of strife away*

*We'll speak no more*
*Of coups and colonels*
*And raids at dead of night;*
*We'll forget the bombs*
*Build scores of tombs*
*And bury the dead.*

*Receive us, mighty one*
*With a cleansing shower.*
Ken Saro-Wiwa (1941–1995)
(used with permission)

## Current Issues in Development

Development in sub-Saharan Africa presents profound issues, such as nonsensical national borders, nonexistent infrastructure, intertribal hostilities, and massive poverty. Tragically, these often intertwine and reinforce one another over time, producing a vortex of antidevelopment. As a result, many African nations have actually become poorer since the end of colonial rule, several despite the existence of quite valuable resources. Thus, Africa represents a unique challenge in international development. The experience of more prominent African nations shows that if hope and perseverance are the parents of progress, despair and fratricide are often their offspring.

## South Africa

South Africa is the bright spot among sub-Saharan African nations, although few would have predicted as much a decade ago. Established in 1652 as an outpost for the Dutch East India Company, Cape Town grew with the expanding trade links between Europe and the Far East. In 1795, the British seized the Cape and instituted laws that antagonized the Dutch Afrikaners, who moved inland establishing two independent states, the South African Republic and the Orange Free State. The discovery of gold in the South African Republic attracted a wave of immigrants, many of whom were English, further aggravating relations between Britain and the Afrikaners. Tensions increased, resulting in the two savage Boer Wars late in the nineneenth century, resulting in English control of South Africa. Chafing under British rule, the Afrikaners resorted to the ballot box, eventually winning control of the government in 1948.

The National Party, dominated by Afrikaners, soon institutionalized the discriminatory practices of the British who had, for example, enacted the Land Resettlement Act of 1936, which set aside reservations ("homelands") for the African tribes. Among other concerns, the Afrikaners were preoccupied with the consequences of intercourse among the races. This led to a 1949 act that forbade mixed marriage, and a 1953 act that outlawed interracial sex. Meanwhile African opposition to apartheid became more intense under the African National Congress (ANC), whose leaders included Nelson Mandela, who was imprisoned in 1964 for sedition (Lamb, 1987: 319–28). The ANC insurgency provoked counterterrorist acts by the government in Pretoria, which not only used the Inkatha Freedom Party of Mangosuthu Buthelezi as a surrogate for attacks on the ANC but also organized police units to persecute ANC sympathizers. Escalating violence compounded by an international boycott on investment in South Africa convinced President F. W. de Klerk to reverse the government's oppressive practices. After 27 years in prison, Mandela was released in 1990, introducing a period of racial reconciliation. De Klerk and Mandela were jointly awarded the Nobel Peace Prize, free elections were held in 1994, and Mandela became South Africa's first black president (Lewis, 1997). During the late 1980s, South Africa had been racked by violence and a deteriorating economy; few would have expected the nation to become a beacon for the continent five years hence.

South Africa is the only sub-Saharan nation with a legitimate claim to membership in the First World; its economy is larger and more integrated than those of other African nations. Table 3.1 illustrates the expansion of the South African economy. South Africa's per capita GNP of $3,160 far outpaces that of Nigeria ($260), Kenya ($280), and Zaire ($120) (*World Development Indicators*, 1997: 7–9).

This is not to suggest that South Africa is devoid of Third World attributes. Of its 41 million people, 23.7 percent subsisted on $1 per day or less in 1993; 46 percent had access to sanitation; and about three-fourths of children were immunized against childhood diseases (*World Development Indicators*, 1997: 52, 80). Still, South Africa's life expectancy

TABLE 3.1    **Gross Domestic Product ($ millions)**

| Nation | 1980 | 1995 |
|--------|------|------|
| South Africa | 78,744 | 136,035 |
| Nigeria | 93,082 | 40,447 |
| Kenya | 7,265 | 9,095 |
| Zaire (Congo) | 14,391 | n.d. |

*Source: World Development Indicators, 1997: 135–136.*

of 63.2 years and its literacy rate of 81 percent approximated First World more than Third World indicators (*Human Development Index,* 1996: 136). The improvement in the social and economic climate encouraged foreign aid. In 1994, South Africa received $214.4 million compared to Nigeria ($47.3 million), Kenya ($400.5 million), and Zaire ($97.3 million) (*World Development Indicators,* 1997: 310–12). On a per capita basis, South Africa received $7 in aid assistance, compared to $2 for Nigeria, $26 for Kenya, and $6 for Zaire (*World Bank Atlas,* 1997: 36–37).

The key to South African prosperity, now that social and racial issues are being resolved, is to increase equity in an industrial economy while diversifying the service sector. In 1996, a former ANC official and Mandela's doctor purchased a subsidiary of the Anglo-American Corporation, the nation's premier conglomerate, for $220 million (Beinart, 1997: 25). Meanwhile, Mandela took pains to reinvigorate a sluggish economy, reducing inflation to 7 percent, the lowest in 25 years (Lewis, 1997: 54) and reducing the budget deficit from 6.9 to 5.1 percent of GDP (Beinart, 1997: 25). Some of the pressing needs of poor South Africans have been addressed, but not with the urgency demanded by activists. In balancing economic growth with the demand for services, South Africa's new leaders have made the commitment to maintain and reinforce basic institutions, as opposed to exploiting them—as has happened in other African nations. With reference to higher education, Mamphela Ramphele, former activist and lover of Steve Biko and now vice chancellor of the University of Cape Town, said, "Contrary to popular myth, poor people did not struggle in order to have equal access to mediocrity… Higher education will be the key to a successful democracy. Without it, South Africa will go the way of the rest of the African continent—a wasteland" (Daley, 1997: 36).

The ultimate developmental lesson to be gained from the South African experience may be the diplomatic role that Nelson Mandela has assumed vis-à-vis the other nations of sub-Saharan Africa. With direct foreign investment to Africa having declined from 2.4 percent of global investment in 1980–1984 to 1.9 percent for 1988–89 (Todaro, 1994:528), it is increasingly important that African nations look to each other for assistance. Given the ineffectiveness of regional syndicates, such as the Organization for African Unity, the burden falls on individual heads of state to cultivate such networks. In this respect, Mandela's serving as a facilitator for the transition of power from Mobutu Sese Seko to Laurent Kabila in Zaire, did more, in all likelihood, than avert a bloodbath in Kinshasa (Duke, 1997b). The import of Mandela's intercession on behalf of South Africa is evident in light of the substantial mineral deposits of Zaire and the extensive experience of South Africa's

Anglo-American Corporation in mineral extraction. Having established himself as mediator, Mandela has positioned the Anglo-American Corporation to exploit Zaire's riches. Since a subsidiary of the Anglo-American Corporation is now black-owned, black South Africans stand to benefit from the provision of such technical assistance.

## Democratic Republic of Congo (Zaire)

The Congo is a volatile region of West Africa that was initially populated by Pygmies. Around A.D. 100, the Hutu, an agricultural Bantu people from the Northwest, settled in the area, subjugating the Pygmies. Hutu rule was interrupted in the 1500s when the Tutsi,[1] a cattle-herding tribe, moved into the area from the Northeast. Though smaller in number, the Tutsi soon dominated the Hutu, who became a subordinate caste ("The Tutsis in Central Africa," 1997). German, Belgium, and French colonists found this stratification complementary to their purposes and furthered Tutsi hegemony by educating leaders of the tribe and moving them into positions in the colonial government and military. With the end of the colonial period, what had been French Equatorial Africa was divided into several nations—Chad, Central Africa Republic, Gabon, Republic of Congo, Congo (Zaire), Rwanda, and Burundi ("The Tale of Two Congos," 1997).

Any expectations that the Congo would exploit its considerable resources for purposes of national development were dashed when Mobutu Sese Seko took power in 1965. Mobutu, a former journalist and army sergeant, inherited a country with a vibrant economy due to its vast copper mines. Mobutu spent lavishly on himself and his cronies, erecting stadiums and monuments to himself, constructing smaller replicas of the World Trade Center in Kinshasa, and hosting the Ali–George Foreman title fight at a cost of $15 million. Relishing his Big Man role, Mobutu changed the country's name to Zaire, ordered all citizens to replace their Christian names with African ones, prohibited wearing of Western attire, ordered his portrait hung in churches then canceled Christmas, and expropriated some $500 million in assets from Asians then expelled them. Soon the remaining whites left, and Zaire slowly succumbed to venality and corruption (Lamb, 1987: 44–47).

During the 1970s and 1980s, political instability spread throughout much of sub-Saharan Africa. Perceiving Zaire as strategically important in its campaign against communism, the United States steadfastly supported Mobutu. Insurgencies in several other African nations obscured hostilities between the Hutus and Tutsis in the former Congo. In 1959, just prior to gaining independence, Hutus, representing 84 percent of the population, overthrew the minority Tutsi leadership of Rwanda in the process slaughtering 100,000 of them. In 1972, in neighboring Burundi, insecure Tutsi leaders moved to exterminate any Hutus who had received an education or held a government job; within three months, 200,000 Hutus had been massacred (Lamb, 1987: 12–13). Tutsis exiled from Rwanda organized the Rwandese Patriotic Front (RPF) and, in 1990, attacked from neighboring Uganda. In an attempt to defuse escalating hostilities, Rwanda's Hutu President, Juvenal Habyarimana, signed a peace accord with the rebels in 1993 (Gourevitch, 1995).

---

[1] The Tutsi, sometimes called the Watusi ("wa" being the plural in Swahili), are a Nolitic people taller in stature and with facial features unlike the Negroid features associated with the Bantu.

Festering tensions between Hutus and Tutsis reignited the following year upon the death of former president of Rwanda Habyarimana in an unexplained plane crash. Suspecting Tutsi insurgents' responsibility for the president's death, Hutus went on a rampage killing suspected Tutsis and Tutsi sympathizers—an estimated 500,000 in two months, hacking entire families to death even as they cowered for sanctuary in village churches. Meanwhile, fighting in neighboring Burundi increased since the Burundi president, a Hutu, had died in the place crash claiming the Rwandan president. Incensed by the Hutu mass slaughter of the Tutsi minorities in Rwanda and Burundi, Tutsis accelerated their attacks, eventually taking control of the capital of Rwanda in July 1994, and later Burundi in July 1996. Despite Tutsi assurances that no reprisals would occur, as many as 1.1 million Hutu refugees near the Zairian border refused to return home and remained in Goma, a large refugee camp of 700,000 Hutus (McNeil, 1997: E4).

In 1996, the alternating genocide between Hutus and Tutsis spilled over the border into Zaire. Apprehensive about the actions of Laurent Kabila, a Tutsi, Mobutu ordered Tutsis expelled from Zaire. Kabila, a Marxist associated with Cuban revolutionary Che Guevara and who had chafed under Mobutu's rule for 30 years, exploited the Hutu-Tutsi conflagration to depose Mobutu (Castaneda, 1997). Fearing mass retribution from Kabila's forces, Hutu refugees fled from Goma, splintered into several large groups, and moved eastward, further confounding Mobutu's ineffective defense. Amid the chaos, relief agencies were unable to locate tens of thousands of Hutus, a large portion of whom were women and children who were dying of malnutrition and disease (Duke, 1997a; Kristoff, 1997a; Wallis, 1997). In a desperate attempt to reverse the tide of refugees and Kabila's insurgency, Mobutu armed the retreating Hutus, a practice that international agencies alleged Mobutu had done for years (Drumtra, 1997). But this was to no avail. In face of Kabila's advancing forces, Mobutu fled, and Kabila became president of the newly declared Democratic Republic of Congo in June 1997.

Despite Mobutu's overthrow, few are sanguine about the developmental prospects of the Congo. Human development indicators rank countries of the region in the lower register of the nations of the world. The ouster of Mobutu signals at least an interruption, if not the end, of the nation's kleptocracy, and this has rekindled interest in the Congo's natural resources among mineral extraction firms (French, 1997). Kabila has yet to offer the international community reassurances that representative political institutions are a priority for his rule, regardless of Zaire's new name. No sooner had he assumed the presidency than Kabila's troops were alleged to have slaughtered thousands of Rwandan Hutus who had gathered in refugee camps for safety (Pomfret, 1997). In Rwanda, some 90,000 Hutu prisoners await trial for genocide against Tutsis, though the fairness of the tribunals is open to question. Rwanda has only 16 practicing attorneys, and most have refused to represent Hutus charged with genocide (Buckley, 1997c). Relief agencies are overwhelmed by the needs of Tutsis who survived the massacres, including the 250,000 Tutsi women who were raped and have been cast out from their native communities (Rote, 1997).

Ominously, the strife that had been expected in Kinshasa in the absence of Mobutu's exit surfaced instead across the Congo River in Brazzaville, as well as southward to Angola. Prior to the political destabilization of Zaire, the Republic of Congo had achieved a reputation for order and modest development. Even though its economy was but a tenth that of Zaire's, it had increased by 26 percent between 1980 and 1995 (*World Development*

*Indicators,* 1997: 134). By mid-1997, however, Brazzaville had disintegrated into private militias that skirmished while looters carted away anything of value, and Western nations scrambled to make any sense of the pillage and anarchy that reigned in the streets of what had been a small, but stable, part of the Congo region. Observers noted the presence of Hutu soldiers from Rwanda in the melee (Shiner, 1997). As disorder overtook Brazzaville, a fragile peace negotiated between the Angolan government and guerrillas to the south began to unravel. Insurgent forces of Joseph Savimbi, an ally of Mobutu, came under attack, threatening to reignite a civil war that had gone on for more than two decades (Daley, 1997b).

As if to negate the progress that had come to characterize many nations of the Third World, leaders of the nations that had once comprised the colonial Congo failed to convert natural resources into foreign exchange with which to invest in education, health, and physical infrastructure, as well as to craft a developing society. Instead, corruption contributed to capital flight, and intertribal strife festered and exploded, leaving international resources invested in refugee maintenance as opposed to nation-building. The magnitude of the antidevelopment of the Congo exceeds the sum of lost opportunities; not only were 500,000 Tutsis slaughtered in Rwanda, but some 220,000 Hutu refugees have simply disappeared into the Congo jungle. If, among the nations of sub-Saharan Africa, South Africa has become a beacon, the Congo continues to manifest a sinister malevolence that had once fascinated Joseph Conrad, provoking his exclamation: "the horror, the horror!"

## Kenya

If any nation mirrored the Western idea of Africa, it would be Kenya. From the lush, verdant forests of the Highlands that reminded British settlers of England to the vast, tawny savannah of the Great Rift Valley, the habitat for some of the continent's most exotic animals, Kenya has captured the imagination of Westerners for generations. Indeed, accounts of East Africa, such as Isak Dinesen's *Out of Africa* and Ernest Hemingway's *Green Hills of Africa*—works that had been in their time modest, yet refreshingly immediate—have become fixtures in the international literature. A quiet moment at Nakuru National Park, amid the acacia trees, the antelope, cape buffalo, and flamingos, can still suggest the enormous majesty of wild Africa. But this is increasingly a figment of the past. The Third World has intruded, and the marvelous charm of untamed Africa has been ruined, replaced by diminishing wildlife, impoverished tribes, and what are arguably the worst roads in the world. As if to signify Kenya's new Third World role, Nairobi has become the regional center for relief agencies serving sub-Saharan Africa.

Kenya was colonized largely by British settlers who were drawn to the Highlands that seemed ideal for cultivating tea and coffee. By the end of the First World War, Kenya was developing a reputation as an island of civilization in the midst of the most extravagant wildlife in the world. Thus, the social institution of the Highland plantations, the British club, was contrasted with the excitement of the big-game safari, making Kenya a particularly agreeable alternative to the artifices of Europe. What was pleasing to British colonists was not necessarily so for the native population, however. The Masai, a cattle-herding tribe, enjoyed the savannah with unincumbered freedom until colonial authorities restricted their raids on other tribes, and the decimation of wildlife impeded the male puberty rite, which required the slaying of a lion. Similarly, the Kikuyu of the Highlands found the tea and coffee plantations proscribing their use of the land, and the ubiquitous missionaries condoned such. A nascent independence movement attracted the attention of Jomo Kenyatta, a Kikuyu who had adopted a Masai name and who became an incisive critic of colonization. "When the missionaries arrived, the Africans had the land and the missionaries had the Bible," Kenyatta observed, "They taught us to pray with our eyes closed. When we opened them, they had the land and we had the Bible" (Lamb, 1987: 59).

In order to regain rights lost to British colonial authorities, Kenyatta traveled to England, where he joined with Malawi's Hastings Banda and Ghana's Kwame Nkrumah to form the Pan-African Federation, which advocated equal rights for all Africans. Upon his return to Kenya, Kenyatta confronted a Kikuyu tribe grown impatient with constitutional reforms and a besieged colonial government. A Kikuyu cabal retreated to the forest and began raiding plantations, killing white settlers and African sympathizers. By the time the British put an end to the Mau Mau insurgency, 13,500 Africans and 95 Europeans had been killed. Implicated in the rebellion, Kenyatta was imprisoned or placed under house arrest until independence was granted. Despite the misgivings of the British colonial government, Kenyatta became Kenya's first prime minister upon independence in 1963. For black Kenyans, Kenyatta's government managed a growing economy, an expanding middle class, and the extension of services into rural areas. At the same time, Kenyatta demonstrated little patience with opposition leaders, occasionally incarcerating those antagonistic to his agenda. The assassination of leaders from the government and the opposition further abraded intertribal relations. Upon Kenyatta's death in 1978, Daniel arap Moi, a schoolteacher with a tribal affiliation independent of the more influential tribes, became prime minister (Lamb, 1987: 58–65).

As a second-generation autocrat, Moi ruled a Kenya that was not unlike other developing nations. Compared to other major African nations, such as South Africa, Nigeria, and Zaire (Congo), Kenya's economy is small, and per capita GNP typical of the poorest nations on the continent. Fifty-three percent of Kenyans have access to safe water, and 77 percent to sanitation and health care. The adult literacy rate is 75 percent. Forty-six percent of births are unattended by trained health workers, and 22 percent of children under age five suffer from malnutrition (*Human Development Report,* 1966: 111, 145). The economy has slowed, increasing only 1.4 percent annually between 1990 and 1995. Slow economic growth coupled with intractable poverty has contributed to negative private investment; between 1990 and 1995, $42 million left the country in capital flight. As rural opportunities stagnate, Kenyans relocate to urban areas; in 1980, 16 percent of the population lived in cities, by 1995 that had increased by more than half to 28 percent (*World Development Indicators,* 1997: 115, 131, 237). Yet, an oppressive central government and protracted poverty make Kenya a major recipient of foreign assistance in relation to other African nations.

In all this, Kenya would be unremarkable except for what may be called the "new exploitation." Since independence, Kenya has experienced a significant degree of abuse of two resources: women and the environment. The adult literacy rate, the ratio of educational enrollment, and earned income of Kenyan women is significantly lower than that of Kenyan men (*Human Development Report,* 1997: 139). Kenya's exploitation of women is typical of the patriarchal nature of traditional African societies. David Lamb has described the consequences:

> The African woman produces 70 percent of the food grown on the continent, according to the United Nations. She works longer and harder and has more responsibilities than her

husband. She is the economic backbone of the rural community, the maker of family decisions, the initiator of social change, the harvester of crops. She is the hub around which the
spokes of society turn. (1987: 38)

Robert Klitgaard made a similar gender observation in Equatorial Guinea:

Alcohol consumption is prodigious given local incomes, and it is true that many men drink
away the earnings from cash crops while many women are guarding for the family the food
and scant money garnered from subsistence crops. Men monopolize formal organizations
from village councils to government ministries. Men are the forces of control but also of a
lack of control, of dissipation. Women are the creators, the sinews of both home and economy. It is the men who are wasting Africa's money on armaments and corruption and luxu-
ries, the women who nurture the young, grow the subsistence crops, tend the houses, and
make markets work. It is a provocative exaggeration to say so: Africa's deepest ills are the
ills of African males. (1990: 173)

In Africa, half of girls enrolling in primary school drop out by the fourth grade, leaving
only 10 percent to advance to the secondary level (Buckley, 1997a: A18). Among the most
troubling indicators reflecting the status of Kenyan women are those relating to procre-
ation. The combination of only one-third of fertile women using birth control and a ban on
abortion yields 5.4 births per woman. Poor maternal health results in 500 maternal deaths
per 100,000 births ("Worldwide Hazards of Childbirth," 1995: H8). Many African tribes
continue to practice female genital mutilation as a puberty rite, including the Masai of
Kenya. While some social indicators for women in Kenya are beginning to approximate
those of men, opportunities are still denied to large numbers of them, particularly in traditional tribes in rural areas.

With an arid climate, only 7 percent of Kenya's land is suitable for agricultural use. An
expanding population strains these few lands, even though large numbers of rural Kenyans
immigrate to cities. Despite these dynamics, 6.2 percent or 35,000 square kilometers, have
been set aside as protected reserves. Even then, many species are endangered. In 1994, 16
species of mammals, 22 species of birds, and 158 species of higher plants were endangered
(*World Development Indicators,* 1997: 95, 99). The most graphic illustration of environmental devastation was the slaughter of elephants and rhinoceros for ivory. In Tsavo National
Park, poachers had butchered so many elephant that the population was reduced to several
thousand. The prospect that these great beasts would be eradicated provoked Richard Leakey
to accept Moi's appointment as director of Kenya Wildlife Services. The charismatic son of
the anthropological team that had made a series of discoveries in East Africa about the origin
of humans, Leakey equipped a paramilitary security force that effectively countered elephant
poachers in the bush. Yet, a problem remained as to the disposition of the tons of ivory that
had accumulated in the government's anti-poaching activities. In a bold stroke that sent a
clear message to ivory traders, Leakey convinced Moi to destroy the ivory. On July 18, 1989,
13 tons of ivory representing 2,000 slaughtered elephants were incinerated before a crowd at
Nairobi National Park (Gallmann, 1991: 297–303). Although Kenya has made considerable
progress in identifying endangered species, the government has been less successful in sal-
vaging endangered habitat. As the Highland plantations are returned to Africans in the form
of small plots, the likelihood of conserving larger tracts of lands becomes more remote.

# Prospects for Development

By the mid-1990s, antidevelopment forces that had checked progress during the 1980s seemed to be propelling sub-Saharan Africa ever more rapidly backward, as evident in Table 3.2. When a research team ranked the corruption of nations, several of the corner-stone nations of Africa featured prominently. Nigeria was listed as the most corrupt nation on the globe, with Kenya not far behind. South Africa registered toward the middle of the scale with other Third World nations. Mercifully, the researchers did not rank Zaire (Congo), presumably for lack of data ("Corruption," 1996).

As sub-Saharan Africa slides from the ranks of the Third World, it creates another developmental category, a Fourth World, one in which the Four Horsemen of the Apocalypse enjoy free rein. The vicious circle of antidevelopment has been graphed by Jeffrey Goldberg, who observed that diseases, such as AIDS, find poverty and anarchy ideal conditions in which to spread. "Disease," he noted, "is also an excellent incubator of chaos. It is an endless cycle of misery: war and corruption mean no health care and no family planning; no health care and no family planning mean too many sick people; too many sick people create desperation and poverty, which lead back to corruption and war" (1997:35). While there have been flashes of success in countries, such as Malawi and Uganda (Kristoff, 1997b), these are dwarfed by the stagnation and chaos that grip much of the region. In sub-Saharan Africa, successful development has come to mean the stagnation of Kenya and the avoidance of the violence of the Congo—with the modest progress of South Africa far away indeed.

Yet, if sub-Saharan Africa is to overcome the forces that pull it downward, several agents will have proven instrumental. Locally, NGOs will assume more responsibility for health, education, and housing. As national governments contend with debt restructuring and economic reforms, they will be less able to provide such services to their peoples, leaving much of development contingent on the capacity of NGOs to weave networks of development. Regionally, South Africa will serve as an anchor, providing a site for African nations to air disagreements and settle disputes. While the record of regional trade alliances is not strong in sub-Saharan Africa, a powerful South African economy and the adept diplomacy of Nelson Mandela may make this conceivable once again. Internationally, the designation of

**TABLE 3.2　Economic Decline in Sub-Saharan Africa, 1980–1990**

| Indicator | 1980 | 1990 | Change (%) |
|---|---|---|---|
| Per capita output ($) | 582 | 335 | –42.5 |
| Per capita consumption ($) | 465 | 279 | –40.0 |
| Investment (% of GDP) | 20.2 | 14.2 | –29.7 |
| Exports of goods ($ billions) | 48.7 | 31.9 | –34.5 |
| Per capita food production ($) | 107 | 94 | –12.2 |
| Total external debt ($ billions) | 56.2 | 147 | +162 |
| Poverty (% below poverty line) | N.A. | 62 | — |

*Source:* M. Todaro, *Economic Development in the Third World,* 5th Edition. ©1994 by Michael P. Todaro.

Kofi Annan from Ghana as Secretary General of the UN will do much to elevate the developmental needs of Africa on the world's political and economic agenda. But Annan will have to be adroit in order to refocus aid to the African Fourth World. Concomitantly, he must corral First World nations, such as the United States, who have been tardy in meeting their contribution requirements, while restructuring the top-heavy UN bureaucracy (Goshko, 1997). Failure on any of these crucial fronts, in all likelihood, means that sub-Saharan Africa will remain a fetid backwater while other regions of the Third World make progress, however modest.

# REFERENCES

Beinart, Peter. (1997a). "The Only Games in Town," *The New Republic*, vo 216, 24, (June 16), pp. 23.26.

Buckley, Stephen. (1997a). "Girls in School," *Washington Post* (April 5).

Buckley, Stephen. (1997b). "Left Behind Prosperity's Door," *Washington Post Weekly* (March 24).

Buckley, Stephen. (1997c). "Trial and Error in Rwanda's Massacres," *Washington Post Weekly* (February 3).

Castaneda, Jorge. (1997). "How Che Saw Kabila," *Time* (April 21).

Conrad, Joseph. (1910). *Heart of Darkness* (New York: Harper Brothers).

"Corruption-An International Comparison." (1996). *World Bank Transition* (July-August).

Daley, Suzanne. (1997a). "The Standards Bearer," *New York Times Magazine* (April 13).

Daley, Suzanne. (1997b). "Zaire's Fall Jolts Neighboring Angola's Frail Peace," *New York Times* (June 8).

Drumtra, Jeff. (1997). "Where the Ethnic Cleansing Goes Unchecked," *Washington Post Weekly* (July 22–28).

Duke, Lynne. (1997a). "U.N. Seeks Out Refugees in Zaire Battle Zone," *Washington Post* (March 10).

Duke, Lynne. (1997b). "Mandela Lauded for a Long Shot," *Washington Post* (May 6).

Estes, Richard. (1998). "The World Social Situation" in Richard Estes, ed., *Encyclopedia of Social Work, Supplement to the 19th Ed.* (Washington, DC: National Association of Social Workers), pp. 343-359.

Franklin, John Hope. (1980). *From Slavery to Freedom* (New York: Knopf).

French, Howard. (1997). "The Great Gold Rush in Zaire," *New York Times* (April 18).

Gallmann, Kuki. (1991). *I Dreamed of Africa* (London: Penguin Books).

Gates, L. G., Jr. (1997). "Going Back," *New Republic* (June 16).

Goldberg, Jeffrey. (1997). "Our Africa," *New York Times Magazine* (March 2).

Goshko, John. (1997). "Haggling Over U. N. Reform," *Washington Post Weekly* (March 17).

Gourevitch, Philip. (1995). "After the Genocide," *The New Yorker* (December 18).

*Human Development Report,* 1996. (New York: Oxford University Press).

Klitgaard, Robert. (1990). *Tropical Gangsters* (New York: Basic Books).

Kristoff, Nicholas. (1997a). "Rwandans, at Rivals' Mercy, See No Justice, or Symmetry," *New York Times* (April 13).

Kristoff, Nicholas. (1997b). "Why Africa Can Thrive Like Asia," *New York Times* (May 25).

Lamb, David. (1987). *The Africans* (New York: Vintage).

Lewis, Anthony. (1997). "Mandela the Pol," *New York Times Magazine* (March 23).

McNeil, Donald. (1997). "In Congo, Forbidding Terrain Hides a Calamity," *New York Times* (June 1).

Naipaul, V. S. (1989). *A Bend in the River* (New York: Vintage).

Pike, John. (1968). *Malawi: A Political and Economic History* (New York: Praeger).

Pomfret, John. (1997). "Maccacres Were Weapon in War of Liberation," *Washington Post* (June 11).

Richburg, Keith. (1997). *Out of America* (New York: Basic Books).

Rieff, David. (1997). "The Threat of Death," *The New Republic* (June 16).

Rote, Elizabeth. (1997). "The Outcasts" *New York Times Magazine* (January 19).

Rupert, James, and David Ottaway. (1997). "Once Wealthy Zairian Leader Said to Be Out of Cash," *Washington Post* (April 6).

Shiner, Cindy. (1997). "Gunfire Halts Evacuation of U.S. Embassy in Brazzaville," *Washington Post* (June 9).

"The Tale of Two Congos." (1997). *Washington Post* (May 21).

Todaro, M. (1994). *Economic Development,* 5th ed. (New York: Longman).

"The Tutsis in Central Africa." (1997). *Washington Post* (June 8).

Wallis, William. (1997). "Zairian Town Suffers in Grip of Hutus," *Washington Post* (March 7).

Wills, A. J. (1985). *An Introduction to the History of Central Africa* (New York: Oxford University Press).

"Worldwide Hazards of Childbirth." (1995). *Los Angeles Times* (July 25).

*World Bank Atlas.* 1997. (New York: Oxford University Press).

*World Development Indicators.* 1997. (New York: Oxford University Press).

# CHAPTER

# 4

# Eastern Europe

Eastern Europe is not so much a collection of states as an assortment of states of mind. Since earliest recorded history, it has represented bewildering diversity, dangerous vulnerability, and an air of constant uncertainty. Asians do not consider it Asian; western Europeans do not consider it exactly part of Europe. Terms traditionally used to describe it are indicative of its position as being suspended in time and place; one of the most common terms used is "the countries in between," without any indication of the entities between which it is supposed to lie. It is an area of such vague and shifting location and such continuous and clamorous conflict that it came early to represent for western Europeans the quintessence of rancorous discord and insoluble problems.

Metternich is alleged to have remarked that Asia starts across the river from Vienna. If the attribution is correct, it is a good example of one of the grand pretensions with which western Europeans enjoy indulging themselves, for if eastern Europe is neither Asia nor Europe, it is because Europe's conception of itself as a separate continent is specious. All the other continents have clear and distinct boundaries (the insignificant exception being the Isthmus of Panama), but the standard definition of Europe is that it is the continent lying west of the Urals. However, to anyone examining a globe, it is patently clear that the "continent" of Europe is actually little more than a major peninsula on the western edge of Asia. Indeed, one of the persistent historical debates is whether Russia, which straddles the Urals, is "truly" a European country.

Uncertainty about their own identity often leads people to try and gain some sense of being grounded by denying others a sense of their identity. Perhaps this principle operates with large masses of people as well, since there is nothing even approaching consensus among western writers about what comprises "eastern Europe". There is substantial agreement that Poland, Hungary, the Czech Republic, and Slovakia, at least, are part of eastern Europe, but the people who live in those countries do not like that designation, preferring to be considered "central-eastern Europe" or "eastern-central Europe", or just "central Europe".

One of the oldest ways of identifying eastern Europe was to describe it as those lands not included in the Holy Roman Empire; that is, east of the Carolingian boundary after the death of Charlemagne in A.D. 814, and north of the Ottoman domains, after the fifteenth century (Shepard, 1932). Another approach, somewhat more precise, was to mark the western boundary of eastern Europe as the Oder River and its southern boundary as the Danube. Neither of these definitions, the first political and the second geographical, could be sustained into the nation-building era of modern times, but this does not mean that agreement was ever reached. Maczak, noting the present lack of consensus, asserted that East-Central Europe "usually" refers to those countries east of the Elbe, extending to, but not including Russia, but "historically" including the Baltic states. To the people living there, he wrote, it means "between Russia and Germany" (Maczak, Samsonowicz, and Burke, 1985: 2) and comprises the (then) countries of East Germany, Czechoslovakia, Poland, and Hungary. Defining eastern Europe as "the lands lying between Central Europe and Russia," Okey (1982: 9) excluded East Germany and added others not in Maczak's list: Austria, Romania, Yugoslavia, Bulgaria, and Albania. (By now, at least one of the problems must be clear: several countries that existed in the 1980s ceased to exist as such before the mid-1990s.) Exclusion of the Baltic states by many scholars may be related to their nonexistence as independent political entities at the time the scholars were writing. This omission is even found in such comprehensive works as that of Rothschild (1985), but the explanation is weakened somewhat by noting that other writers, such as Wandycz (1992: xi) have argued that East-Central Europe means "Bohemia/Czechoslovakia, Hungary, and Poland."

An ethnographic approach suggests the possibility advanced by some scholars of denoting as East-Central Europeans those people whose language roots are Romance or Germanic rather than Slavic (Maczak, 1985) but at least one observer specifically identifies both "Slavic" and "Jewish" in describing the ethnicity of people in the region (Wandycz, 1992).

Lacking definitive designations of what is meant by "eastern Europe," the area included in the following discussion will be stipulated, with the only certainty being that this stipulation will fully satisfy no one and likely will offend many. That caution given, in this chapter, "eastern Europe" refers to the region encompassed by the countries known at the beginning of 1997 as: Poland, the Czech Republic (hereafter shortened to "Czech"), Slovakia, Hungary, Romania, and Bulgaria. Also included and discussed, but in much less detail, are Slovenia, Russia, and the Baltic States of Estonia, Latvia, and Lithuania.

## Overview

The eleven countries that constitute eastern Europe in this discussion contain over two hundred fifty million people (almost three-fifths of them in Russia), who regularly speak over a dozen languages in more than 150 dialects, and practice five major religions (of which three are Christian). They are subject to constantly changing political boundaries. A person still living today could have been born an Austro-Hungarian, later become a Czech citizen, then been a subject of Ukraine-Carpathia, afterward been a member of the Soviet Union, and today, be a Ukrainian—all without ever leaving the community of Ungvar (Hyde-Price, 1996: 7). The present city of Bratislava (in Slovakia) is the same city that appears on maps as Pozsony (Hungarian) and Pressburg (German). Even families have changed the spelling of their names to adapt to external realities: the Zrinius (Latin) family also is known by Zrinyi (Hungarian) and Zrinski (Croatian) (Sugar, 1995: 4).

The geography and climate of the region are nearly as varied as the inhabitants, from the cool, damp winters and dry summers of Bulgaria to the cool, damp summers and wet winters of Estonia. The Baltic countries, Poland, and Romania tend to have showery summers and cloudy, dark winters that can become very cold. The maritime climate along the north coast moderates the cold in summer and the heat in winter. Hungary has warm summers and cold, cloudy, humid winters. The Czech climate is consistently cooler than elsewhere in the region, while Slovenia presents a sharp contrast between the Adriatic coast, which enjoys a Mediterranean climate, and its inland areas, which are considered "continental"—that is, cool, temperate winters and hot, humid summers. The countries range in size from Slovenia, about as big as New Jersey, to Poland, similar in size to Oregon and Washington states together. Topographically, it would be difficult to imagine more variation in an area of only about 1,078,000 square kilometers (excluding Russia), or about 413,000 square miles. In the North, Estonia is largely marshy lowlands; Bulgaria, in the South, is mostly mountainous. Poland comprises a vast, flat plain, while Hungary occupies a rolling plain situated amid mountain ranges. The whole region is divided about in half by the east-west range of the Carpathians, extending roughly from Slovakia and then, in the East, curving southwest to enclose Hungary and western Romania.

Given the topographical variety, it is not surprising that land use and natural resources also vary extensively throughout the region. Forest land still covers much of the region, mostly in the northern portion, representing almost a third of Poland and nearly half of Slovenia and Russia. Mineral deposits lie primarily in the South and include coal (Czech, Poland, Slovakia, and Slovenia); natural gas (Poland and Romania); oil (Romania, shale oil in Estonia); graphite (Czech); sulphur (Poland); metals (Slovakia and Slovenia); and marble (Bulgaria). Land under cultivation also demonstrates the great differences throughout the region. Hungary, Lithuania, Poland, and Romania lead with 51 percent, 49 percent, 46 percent, and 43 percent, respectively, of their territories arable; the proportion is only 10 percent for Slovenia (World Fact Book, 1995).

Although five major religions are found, they tend to be concentrated in irregular patterns. Moslems are a major group only in the South, in the area once dominated by the Ottoman Empire: They are 13 percent in Bulgaria, but in nominal numbers elsewhere, even in Slovenia, where they account for only 1 percent of the professed faiths. Poland and Slovenia are 95 percent or more Roman Catholic, while between them lies arguably the most religiously diverse and historically tolerant country in Europe: Hungary. Sixty-seven per cent of the Hungarians are identified as Roman Catholic; 20 percent as Calvinist; 5 percent Lutheran, and there is one of the largest Jewish populations remaining in Eastern Europe. The Orthodox Church is strong in Bulgaria (85%), Romania (70%) and Russia; Estonia is almost entirely Lutheran. Atheism is strongly professed in the former Czechoslovakia (40% in Czech, 10% in Slovakia) (World Fact Book, 1995).

Religious differences indicate ethnic differences, and the ethnic distribution reflects many past political decisions that have influenced patterns of movement and subsequent homogeneity or heterogeneity of national populations. For example, Poland is 98 percent Polish (essentially all Roman Catholic), although before 1939, Jews were a major group, especially in the cities, making up a third of the population of Warsaw and a quarter of Krakow. The present population resulted from the Holocaust during World War II and the abrupt expulsion of German ethnics after the war. The countries formerly part of the USSR demonstrate the effects of the Soviet policy of removing large numbers of the population eastward and moving Russians into the spaces created. Residents of Latvia, for example, are 52 percent Latvian and 34 percent Russian, with Bylorussians and Ukrainians making up most of the rest. Russians account for 30 percent of the population of Estonia. Large numbers of Hungarians are found in Slovakia (11%) and Romania (9%). Gypsies, one of the fastest growing groups in eastern Europe, live in the South, principally in Hungary (4%), Bulgaria (2.5%) and Romania and Slovakia (2% each). The multiethnic make-up of several of the countries is a source of persistent tension, although all countries with large Gypsy populations seem united in one ethnic response: persecution of them.

As Hupchick (1995) has pointed out, movement of ethnic populations around eastern Europe was quite common until by the end of the nineteenth century, and no national "borders" were strictly legitimate. Until modern times, rulers gained or lost territory through war or marriage, and the ethnicity of the populations involved was of no consequence to them. Occasionally, a king could not even speak the language of the country he ruled, but that was not considered relevant to his right to govern. The people maintained continuity by identifying themselves in terms of family, clan, or ethnic group rather than by nation.

This distinction between citizenship and nationality has been a decisive factor in East European relations (Wandycz: 1992), since eastern Europeans refer to their ethnic identity, not their political identity, as a "nation." The country in which they live is a political identity; at any given time, they are "citizens" of a country, but they always maintain a distinct "nationality." Thus, a person whose family may have migrated from the West to Hungary in the fifteenth century still considers himself (and is considered by others) a citizen of Hungary, but a member of the German "nation" or nationality. This sense of identity also extends to ethnicity, so that the "German" who is a "citizen" of Hungary does not carry either of the significant ethnic identities of Hungary, for he is neither a Slav nor a Magyar. This system of identity classification has made it possible for leaders to distinguish, and then either to favor or to persecute, ethnic populations within their own countries or to identify minority populations as virtual captives in "foreign" countries. It is why Germans in 1938 considered it legitimate to "free" the German ethnics in the Czech Sudetenland, and why the Czechs considered it legitimate to forcibly expel German ethnics from Czechoslovakia less than ten years later, even though many of those "German" families in Czechoslovakia, in both instances, had lived there for hundreds of years. This sense of identity related primarily to ethnicity is difficult for many Americans to grasp, since one is "American" by birth or becomes fully so by naturalization. In at least one European country, the concept of ethnic distinctiveness is so ingrained that citizenship is gained only by the principle of *jus sanguines;* that is, by having the proper "blood," no matter what your residence or where you were born on the Earth. The current American preoccupation with ethnicity is not so much an expression of identity as it is a social affectation or political ploy. Americans could not imagine any justification for deporting everyone with an Irish name "back" to Ireland. Americans may speak with affection about the Old Country, but that affection does not contain the sense of *heimat* (something like "true homeland") that is so pervasive among eastern European ethnics. Neither is it conceivable in the United States that blacks who insist on being called "African-Americans" should be deported to the Africa that many call their "true home." The concept of ethnicity that is the rule in eastern Europe does not, for all practical purposes, exist in the United States, at least from the first native-born generation onward.

Universally considered more backward than western Europeans, eastern Europeans nonetheless exhibit impressively high achievements in critical areas, such as life expectancy and literacy rates. In 1995, only Russia, with a life expectancy of 69 years had a rate lower than 70 years; 73 was the most common figure, with a high of 75 years in Slovenia.

Adult literacy is virtually universal; the lowest reported rate is 97 percent in Romania; 99 percent is common; and Latvia reports 100 percent adult literacy (World Fact Book, 1995). With such literacy rates, it is not surprising to find very high public investment in education. Expenditures for education as a percentage of the GNP reported by UNESCO (1997) for each country include 31 percent for Estonia, 23 percent for Slovenia, and 20 percent for Lithuania. As a point of comparison, the figure for the United States was 12 percent.

The significance of these figures may be greater than is initially apparent. The high literacy rate may be one of the most democratizing phenomena in the region, since it provides access to the intelligentsia. The intelligentsia of Europe represent, according to Longworth (1992, 5), a "distinctive class of which the West has no exact equivalent...educated, thinking people who attach great importance to abstract ideas. . . ." By opening, through literacy, the ranks of the intelligentsia to all on the basis of merit, an entirely new era could emerge in what have been intellectually—as well as economically—deprived countries, by making theoretical ideas and studies available to and welcome from all ranks of society, to the potential enrichment of everyone.

The best ideas from the best minds are required there, because throughout the entire region, ecological disasters remain as a legacy of the command economy. In the Baltic countries, there is heavy pollution of the soil and the groundwater, with especially bad residue from shale oil extraction in Estonia. All the southeastern countries have suffered serious damage from acid rain, leading to degraded forest land and, in Russia, added destruction through extensive deforestation. Heavy toxic pollution in Bulgaria and Slovakia poses serious health risks for the people; soil pollution from various sources is serious everywhere. Some rivers remain unfit for any but industrial uses and, in a few cases, not even for that (World Fact Book, 1995).

As the countries struggle to convert from the command economy to a free market economy, their different levels in the transition are seen to some extent in the income enjoyed by the general populace. The per capita GNPs cover a wide range, from a low of US$2790 in Romania to highs of US$7350 in Czech and US$8100 in Slovenia (1995 figures), with a mean of US$5281. Interestingly, the two countries considered farthest along in their conversion to the market economy fall close to the mean, with one on each side: Hungary at US$5700 and Poland at US$4990 (World Fact Book, 1995).

Although the pace of change varies dramatically from area to area within eastern Europe, certain characteristics are readily apparent. In many places, the agricultural sector retains an almost quaint attachment to traditional methods, and it is possible to see small-scale farming practices not far removed from the Middle Ages. It is in the cities that the most dramatic movement is apparent, of which Prague and Budapest are examples. Less than a decade ago, the buildings in both ancient capitals were encrusted with decades of dirt and grime; buildings and infrastructure were in disrepair; access to public spaces was limited; security forces were omnipresent; a sense of apprehension was pervasive, although private discussion and debate remained vigorous. After dark, one could enter the magnificent square in Prague, the grandest in Europe, and find scarcely another person. The Charles Bridge was just that and no more—a bridge, albeit a stunning and beautiful one. These days, all the old cities enumerated by Churchill in his celebrated 1946 "Iron Curtain" address at Westminster College are cities transformed or, to be more accurate, cities recovering. Whatever the reality of economic transformation, a spirit of energy and enthusiasm can be seen on the streets. The splendid square in Prague is packed with people during the day and alive with people late at night. Both sides of the Charles Bridge are lined with artists displaying their wares, much as they did in times past. The production and export and balance-of-payment figures cannot capture the spirit of optimism that is widely apparent, as well as the notion that anything is possible. There is renewed, subdued murmuring about "the Jews," a group about whom prejudice persists even when there have been none around for many years, and more open expressions of hostility toward the Gypsies, with hardly concealed resentment regarding immigrant ethnics. Yet, in spite of all that, there is a sense of renewal. A small cadre of eastern Europeans has always been able to travel relatively freely between the East and the West, but for most people in the East, the affluence in the West consisted of stories that, however credible, were largely irrelevant to their daily lives. What has changed is the sense of relevance; it is as though life actually *can* be altered markedly for the better.

## Historical Background

The major countries of eastern Europe, but especially Poland and Hungary, long have considered themselves the bulwark of protection for Western civilization. Throughout the ages, endless migrations and invasions from Asia have passed through the territory occupied by these countries, to reach the heartland of Europe. The broad Polish plains have served as a veritable highway for tribes from the Russian steppes and in the South, and the passes through the Carpathian Mountains have been funnels to the Hungarian pasture lands and the riches beyond.

Stopped for centuries by fortified outposts of the Roman Empire, many of these tribes settled in the valleys and river basins just beyond the edges of the Empire to engage in agriculture, herding, and trade. Present-day cities such as Vienna and Budapest are justifiably proud of the Roman ruins they now carefully preserve. In due course, Rome was no longer able to resist the pressure on her borders, and assorted tribes, clans, and confederations such as the Huns, Goths, Visigoths, and Vandals poured into the Empire, looting, burning, and killing, but eventually settling down on the land.

When the Empire was divided in A.D. 395, it was not intended to be a permanent arrangement; however, the rapid decline of the western half eventuated in the establishment of the Byzantine Empire as successor to the eastern half of the Roman Empire. The powerful Byzantine Empire was able to stop the invaders at the Caucasus Mountains and to prevent them from moving down the Balkans. This had the effect of forcing them north through the gap between the Carpathian Mountain range and the Dinaric Alps, or even farther north. Since most rivers in eastern Europe flow east and west, the invaders were assured of reasonably easy passage and ample fresh water. As strong central government in the West collapsed, the sectors that had been part of the old Roman Empire broke away into independent and semiautonomous entities, modifying the old manoral system and adapting many of the established traditions to the changed circumstances. However, divested of a strong central government, these entities could not maintain the roads and aqueducts; they lost the institutions of systematic education; they became increasingly isolated and fragmented as travel became dangerous and trade declined; and they sank into what came to be known as the Dark Ages.

The Romans had never successfully pacified the Germanic tribes to the north, and waves of migrations and invasions from the East and the North did not end, since there was little to stop them from following the rivers and using the unguarded passes to enter the region that was now exposed. The Ostrogoths, Visigoths, and Franks were the most successful in preserving vestiges of Roman order (in the west), but the appearance of the Slavs and the rise of Islam finally cut the old trade routes, and gradually, western Europe fell into a marginal, landlocked agricultural economy.

Over time, various forms of collective defense were developed by the more successful kingdoms that emerged, of which the Franks became the most powerful. By the seventh century, the Franks had begun to conquer the territory of western Europe, and by the end of the eighth century, they controlled the land west of the Elbe in the North and the loop of the Carpathian Mountains in the South. By A.D. 812, Charlemagne had concluded negotiations with the Byzantines by which he became recognized as emperor of the former western Roman Empire in Europe. It was this event of his own doing, not his "illegitimate crowning" in Rome in A.D. 800, according to Barraclough (1976) that marked the beginning of what evolved into the Holy Roman Empire of the German Nation. It was just at this time that a new wave of invasions began, by the Vikings from the North and the Saracens from the South and, a few years later, by the Magyars from the East. The Viking raids grew into systematic warfare for territory, ending with their permanent settlement in Normandy (for "Normans" or north men). The Saracen attacks were confined primarily to Mediterranean coastal settlements, but the Magyars, who were accomplished horsemen, penetrated as far as Bavaria and Saxony, until finally, they were decisively defeated at Lech in 955 and withdrew to the Danube basin, where they created the nation of Hungary.

As the states of western Europe were taking rough early forms, the spread of Christianity was creating a basis for future identity. Canute the Great of Denmark ruled the largest European state of the time. Canute accepted Christianity, as did Olaf of Norway, but it was the conversion of King Stephen of Hungary that had long-term implications for eastern Europe, since it marked Hungarian acceptance of Roman Catholic Christianity over the Byzantine version, and opened the door for Western influence, primarily German, for centuries to come. More importantly, Hungary became a pivotal buffer state between western Europe and non-Christian Asian raiders, and cut the northern Slavs from those in the Balkans. Slavs in the South remained under the influence of Byzantine religion, culture and power; those in the North were soon drawn to Roman Catholicism, and by the end of the tenth century, they had developed two West-oriented states: Bohemia and Poland (Barraclough, 1976). Meanwhile, the Vikings moved down trade routes from Scandinavia to Constantinople and established footholds in places such as Kiev, from which they spread their control. Their close associations with Byzantine culture led them to accept the Eastern version of Christianity, securing it firmly enough throughout that region that it remained predominant after the Vikings themselves had lost their dominance. Thus, many of the regional ethnic and religious divisions that are apparent today already had been set in place a thousand years ago and continued to influence the Western idea of eastern Europe.

By 1100, Bulgaria and Russia had joined Poland and Hungary as major states. They were the states that took the brunt of the next major invasion from Asia, 100 years later. These invaders were the Mongols. Exceptionally skilled horsemen who often spent more than half their lives astride their small, fast mounts, the Mongols who invaded Europe in 1241–1242 were superb warriors, led by brilliant strategists and tacticians, backed by tight and efficient organization. Nothing could stop them, but they seldom encountered much organized and prolonged resistance, anyhow. The princes of western Europe refused to take them seriously, dismissing them as crude barbarians. With only a few thousand in their ranks, the Mongols moved forward along a 600-mile front, their northern wing laying waste to Poland while advancing as far as the Oder before turning south. They confounded the legendary King Wenceslas of Bohemia, whose army never caught up with them while they ravaged Bohemia and Moravia. Their southern wing moved easily across Hungary, reaching the fortifications of Bela IV at Buda-Pest. Soon thereafter, in an inadequately appreciated but decisive battle in which they faced superior arms and superior numbers, the Mongols outthought, outfought, outlasted and then completely slaughtered the cream of European medieval knighthood (Chambers, 1979). Only the death of the Great Khan, requiring them to return to their capital to select his successor, prevented the Mongols from sweeping over the rest of Europe, all the way to the Atlantic and aborting, in the thirteenth century, the illusion that Europeans created early in the seventeenth century that they were a continent, separate from Asia. On the way back to Mongolia, one of the Mongol leaders established the Tatar domain in Crimea, and ultimately in the Ukraine and Russia, where they created a Khanate, while reducing Bulgaria to the position of protectorate, dominating the area until the end of the fourteenth century. Sedlar (1994) claims that they would not have stayed in Hungary or the rest of Europe in any event, because of inadequate forage for their large herds of ponies; but, even if so, this did not prevent their future raids from bases all along the borders of the Eastern European countries. The impact of their brief invasion endured for centuries, and the terror they produced by their raids resulted in lasting changes in practices in the invaded areas. For example, the buildings formerly had been made almost exclusively of wood; after the Mongols withdrew, fortifications of brick and stone, influenced by Western fortifications against the Vikings, became the rule in eastern Europe, too, and where possible, were perched on hills or cliffs. Such fortified castles later became useful to the nobility in maintaining feudalism.

The fourteenth century was a crucial one in the history of Europe. Although it has been described as "calamitous" for western Europe (Tuchman, 1978); it brought a blossoming in the East. In Hungary, farming techniques resembled those elsewhere in Europe, and the economy was vigorous and diverse. Hungary produced more fish than any other country except Norway; wine became a major product. There was mining in the Alpine region; cattle and horse-raising on the plains. Moreover, the social structure remained relatively open and free, including the freedom to move (Makkai, 1985).

Elsewhere, the feudal class was suffering a decline in income, which led to an exodus to less developed areas. Eastern Europe became attractive, and demand for goods gave the East a favorable balance of trade that lasted for the next 300 years (Samsonowicz, 1985), although the goods provided were mostly agricultural products and raw materials. The economic expansion drew migrants who were responding to invitations to settle in the East. Germans flocked to Poland and Bohemia, but elsewhere, the response was more mixed. By this time, eastern Europe had drifted away from its strong economic relationship with Russia which, having been devastated by the thirteenth century Mongol invasions, had remained under their oppressive control.

One of the economic advantages enjoyed by eastern Europe resulted from the most tragic disaster of the Middle Ages. The Bubonic Plague was accidentally introduced from Asia in 1346, and the successively worse outbreaks for the next several years were followed by periodic eruptions for decades thereafter. Called the Black Death, the disease swept north and west, decimating the population of western Europe, in some regions killing as many as two-thirds of the inhabitants. Whole villages were abandoned and forgotten as the land reverted to forest. Perhaps because of their sparser populations, the eastern countries did not suffer as badly from the pandemic; it was actually quite light in Poland (Fugedi: 1985), leaving their social and economic institutions largely intact. In the long run, however, the prosperity that eastern Europe enjoyed as supplier of raw material led it to neglect developing other industry, making it vulnerable to economic changes that lay ahead.

The third major occurrence of the eventful fourteenth century was what Okey (1982) called "the last Asian invasion" of Europe. As soon as Constantinople fell to the Ottoman (Moslem) Turks, they launched an attack on the Balkans. In 1389, they met the combined forces of the Serbs, Bulgarians, Montenegrins, and Bosnians at Kossovo, winning a decisive victory and eliminating any serious opposition south of Hungary. For the next three centuries, the Ottoman Empire moved forward in Europe, overrunning all the Balkan countries and reaching the gates of Vienna in 1683. The countries that fell under Ottoman rule were cut off from changes that were beginning to transform the rest of Europe, preventing them from the progress it was beginning to enjoy.

With its land routes severed, western Europe began to develop trade by sea and, by the end of the fifteenth century, had an extensive maritime economy with seagoing merchant navies run by experienced seamen. These navies ventured farther and farther in search of markets, finally reaching Asia and going on to explore previously unknown places.

By the sixteenth century, eastern Europe had reached a crucial stage. Cut off from Mediterranean trade by the Ottoman occupation in the South, constantly threatened by Russia from the East; and with its economy completely dependent on its agriculture (primarily grain) and livestock shipments, eastern Europe became more and more remote from the West. The Ottoman Moslem advance had led to a fifteen-year war with the Hungarian Christian defenders until, at Mohacs in 1526, the Ottomans dealt the Hungarians the worst defeat in their history, so badly crushing them that their country was partitioned—about a third occupied by the Hapsburgs and the rest falling under Ottoman control. This division lasted for the next 150 years. The Ottoman occupation was especially brutal, with Turkish troops depopulating entire areas of the countryside. By 1699, when the Ottomans were expelled from Hungary, the population of southern Hungary and Romania had been halved (Fugedi, 1985); Hungary had only 10 percent of the population that had existed in 1500. The economy was completely destroyed.

In the North, the situation was better. In the fourteenth century, Lithuania took advantage of Russia's weakened condition as a result of her wars with the Mongols. Lithuania grew to be one of the largest states in Europe, reaching from the Baltic to the Black Sea. Before the end of the century, the Lithuanian Jagiello became king of Poland, joining the two states, a union later formalized in 1569. The Lithuanian nobility rapidly became westernized, but the change did not generally reach the peasantry.

However, economic problems arose, compounded by earlier social developments. As the Atlantic maritime states recovered the population lost during plagues and increased their overseas trade, they also began to acquire colonies abroad and moved toward capitalism. The new wealth allowed the growth of a new class of prosperous merchants, traders and investors. Meanwhile, in Poland, where grain was the major export, the entire economy, including trade, was monopolized by the nobility, who steadily increased their control over the workers. By the end of the 1500s, serfdom had ended in the West, but in the East, the control over the peasants had been extended so far that some historians have referred to it as "the new serfdom." While there was experimentation and innovation in Western commerce, eastern Europe became mired in a stagnant, agricultural system that the powerful Western colony–owning states and the expanding Hapsburg Empire were able to exploit to their advantage. Of all the Eastern states, only Bohemia was able to keep pace with Western change.

During the first half of the seventeenth century, Europe was convulsed by the Thirty Years' War, which involved many countries but was fought largely on German soil. Ostensibly mostly a religious conflict, it actually involved many political, economic, and social issues. As to the religious issues, it was the case, as one historian (Okey, 1982: 23) noted, in which the combatants' "religious fervor took the form of hatred of rival beliefs rather than real knowledge of their own." The Treaty of Westphalia ended the conflict in 1648, bringing recognition to the beginnings of the modern German state and the independence of the Netherlands and Switzerland. The spread of Protestantism in Europe, begun 100 years before the outbreak of the war, was effectively checked, remaining mostly in the northern states of western Europe. The war also ended the ancient dream of a single, unified Christian state for all of Europe.

During the Thirty Years' War, large armies roamed Europe, billeted in small villages and towns and depending on the local economy for their survival. An interesting economic consequence of the war, according to Benecke (1983) was the development of a local system of supplying armies through arrangements between civilian suppliers and military officers, which included price controls. This made it possible for both soldiers and civilians to survive the encampment and led to civilian administrative control of the arrangements for the provisioning of the troops.

Two wars in the second half of the century fundamentally altered the political map of eastern Europe. One was the war between Sweden and Poland. It began shortly after the Peace of Westphalia and lasted only five years, from 1655 to 1660, but when it ended, Poland had lost 25 percent of its population; in some areas, the loss was 60 percent.

During this century, Poland had been a major international trader. In addition to its principle export, grain, it was a supplier of other natural resources to the growing Western economies. Neglecting her own industrial development, Poland exported large quantities of timber, and by the time of the war with Sweden, deforestation already had become a major problem in the country, with the disappearance of several valuable species of trees. This also led to the disappearance of a number of animals that had lost their habitat (Wyrobisz, 1985). With her wealth based primarily on exploitation of her natural resources, and not adopting a policy of replacement of renewal resources such as timber, Poland's economic decline was inevitable as those resources were depleted. A gauge of how depressed the Polish economy became can be seen in comparison of it with the French and Austrian figures (Wandycz, 1992: 107). Using 100 to indicate the French revenue in 1700, Austria's was 26 and Poland's was 3; by 1788, Austria had reached 43 and Poland's had actually declined—to 2.7 Although eastern Europe's economic development lagged behind the West, in some political areas, it was decades ahead. For example, the Polish throne was electoral, not hereditary, and in 1791, Poland adopted the second written constitution in the world (after the American Constitution). Bohemia and Hungary also were trying various sorts of decentralized political systems. The Hungarian experiments were made possible by the second war; the one against the Ottomans. The Moslem armies had entered Austria, and by 1683, they were laying siege to Vienna. In a dramatic cavalry attack, the Polish king John III Sobieski led a relief army that lifted the siege and effectively ended the Ottoman expansion in Europe. It also marked the start of an offensive before which the Ottomans gradually gave up the European land they had occupied for 300 years. However, they retreated slowly, and the struggle continued sporadically until 1912, when it was ended with the Balkan Wars. It was the expulsion of the Turks that allowed Hungary to try more pluralistic forms of politics. However, the constant warfare in the Eastern states tended to offset the advantageous balance of trade that they enjoyed, and as the West found new, cheaper, and more convenient sources, the states of eastern Europe were unable to compete or to find substitute commercial ventures, and their economies suffered. Nor were their bold political ventures to survive. Surrounded by the absolutist states of Prussia, Russia, and Austria, they found their independence slowly crushed.

The important changes that took place in the West had some impact in the East, but significantly, none of them began in the East. The major explorations, the Renaissance, Reformation, scientific revolution, Enlightenment, Industrial Revolution all rose and matured in western Europe and came east late and incompletely. While western European states were involved in Enlightenment discussions and movements, the noose around Poland was tightened. Her economy was in a shambles, and in 1792 and 1793, Poland was partitioned, losing large portions of her territory to Russia, Austria, and Prussia. In a final partition in 1795, the rest of the country was divided among the three adjoining empires; a total of about half the whole country went to Russia, and Poland as an independent nation disappeared from the maps of Europe, becoming what Wandycz (1992: 107) called a "stateless nation."

These three great empires were able to exercise complete control over the economy of eastern Europe, but they could not control the penetration of ideas from the French Revolution. Each empire included a variety of ethnic populations that were being influenced by the idea of independent nationhood. The Hapsburgs, for example, allowed relatively unrestricted travel within their empire, and one result was that the mix of distinct and separate groups was extensive: Germans, Croats, Slavs, Czechs, Serbs, Slovenes, Poles, Russians, and others.

By the time of the Napoleonic Wars, central Europe consisted of an assortment of Germanic states, later known as the German Confederation, bordered by France and the Netherlands on the west and the Russian and Hapsburg empires on the east. All of eastern Europe except part of the Balkans fell within one of these competing empires. The French Enlightenment was taken everywhere by the French army, but in eastern Europe, there were no independent states; and in 1815, the Congress of Vienna put an end to hopes of eastern Europeans for major reforms. In fact, the Congress closed without reaching agreement on what to do about the "Eastern Question."

There was some improvement in farming methods and a degree of industrialization, but economic performance in eastern Europe continued to fall behind the West, and the area remained under absolutist rule. The public political debate that took place in western

Europe was suppressed in the East, and universities, rather than legislatures, public forums, or the press became the centers of political ferment. These universities had long and distinguished traditions of intellectual achievement; both Charles University in Prague and Jagiellonian University in Krakow had been established in the middle of the fourteenth century and enjoyed a special status. The literacy rate rose sharply after 1860, and Marxist ideas began to penetrate the East European censorship. Despite strong attempts to repress them, workers began to organize, and even agrarian workers' parties appeared. Capitalist farming was started, but no industrial class developed, as in the West. Instead, the landowning aristocracy dominated politics and diverted funds that could have been used to create industry into the arts and cultural pursuits for the elites (Okey, 1982).

While unrest grew, the economy continued its downward spiral. There were crop failures in 1845 and a depression in 1847, which intensified the political tension. The Revolutions of 1848, starting in Paris, swept over Europe but promptly were put down by the ruling conservatives. Throughout eastern Europe, nationalism was sought; the idea of "nation" having become "an ethical ideal" (Wandycz, 1992). In Poland, uprisings demanded Polish independence in 1806, 1830–1831, 1846, 1848, and 1863–1864, but each was crushed by Prussia and Russia, although Russia freed the Polish serfs in 1864. Liberals continued to be active in the West, but the suppression was so severe in eastern Europe that many liberals were forced to flee. Still, the movement was not entirely swept away, and by 1900, some moderate reforms had taken place everywhere in eastern Europe except Poland (Okey, 1982). Hungary had declared its independence in 1849 and, although thoroughly defeated by the Austrians, had still managed to free its peasants. By 1868, the Hungarians forced the Hapsburgs to give them semiautonomy and henceforth were part of the Austro-Hungarian Empire. Having succeeded in winning concessions from the Hapsburgs, Hungary set out on a program of "Magyarization" of the Romanians and Slovaks (Wandycz, 1992), a move that was vigorously resisted.

A combination of political oppression and economic need led to extensive emigration from eastern Europe. Although some industrialization had started there, it was not adequate to absorb the peasants fleeing to urban centers. Major waves of Polish and Hungarian migrants made their way to America. By 1900, over 40,000 Hungarians a year were entering the United States; in 1907 alone, almost 1 percent of Hungary's entire population crossed the Atlantic (Vardy, 1983). The attraction doubtless was related to a longing of the people for freedom, but their decisions to move surely were not hurt by the fact that U.S. workers' wages were 500 percent to 600 percent higher than in eastern Europe.

Eastern Europe was not without industrial development. Railroads extended their lines; coal and steel output rose; certain industries such as food processing grew, but the pace was not competitive with the West, except in Bohemia. By 1900, Prague was the largest eastern European city, making steady progress in modernization and industrialization and achieving a dominant position in textiles. By the 1860s, a major credit bank had been formed there. Strong foreign investment might have moved the development faster, but a large peasantry, especially in the East, and state bureaucracies drained much of the money, delaying capital accumulation. Throughout eastern Europe, Germans and Jews began to form the nucleus of an emerging middle class (Wanducz, 1992; Stokes, 1997). The industrial development in Europe during the latter part of the nineteenth century was accompanied by an unusual, extended period of peace. Germany under Bismarck was moving toward unification and increasing its influence on a solid base of industrial progress and skillful diplomacy. The Franco-Prussian War of 1870–1871 indicated the new alignment of powers, and from the end of that war, Europe remained uncharacteristically peaceful until the outbreak of World War I, over 40 years later.

On the eve of World War I, Germany occupied all of northcentral Europe, extending along the Baltic coast past Konigsberg to Lithuania, where it abutted the Russian Empire. The rest of eastern Europe was divided between the Austro-Hungarian Empire and Russia; the former reached from the Adriatic north, including Bohemia, sharing a common border with Russia, and south into the Balkans, the Ottoman Empire having retreated to the southern Balkans, with Serbia and Bulgaria as nation-states carved from the remains of the Ottoman European territory. Disaffection among ethnic populations was widespread within both the Russian and Austro-Hungarian Empires. In fact, it was the act of an ethnic "freedom fighter" (from the Serbian viewpoint) or "Slavic terrorist" (from the Austro-Hungarian viewpoint) that set the countries of Europe and elsewhere on the final path to total war in 1914. In the kind of coincidence that occurs in real life but would be considered much too far-fetched for fiction, a number of men who would figure prominently in European and world affairs after the war all lived in Vienna some months before the outbreak of hostilities: Sigmund Freud, psychoanalyst; Leon Trotsky, editor of *Pravda;* Adolf Hitler, unsuccessful artist; Joseph Stalin, Bolshevik organizer and messenger for Lenin; and Josip Broz Tito, auto mechanic.

When World War I ended in 1918, the peace conference altered the boundaries in Europe again, arguably more dramatically than by any such previous conference. Nationalism, the predominant political movement of the nineteenth century, was recognized in forming new nations, purportedly to address the desire of the peoples for ethnic cohesiveness and "self-determination." The medieval principle that the will and convenience of monarchs and aristocrats, not ethnicity, is what mattered in setting political boundaries supposedly received its "final repudiation" (Hupchick, 1995) at Versailles. Eastern Europe became identified by the "successor states" thus created: Poland, Czechoslovakia, Hungary, Romania, Yugoslavia, and Bulgaria. However, as already noted, the ethnic populations of eastern Europe had become so intermixed that no national borders based on ethnic homogeneity were possible, and the new nations did not have such ethnic homogeneity. It may be said that the one ethnic characteristic common to virtually all the separate groups was their virulent hatred of Jews and Gypsies (Hanak and Held: 1996). As Korbonski (1996: 233) put it: "the official policy toward the minorities was hostile from the start...."

Although the Armistice was declared in 1918, active fighting continued in eastern Europe. In 1920, Poland attacked Russia (by then, part of the Union of Soviet Socialist Republics) with great success, and by the time the fighting ended in 1921, the Polish border was much farther east than had been intended, taking in territory where the people were predominantly Bylorussian and Ukrainian. Poland was two-thirds Polish. More vast amounts of Russian territory were taken to create Finland, Latvia, Lithuania, and Estonia. The Austro-Hungarian Empire also was dismembered; Czechoslovakia was created from its northern territory and Yugoslavia from its land in the Balkans. Yugoslavia actually was the name taken at a somewhat later date by the new nation that originally had been called the "Kingdom of the Serbs, Croats and Slovenes" (Shepard, 1932), reflecting the complex ethnic mix of the region and, in all likelihood, the puzzlement of the peacemakers over what to do with it. Although Hungary became an independent nation, in some respects, she suffered the most in the peace settlement. She had suffered a million and half people killed, wounded, or captured during the war; in the peace, she lost Slovakia and Transylvania, both of which contained large numbers of ethnic Hungarians. Hanak (1996) compared this loss with the disaster at Mohacs in 1526. In the new division of land, Hungary lost 68 percent of her geographic area and 59 percent of her population; nearly a third of all ethnic Magyars were in territory outside the country (Hyde-Price, 1996).

The war had been fought under the guise of making the world "safe for democracy," and the successor states were intended to be democratic, but in rather short order, they became neither safe nor democratic. They were "a naïve invention of the West," not supported by the indigenous church, monarchy, or army (Fischer-Galati, 1996), although they represented the closest approximation yet to the kinds of governments found in the West. They were intolerant of ethnic and religious differences and probably predisposed to autocratic rule from centuries of experiencing it. Perhaps, in the long run, the same was true for western Europe. By 1922, the Fascists controlled Italy; in 1933, the Nazis took over Germany; totalitarian regimes soon followed in Portugal and Spain, in all cases with extensive internal support. In eastern Europe, the decline of democratic government was even faster. In 1920, even before the signing of the Trianon Treaty that savaged Hungary, Horthy became Regent there; in 1926, Pilsudski staged his takeover in Poland, followed by King Alexander of Yugoslavia in 1929, King Carol in Romania, and Tsar Boris in Bulgaria. By 1927, Stalin had seized complete control in the USSR. Within a few years, Nazi-like organizations had begun to appear in eastern Europe: the Arrow Cross in Hungary and the Iron Guard in Romania. One by one, the eastern European governments were taken over by right-wing movements; even during a time of relative prosperity and peace, democracy could not succeed there.

American and French investment in Polish development was heavy initially, but Polish productivity fell regardless, sometimes to 1870 levels. The British invested in Czechoslovakia, which maintained its prewar position of leading the other eastern European countries in industrial growth (but only in the Czech sector). It also was the country that maintained democratic government longest—until 1938. The development prospects for the new countries were not promising, even with outside help. "Peasant Eastern Europe...was a hopelessly under-capitalized, overpopulated bottom rung of the European economy" (Okey, 1982: 196). As the Great Depression settled over Europe, the effects were most serious in the industrialized West. Eastern Europe, which had remained largely agrarian, had reformed and modernized many of its agricultural practices, and was less susceptible to the capitalist boom and bust cycle. Where industry existed in the East, efforts were made to reform and modernize it. As the 1930s progressed, the countries of eastern Europe saw support and investment from the western democracies decline sharply and they shifted their trade increasingly to Germany, which was eager to have economic ties to the East. As in centuries past, eastern Europe represented a vast store of raw materials, such as oil, that were essential for Germany's efforts to rebuild itself.

The intention of western Europe after World War I had been to isolate the USSR and to permanently cripple Germany. Caught between them, the eastern Europeans feared aggression from both the USSR and Germany. Trade arrangements seemed to be good economics and perhaps good insurance, as well. Germany may have seemed important protection from the Soviet Union's growing strength and inevitable expansion. Stalin had embarked on a campaign of dragging his people out of their feudal backwardness at any cost and was beginning to industrialize the country. It is unlikely that the traditionally conservative peasants in eastern Europe were not aware of Stalin's ruthless campaign against the peasants and of the brutal collectivization of farms with a loss of millions of lives. As the Depression ground on, and the economies of the industrial democracies seemed unlikely to recover any time soon, if at all, the booming German system must have seemed very attractive. Men were working, the infrastructure was being improved and expanded, life seemed secure and pleasant. The autocratic government might not have seemed much different from the kinds that eastern Europeans had endured for generations. Even the ugly anti-Semitism was a familiar and not unwelcome public policy for them. The largest concentration of Jews outside the Soviet Union was in Poland, where they had lived for 700 years. Most lived in the cities; about a third of the population of Warsaw, Krakow, and Lodz, Poland's largest cities. They were prominent in the professions and trades, competing successfully with Catholic Poles, whose feelings of resentment were not opposed by the Church, so that widespread anti-Semitism was "not surprising" (Korbonski, 1996). When the German reoccupation of the Rhineland was unopposed, it just seemed to underscore the weakness and indecisiveness of the Western democracies. Even the Anschluss with Austria in the Spring of 1938 was not necessarily alarming to eastern Europeans, since it was still a case that involved "only Germans." The betrayal of Czechoslovakia later the same year was still "a German matter" and may well have seemed confirmation of the inability of the Western democratic governments to confront the determined German will or to match the German "economic miracle." Scarcely fifteen years after Germany had been smashed and forced to accept the cruel and humiliating treaty of Versailles, it had made itself the major industrial power in Europe, investing heavily in eastern Europe, while France and England were struggling just to survive economically and to counter the sympathy for fascism that was growing in those countries.

However, none of the countries anywhere in Europe could overlook the ominous implications of the 1939 German-Soviet nonaggression agreement. Under certain secret provisions of the pact, Russia was to recover the territory she lost to Poland in 1921; Germany was to get the industrial western half of the country. The month after the pact was signed, Germany invaded Poland from the west, followed after a short delay in the east by the USSR, which also invaded Finland. The Soviet invasion was vigorously if unsuccessfully resisted. However, as the Wehrmacht moved deeper into eastern Europe, the German troops often found themselves welcomed. In the Ukraine, for example, they were initially considered liberators of the people from the Russians. The affection did not last very long, as the Nazis proved to be at least as oppressive in their occupation of the country as were the Soviets.

The most savage fighting of the war took place in eastern Europe, in the years during which the Soviet army drove the Nazis steadily back. Both sides practiced a "scorched earth" policy—both when they retreated and when they advanced. It was in the East that the Nazis built their major concentration camps and the death camps of the Holocaust. By the end of six years of war, the region again had been thoroughly devastated and the populace decimated. The Allied conference at Yalta near the end of the war decided the future boundaries of Europe and, as usual, there were major changes in eastern Europe.

Only the Soviet Union gained substantial territory. At the Potsdam Conference, just after the war was won, it was agreed to leave undisturbed the Soviet occupation of the eastern half of Poland, roughly along the line suggested by Curzon after the First World War. To compensate Poland, territory was taken from Germany by moving the Polish border west to the Oder for the first time since the eleventh century. The USSR also continued to occupy the Baltic States, took the northern third of Romania, and absorbed the eastern "tail" of Czechoslovakia and a large part of Finland. Then, with the approval of the victorious allies, Poland and Czechoslovakia expelled the ethnic Germans living within their borders, 8,000,000 and 3,000,000 respectively, often subjecting to terrible atrocities families that had lived peaceably in the region for hundreds of years.

The expectation of the West was that the war would be followed by democratic elections in the eastern European states, following the principle of self-determination, even though the ethnic groups there had squabbled incessantly between the wars. The USSR agreed to permit such elections. Almost at once, the agreement broke down. The West suppressed Communist attempts to take power, beginning with the British sending troops to Greece. A Communist coup in Bulgaria was beyond the reach of the West and when elections were held in November 1945, the Communists received 90 percent of the vote, to the surprise of no one at all. Through a combination of Western ineptitude and Communist opportunism, the Party spread its control until by 1948, all the countries in eastern Europe were under Communist governance, which quickly ended free elections and stopped early attempts to develop liberal capitalism. Instead, command economies were put in place, ultimately dictated by Moscow.

The United States undertook to help the countries that had been ruined by the war rebuild their economies. The Marshall Plan was announced by President Truman in 1947, and all European countries were invited to apply for aid. Requests were answered throughout the West, but initial applications from the East were withdrawn under Soviet pressure and no more were permitted. With the help of the Marshall Plan, the West recovered rapidly, while eastern Europe again found itself lagging behind and people began to flee to the West. Between 1949 and 1961, when the Soviets erected the Berlin Wall, East Germany lost 15 percent of its population—2,500,000 people (Hanak, and Held, 1996). The Soviets tried to tighten their grip on East Germany by blockading all roads into Berlin in order to starve the city into submission, but an allied airlift thwarted the effort and the blockade was lifted a few months later. Throughout eastern Europe, except Yugoslavia, the Soviet eliminated any threats to their hegemony. Poland, for instance, had lost 6,000,000 people in the war (half were Jews); after the Communist takeover, another 1,250,000 to 1,500,000— mostly clergy and intelligentsia—were sent to Soviet Asia, where about half of them died.

Stalinization proceeded quickly in the countries under the Soviet aegis, with a program of industrializing that had been successful in dragging the Russian people into the twentieth century and had made the country strong enough to defeat the Nazi invasion. As recovery accelerated in the West, the Soviet Union organized the Council for Mutual Economic Assistance (CMEA or COMECON) to provide a basis for collective recovery and to avoid competition. CMEA countries were assigned what seemed most appropriate for them, but when Romania refused its assignment to limit industrial growth and focus on agriculture, the guidelines were made somewhat more flexible.

The Communist takeover in eastern Europe often was well supported within the country, despite ancient misgivings about the Russian bear. Poland, once the Jews had been killed, the Eastern Orthodox portion taken by the USSR, and the Germans expelled, was left virtually a monocultural, Polish, Roman Catholic country. The Soviets were resented at first, but it had been Soviet troops that drove back the Nazis and the USSR that supported the westward extension of the Polish border. Moreover, Eastern Communists generally acted on behalf of their nationalist aspirations, not as Soviet operatives, and besides, what democratic movements did manage to get started did not receive support from the West. In Bulgaria, for example, the monarchy was abolished after the war and replaced by the Petrov government, which was anti-Soviet. But the West failed to include Bulgaria under the protective umbrella that covered Greece. The day after the United States signed the peace treaty, which left him vulnerable, Petrov was arrested on the floor of the Bulgarian parliament and subsequently hanged (Rothschild, 1989). The Czechs did not even consider the USSR a hostile power. In their only free election, in 1946, they gave the Communists 38 percent of the vote. Although they were a minority party, the Communists were able to exploit a political crisis and seize power in 1948. In Hungary, the Communists also were a minority party, with 22 percent of the vote, but in 1949, they were able to take power even though Cardinal Mindszenty led a vigorous opposition to their rule until his arrest (Rothschild: 1989). Hungary quickly felt the weight of Russian authoritarianism: between 1949 and 1953, over 750,000 people from a population of 10,000,000 were investigated for political crimes; 150,000 were imprisoned; about 2000 were executed (Hanak and Held, 1996). As in other eastern European countries, the intelligentsia was a major target for suppression; for years, several of the CMEA countries forbade the teaching of certain social science disciplines in the universities: psychology and sociology in Hungary and Czechoslovakia and anthropology in Bulgaria (Stokes, 1997).

In 1953, Stalin died, and it was widely believed that any new regime would allow more economic diversity and a greater voice for the people. It did not happen as expected. Three months after Stalin's death, workers in East Berlin took to the streets to protest new work quotas. In the ensuing conflict, 21 were killed, 187 injured, and more than a thousand jailed. In Poland, there were persistent periodic protests. Gomulka had actually resisted Stalinization after the war and was imprisoned in 1951. A few years later, a protest over food prices ended with over 50 Poles killed and 300 arrested by the military. Gomulka was released from prison and returned to power, which he used to follow a strategy of keeping Poland Communist, but making it more nationalistic than a client of the Soviet Union, although the homegrown version was no less oppressive. Pressure for changes in the economic system persisted throughout most of the region. Some revision was allowed, so long as it was couched in Marxist terms and did not include a break from the East European bloc.

Leadership in these changes was taken by Hungary after Nagy became premier. He tried to introduce modest economic reforms, mainly to reduce the amount of heavy industry and to eliminate the farm collectivization. He was deposed in 1955, but a year later, student demonstrations brought him back to office. Once again, he initiated reforms, which were tolerated until he tried to take Hungary on a more independent political road. The Soviets sent tanks into Budapest, crushed the street demonstrations, and placed in power Janos Kadar, who put an end to the Nagy reforms and under whom, two years later, Nagy was hanged. Despite this inauspicious beginning, Kadar eventually began to introduce and, more importantly, to permit economic changes that had a long-range positive effect for the country. Eventually, Hungary adopted the New Economic Mechanism, which significantly overhauled the economic system and even allowed some private ownership (Rothschild,

1989). The regime maintained tight control and was certainly an oppressive one, but the economic improvement enhanced Kadar's image with the people. By the 1960s, there was increased communication with the West to the extent that the Hungarian intelligentsia sometimes were more aware of what was happening in Western Europe than of events in other CMEA/Warsaw Pact countries. The Warsaw Pact was a common defense alliance created in 1955 to counteract the North American Treaty Organization (NATO), a Western mutual defense pact. Nagy's attempt to withdraw Hungary from the Warsaw Pact is believed to have been the proximate cause of the 1956 Soviet invasion of the country.

Romania was so effectively controlled that it was able quite early to try a few small economic reforms, and, by 1958, the Soviets were sufficiently confident of the regime that they began to withdraw their troops. By the 1960s, Romania was introducing selected Western technology. The leadership remained more constraining than ever, particularly after Ceaucescu took power in 1965, placing members of his family in all key positions. The adjacent country, Bulgaria was the one that never directly challenged Moscow, but it began to shift from agriculture to food processing and light industry. By the 1970s, Bulgaria was allowing private peasant plots and accepting some capital investment from the West.

In some respects, the most dogmatically Stalinist East European country was the most industrial: Czechoslovakia. The economy worked quite well and modest reforms were introduced in 1966. Two years later, Novotny was replaced by the more liberal Dubcek, who began some serious reforms. In the Eastern countries that were able to start some reforms, care was taken not to oppose socialism, but to suggest ways of making it work better. Even Dubcek worked within the party, but his attempts to institute a market economy precipitated the so-called Prague Spring, a savage suppression of the reforms by the countries of the Warsaw Pact, spearheaded by the USSR. The overthrow of Dubcek's reform was followed by even more centralized control of the economy. So strong was the resistance to reform by Husak in Czechoslovakia that it held on to the old, outmoded system after Hungary, Poland, and even East Germany and Russia were exploring new forms. During the 1970s, Hungary seemed to be leading the reforms and Poland was leading the protests, which were usually bloodily put down.

Both Poland and Hungary had begun borrowing from the West. In Poland, the money was not spent prudently, going more for consumer goods than economic development. Moreover, the borrowing was excessive; the oil crisis in the West had resulted in gigantic holdings that banks were eager to invest. The protests became more vocal after Woityla was made Pope John Paul II in 1978. His visit to Poland the next year produced a massive demonstration. By 1980, Poland's debt to the West was over US$21 billion, and when the government raised prices again, the students were joined by the workers and the intelligentsia, forming *Solidarity* and winning major civil and economic concessions. The Polish Communist leaders were exposed as representing their own interests, not those of the workers (Rothschild, 1989) and resentment ran deep. The country was taken over by the military, led by General Jaruzelski, who somewhat later imposed martial law. This was seen as a victory for the Poles, since the takeover had not involved Soviet troops.

Throughout eastern Europe, centrally planned economies were not succeeding. Starting in the 1970s, they were plagued by slow growth, inflation, rising indebtedness, and poor balance of trade. Meanwhile, the West's Common Market was proving to be a great success, and by 1984 had abolished tariffs on all industrial goods. "Actually existing socialism" did not seem "able to provide in practice what the ideology claimed" it would (Swaim and Swaim, 1993). Belatedly, some reforms were introduced. There was a certain amount of decentralization of production, as well as limited attention to consumer demands; the profit motive was allowed to influence some prices; and there was a shift in financing from state banks to independent groups motivated by return on investment rather than ideology (Okey, 1982). Yet, despite the efforts to liberalize the economy, it became clear that the reforms were being undermined by entrenched bureaucracies. Success of the economic liberalization could not be completely separated from the need for relaxation of the party control. As this idea was sinking in with Eastern economists, technological advances in the West were widening the gap.

In a broad sense, socialism had been extraordinarily successful in eastern Europe. It had taken over backward societies with a history of autocratic regimes that exploited docile, ignorant workers. Despite the oppressiveness of the socialist system, it had cut the death rate in half; virtually eliminated adult illiteracy; opened access to education, sharply increasing education of physicians and teachers; provided better health care; and raised real wages over 300 percent (Okey, 1986). After 1970, the economies had begun to improve. Exports, which previously had been almost exclusively agricultural products, primarily consisted of manufactured goods; the agrarian societies had been urbanized. By 1980, the rise of industrial output since 1955 had been 600 percent for Hungary, 700 percent for Czechoslovakia, over 1100 percent for Poland, 1600 percent for Bulgaria, and nearly 2000 percent for Romania (Okey, 1982). Nevertheless, the base for this progress had been so low that the quality of life in the East still compared unfavorably with that in the West. Disillusion with the command economy grew, and the interference with serious reforms by government officials became more intolerable. It became clear that the centrally planned economy could not "create wealth in conditions where prices bore no relation to costs," which, instead of being absorbed by inefficient operations, were being passed on to the public. The "once inspirational ideology" had "turned concrete" (Swaim and Swaim, 1994), in more ways than one. There was resentment by urban intellectuals over human rights abuses and restriction on personal liberties, but for most of the population, even more objectionable was the elimination of private property and, in rural areas, the endless attacks on religion (Fischer-Galati, 1996). The irony of the socialist system in eastern Europe is that by the end of the 1980s, it was still trying to sustain a rigid and repressive political structure to rule a population it had helped make stronger, healthier, better educated, more informed, and longer lived.

In the USSR, Gorbachev addressed the twenty-seventh Party Congress (1986), calling for extensive reforms. He recognized that the USSR could not simply be "a Third World state with missiles" (Stokes, 1997), but every leader of the eastern European countries rejected his idea of *perestroika.* Three years later, the inflexible socialist governments in eastern Europe went into the political equivalent of cardiac arrest, one after the other collapsing. The East German Communists announced their intent to "pursue their own road to socialism"; the Red Army did not invade. Almost at once, Hungary eliminated security at its border with Austria and East Germans poured into Hungary "on vacation," quickly passing unimpeded into Austria on their way to West Germany. In the fall of 1989, the Berlin Wall itself was torn down by exultant crowds as the Red guards looked on; the next day, Zhivkov resigned in Bulgaria. Later the same month, demonstrations in Prague, the "velvet revolution," led to the election of Havel as Czech president. Within a month, Ceaucescu had been overthrown and executed in Romania.

Socialism had reduced poverty in eastern Europe, but had retained stifling, bureaucratic political/economic controls. As Rothschild (1989: 225) pithily observed, socialism had transformed "sullen and alienated peasants into sullen and alienated proletarians." As modest freedoms grew, capricious laws were more and more ignored; resentment of authority increased; a vigorous black market economy developed to offset the "shortage economies" (Longworth, 1992). The fault lines in the economy, such as inequities in work and the provision of social welfare benefits, became more apparent and widened—for example, the ballooning "gifts" that had to be given to physicians in order to get adequate medical treatment or a bed in a particular hospital. When they were out of power, the Communists were popular because they had opposed government oppression; by the end of the 1980s, they had become the embodiment of that very government oppression. Moreover, despite the benefits that socialism had brought, it had not managed to develop real, voluntary cooperation among the eastern European countries. In June 1991, the CMEA/COMECON, already long moribund, was formally dissolved; weeks later, the Warsaw Pact was dissolved, and in the last month of the same year, the Union of Soviet Socialist Republics declared its union to be ended.

The "fall of Communism" seemed dramatic and spontaneous, but it is widely argued that it was neither; in fact, the economic systems based on central planning had been slowly changing for several years. Trade with the West had been increasing, and indebtedness to Western lending institutions had reached gigantic levels. The widespread existence of black markets and the underground economy had been supplying consumer goods when the economy was not allowed to produce them in anything near demand levels. Services and small businesses had been socialized, inviting under-the-table arrangements, such as the physicians' "gifts" and the "tip system" for public services. In some of the countries, money borrowed from the West went to meet consumer demand rather than development (Adam: 1996), which raised expectations that could not be met, and also raised debts that could not be repaid. Historic fear and suspicion of Russia had been fueled by the Hungarian and Czech invasions; by the 1980s, there was a whole generation of young leaders who could remember neither the Depression nor the Russian liberation during World War II, further weakening the bonds that tied the eastern European countries to the USSR and to each other. Ideological considerations were less important to workers than quality of life issues, and the quality of life in the West was patently more attractive. The CMEA countries had been looking west for trade and by 1990, Hungary's main trading partner was Germany rather than the Soviet Union (Hyde-Price, 1996). Moreover, for years, there had been smoldering outrage among the intelligentsia over government constraints and lack of status, as well as the rigid controls over academic instruction. As travel restrictions eased in the 1980s, more scholars were able to leave their countries and attend overseas conferences and seminars, sometimes assisted by research grants. This became a kind of de facto subversion technique by the West for getting market economy and other ideas into the CMEA countries, and it was one that proved highly effective, given the long tradition of universities in the East of serving as centers of dissent and opposition to the government.

When the COMECON/CMEA ended in 1991, the favorable arrangements for trade credits and other benefits from the Soviet Union to member countries ended, as well, and resulted in a sharp drop in exports to the former USSR; on its part, Russia raised the prices of many vital commodities, most notably fossil fuels, to capture something closer to market prices.

The euphoria over the collapse of the command economy and autocratic governments did not last very long. It had been a wonderful binge, but the hangover was severe. There had been an expectation on the part of Eastern leaders that the West would promptly welcome them as partners, with the inevitable boom in their economies, but the reception was restrained (Korbonski, 1997). France vetoed a move to give them easier access to the Common Market, and with the collapse of trade with Russia, there were few other places to go. Turning to each other, the most advanced of the eastern European countries, Poland, Hungary and Czechoslovakia created a free trade zone among themselves. CEFTA, or the Visegrad Agreement took effect in 1993. During the first phase, it was agreed to eliminate border checks and, by 2001, to have free trade comparable to that of the European Union (Stokes, 1997).

Another expectation had been that introduction of the market economy would bring a fast increase in the standard of living. Instead, the opposite happened. Hungary had chosen the path of gradualism, or movement into the market economy by steps or degrees; Poland had chosen "shock treatment," or rapid change.

Poland instituted the Balcerowicz Plan, which aimed at privatization of state-owned industry, liberalization of the market, and holding down inflation. The intention was to take the market quickly to production and pricing driven by demand rather than central planning (Cannon, 1997). The first results of the plan were disappointing and potentially inflammatory. Solidarity leaders had intended to take over the state industries or to control them through memberships on the boards of directors. The changeover did not happen as they expected; instead government bureaucrats manipulated the process, often for their personal enrichment. Despite the slow pace of privatization of large industries, small private-sector businesses flourished. The economy began to revive, buoyed by the success of small private business. In 1993, the real gross domestic product grew by 3.8 percent; by 1995, it was growing by 6.5 percent (Cannon, 1997).

In the eastern European countries in general, the growth did not surpass the 1960–1985 period, and after 1990, it dropped sharply (Human Development Report, 1996). In Russia, the sharp decline that began in 1990 had not been reversed by 1997. All through the region, the rate of transformation to a market economy slowed. Almost everywhere, the old Communist party (sometimes renamed, sometimes reformed) made gains. In the 1993 Polish elections, post-Communist parties won 65 percent of the seats in the parliament and have returned throughout the East; in Romania, they never lost control.

Problems notwithstanding, by 1995, the Visegrad countries were essentially market economies. After 1993, production there grew quickly, although it continued to fall in Russia (output declined by 40 percent between 1990 and 1995). In the Czech Republic, Romania, and Bulgaria, the decline was checked by 1995, but the stabilization was at a level below that of 1989 (Gelb, 1996). In Hungary and Estonia, privatization moved well through direct sales, while Romania and Slovenia favored worker-management buy-outs. Foreign investment as a share of the GDP boomed in Hungary and Poland, matched elsewhere in the world only by China (Gelb, 1996). Foreign aid increased, with Germany "by far the largest source," accounting for "nearly two-thirds of total official and private flows to these countries" (Assistance Programmes, 1996: 32), with the largest amounts going to Russia. However, the recent general flow of aid from Western countries has declined significantly, except for Canada and the United States; long-term commitments are made only by Germany and Sweden, and they tend to be for the same amount each year over a five-year term. As the economic transformation continued into the late 1990s, a more realistic view was replacing the utopian expectations with which the era began.

## Current Issues

One shortage eastern Europeans have never had to face is that of problems. As so often in the past, the current development problems relate to economic viability, political stability, international relations, quality of life issues, and the environment. As before, they do not lend themselves well to seriatim solution, but require simultaneous attention.

A majority of observers seems to feel that the command economy is dead and that the transformation in the East to a market economy is irreversible. "Shock therapy" in Poland and Czech/Slovak has produced serious dislocations. The major economic growth has been in new private business, not in privatized major state industries. The myths of the Western economy, including the expectation of strong commitment and aid, were not fulfilled, although the gap was filled partly by Germany. The region still faces the residual effects of investors and "consultants" who descended on eastern Europe after 1989. Some of them were "both genuine and capable, and they did good work" but others "had neither quality" and left a bad aftertaste in the mouths of the people who had trusted them. Brown (1994) refers to many of them as being simply "opportunists." The development of the economy has been described as "spectacular...for some countries—and unprecedented decline for others" (Human Development Report: 1996).

The gradual reform strategy was adopted in Hungary and, later, by Bulgaria and Romania. This approach allows for development of the private sector while the state continues to provide certain social protections. The ultimate dismantling of the state welfare system is delayed to allow people who are at risk to adjust their lives to the new situation. In some places, this strategy seems simply to have prolonged the agony rather than get it over in one jolt; in other places, it seems to have been very successful. China is the prime case of gradual market development of the economy under socialist control of the government.

In either strategy, the ultimate tasks remain the same: trade liberalization; privatization, especially of public heavy industries; tax reform; modernization of production; overhaul of the legal system; and modification of the financial sector. None of them is easy to do and, in some cases, such strategies are easy to derail. As the reforms got underway, prices rose sharply, a phenomenon that under the early system produced the sorts of public outcry that finally toppled the system. Productivity plummeted and inflation soared. Productivity is still declining in Russia, but seems stabilized elsewhere. The rise of inflation has stalled, but remains a serious problem that will become gravely worse if it begins to occur again. In this area, too, Russia is much the worst off with a 1995 inflation rate of 120 percent. Rates in some other East European countries were equally horrendous, but have been brought back down. Lithuania, for example, had an inflation rate of 165 percent in 1993 and, within two years, brought it to 37 percent. In a competitive economic situation, however, inflation is a vital factor, and none of the countries in the East can expect to enjoy stable economies until they can tame inflation. Rates in 1995 were: Poland, 30 percent; Hungary, 21 percent; Czech Republic, 10 percent; Romania, 62 percent; Estonia, 24 percent (but going down); Slovakia, 12 percent; Slovenia, 20 percent; and Latvia, 24 percent (World Fact Book, 1995). These estimates of inflation rates do not represent consensus, but there is general agreement that as inflation has been brought down, growth has resumed.

Unemployment rates vary extensively by occupation, but in most places, the private sector is beginning to absorb significant numbers of workers who lost their jobs to modernization and downscaling. Poverty has grown throughout eastern Europe, with the most seriously affected the elderly, families with many children; and single-parent families (Gelb, 1996). As support programs such as day care have been cut back, women have been squeezed out of the paid work force, and open discrimination in hiring has become rampant. Employers openly advertise in newspapers for women who are young and attractive; some require a photo with the job application. In "gender development," an indicator of the status and progress of women used by the UNDP, 137 countries were ranked (Human Development Report, 1996). The United States was ranked fourth; rankings of the East European countries were: Czech, 23; Slovakia, 24; Hungary, 28; Latvia, 36; Poland, 37; Russia, 40; Estonia, 48; Romania, 53; and Lithuania, 57. Discrimination against ethnic minorities was suppressed during the years from 1945 to 1990, but with the new freedoms came a return of widespread oppression. Women are not the only target. Gypsies are the fastest-growing ethnic group in the region, numbering about 2,000,000 in Romania; 800,000 each in Czech and Bulgaria; 600,000 in Hungary; and 50,000 in Poland. Gypsies are singled out everywhere for abuse at all class levels: Even university professors may be heard making disparaging, derogatory remarks about them. Anti-Semitism has proved to have remarkable powers of survival, even though the region was virtually emptied of Jews. Brown (1994: 224) called it "Antisemitism without Jews." In a 1991 survey, people were asked to respond to the following statement: "I do not have much in common with people of other ethnic groups and races." The percentage of "Yes" replies was reported by Terry (1996): Poland, 74 percent; Czech, 31 percent; Hungary, 27 percent; and Bulgaria, 17 percent. People in this region, which in the present century has been the birthplace of two world wars and the cold war, gave a "Yes" answer in the following percentages to another statement: Poland, 58 percent; Hungary, 34 percent, Bulgaria, 26 percent; and Czech Republic, 20 percent. The statement was: "The best way to ensure peace is through military intervention."

As social problems have mounted, life expectancy has declined. By the 1960s, the life expectancy gap between the West and the East had been closed, but recently, it has begun to open again, especially among the middle-aged. According to Gelb (1996: 127), "by the late 1980s, Hungarian men aged fifteen to fifty-nine stood a greater risk of dying than their counterparts in Zimbabwe." Although CIA figures reported earlier placed Russian life expectancy at 69 years in 1995, UNDP figures in 1996 placed the age at 67.4 years (Human Development Report, 1996), and Gelb (1996) reported that it had dropped to 59 years. It should be noted that UNDP figures for East European life expectancy were consistently lower than those used by the CIA for the same period.

Political reforms have been the rule, but they also have been uneven. Ancient ideologies of autocracy die slowly, and in some countries, the transformation of the economy has been perverted to enrich the old bureaucracy. In comparing Latin American regimes with those in eastern Europe, Rosenberg (1995, 401) concluded that the dictatorships in Latin countries have been "regimes of criminals"; those in East Europe have been "criminal regimes." The distinction seems apt, but the attraction and strength of political extremists is still apparent in support for such as Zhirinovsky in Russia and Tyminski in Poland, who blame ethnic minorities for whatever complaints their citizens have.

Intrinsic in political and economic reforms are overhauls of the legal systems. The old socialist governments used their legal systems largely to maintain their control and to punish dissent. Much remains to be done in changing holdover systems of jurisprudence into fair and objective ones. For example, as recently as 1995, a reporter in Romania could receive a seven-year sentence for publishing evidence that a policeman accepts graft, even if can be proved that he does (Rosenberg, 1995). Eastern European civic and legal systems retain much of the flavor of those set in place by the old aristocracies. In some of the countries, no one was allowed to practice law (Zacek and Kim, 1997), and the judiciary was anything but independent. One obvious target for early reform is property law. Not far behind is the need for a revised code of taxation and the instrumentality to enforce it.

All the economic, political, and legal reforms are essential to save the environment. As already noted, the Soviet development of heavy industry using outmoded, wasteful, and polluting equipment has left all the countries in the East with toxic environments. The water, soil, and air all suffer from disastrous levels of pollution that it may take decades of all-out effort to reverse. Failure to take prompt action could have serious long-term effects on the health and safety of the people, but none of the governments has sufficient available capital to undertake the needed clean-up.

It is not clear how long the people will be willing to wait for the benefits of the reformed economic and political systems to become widely available, or how long they will endure the discomforts, inconveniences, and pain of the transformation. Stokes (1997: 163) asserts that "the legitimacy of modern governments rests on their ability to deliver economic success," but success that is merely economic may not be enough." According to Adam (1996, 207), "most people judge systems of government according to the welfare effects they get from them." Both of these claims were made in the context of analyses of eastern Europe, but seem to overlook the inevitable harm some people suffer during the changeover period. Brown (1994: 6) has described the problem with disturbing candor. "Economic reform...," he wrote, "effectively means social disenfranchisement of hundreds of thousands of workers [who] must become extinct if the new Eastern Europe is to have a future. The prospects of these [workers]...ever retraining, redeploying, or being reincarnated as entrepreneurs are practically nil." Without some sort of social democracy with social supports, it is difficult to imagine that hundreds of thousands of marginalized workers will long tolerate the new governments *or* their economic systems.

# Future Prospects

The glum and forbidding assessment of Fischer-Galati (1996) is that "present conditions are no better for making eastern Europe safe for democracy than they were at the end of World War I." Others have a somewhat more optimistic outlook, arguing that the reforms already in place cannot be undone and eventually will lead to better conditions for all. Still others prefer to hedge their bets by describing the situation as ambiguous, noting that "the chances of the Eastern European revolutions leading to secure multi-party democracies are at best uncertain" (Swaim, and Swaim, 1993). The economic picture in the Visegrad Alliance countries began improving in 1993 and appears to be staying on a fairly steady upward trajectory. Although it is difficult to make predictions for other East European countries, they have a history of following the lead of the Visegrad group. The present pattern is that improvement will progress more quickly in those countries that already are ahead, and none of them has achieved optimal development (Zecchini, 1997).

In devising a projection for prospects in eastern Europe, it is helpful to have a clear understanding of why the command economies suddenly seemed to implode in the late 1980s, but there are conflicting interpretations and explanations of the events. Most theories focus on flaws inherent in the system, which failed to provide consumer goods in favor of heavy industrial development, but failed in that, too (e.g., Adam, 1996). Others discuss the high cost of guaranteed employment and the obsolete technology used to sustain it, which produced inefficiency and corruption (the standard joke was that "we pretend to work and the government pretends to pay us"). Another popular theory is that the overthrow of Communism "was motivated primarily by the elimination...of private property rights" and the impoverishment of the people (e.g., Fischer-Galati, 1996). In a closely reasoned discussion, Sugar (1995) asserted that the cause that ignited the region was simple nationalism, the same cause that led to the organization of the E.U. as well as warfare in the Balkans. In many respects the most original and persuasive interpretation of events was made by Longworth (1992: 2), who concluded that the eastern European countries did not win their freedom from Moscow at all; they simply "had become too expensive to maintain," so the Soviet Union "dismantled its own empire," cutting its client states loose to fend for themselves in the new global economy. Longworth's evidence is as fascinating as his conclusion; he claimed that every specific and celebrated "freedom incident" was actually staged: Honecker declared in public that the opening of East Germany was planned in the Kremlin; the Czech incident that produced the street demonstrations was faked by the KGB; the intent to arrest the pastor in Romania that resulted in riots had been announced well in advance; and so on.

Each of these interpretations has implications for how future prospects look for the region. As early as 1994, the U.S. Congress was advised that the "reforms have become largely irreversible" (*Eastern Europe: Reforms Spur Recovery:* 1994), but this seems unrealistic in light of the proven ability of this region to go through unpredicted and basic change.

It may well be that the future of development in the region is related to the vigor and reliability of encouragement, commitment, and assistance from the West. What the Marshall Plan did for western Europe in the 1940s could help eastern Europe succeed half a century later. Prospects for any such plan are dim. In another of history's delicious ironies, it is Germany, the country that brought death, destruction, and dismay to the region and effectively consigned it to 50 years of Communist domination that is the most reliable support East European countries have.

The OECD (1996) recently warned that the present situation is "critical." Far from being passive in the wake of the end of central planning, the eastern Europeans are involved in enormous activity. They are not satisfied with the progress so far. A recent study conducted in the Visegrad countries plus the former East Germany found about as many people feeling much worse off as felt much better off since the change. Many people are able to look back on the time of Soviet occupation as "the good old days," when there was employment, not meaningful, but steady; health benefits, not very good, but available; education, not open, but free; and pensions, not large, but assured. Without what Burg (1996) called "preventive engagement," the people who are not beneficiaries of the new market economics may become its pallbearers. As Zsuzsa Ferge (1997, 172), the lead researcher in the satisfaction study mentioned above, found:

> Five years after the victory of the new democracies, the balance sheet is ambiguous. There are clear gains: in political terms for everybody, in economic terms for a minority...Whether the present situation was inevitable...is an open question. The main gain of the transition is freedom and democracy...but freedom [and] democracy...cannot flourish, perhaps cannot even survive, without potent social forces supporting and defending them.

Clearly, the final chapter in the story of development in eastern Europe has yet to be written.

# REFERENCES

Adam, J. (1996). *Why Did the Socialist System Collapse in Central & Eastern European Countries?* (London: Macmillan).

*Assistance Programmes for Central and Eastern Europe and the Former Soviet Union.* (1996). (Paris: OECD).

Balcerowicz, L. (1997). "The Interplay Between Economic and Political Transition." In S. Zecchini (Ed.), *Lessons from the Economic Transition* (Boston: Kluwer Academic Publishers).

Barraclough, G. (1976). *The Crucible of Europe* (Berkeley: University of California Press).

Benecke, G. (1983). "The Economic Policy of 'Kriegsraison' in Germany During the Thirty Years' War." In Vardy and Vardy (Eds.), *Society in Change,* (New York: Columbia University Press), pp. 39–51.

Brown, J. (1994). *Hopes and Shadows* (Durham: Duke University Press).

Burg, S. (1996). *War or Peace?* (New York: New York University Press).

Cannon, L. (1997). "Polish Transition Strategy." In J. Zacek and I. Kim (Eds.), *Society in Change* (New York: Columbia University Press), pp.142–158.

Chambers, J. (1979). *The Devil's Horsemen.* (New York: Atheneum).

*Eastern Europe: Reforms Spur Recovery.* (1994). (Washington: Central Intelligence Agency).

Ferge, Z. (1997). "Major Problems and Crisis Phenomena of Five Transitional Economies in Central Europe." *Economies in Transition: The Growth and Maintenance of Market Economies in Developing Countries.* Special issue of *Regional Development Dialogue* 18 (1), Spring.

Fischer-Galati, S. (1996). "Eastern Europe in the Twentieth Century: Old Wine in New Bottles." In J. Held (Ed.), *The Columbia History of Eastern Europe in the Twentieth Century* (New York: Columbia University Press).

Fugedi, E. (1985). "The Demographic Landscape of East-Central Europe." In A. Maczak, et al. (Eds.), *East Central Europe in Transition* (New York: Cambridge University Press), pp. 47–58.

Fullard, H. (1971). *World Patterns* (New York: Aldine).

Gelb, A. (1996). *From Plan to Market* (Washington: Oxford University Press).

Hanak, P. and J. Held. (1996). "Hungary on a Fixed Course: An Outline of Hungarian History." In J. Held (Ed.), *The Columbia History of Eastern Europe in the Twentieth Century* (New York: Columbia University Press).

Held, J. (Ed.). (1993). *Democracy and Right-Wing Politics in Eastern Europe in the 1990s.* (New York: Columbia University Press).

Held, J. (Ed.). (1996). *The Columbia History of Eastern Europe in the Twentieth Century.* (New York: Columbia University Press).

*Human Development Report* (1996) (Washington, DC: World Bank).

Hupchick, D. (1995). *Conflict and Chaos in Eastern Europe* (New York: St. Martin's Press).

Hyde-Price, A. (1996). *The International Politics of East/Central Europe* (New York: Manchester University Press).

Korbonski, A. (1996). Poland: 1918–1990. In J. Held (Ed.), *The Columbia History of Eastern Europe in the Twentieth Century* (New York: Columbia University Press).

Korbonski, A. (1997). "The Security of East/Central Europe and the Visegrad Triangle." In J. Zack and I. Kim (Eds.), *The Legacy of the Soviet Bloc* (Gainesville: University of Florida Press). pp. 159–177.

Longworth, P. (1992). *The Making of Eastern Europe.* (New York: St. Martin's Press).

Maczak, A., H. Samsonowisz and P. Burke (Eds.). (1985). *East Central Europe in Transition.* (New York: Cambridge University Press).

Makkai, L. (1985). Economic Landscape: Historical Hungary from the Fourteenth to the Seventeenth Century." In A. Maczak, et al., *East Central Europe in Transition* (New York: Cambridge University Press), pp. 24–35.

Okey, R. (1982/1986). *Eastern Europe 1740–1980* (Minneapolis: University of Minnesota Press).

Rosenberg, T. (1995). *The Haunted Land.* (New York: Random House).

Rothschild, J. (1989). *Return to Diversity.* (New York: Oxford University Press).

Samsonowicz, H., and A. Maczak (1989). "Feudalism and Capitalism: A Balance of Change in East-Central Europe." In A. Maszak, et al. *East Central Europe in Transition* (New York: Cambridge University Press), pp. 6–23.

Sedlar, J. (1994). *East/Central Europe in the Middle Ages, 1000–1500.* (Seattle: University of Washington Press).

Shepard, W. (1932). *Atlas of Medieval and Modern History.* New York: Henry Holt.

Stokes, G. (1997). *Three Eras of Political Change in Eastern Europe.* (New York: Oxford University Press).

Sugar, P. (Ed.). (1995). *Eastern European Nationalism in the Twentieth Century.* (Washington: American University Press).

Swaim, G., and N. Swaim. (1993). *Eastern Europe Since 1945* (New York: St. Martin's Press).

Terry, S. (1996). "What's Right, What's Left, and What's Wrong in Polish politics?" In J. Held (Ed.), *Democracy and Right-Wing Politics in Eastern Europe in the 1990s* (New York: Cambridge University Press).

*Transition at the Local Level.* (1996). (Paris: OECD).

Tuchman, B. (1978). *A Distant Mirror.* (New York: Knopf).

*UNESCO Statistical Yearbook.* (1997). (New York: Bernan Press).

Vardy, S. (1983). "The Great Economic Immigration from Hungary: 1880–1920." In S. Vardy and Vardy (Eds.), *Society in Change* (New York: Columbia University Press), pp. 189–216.

Vardy, S., and A. Vardy (Eds.). (1983). *Society in Change* (New York: Columbia University Press).

Wandycz, P. (1992). *The Price of Freedom.* (New York: Routledge).

*World Fact Book, The.* (1995). (Washington: Central Intelligence Agency).

Wyrobisz, A. (1985). Economic Landscape: Poland from the Fourteenth to the Seventeenth Century. In A. Maszak et al. *East Central Europe in Transition* (New York: Cambridge University Press), pp. 36–46.

Zacek, J., and I. Kim (Eds.). (1997). *The Legacy of the Soviet Bloc* (Gainesville: University of Florida Press).

Zecchini, S. (Ed.). (1997). *Lessons from the Economic Transition* (Boston: Kluwer Academic Publishers).

# 5 Missionaries and Development

## Introduction

The word "missionaries" is likely to conjure up images of robed or suited men armed with holy books and rigid moral codes, speaking to hordes of skeptical savages about their souls. In fact, it is true that the central message of missionaries is spiritual, but that spiritual message almost always has links to an economic message, either directly or indirectly. It also is likely to be the case that the reluctant converts are more interested in the message that influences their economic status than the one pertaining to their spiritual status.

For hundreds of years, the cross of Christianity and the crescent of Islam have been carried throughout Africa and Asia and, particularly in the case of Christianity until recent times, to both of the Americas. The spread of these two faiths, in particular, has been accompanied by social and economic consequences such as those that transformed Indian societies into the present-day nations of Mexico and Peru. Any notion that the zeal to proselytize has disappeared will be dispelled by the most casual look at the activities of missionaries around the world today.

Even the term "missionary" usually evokes a set of concepts far simpler than the reality. In fact, missionary activity always has taken place in a number of spheres, comprising a complex network of spiritual pursuit, with separate sectors sometimes competing with each other.

## Varieties of Missionary Work

Five types of missionary work are apparent. First, missions to peoples living in primitive societies such as tribes engaged in subsistence economies—typically, those formerly found in the Congo, and still found in the Amazon. The native religions of such groups tend to be animist. Second, missions to peoples living in advanced civilizations with more developed, but still primarily agrarian, economies, such as the Maya or Inca empires in pre-Columbian America or in late medieval Japan and India in Asia. Religions in these societies may be pantheistic, or based on philosophical tenets, or both. Third, missions to coreligionists, but with whom there are fundamental differences, even though all proceed from the same basic assumptions and from the same doctrinal sources. Examples might include organized attempts to convert Protestants to Roman Catholicism or vice versa; or such missions might be illustrated by differences between Sunni and Shiite Moslems. In the Christian example, both Protestants and Catholics accept the Holy Bible as sacred scripture and Jesus Christ as their Savior, but have basic differences in versions of the Bible, interpretation of Holy Writ, and ordained organization of the church. Fourth are missions to coreligionists within the same basic sector or division, but with whom important—although less basic—differences exist. Catholics are divided between those who follow the Church of Rome, with its supreme leadership vested in the Pope, and other Catholics who reject the supremacy of the Holy See; Protestants are divided into many groups, all of which reject the leadership of Rome in favor of a more congregational basis for organization of their members, but who disagree with each other on assorted doctrinal interpretations. The fifth mission is aimed less precisely at distinct populations of believers or unbelievers, but rather at the generally uncommitted who may or may not profess a particular faith, whose circumstances do not suggest clear adherence to any position, irrespective of their frequent professions to the contrary. Such missions are typically found in large urban centers and are directed at unchurched poor people. They are frequently, but not exclusively, Protestant.

Historically, the various sorts of missions have been distinguished by different sorts of organizational structures and have favored different methods of pursuing their calling. The organizations range from global networks bound by oaths of allegiance and tight management structures sending out clusters of missionaries, backed by appropriate logistical supports, to small sects sending individual missionaries who must depend upon their own resources and sagacity. The Franciscan Brotherhood is an example of the former; the latter could include any of myriad Pentecostal groups.

Variation in method is equally extensive, with a range from violence delivered by armies of the faithful offering the choice of conversion or death, to attempts at compassionate suasion through good works, example, or argument. Again, plentiful examples can be found in the two largest world religions that are also arguably the most forceful in their mission work, Christianity and Islam. A premiere Christian example is the relentless campaign to convert Jews, an enterprise pursued with equal vigor by both Catholics and Protestants; the Moslem *jihad* or holy war could be based on doctrinal differences or on determination to convert the infidel. The objective of conversion and the objective of destruction are not always clearly distinguishable from each other, so that a *jihad* may have as its goal the death of the infidel rather than mere conversion, just as the series of campaigns by Christians against Islam, known as the Crusades, displayed a similar lack of consistency of objective. Most frequently, methods have been related to the objective, but they also have shown an understanding that adaptation to venue is always necessary. Missionaries to villages of natives living in a Stone Age culture need not exhibit the sophistication or subtlety of purpose required in approaching the court of a sovereign at the head of a powerful, extensive, wealthy, and entrenched society.

Although the differences in missions are manifold and significant, all seem to share one common feature: Whatever the ultimate spiritual goal and whatever the methods selected for achieving it, all successful missionaries seem to have understood the importance of an economic element in their work. Some have expressed it explicitly, others implicitly, but all seem to have agreed to some extent with the observation of the famous Scottish divine Thomas Chalmers, who pointed out that missionaries who approach a hungry person with food in one hand and a Bible in the other will find that the hungry person's attention to the Bible cannot be maintained until the person's hunger has been satisfied by the food.

In reviewing the work of the missionaries, it is important to be clear that they were (and are) not the same as explorers, conquerors, and colonizers. Although missionaries often accompanied and sometimes even preceded all those groups, the primary goal of the missionary was always spiritual, not worldly. Explorers and conquerors seek wealth and power; colonizers seek land or trade and economic improvement; missionaries seek the souls of those they encounter. To explorers, indigenous populations may be curiosities to be ignored, shunted aside, or used; to conquerors, they are more likely to be considered dangers to be eliminated; to colonizers, indigenous people may be impediments to be removed or labor potential to be exploited; to missionaries, whatever their opportunistic or instrumental interaction with indigenous peoples, they are always souls to be saved. The implications of these differences are profound, but not always readily apparent.

The sixteenth century constitutes the hallmark era of European missionary activity in modern times. The newly discovered American continents were filled with millions of souls to be saved by Catholic missionaries who almost always accompanied or followed the predominantly Spanish and Portuguese Catholic explorers. The Spanish Crown was militantly and aggressively Roman Catholic, flush from driving the last of the Moslems from the Iberian peninsula and, thus, from western Europe. Spanish Jews, including the financial advisor to the Crown, had been given the choice of conversion, exile, or death, leading to another great exodus of Jews from a land where they had lived and to which they had made significant cultural contributions for generations. In northern Europe, the Protestant Reformation challenged the roots of Roman Catholic authority in the most fundamental ways, leading to another sort of religious exodus, which the Church of Rome answered by launching a counter-Reformation.

Explorers reached Asia by sea and with them went missionaries. In all, it was a dramatic, dangerous, and startling time in which spiritual activity followed a breathtaking course: missionaries to primitive people, missionaries to ancient higher civilizations (sometimes more civilized than the ones from which the missionaries came), missionaries to convert believers from other mature religions, missionaries to retrieve "fallen away" Catholics from the Protestant movement, and Protestants seeking to enlighten each other about the nature of the true faith. There was endless spiritual work on all sides, offering the outstretched palm of peace and also threatening the point of a blade.

Although the course of missionary activity in the Americas during the sixteenth and seventeenth centuries is well known, it was not an historic artifact that either succeeded completely or was decisively thwarted in its quest for souls. In fact, the movement never stopped. Right to the present day, the churches in Latin America remain heavily involved in social and political activity, and church representatives of whatever denomination remain at mortal peril in many places—perils as real as any their predecessors faced four hundred years ago.

## The Cross and the Sword

There always were important distinctions between missionaries and other people who entered territory unknown to them. Explorers and colonizers of the sixteenth century, who were succinctly described by Boxer (1969) as "fanatical, filthy, and ferocious" were not particularly interested in salvation for the Amerindians. They considered the indigenous peoples to be best suited for enslavement, not salvation. It was the missionaries who most vigorously fought to prevent—and later to reverse—that sort of exploitation. One prosperous merchant and slave owner was converted in 1514 to being a crusader for the natives. In his time, Father Bartolome de las Casas (Dominican) became the most persistent and articulate spokesman for native rights in the Americas, through books, speeches, and direct petitions to the Crown. Although he initially supported black slavery as a way to relieve the exploitation of Amerindians, he subsequently opposed that practice, too. The long struggle finally did bear fruit when, in 1537, Pope Paul III issued his famous Bull *Sublimis Deus,* which forbade further enslavement of Indians, even if they were not Christian.

The objections to Indian slavery were based on the view of the missionaries that it was immoral to enslave others, but there was another compelling reason as well. The mission system comprised a series of self-contained Indian communities, organized and led by the Holy Fathers. The missions were supported by farming and crafts, and sometimes with trade as a major source of income. Although paternalistic in structure, the missions were not based on slave labor. The lives of the Indians were modest by any standard, but, in general, they seem to have been better than the lives they lived before the missions were established. For one thing, the introduction of new methods of managing crops produced a consistent surplus in many of the missions. This surplus money did not go directly to the mission residents, but to support the opening of new missions. The Jesuits were singularly successful in raising the standard of living of the mission congregants and in creating a surplus economy in their missions throughout northwestern Mexico.

In her study of the Yaqui Indians, Hu-DeHart (1981) found that the mission system improved the standard of living and also protected the Yaqui from "encroachment on their lands" as well as "indiscriminate uses of their labor." The "indiscriminate uses" to which she referred were the frequent raids on Indian villages to carry off able-bodied men for work in the mines. These raids threatened to deplete the labor supply of the missions and thereby to undermine their productivity and self-sufficiency. Far from being oppressed by the missionaries, the Yaquis found themselves with a much higher degree of economic security than in their former social structure, and protected to an extent from forced labor in the mines, work that usually significantly shortened the life span of the workers. Moreover, the missionaries quickly established schools and hospitals that also improved the quality of life among the Indians. As Hu-DeHart (1981: 3) pointed out, the missionaries understood that "only when the indigenous peoples remained healthy and intact could missions endure."

Partly out of spiritual motivation, but partly for economic reasons as well, the Catholic missionaries remained the leading defenders of the Amerindians throughout the colonial period. By 1573, they had induced Philip II to issue an ordinance that forbade further armed expeditions against the Indians. Because Philip was several thousand miles away, royal orders were not scrupulously obeyed and, indeed, missionaries themselves entered new territory with small armed escorts (Boxer, 1978), but the ordinance was a major victory in the fight by the clerics to prevent the secularizing of the missions.

Secular authorities wished to take control of the missions in order to have unfettered access to the manpower needed for mining and other purposes, but also to seize the vast surpluses which the mission system was producing. Unfortunately, under the patriarchal organization, little of that surplus reached the Indians who produced it; their benefit was a safer, healthier, more economically secure way of life and, of course, Heaven. But the charge that withholding the surplus and using it for other purposes (new missions) was a brutal or exploitative policy seems somewhat overdrawn, since the missionaries themselves shared the austerity they required of the Indians. Secular authorities had taken no oath of poverty, and to them, the surplus was a pathway to a luxurious life, not a resource to assure better living and working conditions for the Indians or new missions for those beyond the frontier. There were instances of revolts in which frustrated Indians killed all the Spaniards they could reach, without making fine distinctions between clerical and secular. Those outbreaks notwithstanding, it is important to distinguish between the work of the missionaries and the operations of the colonists.

The weakness of the mission system was that its patriarchal structure did not allow for development of an indigenous leadership, so that when the secular authorities finally won the battle with the Jesuit missionaries, leading to their expulsion in 1767, the Yaqui, after more than 100 years of consistent and enormous surpluses, soon reverted to subsistence farming (Hu-DeHart, 1981). Elsewhere in the Latin colonies, wherever the secular authorities managed to weaken the mission system and replace it with the colonial system, the Indian populations were decimated. Whatever the faults of the missionaries, their primary concern for the souls of the indigenous peoples tended to moderate treatment of them which, in any event, was infinitely more humane than the human sacrifice practiced in the pre-Columbian Indian Empires, or exploitation by the secular colonial system, which had little interest in Indian traditions and customs and even less regard for the quality of their lives. Moreover, the agrarian communities that comprised the missions, consisting of many hundreds of Amerindians and very few missionaries, proved far more effective in maintaining a peaceful, prosperous way of life for all, and especially the native population, than did whole occupying armies. "The Iberian colonial world," Boxer (1979: 77) noted, was held in place by the Catholic priesthood "in the absence of substantial military garrisons."

Work among the native peoples of southwestern North America was undertaken largely by the Franciscans who, from 1540 on, spread the faith but also "cared for the sick and poor, introduced new crops and livestock into the area's economy, taught reading, writing, crafts, and music, and built churches" (Walker, 1991: 5). As did other Catholic orders, the Franciscans practiced strict personal poverty, which doubtless influenced their judgment about what constituted poverty among the Indians. All of the territory that comprises the present southwestern United States was then part of Mexico, and from 1540 until the nineteenth century, members of religious orders were more significant in the lives of the Amerindians than were the state authorities, who held them in low regard. Not until 1834 did Mexico grant Indians full rights as citizens.

Missionary successes in Mexico had their parallels farther south, in present-day Uruguay, Paraguay, Bolivia, and Argentina. Here, too, the missions ended intertribal warfare, provided political stability, and improved the native economy. The mission communities excluded non-natives, effectively undermining strong efforts at colonization by secular authorities (Carriker, 1995). In Brazil, the Jesuits encountered natives in very primitive societies and quickly converted them to Christianity, establishing communal agricultural economies, while simultaneously defending the natives from colonizing efforts of Portuguese civil authorities (Boxer, 1963), although in the end, their 150-year resistance to secularization throughout Latin America ended with their expulsion.

The time of Roman Catholic mission work in the Americas throughout the 350 years before secularization was an era of general peace and relative prosperity for the Indians, often in spite of tumultuous political upheavals by the colonists. It was not an era of democracy, even on the missions, for the Fathers did not recognize that sort of organization as necessarily a virtue, but neither did secular authorities acknowledge the rights of indigenous peoples and, unlike the missionaries, did little to provide the wherewithal to improve their lives. The friars, in seeking to save the souls of the Indians, added to the economic resources available to them; the secular authorities, in seeking to lift the level of their own lives, extracted economic resources from the Indians. The resentment of the Indians toward the missionaries was based on being treated as children; their resentment toward secular authorities was based on being treated as expendable labor; it is the latter resentment that can still be seen in resistance movements such as the recurring outbreaks in the Mexican state of Chiapas.

The intense missionary work in the Americas was matched by similar, albeit much less successful efforts in Asia during the same period of time. Traveling by sea with traders, missionaries encountered long-standing, highly developed civilizations in which mature religions already were firmly established. Far from the animistic and primitive beliefs of the American Indian civilizations, they found Buddhism, already at least five centuries old when Jesus was born; Confucianism, with equally ancient origins; and Hinduism, perhaps a thousand years older than the other two. These were religions with deep philosophical roots and richly elaborated written doctrines, supported by a powerful and well-developed state structure.

## Christ and Commerce in Asia and Africa

It was not the first appearance in Asia of Christian missionaries from Europe. As shown by LaTourette (1929) and others, as early as the thirteenth century, Mongol conquests actually facilitated missionary activity because they assured the relative safety of the trade routes taken by missionaries and also because the Mongols themselves were intrigued by, or at least tolerant of, the many different religions within their empire. After the dissolution of the Mongol Empire and the closing to Christian merchants of land trade routes over territory controlled by the Moslems, missionaries were forced to take to the sea, along with European traders. Trade with Asia was opened again when Portuguese ships reached India at the very end of the fifteenth century, an event that was closely followed by vigorous proselytizing.

The missionaries recognized the importance of adapting to the complex Asian cultures they sought to bring to Christ. In Japan, one of the leaders of the missionary movement, Father Alessandro Valignano, urged his Jesuit brothers to conform "to the Japanese way of life so far as they possibly could" (Boxer, 1951: 212). By the early 1600s, the padres were required to make "a detailed study of the minutiae of Japanese etiquette, and conform closely to Japanese customs" (Boxer, 1951: 212), even to the extent of living in quarters designed and furnished in the Japanese style. The work of the missionaries was rather effective in Japan until 1613, when the Tokugawa dynasty banned the missions, an edict whose effects lasted for almost 300 years.

The association between traders and missionaries was not always a happy one. There was effective merchant interference with missions to China on the grounds that they could injure trade (La Tourette, 1929). One of the most memorable examples of this resistance was the delay by secular authorities of Francis Xavier, who sought entrance to China but was repeatedly delayed until he finally died after spending months virtually at the door. Successful work in China did not come until after 1580, when leadership was assumed by Matteo Ricci, who adopted the approach of showing respect for Chinese culture and customs. Despite his long years of work (1583–1610) and that of many other diligent missionaries, conversion of the Chinese never achieved the high level of success enjoyed in other places (Rienstra, 1986). Elsewhere in Asia, missions fared unevenly—although sometimes very well, as in the Philippine Islands. There, the religious orders displayed an economic skill that was the equal of their religious skill—the Jesuits in trading, the Franciscans in cultivation, and so on. Where the religious communities seemed to thrive, the profits were used for charitable purposes. The priests and friars themselves lived frugal lives (Boxer, 1951) with little indication that they diverted resources for their personal use (even though their orders often became very wealthy, giving them, as it were, a kind of communal stake in the wealth).

Sixteenth- and seventeenth-century efforts of Christian missionaries in Africa were largely unsuccessful, particularly where Islam had preceded them. In fact, Christian missionaries were almost uniformly unsuccessful everywhere in the conversion of Moslems. Missions were opened in the Congo during the early 1500s, at the request of the Bantu ruler who sought the benefits of the European artisans who lived in the missions (Boxer, 1969), including blacksmiths, bricklayers, and other skilled workers. These operations were quite successful until the slave trade developed and was extensively expanded. Although some missions are reported to have received support from the slave trade, Boxer (1963) argues that missions in Africa failed where religious efforts collided with commerce, because commerce usually won.

Augustinians opened a mission in the key West African city of Mombasa in 1597, but as the country was Moslem, it achieved no more success than elsewhere in the Moslem world (Boxer and De Azevedo, 1960). In West Africa, the massive failure of missions was largely the consequence of susceptibility by European friars to diseases of the tropics. Eventually, assignment to West Africa was resisted by missionaries. Throughout East Africa, Islam was already well-established and well-defended. Where some measure of success was achieved by missionaries, it seemed to be related to missionaries' teaching natives new crafts and the use of European agricultural methods and implements. Here, as elsewhere, missionaries and traders often were sharply divided on their evaluation of and relationships with local peoples. In Mozambique, for example, immigrants from India comprised an influential merchant population whom Portuguese traders considered "unscrupulous" and "parasites," but who were described by the Jesuits as "frugal and hard-working" (Boxer, 1963: 48–49). Similarly, traders described mulatto inhabitants of the West African islands as "the most vicious and immoral [people] on the face of the earth," while missionaries acknowledged their "great intelligence and ability" and claimed that they were different from Europeans only in being black (Boxer, 1963: 14).

Overall, the era of exploration was marked by massive changes in the world economy, particularly in the opening of new routes to reestablish access to trading centers that had been blocked, and the discovery of hitherto unknown and vast sources of raw materials, markets, and human capital to exploit. Wherever trade went, missionaries, primarily Roman Catholic missionaries, also went.

## Protestant Competition

The Protestant revolution taking place all over Europe during this time was preoccupied with its own internal disagreements over scriptural interpretation and with defending itself against the campaigns of suppression that were launched by Rome. Moreover, in the early years of the Reformation, most Protestants did not accept the legitimacy, or at least the importance, of converting others.

In reviewing the years of exploration, it seems clear that the most successful missions were those in which the spiritual enlightenment brought by the reverend fathers was accompanied by economic enlightenment, and by a marked improvement in economic status for the proselytes. Everywhere they set up missions, missionaries brought artisans and skilled craftsmen to modify local practices in ways that enhanced the quality of life of the natives. From Mozambique to Brazil to Mexico, the parties of missionaries often included a small armed escort, but also almost always included skilled workers to teach new ways to the local populace. From Portuguese missions in the Congo and Brazil to the Spanish missions in Mexico and Peru, missionaries brought the cross as a representation of the new faith and a glorious hereafter; but they also brought new techniques and tools as representations of a new economy and a more fulfilling present life. Whatever the shortcomings of the early missions, they profoundly influenced the nature of European expansion. As La Tourette (1929: 82) observed, the course of exploration and settlement without the missions can only be conjectured, but "with the economic and political factors left unbalanced by any religious elements, the results would have been far different and in all probability, far worse."

The dual spiritual/economic style of the Catholic missionaries continued into the modern era, as did their attempts to protect their converts from secular exploitation. The missions established in the western territories of North America that later came into the American union as states displayed the same pattern as that seen hundred of years earlier, and hundreds of miles south. Father De Smet became beloved for his defense of the western tribes against fur traders, the sale of alcohol, and persistent government drives to force the Indians to reservations (Carriker, 1995). Jesuits in the Oregon Territory pressed the federal government of the United States for schools, mills, and hospitals for some of the most depressed and oppressed tribes. Studies of missionaries pursuing similar efforts among the Navaho and other southwestern tribes in the 1950s have engaged the interest of scholars right into the decade of the 1990s (Rapoport, 1991).

The shift of supremacy in trade and settlement from the Iberian countries to the countries of northern Europe brought with it a dramatic shift in both the status and methods of the missionaries. The northern missionaries were usually Protestant, and their style reflected vast differences from the Catholics friars in the ways in which they perceived the subject populations. Essentially, they usually remained aloof from those they sought to bring to the Christian faith, irrespective of their level of civilization, or their acceptance or rejection of the missionaries themselves. With few exceptions, primarily among smaller denominations such as the Quakers or the Mormons, Protestant missionaries conducted their calling in the clear and firm belief that they were dealing with inferiors. Catholic missionaries believed they were saving souls through Jesus; Protestants believed they were bringing the light to benighted heathens. Although important exceptions exist, such as the Mormon belief that native Americans were lost tribes of Israel, the rule was remarkably consistent among Protestant missionaries that the conversion of the heathen should be accomplished in the most parsimonious manner and primarily through preaching. Goods and provision of services intended to better the economic level of the people did not seem to occupy the same central position for Protestants that it did with Catholic missions; or, more precisely, the role played by economic factors was based on radically different assumptions, both about the native populations and about the objectives of the mission. The distinctions were imbedded in variations with respect to the basic purposes of the faith. Nida (1969: 5) provides a terse description of this difference: "Catholicism is a method to get through crises of life for spiritual benefits now and in the hereafter; Protestantism is a way to 'transform' life, not to survive it."

Perhaps nowhere was this divergence more clear than in the perception of work. In missions to more primitive populations, essentially those of the Americas and Africa, work was an integral element in the interaction between the missionaries and their proselytes. However, the Catholic friars treated work as a necessary evil for the survival of the mission and worked alongside their flocks; the Protestant pastors held work to have inherent value for the natives quite aside from its instrumental usefulness, and they usually occupied themselves in overseeing the work. Work as "divinely ordered activity" Nida (1969) noted, was a "distinctly northern European concept." Catholic missionaries labored out of piety, with much the same motivation as that which led them to take oaths of poverty, and they required the natives to work out of necessity. When their necessary work was done, rest was considered appropriate and even commendable. Protestant missionaries viewed labor as virtuous in itself, without necessarily conferring an improved state of existence at present. What Catholics considered reasonable relaxation, Protestants often considered sloth. They made even recreational activity seem like work, a characteristic apparent even in the present day.

English missionary work did not begin in earnest until the early eighteenth century, when it was promoted by the establishment of sponsoring organizations such as the Society for the Propagation of the Faith in Foreign Parts, inaugurated by the Anglicans in 1701. In the Americas, conversion efforts were aimed first at the Indians, only somewhat later encompassing blacks, including black slaves.

The ministry to the slaves brought problems between the missionaries and the slave owners, similar to the tensions experienced between Catholic missionaries and the traders and settlers around them. A major source of this tension was what Van Horne (1985, 29) called the "tenacious" and "pervasive" belief among Protestant missionaries that "Christians could not be enslaved." Property issues continued to plague the missions until, by 1710, proposals were put forward to assure slave holders that conversion did not confer emancipation. Many slaves owners began to forbid their slaves from taking part in any religious activity anyhow, not on religious or spiritual grounds, but as a property rights issue. Even with the assurances that Christian slaves would not be automatically freed from bondage, the owners worried that converting slaves to Christianity (which also involved teaching them to read and write in order to be able to study the Scriptures) "bred egalitarian notions among [them], rendering them more intractable and potentially rebellious" (Van Horne, 1985: 30).

Protestant missionaries in North America followed trappers and explorers in advance of the general westward movement that was virtually continuous from the early seventeenth century until the closing of the frontier in 1890. The Puritans were among the first to consider penetration of the wilderness to be a divine duty. They saw the forests that seemed to extend endlessly from the coast of New England as a wilderness to be cleared in order to make the land "blossom as the rose." However, as Rohrer (1995) has pointed out, in America, the "wilderness" has always been a relative concept, and for the Puritans, it began "at the edge of the clearing." The Indians who lived beyond the clearing were seen alternately, and at various times, as "children of Nature" and "God's simple creatures," and as "ruthless and impious savages." These changing views influenced the intensity and form of the Protestant missions into the wilderness. The westward pressure of settlement was so relentless that missionaries often barely stayed ahead of the wagon trains of the pioneers.

After the Revolution opened the trans-Appalachian lands, which had been closed to settlement by the British government, the pace of westward population shift accelerated sharply. In the forty years between 1790 and 1830, over three-quarters of a million settlers moved into the frontier (Rohrer, 1995). By the end of that time, both settlers and missionaries were encountering a different problem. Instead of facing primitive and often nomadic Indian tribes, they reached the Spanish settlements and missions, many of which had been established for generations. The Catholic missionaries were still very active, their mission system still very much alive, and the economic development that sustained it still fully operational. In fact, some of the Catholic orders, particularly the Jesuits, were familiar in Washington, D.C. through their lobbying efforts on behalf of the Indian tribes north of the territories of New Spain and well inside territories acquired by the United States in the Louisiana Purchase. Protestant denominations that had been competing with each other now had to compete with the far more formidable, organized, and successful Catholics.

In this confrontation, during the antebellum years of the nineteenth century, Protestant missionaries struggled not only to convert Indians from their native religious beliefs, but also to sway other tribes from their Catholic faith. This pressure on Catholic missions extended into the twentieth century as Protestant missionaries emphasized their goal of Indian "freedom from priests" (Walker, 1991). Their primary strategies for achieving this goal were to open schools where Indians could learn to read the Bible, and to teach Indians the importance of hard work in order to improve their economic condition. In this, the Protestants found themselves at the same disadvantage that Catholics had experienced in trying to convert Moslems; it was one thing to bring a new spiritual message to fragmented and impoverished, scattered and weak tribes, but quite another to deal with an entrenched belief system that was working very well, often tied to an equally well-developed political and social system. Unless the target groups could see some advantage in changing, particularly in terms of some measure of economic advancement, they saw no reason to shift their spiritual allegiance. Where Catholic missions already existed, Protestant recruitment campaigns did not meet with much success, even after social and political control of the area was settled solidly in Protestant hands.

Protestant missionaries also made their way to other parts of the world with their message of hard work and salvation. In some cases, they understood the basis for the success of the Catholics and sought to emulate their methods. A singular aspect of the Catholic missionary strategy was to introduce a new economic order that held the promise of a better life in this world, while preparing one for the next. Most Protestant missionaries had their eyes securely fixed only on the next world. Some of the Protestant missionary guide or instruction books did recommend taking Western technology such as weaving and carpentry to the primitive cultures; one such text noted that the Catholic missionaries "have always made a specialty of industrial work…" and argued that "Protestants might learn much from them…" (Smith, 1912: 167). However, such advice seemed the exception rather than the rule.

The first formal party of Anglican missionaries to the South Sea Islands appeared to have learned from the Catholics when it left England in 1796. The clergy were accompanied by carpenters, blacksmiths, and other workmen skilled "in the mechanical arts" (Hutton, 1874). Within five years, they had introduced new seeds and vines into the local horticulture, with the intention of improving the native diet. However, their custom of remaining detached from personal contact with the native population kept them from teaching the indigenous people how to cultivate the new plants, with the result that the suspicious natives soon destroyed them. Protestant views of native customs, particularly if they included a high degree of sexual freedom, were that they were ungodly and immoral. This view led the missionaries to treat the natives as "disobedient unbelievers" in need of discipline and moral reform. Typical was the mission of Hiram Bingham (Rennie, 1989), who twice traveled to the Gilbert Islands between 1857 and 1873 to lecture the inhabitants about Christ's Kingdom on Earth. He had little respect for the natives, and his rejection by the Gilbert Islanders was complete—both of his doctrine and of his person.

Western gunboats were able to carry commerce into the seaport cities of Japan and China more effectively than could Western missionaries penetrate the ancient religious cultures in those and other Asian countries. For example, English missionaries arrived in Bengal (India) about 1800, where they encountered a variety of traditional religions. They selected the Hindus for their major efforts, and while they met with some success, it was not extensive. When they turned to the Moslems, they had no effect at all. Other Protestant denominations, such as the Baptists, were equally unfulfilled in their dreams of mass conversion (Laird, 1972). As did most Protestants, they opened schools, but they relied on education and preaching to win over converts, and their message was both too austere and idealistic and too impractical to make much impression (Rennie, 1989).

By the beginning of the twentieth century, Protestant missionaries had come to understand the importance of the economic element in their spiritual message. This appears to have been tied to the fierce commercial competition brought on by the Industrial Revolution, as well as the policy of aggressive colonial expansion by industrial countries in search of plentiful raw materials and cheap labor to extract them. This commercial competition fit well with the Protestant message of hard work. Africa became a major arena for this competition, and German missionaries entered it with their customary vigor.

Moravians, for example, did not support colonization, but in Tanganyika, they sought to "encourage a cash economy," setting up trading companies to "encourage economic development" in Nyasa Province (Wright, 1971). There, and elsewhere, missions were most successful when administration gradually was turned over to indigenous people.

However, after 1933, German missionaries had to contend with Nazi race policies. They continued to ordain Africans, but administrative control was increasingly taken over by Berlin and by 1940, the last German missionary was recalled.

## Missions and Development: "Render unto Caesar..."

Other missions were similarly influenced and transformed by twentieth-century political and economic developments. In the American southwest, the agrarian-based Catholic missions could not survive the railroads, industrial growth, and most of all, statehood that was an instrumentality of the Protestant political system (Walker, 1991). Some Protestant denominations increased their influence in the area by mimicking the Catholic tradition of studying and adapting to local cultures, although most of them might be offended by the suggestion that they followed a well-trod pathway.

One interesting instance of such a development is seen in the vigorous and highly effective mission system of the Church of Jesus Christ of Latter-Day Saints, or Mormons. Mormon missionaries study the language and traditions of the countries they will visit. They accommodate themselves, to the extent that their own religious beliefs permit, to local customs. A major goal, to "subdue and beautify the earth" (Tullis, 1987: 173ff), is reminiscent of the Puritan goal to tame the wilderness and make it fruitful. As did the Puritans, the Mormons identify with early Jews, and the nineteenth-century westward trek of the Mormons was to them clearly an exodus into the desert. However, unlike the Puritans and most other Protestant groups, they worked to understand and adapt to local traditions and culture. For example, in Mexico, they related to Mexican village models when working in the villages, while in the great metropolis of Mexico City, they built a Mormon temple that reflects principles of Mayan architecture (Tullis, 1987: xiv).

Adaptation to and absorption of the culture of the target population was a major device of the earliest Catholic missionaries. In this, they were guided for over a thousand years by the recommendation of Pope Gregory the Great, who in 597 instructed Christians not to destroy the religious shrines of pagans and not to suppress their rites, but to adapt them to Christian usage, advice which came to be reflected in virtually every major Christian holiday. For their part, the intended converts displayed an impressive ability to do the same with Christian ideas and ceremonies; that is, to turn them to their own use.

Vogt (1976) described such a case among the Mayans of Chiapas Province in Mexico. He found that the Christian Mayan Indians have remained keenly aware of their pre-conquest history; they incorporated Latin ideas into their traditions, turning them to good use. Even in present times, the Zinacanteco Maya retain old rituals, but they "have been quick to take advantage of material objects and economic opportunities which have benefited their lives without fundamentally distorting more crucial customs" (Vogt, 1976: 208).

Those missionaries who have had the greatest and longest-lasting impact historically have accepted and put into practice certain central principles of relating to and influencing populations different from themselves. First, as observed about the Mormons, they have sought to understand the culture of the peoples with whom they intend to work. This has involved fundamental activities such as learning the local language; but it also carries the implied expectation that with understanding comes respect. Second, they have sought to bring a spiritual message of salvation and eternal bliss, but also to bring an economic message of a better life in the present, including an equitable share of the products of their labor, improved health, better education, and other benefits. Third, they have identified with the dreams and aspirations of the indigenous peoples and allied with them to prevent exploitation, whether social, political, or economic, but especially economic. In short, successful missionaries have sought acceptance of the indigenous people largely through identifying with them, without losing their own identities; and they have sought to bring economic improvement along with spiritual enhancement. It is a stance that Catholic missionaries have used for centuries, while Protestant missionaries seem to have begun applying it in earnest only about 100 years ago.

Given these principles, it is easy to understand why missionaries have been able to exert their greatest influence with primitive tribes or in situations in which an established order is in disarray or under assault. In the former case, their message of a better life has been relatively easy to demonstrate, even in the short run. In the latter case, chaos, fear, and confusion, or hostility and deep disenchantment with an existing social, political, and/or economic order has made people susceptible to whatever changes offer to bring meaning and order to their lives. Missions to the Brazilian Indians living in virtual Stone Age societies exemplify the former circumstance; missions to Mexican Indians living under Aztec rule illustrate the latter. After all, the conquest of the Aztec by Cortez and a few hundred Spanish soldiers was accomplished only because that small band was joined by tens of thousands of Indians from tribes oppressed by the Aztec. The missionaries took to those tribes a message of a Christian god, which doubtless had a special appeal for them after their experience with generations of blood sacrifice in which their tribal kinfolk had been slaughtered, sometimes hundreds at a time, to appease the Aztec gods. To succeed, missionaries had to understand, as Tullis (1987: 3) put it, that "belief systems orient people to their world...and establish the patterns of rewards and sanctions that motivate their actions." Missionaries seek to replace one set of beliefs with another, but there must be clear rewards in what they offer, or their message is meaningless. The message must provide hope, but it must be delivered on the basis of respect; it must express concern for brothers and sister, not for inferiors. It was an expectation that Catholic missionaries grasped and met with skill and style. Protestant missionaries often were frustrated because they held the locals in disdain, considering them to be willful, ignorant savages who had nothing to teach their betters. As recently as the 1950s, research on missions to the Navajo found that Catholic missionaries learned the Navajo language and ceremonies and treated the people and their customs with genuine respect; Protestants, particularly fundamentalists, sought only to convert the Navajo, considering them pagans whose souls would be doomed without (Protestant) salvation (Rapoport, 1991).

Attempts to overcome this strategic weakness in the typical Protestant approach were addressed from time to time, even in the nineteenth century. According to his sister's account of his work (1890/ 1970), A. M. Mackay, an early missionary to Uganda, urged his brethren to learn Swahili and to banish their "ideas of race superiority," but his admonitions appear to have fallen mostly on unhearing ears. When missionaries spoke in terms familiar to the listeners, they were not assured of agreement, but there was a strong likelihood that their ideas would at least be considered; when they addressed natives in abstractions, they did not make "the slightest impression upon either their understanding or their heart" (Hutton, 1874: 48). A major element in the success of the Catholic missions was the economic changes the missionaries brought about. These changes brought benefits to the natives and provided the base that was the "foundation" of the mission system (Hu-DeHart, 1981).

Deep divisions still exist in the techniques and objectives of different missionary groups. In a sense, the economic aspects of spiritual uplift have been accepted universally, but appear in very different guises. Protestant missionaries often seek to expand the reach of Christianity by extending the reach of corporate capitalism. While Catholic missionaries in colonial times worked alongside traders and even engaged in trade themselves, their objective was to serve the immediate temporal needs of their converts as a way of eventually being able to serve their spiritual needs. "The genuine concern for the worldly well-being of the convert has continued into the present; Mother Teresa of Calcutta is a superb example of why so many missionaries were beloved to those to whom they ministered." Protestant missionaries sometimes were indistinguishable from traders among them, and their text must have seemed the gospel of American commerce. Tyler Dennett (1918: 212) described this concept with remarkable candor when he wrote that "the missionary as a business man is an important representative abroad of American business life." He noted that in Asia, the "distribution of American-made goods through the missionaries reaches proportions which few people realize" (217). It is a surprisingly contemporary observation, considering that he published these views 80 years ago. Expanding upon the theme, he expressed delight over the success of mission schools in making much more affluent consumers (albeit Christian consumers) of every mission-educated Asian child, who "insists on wearing European-style clothes and foot-wear" (Nikes?). After describing other product demands of the educated Asians, Dennett noted that this knowledge helps one to realize "how very great is the influence of the missions in developing new markets in Asia" (218).

Missions continue to play an important economic role in the world today. The economic issues they address have tended to shift from simply raising the standard of living of working-class populations to helping them get a more equitable share of the massive wealth being created by a growing, but very exploitive, global economy. Usdorf (1994), in disagreeing with a claim that "rich missionaries" are a Third World problem, declared that the real problem is the "fundamental inequality" in the developing countries—an inequality that is being exacerbated by a global economy that seems to place policies and practices of major industries beyond the control of the people, and even beyond the reach of individual nations. Economic issues and human rights issues still overlap, and religious leaders find it increasingly difficult to deal with one without facing the other, and even more difficult to avoid dealing with either issue.

Missionaries of the past were moral leaders, but also carried responsibilities for the daily lives of the people under their spiritual guidance. Religious, moral leadership today still carries the additional weight of temporal burdens, often in altered forms. Protection of vulnerable people from oppression and exploitation has grown from the villages to the major cities; present-day issues contain the kernels of earlier concerns, but have grown in proportion to the growth of industrial society. Although the connections to the past may be obscure, they can be identified. For example, establishment of schools and colleges for ex-slaves was an important initiative of American religious societies in the years following the Civil War. The celebrated Tuskegee Institute developed from the Hampton Institute, which was founded by the American Missionary Society (Luker, 1984). In fact, Luker (1984) argues persuasively that the American settlement house movement was not so much modeled after its London predecessor as it was an outgrowth of Protestant urban missions in the North, seeking to preach the same spiritual message to black ex-slaves as they gave to western Indian tribes; essentially: praise God in the church, get a job in the factory, and get to both on time.

## Modern Missions and Development

More dramatic and much more current is the struggle by the religious leaders on behalf of the poor in a number of Latin American countries. It is a struggle that has pitted many Catholic clergy against extreme radicals on one hand, and against the central church bureaucracy on the other, in an alignment reminiscent of the colonial-era struggle of Jesuit missionaries against the conquistadors and their secular successors and also against the central church bureaucracy. It is seen in the development several decades ago of "liberation theology."

Initiated by the Peruvian priest Gustavo Gutierrez, liberation theology reconceptualized the term "liberation." Early missionaries had conceived it as striking off the chains of sin; the new meaning retained this idea, but added the idea of freedom from psychological and sociopolitical bondage, as well, and thus, from the prison of poverty (Schutte, 1993). Expanded through the writing and preaching of Juan Luis Segundo, Leonardo Boff, and others, liberation theologians demanded liberation of the people from poverty and exploitation.

Critics charged that liberation theology was "little better than Marxist infiltration" (Lehmann, 1990), but the movement grew, despite attempts at suppression by civil authorities and denunciation by the traditional church hierarchy. Liberation theologians defended their positions by pointing out the wretched conditions in which the people lived—all children of the Church—and referred for justification to the magisterial authority of Pope Leo III, whose famous 1891 encyclical, *Rerum Novarum*, called for decent treatment of laborers. The bitter reaction of civil authorities was to try to suppress "Communist" priests, who were seen as a threat to the control of their governments. Simultaneously, liberal priests were prime targets of movements on the left, such as the Sandinistas in Nicaragua and the Shining Path in Peru.

Although also targets for Maoist radicals, Protestant missionaries in Latin America have not generally involved themselves in sociopolitical movements, but they have faced their own special kinds of problems. Facing a well-entrenched Catholic church as the primary spiritual institution, Protestants nevertheless often send female missionaries, despite their certain knowledge that Latin men tend to resent women who seek to occupy what the men perceive as dominant "male" positions (Nida, 1969). As in times past, the Protestant missionaries prefer to bring their own ideas of justice and equality with them, rather than to seek understanding of the local culture and the basis for its traditions.

Partly inspired by the ideas of liberation theology, new economic initiatives have begun to appear throughout Latin America. A lay organization, Communidades Eclesiales de Base (CEB) is a grassroots organization that may be merging with the clergy in some of its operations (Lehmann, 1990). A small community development movement, it focuses on the oppression experienced by poor workers in daily life, such as insecurity in employment (and consequent migrant labor), concentration of land ownership among the wealthy few, and the scarcity of adequate schools and health facilities.

As was the case with the most successful missionaries in times past, contemporary spiritual leaders who have reached the hearts of the people have done so by first learning about them—about their hopes and problems, dreams and troubles, and then, by seeking to help them improve their immediate life conditions. Such missionaries are more than spiritual guides to the celestial afterlife; they stand for practical change and needed improvement in the quality of present life.

The most effective community development can be expected from the missionary who is, as Van Der Geest (1990, 595) put it, "the outsider who becomes an insider, understands and respects 'the others' and takes their side." Effective missions share many methods with effective community economic development projects. In a sense, both use the techniques of the anthropologist. Van Der Geest (1990) calls missionaries and anthropologists "brothers under the skin"; Rapoport (1991) claims that good missionaries have the souls of anthropologists. What effective missionaries, anthropologists, and community development leaders share is a genuine interest in the people among whom they work; and a diligent and sophisticated study of their belief systems, customs, rituals, and the sources of their spiritual strength and needs. Living among them, learning their language, understanding and respecting their traditions, and working closely with them provide the basis for collective activity toward the goal sought by the indigenous people, and also toward the additional goals to which the outsiders aspire. Missionaries have long understood that it is normal for them to expect indigenous populations to have two faces, one of which is shown to the outsider and the other only to intimates. The task of the change agent is to become someone to whom the "intimate" face is shown—not in order to impose outside conceptions, but to become an "insider" whose ideas are worthy of consideration because they come from "one of us."

What successful missionaries have demonstrated is that their efforts are based on the interests of the indigenous people and are undertaken with the goal that the indigenous people own the results of that work. In the case of the mission system of past times, it is true that the mission system's surplus was not distributed to the people who produced it, but neither was it appropriated by secular authorities for their own enrichment. It was used for the good of the mission people and to support additional missions so that, in a sense, it remained with the people. It also provided the resources needed for the schools, hospitals, and other services that improved the lives of the mission people. While it is true that the mission population was required to work hard to create the surplus, it is also true that the missionaries protected them from far worse and more dangerous work for which secular authorities sought to conscript them. The fatal flaw in the mission system was its failure to allow indigenous leadership to emerge, which would have allowed the whole structure to be passed on to a local elite and continued after the missionaries were gone. As a consequence, when missionaries left the missions, the indigenous people tended to revert to their earlier primitive ways, with a consequent loss of the economic gains they had made. Evidence that this lesson finally was learned is apparent in the methods of liberation theologians, who wrote and preached and organized, but ultimately left the movement in the hands of the oppressed populations among whom they worked. Unlike the secular government leaders, they clearly were seeking not personal gain, but to build a systematic spiritual philosophy that would serve as the foundation for a stable, constructive lay organization. In this way, any dependency of the indigenous population would be not to an ecclesiastic hierarchy, but to a mutual, symmetrical organization of their peers.

It is an impressive model for organization in developing countries. Sermons of love and peace may be welcomed by those in comfortable circumstances, but to the poor and fearful, the message must be attached to the hope of a better life in the near future if it to be attractive to them. Development efforts that do not take this principle into account are likely to be as welcome in the international development movement as were preachers against sin, who offered only damnation terror to the hungry who steal food and a pleasant afterlife to the oppressed who meekly accept their oppression.

# REFERENCES

Boxer, C. R. (1978). *The Church Militant and Iberian Expansion, 1440–1770* (Baltimore: Johns Hopkins University Press).

Boxer, C. R. (1951). *The Christian Century in Japan, 1549–1650* (London: Cambridge University Press).

Boxer, C. R., and C. De Azevedo. (1960). *Fort Jesus and the Portugese in Mombasa, 1593–1729* (London: Hollis & Carter).

Boxer, C. R. (1969). *Four Centuries of Portugese Expansion, 1415–1825: A Succinct Survey* (Johannesburg: Witwatersrand University Press).

Boxer, C. R. (1963). *Race Relations in the Portugese Colonial Empire, 1415–1825* (Oxford: Clarendon Press).

By His Sister. (1890/1970). *A. M. Mackay: Pioneer Missionary in Uganda* (London: Frank Cass & Co.).

Carriker, R. C. (1995). *Father Peter John De Smet* (Norman: University of Oklahoma Press).

Dennett, T. (1918). *The Democratic Movement in Asia* (New York: Association Press).

Hu-DeHart, E. (1981). *Missionaries, Miners and Indians* (Tucson: University of Arizona Press).

Hutton, J, (1874). *Missionary Life in the Southern Seas* (London: Henry S. King & Co.).

Laird, M. A. (1972). *Missionaries and Education in Bengal, 1753–1837* (Oxford: Clarendon Press).

LaTourette, K. S. (1929). *A History of Christian Missions in China* (New York: Macmillan).

Lehmann, D. (1990). *Democracy and Development in Latin America* (Philadelphia: Temple University Press).

Luker, R. E. (1984). "Missions, Institutional Churches, and Settlement Houses: The Black Experience, 1885–1910," *Journal of Negro History* 69 (3,4), Summer, Fall, pp. 101–113.

Nida, E. A. (1969). *Communication of the Gospel in Latin America* (Cuernavaca:CIDOC).

Rapoport, R. N. (1991). "Missionaries and Anthropologists," *Man* 26 (4), December, pp. 740–743.

Rennie, S. (1989). "Missionaries And War Lords: A Study of Cultural Interaction in Aaiang and Tarawa," *Oceania* 60 (2), December, pp. 125–138.

Rienstra, M. H. (1986). *Jesuit Letters from China, 1583–84* (Minneapolis: University of Minnesota Press).

Rohrer, J. R. (1995). *Keepers of the Covenant* (New York: Oxford University Press).

Schutte, O. (1993). *Cultural Identity and Social Liberation in Latin American Thought* (Albany: State University of New York Press).

Smith, A. H. (1912). *The Uplift of China* (New York: Young Peoples' Missionary Movement).

Tullis, F. LaM. (1987). *Mormons in Mexico* (Logan: Utah State University Press).

Usdorf, W. (1994). "Missions and Money," *Scottish Journal of Theology* 47 (3), pp. 389–390.

Van Der Geest, S. (1990), "Anthropologists and Missionaries: Brothers Under the Skin," *Man* 25 (4), December, pp. 588–601.

Van Horne, J. C. (Ed.). (1985). *Religious Philanthropy and Colonial Slavery* (Urbana: University of Illinois Press).

Vogt, E. Z. (1976). *Tortillas for the Gods* (Cambridge: Harvard University Press).

Walker, R. J. (1991). *Protestantism in the Sangre de Cristos, 1850–1920* (Albuquerque: University of New Mexico Press).

Wright, M. (1971). *German Missions in Tanganyika, 1891–1941* (Oxford: Clarendon Press).

# 6 Strategies of Economic Development

*João wakes up in the doorway of a Rio de Janeiro jewelry store. Behind the sliding steel door before which he sleeps are the treasures of Brazil: smoky topaz, garnet, aquamarine and amethyst stones set in gold and platinum. In front of him is a world in which his greatest fears are police brutality, assassination squads, and the pervasive hunger and want of a life on the streets. Before the day is out, this nine year old boy will have begged for scraps at streetside cafes, carried groceries to the new cars of city shoppers, huffed some industrial solvent, and bathed in the seas of the famous Copacabana Beach. He has a home in the* favelas—*the slums that pour down the green hillsides of one of the most beautiful cities in the world. But, his mother isn't there much, working as she does as a maid in a luxury high rise, so he stays with his friends and makes a living, such as it is, by odd jobs, begging, and petty theft. If João turns out like many of his older colleagues, he will soon be involved as a courier in Rio's lucrative drug trade. If he doesn't wind up in prison, he may live to twenty.*

Among the most perplexing subjects studied by economists is the wide divergence of wealth in countries both rich and poor. In a country that manufactures airplanes for the American market, produces its own automobiles, powers its cities with nuclear energy, and sits astride a huge land mass of enormous natural resources, half of João's fellow Brazilians live in squalid poverty. In this respect, he is not unlike his colleagues in India, Kenya, and North Korea, maybe even luckier. Under differing forms of government and market policies, vast segments of the globe's population remain untouched by the tremendous accomplishments of economic development in this century. João is among the one billion worldwide who live in abject poverty.

In this chapter, we briefly explore the topic of economic development as viewed from a larger institutional perspective. Many private, church, and nongovernmental entities seek to remediate the situation of João and his counterparts through localized strategies that stress community resources, grassroots development, and self-reliance. This is not the primary concern of economic development institutions or agencies. While all contemporary economic development strategies stress improved human welfare as the primary goal of economic progress, economic strategies generally seek to accomplish this by large-scale structural changes, policy interventions, and program investments.

Economic development and human progress are grounded in growth—the increased capacity to produce goods and services at lower costs for the greatest number. While there has been some historic antagonism between those who concern themselves with economic development and those who stress social development, the two approaches are interdependent. As long as population increases, there must be economic growth to offset burgeoning demand and provide for growing human needs. Similarly, growth itself is no indicator of social welfare and must be attenuated to improve human development.

# Malthusianism

With legions of street children wandering through the great cities, the hillsides of Nepal stripped by the poor to stay warm, the forests of Brazil slashed and burned to make way for teeming urban emigrants who will deplete the soil, and the slums of Calcutta bulging with death and torment, it is easy to see why economics has been called "the dismal science." Among the most pessimistic of those who have sought to unravel the mystery of economic growth and development was Thomas Malthus, an English parson whose anonymous treatise, *An Essay on the Principle of Population as it Affects the Future Improvement of Society,* set the tone for generations. Publishing at the end of the eighteenth century when romantic and utopian views of the future prevailed, Malthus quickly got to the bottom line by asserting that population would inevitably outstrip resources as the human demand for food and energy progressively decimated the natural world's capacity to support a rapacious species. And while his predecessor Adam Smith who, in essence, invented modern economics, took a much more optimistic view, Malthus and his contemporary, David Ricardo, laid a platform for future development theory.

Many of Malthus's assumptions proved to be false. His demographic projections that the world population, growing exponentially, would double every 25 years was but one among them. It is widely acknowledged today that his rather fixed view of the globe's capacity to increase food production while population burgeoned did not anticipate the mechanization of agriculture, the refinement of irrigation engineering, or the development of modern agronomy. The Green Revolution, which in this century transformed food deficit nations such as India and Mexico with the introduction of new seed varieties and scientific agriculture, was beyond Malthus's crystal ball. He could not have anticipated at the time of the horse-drawn plow that vast tracts of new lands would be covered with irrigated crops under mechanical cultivation. Nonetheless, even the father of the Green Revolution, the Nobel Laureate agricultural scientist Norman Borlaug, has expressed apprehension at the prospects for the continued capacity of the planet to feed itself.

> In 1975, when world population reached 4 billion, the world produced an all-time record harvest of 3.3 billion metric tons of all kinds of food…It took from the beginning of agriculture and animal husbandry (some 12,000 to 14,000 years ago) until 1975 to gradually increase production to those record levels. If human population growth continues at the 2% levels of 1975 it will double to 8 billion in 40 years; consequently, food production must be doubled and more equitably distributed in the same period. (Borlaug, 1987: 394)

Economic development is not just a question of how the larger economy functions and "develops," the traditional concern of Smith and subsequent macroeconomists, but also how it relates to the fundamental issues of the balance of natural resources, human

deprivation, and population. Today, Malthusianism is practically an epithet among economists, yet again and again, development theory confronts the basic question of balancing
population growth and distribution—how indeed to account for the vast majority who do
not benefit from the accumulation of wealth. Any approach to development theory that
evades the fundamental link between long-term population growth and natural resources
would be irresponsible.

# Economic Development

Economic development theory and practice are products of the world view of a given era.
Far from a mathematical exercise in calculating Lorenz curves and GNP, development economics is inextricable from its social, philosophical, and political context. From the deep
pessimism of Malthus to the post–World War II obsession with growth, economists have
labored in a broader context that sets the tone for their work. What are the important variables and what are the desirable outcomes? If the production of wealth drives our thinking,
we arrive at completely different perspectives than if we are concerned with maintaining
the environment or assuring that the weakest among us may thrive.

Definitions and models of economic development have responded to the challenges
of a particular period. Contemporary competing paradigms of development variously
focused on social class, structural adjustment, sustainability, or basic human needs are
grounded in the challenges of a new global economy. Earlier narrower approaches to economic development have provided the context and background for a continuing debate on
what variables are important to manipulate for which preferred outcomes.

# Classical and Neo-Classical Theory

At the outset of the development of modern economics, the primary concern was not with
the uneven international development that has come to preoccupy many contemporary
economists, but rather with the development of a system of thought that empirically
describes the relationships between labor, capital, resources, and markets. The Industrial
and Agricultural Revolutions of eighteenth-century Britain provided the intellectual fodder
for building a comprehensive, scientifically based paradigm that formed the basis of
modern economic thought. It was at this time that production accelerated, new trade routes
opened, job specialization increased, and new technologies dramatically improved efficiencies. From the writings of Adam Smith and David Ricardo came a perspective on the
relations between people, capital, and markets that had remained vaguely described, at
best, under the prevailing social philosophies of the day. It is a school of thought based on
the idea of "progress"—that nations and civilizations grow in a positive and desirable
direction and that this growth is directional, organic, purposive, irreversible, and cumulative (Hettne, 1995).

Contemporary development economics, although firmly grounded in this tradition, did
not emerge as such until the 1940s and 1950s, when economists sought to use the prevailing
grand theories (such as Marxism and Classical Economics) to account for the difficult-to-
explain predicaments of Africa, South Asia, and Latin America. Yet the classical theorists

were not mute on the process of development. The opening paragraph of Adam Smith's *An Inquiry into the Nature and Causes of the Wealth of Nations* (1776) reads:

> The annual labor of every nation is the fund which originally supplies it with all the necessaries and conveniences of life which it annually consumes, and which consist always, either in the immediate produce of that labor, or in what is purchased with that produce from other nations. Accordingly therefore, as this produce, or what is purchased with it, bears a greater or smaller proportion to the number of those who are to consume it, the nation will be better or worse supplied with all the necessaries and conveniences for which it has occasion. But this proportion must in every nation be regulated by two different circumstances; first, by the skill, dexterity, and judgment with which its labor is generally applied; and secondly, by the proportion between the number of those who are employed in useful labor, and that of those who are not so employed. Whatever be the soil, climate, or extent of territory of any particular nation, the abundance or scantiness of its annual supply must, in that particular situation, depend upon those two circumstances.

From the outset, there was a fundamental preoccupation with how nations accumulate wealth, how it is distributed, and what factors account for the differences between nations. In Smith's preamble, we already see the unfolding of a model that emphasizes human capital (skill, dexterity and judgment), population, employment, and natural resources.

Classical economics set the context for contemporary development theory by elaborating a paradigm that continues to dominate, albeit in altered form. The classical model emphasizes the efficient allocation of labor and resources, production of wealth, and growth of output to thereby generate self-sufficiency, increase commerce, and improve general welfare. At its simplest level, the paradigm assumes perfect information, lightly regulated or "free" markets, minimal state involvement, and the economic rationality of those involved: That is to say, people will, all things being equal, act in self-interest and seek to maximize utility by choosing more over less with the least input and cost.

Although the assumptions of classical and neo-classical theory are not without exceptions, they work well. Even with less than perfect information, modest state oversight, and some economic irrationality, markets tend to strive toward the efficient allocation of resources and the creation of wealth and welfare. But when state intervention becomes corrupt, monopolistic, or burdensome, the intrinsic mechanisms of the market cease to function. When information is limited, erroneous, or controlled, prices and costs cannot fluctuate in accordance with value and preferences. And when the capacities of individuals to act in their self-interest are overshadowed by political coercion or cultural constraints, their decisions are distorted.

Thus, the challenge of development (or growth in this framework) is to increase the quality and supply of information (about such things as prices and buyers), reduce unwarranted and intrusive intervention by state actors (such as tariffs, overtaxation, coercion, and corruption), and, by building human capital, reduce the distortions caused by irrational actors (such as zero sum thinking, in which another's gain is perceived as one's loss). The policy and development implications of classical theory are to reduce or eliminate those factors that interfere with the market's innate tendency to achieve dynamic equilibrium through efficient allocation and trade.

The term "development," as it is now understood, was not at the core of classical theory, which has concerned itself with the division of labor, the availability and investment of capital, and economic growth. Economic expansion is seen not only as the by-product of acquiring more natural resources, labor inputs, and capital, but also related fundamentally to increasing productivity. Enhanced productivity is seen as due in large part to the expanding division of labor, mechanization, specialization, and improved tools and technology—doing more with the same inputs (Hunt, 1989).

These ideas came to be refined by neo-classical theorists to adjust to the changing economic environment of the Industrial Revolution and later by those who sought to refute the statist[1] implications of Marxist and Neo-Marxist economics. Neo-classical economists, such as Roy Harrod (1939) and Robert Solow (1956), emphasized the growth of aggregate economic welfare through liberalized national markets that are subject to international competition. Open markets attract foreign investment, increase capital savings, and improve the ratio between capital and labor. Long-term growth requires increased savings and investment. Increased capital availability for technological improvements will expand labor output and worker productivity. These relationships will function best when unimpeded by government interference and will be maximized when an economy is open to unimpeded international trade and investment. Closed economies, such as are common in LDCs, impose tariffs, fix exchange rates, pursue import substitution, retard internal savings, promote capital flight, and discourage foreign investment. Developing economies that pursue economic *dirigisme* retard their economic growth. Instead of producing wealth, they are forced to redistribute poverty. One of the problems with the model is that it implies that over time returns on new investment will diminish and, barring external shocks, an economy's growth will decline to an equilibrium of zero.

The common themes of classic and neo-classic thinking include:

- Individuals and firms act in their own self-interest to improve their welfare by husbanding their labor, reducing their expenditures, increasing their savings, and purchasing quality goods and services at the least possible cost.
- Competition among these individuals and firms regulates self-interest by pitting competitors against each other to produce the best-quality goods and services at the least cost in order to gain market share and increase income, thereby benefiting all competitors.
- Labor is also subject to the forces that determine the price and supply of goods and services. Its value is likewise a function of its supply, quality, and price. Competition among workers and producers creates a dynamic equilibrium in which labor is divided and specialized so that individuals may increase their productivity and income by identifying and preparing for specific skills and worker qualities.
- Goods and services are allocated in the market via the price mechanism, which itself reflects consumer preferences, supply, and demand.

---

[1]Statist, or growing out of statism. Statism, also called *dirigisme,* is the view that a powerful interventive national government is needed to control the "excesses" of the market by using the power of the state to direct the economy in politically desirable ways so as to maximize national output, prevent external domination, achieve national self-sufficiency, and address inequality of income.

- Economic growth is dependent upon savings and investment in new technology.
- Markets tend to regulate themselves to maximize growth and output when unimpeded by monopoly, regulated trade, excess taxation, government manipulation, and inadequate information.

The contemporary implications to development policy are fairly straightforward and are echoed today in the work of so-called neoliberals who advocate for open international markets and free trade, reduction of the state sector, privatization of state-owned enterprises, tax reform, and reform of the social welfare state.

## Marxist and Neo-Marxist Perspectives

Adam Smith and Karl Marx developed their theories during the Industrial Revolution in response to the massive changes that were affecting western Europe in the early eighteenth century. While Smith concentrated on the considerable growth in output and the means by which it was being achieved at the outset of industrialization, Marx, writing somewhat later, focused on the changing structure of social class and the role of workers.

The early stages of capitalism and industrialization displaced significant segments of the population. Agricultural workers and farm families migrated to cities as the countryside was similarly affected by mechanization, specialization, and the improvement of transportation. This urbanization process produced an ample labor supply to fuel the factories and mills, but carried with it the unforeseen costs of large-scale unemployment, underemployment, low wages, long work hours for those who could find work, and labor conditions that were appalling by current standards. To increase household income, even children were forced to work in mines and mills. The distribution of income widened, and employment was by no means an assured way of escaping poverty. Cities became crowded and affordable housing was scarce, public health declined, occupational hazards abounded, and society had yet to create any policies or programs to ameliorate the plight of workers.

In such a context, Marx focused not on the strengths of the growing economy, but on its social repercussions. Perhaps best known for his *Communist Manifesto,* an easily accessible utopian call for the defeat of capitalism, his theory of political economy was of far greater importance, as it profoundly affected socioeconomic policy around the world for the next century. While it is beyond the scope of this chapter to elaborate the theory, those key concepts that continue to drive many contemporary national policies need to be elucidated.

Central to both Smith's and Marx's analysis is the production of surplus value. For capitalists, surplus is generated through increased efficiencies brought about by mechanization, specialization, improved labor productivity, enhanced distribution systems, and marketing. For Marxists, surplus is created by workers who, through the capitalist system, generate an excess over subsistence; in other words, the value that is created by production is greater than its inputs, with the effect that the owner of the means of production is able to capture that excess value through profits. Such profits are reinvested back into production in order to accelerate earnings at the expense of those who create it—the workers themselves. This Marxian idea of *surplus value* implies that workers are divorced, or alienated, from the means of production as the ownership class, or *bourgeoisie,* concentrate wealth further to amass even greater assets in the form of land, capital, machinery, and infrastructure. In this way, the class system, which itself is rooted in the feudal period, becomes even more firmly entrenched, and workers find themselves in the position of having only their labor to sell. Detached from the land and unable to ply a trade (in which the tinker or tailor owns the means of production), a worker becomes a labor input rather than a participant.

While capitalists saw the division of labor as a positive feature of development in which people find a productive niche in the overall economy, Marxists argued that the skills and labor of workers were devalued and forced into a narrow band of repetitive tasks. Detached from self-sufficiency and unable to generate surplus earnings, workers are obliged to seek credit from capitalists to purchase housing and consumer goods, thereby spiraling them further into dependency and alienation.

Industrialization requires an ongoing and reliable supply of natural resources as inputs are transformed into marketable goods, such as steel, shoes, or soap. With expansion of production, industrial nations turn to their colonies to provide abundant raw materials and cheap labor. The vicious circle is completed as the industrial nations export back to the colonies their processed goods, which are sold at oppressive prices. Thus, the developed industrial world expands at the expense of the developing world perpetuating the developing world's dependency upon the "North," that is, the countries of the northern hemisphere. Even with decolonization, the fundamental relationships between the two hemispheres is presumed to continue (Frank, 1967).

As the developing nations achieve independence, colonial officials are replaced with internal elites who benefit as a resident capitalist class, and the nation continues to carry out its subordinate role. José Mariátegui (1972), a Peruvian Marxist, goes on to observe that within the developing nations are peripheral groups, most notably indigenous peoples, who, like feudal serfs, serve landlords by providing cheap labor and a market for industrial goods (1972). These groups and the oppressed urban working class become "internal colonies" that are at the edge of the periphery, a Fourth World if you will (Chilicote, 1984). The only upside to this process is that workers in the industrial world develop "class consciousness" and the neocolonial nations of the Third World crystallize a "national consciousness," thereby affirming their class and nation and leading them toward self-determination (Fanon, 1963).

The Marxist and Neo-Marxist perspectives generated a powerful critique of capitalist economies and affected, at one time or another, the policies governing a majority of the world's people. The Leninist variant framed Soviet society, the Maoist version China's, while the developing nations of the southern "periphery" carried out a more muted process of social change that stressed the ostensible economic equality of peoples and firmly entrenched the state as the arbiter of economic policy and the employer of first resort.

The themes and implications of the Marxist and neo-Marxist strategies of economic development include:

- Models of development followed by the industrial nations are not applicable to the developing world and work against their economic independence and national self-determination.
- Limited or broad appropriation of production (factories, farms, and infrastructure) by the workers themselves is pivotal to self-determination.

- The state, as the representative of the people, is entrusted to control public property, to limit the powers of the private economy, and to assure economic equality.
- Dependency upon the industrial nations must be ruptured by a process of nationalizing some or all foreign-owned assets and limiting the influence of international elites.
- Multinational corporations, as the modern instrument of neo-colonialism, must be reined in by international cooperation of the nonaligned LDCs.
- Development strategies for the Third World must be "home grown" to avoid the pitfalls of Western models.

# Modernization Theory

An approach to economic development that bridges sociology and economics, modernization theory argues that the divergent paths of development in the Western and non-Western worlds are fundamentally linked to culture. It posits a continuum between traditional and modern societies in which the latter are characterized by cultural attributes that favor economic development. These include a propensity to save, an emphasis on formal and legal relationships, a future orientation, a rational and scientific outlook, entrepreneurship, ambition, and political and economic self-determination.

Modernization theory has its roots in the work of Émile Durkheim who was strongly opposed to the socialist ideas that were capturing economic philosophy during his lifetime (1858–1917). His work as a positivist focused not on class conflict, but on the organic integration of social classes in a dynamic economy. He argued that the transition to modernity was dependent upon a shift from rather limited, kinship-based economic relationships to formal, complex, innovative economic associations (Webster, 1990).

The Marxian school also provoked a refinement of classical development theory by German economist Joseph Schumpeter who, in 1911, stressed the centrality of entrepreneurship to democratic capitalism (Harrison, 1985). He rejected both the egalitarianism and the leveling implications of socialist thought and argued that competition was critical to growth because it allows for individuals to exercise their creative abilities and ingenuity to develop new ideas and technologies. Democratic capitalism is seen as nurturing the capacity of people to get things done by providing them with the freedom and the incentive to achieve (Schumpeter, 1911/1961). Schumpeter's emphasis on individualism, entrepreneurship, and civil society has been echoed throughout modernization theory and is still influential today among neo-liberals such as Francis Fukuyama.

Max Weber, in *The Protestant Ethic and the Spirit of Capitalism* (1958), argued that the development of modern capitalism was dependent upon the rational organization of formally free labor. The accumulation of wealth has been a goal in many precapitalist systems, but under modern capitalism, such accumulation is not an end in itself. It is instead a moral endeavor that is regulated by a normative system that stresses frugality, future-orientation, savings, restraint from self-indulgence, and service to others. The production of wealth and the development of society is facilitated by an ethical, industrious, and free labor force that strives for success in a "calling." Weber noted that such characteristics were evident in Western Europe and the United States, thereby accelerating their growth.

This development or "modernization" could be partly attributed to a culture that generates an adequate pool of capital for investment in innovation and technology, stresses education as central to a child's success, frees government and business from the pervasive corruption characteristic of so many developing countries, and allows free individuals to compete. In essence, these values are preconditions to the modern industrial capitalist economy.

Weber also stressed the importance of religion by noting that those faiths that stressed achievement in the present world were conducive to economic development. The core ethics of thrift, honesty, work, and rationality mediate the acquisitive individualism of citizens. Religions that propose magical explanations of phenomena, which provide ready means of repentance, or stress life in the hereafter are far less inclined to support civil conduct, cooperation, trust, the rule of law, and the community of democratic institutions that form the crucible of progress.

Rostow (1960) elaborated modernization theory by identifying the stages of growth through which developing nations must proceed in order to develop a modern capitalist structure. His book on modernization, *Stages of Growth: A Non-Communist Manifesto,* was a product of the Cold War in which the competing ideologies of the industrial West and the socialist East vied for supremacy in the emerging Third World economies. Development was seen as an instrument of Western foreign policy whereby the affluence and freedom of Western societies could be exported to the LDCs as a means not only of improving living standards and self-determination, but also of stemming the growing influence of the Soviet Union throughout the Southern Hemisphere (Memet, 1995). A developing nation would proceed, with international foreign aid and technical assistance, in a linear and deterministic way toward advanced capitalism. Like the work of Francis Fukuyama, who writes in the contemporary neo-liberal school of development, Rostow believed that the capitalist system would inevitably prevail as the only integrated and self-sustaining means of national development that could assure long-term economic growth and democratic self-determination.

The Rostow stages include: traditional society, the preconditions of take-off, take-off, the drive to maturity, and the age of high mass-consumption. To proceed along the continuum requires shedding the fatalism, present orientation, and kinship or tribally based economic relationships that characterize traditional societies (Foster, 1973). Moreover, development requires that social and economic roles not be *ascribed* through inheritance and tradition, but *achieved* or earned through education, skill, leadership, and work (Webster, 1990).

The stress on achievement is best elaborated by McClelland (1960), who in seeking to empirically explain the wide differences between the economic progress of cultures and nations, identified a cluster of economic and cultural values that facilitate and account for development. Among the most important factors are:

- *Universalism,* as opposed to particularism, in which modern societies develop a universal set of codes, norms, and laws that apply to all people "regardless of who they are in particular" (p. 180).
- *Antitraditionalism,* in which pressures for conformity are superceded by the individual's drive for economic success through impersonal entrepreneurial behavior.

- *Specificity of role relationships,* a characteristic that stresses individually motivated contractual economic arrangements rather than diffuse, informal, traditional, and kinship based arrangements.
- *Achieved status,* as contrasted with ascribed or inherited status.
- *Collectivity,* in which individuals must, to some extent, put the goals of the public interest above those purely individual aspirations.
- *Rationality and planning,* emphasizing the formal, scientific, and future orientations instead of magic or supernaturalism.
- *Optimism* and faith in the future, in particular, the idea that progress is not constrained by nature and fate, but is a function of human capacity.

The idea that achievement is a precondition of development carries with it an economic interpretation for McClelland, who argues that achievement is not solely the cultural propensity to seek social status, but more importantly for economic development, the "desire to do something better, faster, more efficiently, and with less effort" (1960: A).

Among the more provocative of those who emphasize the importance of culture to development is Larry Harrison. A former USAID officer and administrator in Latin America, Harrison undertook a systematic study of development in that region while posted at the Harvard Center for International Affairs. Harrison acknowledges the many factors that facilitate economic development including natural resource endowment, human capital, government policies, history, and leadership, but unequivocally states:

> …more than any of the other of the numerous factors that influence the development of countries, it is culture that principally explains, in most cases, why some countries develop more rapidly and equitably than others. By "culture" I mean the values and attitudes a society inculcates in its people through various socializing mechanisms, e.g., the home, the school, the church. (1985: xvi)

Echoing Max Weber, Harrison makes stark contrasts between more successful countries and nations with comparable resources that have failed to progress. He contrasts Nicaragua and Costa Rica, Barbados and Haiti, as well as Argentina and Australia. His analysis pointedly concludes that seven conditions describe a functional modern democracy:

- The expectation of fair play
- Availability of educational opportunities
- Availability of health services
- Encouragement of experimentation and criticism
- Matching of jobs and skills
- Rewards for merit and achievement
- Stability and continuity

Although some have criticized his work as ethnocentric at best, many of his ideas are accepted as common wisdom among development workers who regularly confront the challenges of dealing with corrupt bureaucracies that expend their resources to benefit elites, distribute perks, obstruct innovation, sell jobs, ignore contracts, and take kickbacks. A compelling example of the frustration of well-intended development specialists, Harrison's work identifies those cultural factors that can work against the best-laid plans of development specialists who confront many of the unique attributes of developing societies.

Modernization as a strategy of economic development has the following themes and implications:

- Traditional societies are restricted by cultural values that emphasize the present, utilize supernatural explanations for rationally ordered phenomena, and seek to maintain the status quo.
- Zero sum thinking also restrains development and has a leveling effect. The idea that another individual's gain comes at one's own loss exerts a conservative influence on innovation and entrepreneurship.
- Modern economies require the rule of law. The use of contracts should mediate the economic interaction of unknown individuals operating self-interestedly in the formal social system. The law must be equally applied to all individuals regardless of rank or status to assure fair competition.
- Modern economies are based on democratic institutions. Open and equal access to political decision making restrains the propensity of self-interested individuals to unfairly use political processes on their own behalf.
- A modern government must assure equal access to all of its services, especially universal education.

## Structuralism

According to Argentinean Raúl Prebisch (1984), neo-classical economics did a poor job of explaining the worldwide depression of the 1930s and a poorer job yet of accounting for the situation of the developing nations, particularly those in Latin America (1984). Many developing countries have sought to exercise comparative advantage in which they export those goods that they produce most efficiently and import those at which other nations excel. The problem for LDCs has been that their comparative advantage was in primary products (e.g. natural resources, agriculture) and as the price of these goods remained stable while manufactured import prices increased, the developing economies were squeezed in such a way that it was impossible to carry out long-term recovery (Hunt, 1989).

Prebisch and his contemporary, Brazilian Celso Furtado, began in the 1950s to argue for economic policies that were seen as providing the means for developing nations to compete successfully. The structuralists thus advocated import substitution whereby a domestic economy might be protected over the short term as it strove for industrial self-sufficiency. This would ease the balance of payments difficulties of developing countries and allow them to develop domestic markets. For them, development was based not solely on the growth of output, but also on the expansion of the sectors of the economy that use current technology (Hunt, 1989).

In contrast with a laissez-faire approach to trade, the structuralists advocated for protection while the domestic economies at the "periphery" of the capitalist center made the transformation to an advanced industrial base. Advanced nations and LDCs are seen as engaged in a process of *dual development* in which the former exercise their comparative advantage. The First World economies' edge on the international market and its terms of trade is attributable to their technological lead. To narrow the gap of dual development requires domestic industrialization, changing the terms of trade with advanced nations, investment in infrastructure, and strong domestic planning (Prebisch, 1984). The neo-Marxists used many of the same observations to arrive at Dependency Theory, but, unlike them, the structuralists did not dispute the soundness of capitalism. They have sought to refine it to meet the needs of nations outside of the capitalist center.

# Institutional Reform

Western economists have argued on behalf of a modest role for the state, but have given greater attention to "market failures." Market failures occur when the self-regulating dynamism of supply and demand is significantly distorted by forces that operate within the private sector. They also occur when the market passes on its externalities (costs and problems) to the community at no cost to itself. Examples of market failures are industrial pollution, private monopoly, and consumer fraud. A legitimate role of the modern state in the economy is to mitigate the failures of the market.

More recently, attention has also been given to "state failures" in which the intervention of government into the marketplace introduces distortions. The market produces goods and services for individual demand at prices determined by competition, supply, demand, infrastructure, scale, and other factors. The state produces nothing, but does supply services for the collectivity that are not provided by the private sector, such as law enforcement, interstate highways, and primary education. State failures occur because the public sector is not subject to any of the forces that compel private providers to strive toward efficiency. The result is "…the profligate use made of tax revenues by public servants and the excessive price of state services" (Janicke, 1990: 31). To put it another way, public bureaucrats spend other peoples' money, have no incentives to reduce the size of their budget, and no reason to introduce efficiencies. They are not elected and thus do not respond to a market or electorate. Rarely are they subjected to the forces of competition, infrequently is their remuneration linked to their performance, and their own personal welfare is almost never a function of the effectiveness of their projects or programs (Knott and Miller, 1987). Indeed, the most successful bureaucrats are those with the largest budgets. These factors imply the necessity for institutional reform.

State failures fall into three broad categories, those having to do with political, economic, and functional incapacity (Janicke, 1990). Political failures reflect government propensity to avoid action on critical policy issues. Economic failures are the substandard services provided by government at high cost. Functional failures include the ineffectiveness of government programs and projects.

Economists who are concerned with state failures advocate institutional reform—changes in policies and bureaucracies. Among the reforms most commonly identified are downsizing the public sector, deregulation of the marketplace, balancing national budgets, bureaucratic reform and reorientation, privatization of state-owned enterprises elimination of tariffs, and improved accountability in political decision making.

## Downsizing

Economists from Adam Smith to Milton Friedman have written about the inherent ineffi-ciencies of government planning and administration and the need to downsize government and reduce public spending. The tradition was all but forgotten during the West's long experiment with Keynesian economics[2] and the Third World's endorsement of statism, but attracted increased attention over the past two decades as the proportion of national income spent by government grew to alarming figures.

The Conservative Revolution of the 1980s changed the ideological landscape world-wide in identifying the proper role of the state. It provided a fresh opportunity for empiri-cal economists to demonstrate that when it comes to government, less is better. For the first time since the Great Depression, leaders of advanced economies took significant steps in the eighties to stem the growth of public institutions. Despite their efforts, during that decade, the average proportion of national income spent by advanced countries increased from 42.5 percent to 45 percent ("The Visible Hand," 1997). Today the figure has reached 46 percent; Sweden's government spends 64 percent of national income, the United States government spends 33 percent ("The World Economy," 1997). The institutional reform movement set into motion during the 1980s did have the effect of slowing the rate of gov-ernment growth in the industrial economies. It also drew attention to high taxes, deficit spending, and government bloat and the drain that each produces on economic prosperity.

During the past two decades, progress was also made in reducing the size of public expenditures in poor nations. In Latin America, large foreign debt, statist policies, and extensive regulation forced governments in the region to review their interventionist approach to macroeconomics. During the 1970s, Latin American governments were not providing needed public functions such as price stability, law enforcement, and high qual-ity, low-cost public education (Holden and Rajapatirana, 1995). While failing to carry out needed public functions, governments in the region interfered with the capacity of entre-preneurs to establish new firms and implemented complex and contradictory regulations on business. By the 1980s, it was clear that long-term growth in Latin America was down, inflation was out of control, and import substitution was not working. During the past two decades, many nations in the region have come out of a long slump after implementing changes in trade policy, imposing fiscal discipline, privatizing state enterprises, and estab-lishing clearer property rights.

The collapse of the former Soviet Union and the reform of its allies also represented an historical rejection of central planning and government domination of the economy. The transformation of the centrally planned economies of eastern Europe, central Asia, and Russia has been profound. While the transition of these economies into the market has proved more difficult than originally envisioned, the reform period is showing early suc-cess in revitalizing business.

---

[2]"Keynesian," from John M. Keynes, is a model of economics that aims to reduce the threat of depression and unemployment by increasing aggregate demand through government spending.

## Privatization

One approach in the toolbox of downsizing is privatization—the transfer of public property rights to the private sector and the increase of private return on state assets. The most dramatic example of privatization is in the former Soviet Union and Warsaw Pact nations. Since 1990, the Russian Federation, for example, has transferred 70 percent of its enterprises to some form of private ownership (Summers, 1997). Over 10,000 enterprises have passed into private hands. Formerly state-owned enterprises (SOEs) now employ more than 11 million people (Lieberman and Rahuja, 1995), and private-sector output has reached nearly 60 percent of GDP (World Bank, 1996). Although this transition has not been without its difficulties, such as inflation and high unemployment, it represents the largest transfer of state property in history.

Privatization is a type of institutional reform that reduces the role of government in the private economy by spinning off those aspects of public spending to nongovernmental entities. This is done to reduce public spending and to put selected public activities into a market environment that will transform them through the forces of competition. It reduces taxes and improves efficiencies. In addition, it depoliticizes businesses that had been administered by public bureaucrats. Public businesses, such as a state-owned airline, railroad, farm, or industry, are ostensibly owned by the "people," but in fact the public do not profit and the business is run as the de facto property of bureaucrats and politicians (Poole, 1995). Thus, privatization also creates "ownership" wherein the economic entity can be sold to shareholders or firms who have a stake in the outcome.

In developing countries, where public ownership of businesses and services is widespread, there are several advantages to privatization beyond the immediate benefit of load-shedding a costly state enterprise. Privatization raises capital that can be used to reduce foreign debt, develop national infrastructure, modernize industry, and broaden capital markets by creating new shareholders (Poole, 1996).

International interest in privatization grew after the early successes of the Thatcher government in Britain and is rapidly gaining popularity worldwide as a tool of economic reform. Nearly any type of government-owned enterprise has been privatized in the past two decades including: automobile manufacturing (Mexico), public housing (Britain and the United States), state farms (Kazakstan and Russia), banks (Russia and eastern Europe), telecommunications (Japan and Italy), ports (Peru), insurance (France), and dams and bridges (Turkey) (Cowan, 1987; World Bank, 1997).

## Bureaucratic Reform

The economic drag created by public bureaucracy in the developing world is well understood by anyone who has worked or lived there. For the foreigner it can range from the difficulty cashing a traveler's check in Tanzania to buying a factory in Russia. For residents, it can be the challenge of getting a phone line installed in India or obtaining a legal land title in Kazakstan. The price of doing business in the Third World can include paying off government bureaucrats, buying licenses, evading government expropriation, paying onerous taxes and fees, insecure property rights, ignored and unenforceable contracts, hours of meaningless paperwork, avoiding organized crime, evading corrupt security forces, and huge impediments to securing credit at affordable prices. Consequently, many entrepreneurs in the developing world, both large and small, have moved into the informal sector.[3]

Hernando de Soto, a Peruvian economist, carried out an experiment in that country to document the "costs of legality." His Institute of Liberty and Democracy established a fictitious garment business in Lima, which the Institute group tried to register legally in the official economy. Deciding that they would pay no bribe or hidden fee, they spent 289 days navigating various bureaucracies without successfully registering their firm. Recognizing that it would never be registered without the usual sleight of hand, they were able to obtain legal status after $1,231 in bribes and lost production. For a country in which the annual GNP per capita is about $2000, this is no small sum, and at these rates, any small or micro entrepreneur would be unable to establish a bona fide enterprise. They concluded that legality is a privilege that is accorded only to those with political and economic power. Hernando de Soto documented that 43 percent of Lima's housing was unofficial, 274 of its markets were informal, and over 91 thousand of its street vendors worked without documents. Much of the country's public transportation, services, sales, food production, and light manufacturing is carried out "at the margins" (de Soto, 1987).

Peru is in no way unique in this regard. Informality is pervasive through Latin America, the developing world, and the former Soviet Union because rational and cost-conscious economic actors will seek any means to earn a living, "official" and legitimate or not. When the business environment discourages the creation of firms or imposes high transaction costs on existing businesses, the incentive is to function informally. In addition, high transaction costs and state monopoly encourage rent-seeking behavior. Distinctly different from profit seeking, rent seeking is the "diversion of entrepreneurial energies toward the extraction of a surplus from public agencies and away from productivity-enhancing market activities" (Birdsall and James, 1993: 339). Examples include lobbying to seek a monopoly, soliciting to protect a domestic industry with import tariffs, bribing of public officials, or trying to acquire exclusive licenses, tax benefits, subsidies, or quotas (Gallagher, 1991). The result of rent seeking is that real income becomes tied, not to production in the market, but to access to political and bureaucratic power. Rent seeking distorts incentives and diverts capital away from productive enterprise. It also slows growth because a portion of a nation's investment and labor are engaged in the capture of rents rather than in the production of profits. In addition, the incentives to work and save money are reduced. Informality and rent seeking are widespread among developing economies; in Africa, the median rents are 20 percent of GDP (Gallagher, 1991).

For de Soto, the implications of informality and rent seeking are to establish clear and incontrovertible property rights for land owners, business people, and farmers. It means that the "property disowning bureaucracy" must be downsized and reconfigured away from its obsessive interest in paperwork authenticity and self-enrichment (de Soto, 1996). Another implication points toward democratization. When public agencies are

---

[3]The informal sector is comprised of all undocumented and unofficial economic activities that escape regulation, taxation, and public oversight. Informal activity, though often profitable, is not governed by legal contract or clear property rights, but is carried out to avoid the costs of doing business in the formal economy.

transparent and accountable, the ability to capture rents or move toward informality is reduced. Democracy and institutional reform are mutually reinforcing.

Institutional reform strategies stress *structural adjustment* as well as internal bureaucratic reform, privatization, and government downsizing. Structural adjustment broadly emphasizes economic growth and financial stability by reducing price distortions, liberalizing trade policies, opening up the domestic market to more competition, and devaluing currency (Klitgaard, 1990). Economic development strategies that emphasize institutional reform recognize the unique environment of each developing country, both obstacles and strengths. Interventions to change institutions seek to build on identified strengths (such as clear property rights) through policy supports and replication and to alter institutional obstacles (such as widespread corruption). There is no room for a romantic view that self-interest is not an issue in economic development; the idea is to create the institutional incentives for self-interest to be actualized in a prosocial and developmental direction. Sanctions for corruption and bureaucratic abuse must be enforced, and economic transactions by public and private actors need to be transparent.

The institutional reform perspective has the following themes:

- Economic development is conditioned on clear property rights.
- Property must be fully transferable in the market.
- Government spending is growing in absolute terms and in relation to percentage of national spending; the government share of national spending must be reduced.
- Government transactions and policies must be transparent and equally applied.
- Privatization of state-owned enterprises improves efficiencies, creates new owners, increases capital availability, and promotes economic growth.
- Institutional reform is inextricable from fiscal relief.
- Obstacles to economic development must be dismantled, including short time horizons, bureaucratic corruption and nepotism, land tenure insecurity, and obstruction by power elites.
- Those incentives that work in the private sector must also be applied to the public sector.
- Rent seeking should be replaced by profit seeking.

## Basic Needs Strategies

The emphasis on growth as the engine of economic development has been criticized as failing to address human development. Although the classical and neo-classical models make ample reference to human welfare, the emphasis has been on aggregate economic expansion. To some degree, it was assumed that aggregate growth would entail a net gain for all sectors of the population because as a society becomes richer, demand is increased and unemployment tends to decline. The "trickle down" of wealth would tend to improve welfare indicators. This would entail the development of the poor as spending increased and was felt throughout the economy through the multiplier effect. Wealth invested in infrastructure would also benefit the majority and improve employment and earnings.

Development can be a highly uneven process and growth in average GDP per capita does not necessarily translate into improved prospects for the poor. In many Latin American, African, and Asian countries, aggregate growth has not been accompanied by an increase in the living standard of the poorest segment of the population nor has income distribution become more equitable. In fact, the poorest quintile of the world's population experienced both a real and relative income decline over the past thirty years (United Nations, 1996). Since 1965, the percentage of world income taken in by the highest 20 percent of the population has increased by 14 percent; the richest quartile earns about 60 times the poorest twenty percent (Income distribution, 1997) (Table 6.1).

Simon Kuznets examined the relationships between economic growth and income distribution and found that, initially, economic growth seems to worsen income distribution, but that with continued growth in GNP/capita, inequality tends to decline (1955). One implication of Kuznets's work is that unless a nation takes specific redistributive steps to ameliorate the situation of its poorest citizens, economic growth alone may be insufficient over the short term to assure a minimal standard of living. The recent experience of numerous success stories such as Singapore, Taiwan, Costa Rica, and Malaysia for example, indicates that his hypothesis is not uniformly accurate. In these countries, growth has been rapid, the poor have benefited significantly, and investment in social transfers has been primarily in human capital.

An influential approach to economic development stresses the *basic needs* of people in developing economies. The founding premise of this school of thought is that economic growth is a necessary, yet insufficient, condition for assuring the human development of a cross-section of the population. Mohandas Gandhi's definition of development is illustrative:

> Whenever you are in doubt…apply the following test. Recall the face of the poorest and weakest man whom you may have seen, and ask yourself if the step you contemplate is

**TABLE 6.1    Income Distribution in Selected Economies**

| Country | Lowest 20% | 2nd Quintile | 3rd Quintile | 4th Quintile | Highest 20% |
|---|---|---|---|---|---|
| India | 8.5% | 12.1% | 15.8% | 21.1% | 42.6% |
| Ghana | 7.9% | 12.0% | 16.1% | 21.8% | 42.2% |
| Egypt | 8.7% | 12.5% | 16.3% | 21.4% | 41.1% |
| Bolivia | 5.6% | 9.7% | 14.5% | 22.8% | 48.2% |
| Guatemala | 2.1% | 5.8% | 10.5% | 18.6% | 63.0% |
| Kazakstan | 7.5% | 12.3% | 16.9% | 22.9% | 40.4% |
| China | 5.5% | 9.8% | 14.9% | 22.3% | 47.5% |
| Russia | 3.7% | 8.5% | 13.5% | 20.4% | 53.8% |
| United States | 4.7% | 11.0% | 17.4% | 25.0% | 41.9% |
| Japan | 8.7% | 13.2% | 17.5% | 23.1% | 37.5% |
| Sweden | 8.0% | 13.2% | 17.4% | 24.5% | 36.9% |

*Source:* From *World Development Report 1997* by World Bank. Copyright © 1997 The International Bank for Reconstruction and Development/The World Bank. Used by permission of Oxford University Press, Inc.

going to be of any value to him. Will he gain anything by it? Will it restore him to control over his life and destiny? (Mamen, 1990)

By this measure, many, if not most, development projects could be counted as failures. It is not for the poorest and weakest that bridges and airports are financed and built by international capital.

The basic-needs approach functions as a counterpoint to classical and neoliberal growth strategies because it stresses human development of the one billion people who occupy the lowest quartile of income. The emphasis on providing for the basic needs of the poorest is certainly not a new idea; it has been an underpinning of most of the world's religions and has been supported by charitable organizations and nongovernmental organizations for a very long time. Yet it became a major issue for the international development community in the 1970s when the International Labor Organization (ILO), the United States Agency for International Development (USAID), and the World Bank began to incorporate basic needs strategies into policy and program designs.

The basic needs approach argues that investment in the living standards of the poor has the immediate impact not only of improving the quality of people's lives, but also of increasing aggregate demand and sustainable economic growth. A more equitable income distribution will increase small-scale savings, promote trade between developing nations, and reduce food imports (Hunt, 1989).

A major objective of the basic needs strategy is to improve human welfare in economic, health, social, educational, and political terms. Economic policy would aim at improving incomes of the bottom two quartiles. Health policies would be designed to improve life expectancy, reduce infant and maternal mortality, increase caloric intake quantity and quality, and reduce morbidity, especially for infectious and parasitic diseases. Social policies would be aimed at improving the opportunities for children and closing the "gender gap" in which women in the developing world work far longer hours for less income than men. Educational policy would aim for universal and affordable primary and secondary education with particular attention to girl's education and the rural poor. Political reform would address the democratic empowerment of marginalized populations by expanding the participation of indigenous cultures, women, rural groups and urban slum dwellers. The model gives particular attention to child welfare, land reform, and the development of human capital (Selowsky, 1979).

The basic-needs approach relies on continued aggregate expansion, but aims at directing the benefits of growth more equitably. Several means can be used to gauge the success of development from the basic-needs perspective. These include the Human Development Index, a comprehensive scale of measures of welfare developed by the United Nations Development Program (United Nations, 1996: 136–137); the Index of Sustainable Economic Welfare, a similar scale which gives particular attention to the environment (Daly and Cobb, 1989: 401–455), or the Social Development Indicators (World Bank, 1995).

Themes and implications of the basic needs approach include:

- Economic growth is a necessary, but insufficient condition of development.
- The elimination of absolute poverty is the major goal of economic development.

- Providing for basic needs increases domestic demand, enlarges small-scale savings, and acts as a stimulus to aggregate growth.
- Obstacles to small-scale business development and labor-intensive production must be removed to thereby empower the microentrepreneur and small farmer.
- Women and children are particularly at risk in the developing world, and policies should be specifically aimed at equalizing their opportunities and standard of living.
- Economic development, to be effective, must be intertwined with supportive policies in the health, education, and political sectors.

## Technocratic Development: Multilateral Banks and Development Assistance

The period between the two world wars was characterized by international economic chaos: worldwide depression, falling trade, widespread unemployment, commodity scarcity, and massive currency fluctuations. It was a time when commodity prices were below farm production costs, land values plummeted, and factories were closed for lack of markets. Currency lost its value and there was wide speculation in gold. The prices of goods worldwide fell by 48 percent between 1929 and 1932; international trade declined 63 percent during the same period (Driscoll, 1995). Near the end of World War II, the leading economic thinkers of the Western nations (including John M. Keynes and Harry D. White) began to devise an institutional framework that would stabilize the world economy and combat those policies that led to economic anarchy. Nations at the time sought to export their unemployment, manipulate currency exchange rates, set up import barriers, and engage in restrictive bilateral arrangements, all in an effort to control the internal anguish of unemployment, food lines, and soup kitchens, but with the result of accelerating rather than diminishing the crisis (McCormack, 1984).

After over a decade of negotiations, a new international financial system was created in 1944 at a conference in Bretton Woods, New Hampshire. This new international system was to be brokered by two new global institutions—the International Monetary Fund (IMF) and the International Bank for Reconstruction and Development (The World Bank). While the wars in Europe and Asia continued, delegates from 44 nations, rich and poor, signed the accords. A primary intent of the delegates was to guarantee free trade and an end to the import quotas, tariffs, restrictions, and currency depreciations that had brought the world economy to a standstill (George and Sabelli, 1994).

The IMF opened its doors in 1946 with 36 members and has grown to include 179 member states. It was designed to encourage the unrestricted conversion of currency, establish clear value for each national currency, and eliminate monetary restrictions. Each participating nation agrees to inform the IMF of how the value of national currency is determined and also to avoid any policy that restricts the exchange of its money (Driscoll, 1995). A key benefit of membership is access to large-scale IMF loans that can be used to stabilize currency and meet public obligations—especially obligations to other members. Member nations, particularly developing ones, often face payment problems because they are not taking in adequate income to meet obligations. This may be a function of balance of payments in which imports exceed exports, and international aid and private investment are insufficient to offset its losses; thus a nation may be unable to garner sufficient tax or external income to pay its bills. Financial insolvency in developing nations is commonly a by-product of large expenditures on military hardware, an unrealistic government payroll, an unregulated and untaxed informal sector, and the repression and overregulation of its business sector. Thus, IMF loans are conditioned on the recipient's taking action to reform those economic policies that are leading to its insolvency—not by addressing specific expenditures, but by putting into place the liberal trade, investment, fiscal, and monetary policies that lead to economic growth. It is expected that IMF loans will be paid in three to five years, with extensions of up to ten years possible. A presentation of planned reforms that will lead to economic growth is a precondition of a loan, and future loans are contingent upon compliance with those reforms.

During the 1970s, international lending accelerated sharply to offset the budget deficits that grew partly out of the oil crisis and the recessions it provoked. Economic restructuring was quite difficult during the recession and debts exploded, with the result that some nations began to default on their loans and were forced to renegotiate the terms of repayment. With debt service growing as a percentage of GNP, many nations, such as Mexico and Brazil, were unable to make the domestic investments needed to spur growth. By the decade of the eighties, debtor countries were remitting an average of $6.6 billion a year in interest payments to the IMF, World Bank, and other lenders (George and Sabelli, 1994).

Some have described the debt crisis of the developing world as a form of extortion designed to keep the Third World in economic check. It is argued that the growing recession of the 1970s, coupled with the debt crisis, led to the phenomenon of the Lost Decade. During the late seventies and early eighties, growth all but stalled in Latin America and Africa, and those living in the poorest quartile saw their share of the economy dwindle. Many critics surged forward to criticize the arrangement by which growth had spiraled downward, and it became de rigueur to describe the debt crisis as the by-product of overzealous and highly profitable financial institutions making money on the backs of the Third World's poor (cf. Rich, 1994a). Only occasionally was it observed that massive *borrowing* is a precondition of huge lending or that debtor nations were wildly spending on military hardware and engineering monuments to benefit the elite. It was also rarely noted that billions of dollars in debts were simply written off by the advanced economies. Moreover, it was increasingly the commercial banks who were making the loans rather than the multilateral banks and agencies. Nonetheless, it was clear by the mid-eighties that the situation was untenable and was not moving the international economy toward greater integration and stability, as had been originally intended when the IMF and World Bank were founded.

Several techniques were used to restructure debt and reduce its burden. Most commonly, the loan was renegotiated at terms more favorable to the borrower, including lower interest rates, longer repayment periods, and partial cancellation of outstanding principal. Sometimes debt to banks in the North has been exchanged for equity in weak banks in the South. More infrequently, debt has been swapped for environmental concessions such as the preservation of tropical forests and parks (Todaro, 1997). Because a large share of debt was to commercial banks who were less able to be flexible, nations were required to renegotiate loans with IMF support. This entailed the application of the IMF's Stabilization Policies, which reflect an effort to control inflation and balance national budgets. These measures include:

- Compliance with IMF membership rules on the full convertibility of currency
- Devaluation of national currency as needed
- Reduction of government expenditures
- Opening its markets to direct foreign investment
- Removing import barriers
- Reduction or elimination of consumer subsidies, especially on agricultural products
- Privatizing state-owned enterprises

These interventions are not without their costs, and many nations bear them unwillingly. Nonetheless, the debt crisis has subsided in the wake of large-scale debt restructuring. Countries that had negative economic growth and suffered from the largest debt are now in a growth phase. The annual GDP of two of the largest debtors, Brazil and Mexico, are currently growing at 5.0 and 8.8 percent respectively ("Emerging Market Indicators," 1997). The evidence is not yet in on whether the resurgence of growth in the developing world will continue.

The International Bank for Reconstruction and Development (The World Bank) has a related, but different role than the IMF. The Bretton Woods Protocol was designed to stabilize the international economy of the postwar period. The industrial world had three goals in particular: assurance of free and unrestricted international trade, open international investment, and access to raw materials (George and Sabelli, 1994). The International Bank for Reconstruction and Development, as its name implies, was created to provide the financing necessary to achieve the reconstruction and development of economies ravaged by world war. Indeed, its first loans were to European nations to finance imports. The Marshall Plan supplanted the bank's role in Europe, and as the economies of the war-affected nations recovered, the bank turned its attention to the development of "the resources and productive capabilities of the less developed countries" (Mason and Asher, 1973).

The World Bank (IBRD) is quite unlike other banks. It lends money only to governments, it does not receive deposits per se, and its principal function is to guarantee and encourage private investment. Member nations "own" the World Bank and must pay a capital subscription to join. The subscription serves as a sort of collateral, but does not comprise the money lent by the bank; most of this comes from bonds sold on world financial markets. The terms of its loans are slightly higher than the interest rate of its bonds, providing it with operating capital and profits that can be directed toward new loans.

IBRD loans can be taken for specific projects such as major construction, agriculture, infrastructure, hydroelectric, and other activities that contribute to economic growth. A nation may also borrow to develop a particular sector such as agriculture or energy (George and Sabelli, 1994). In addition, a country may use a loan to ease its debt problems under certain conditions. These *structural adjustment* loans require that specific policy measures be taken to address the underlying causes of debt, most notably the excessive expenditures of government and deficit budgets. Structural adjustment aims to integrate a developing nation into the global economy by developing a domestic free market. It stresses the expansion of exports in order to generate foreign currency, the elimination of subsidies that artificially support noneconomic industries or sectors, and policies that improve a nation's comparative advantage in specific products and industries.

Structural adjustment loans have generated enormous criticism because, over the short term, there is a tendency for incomes to stagnate and demand to flatten. Critics of the structural adjustment requirements claim that the status of women, children, and indigenous peoples declines, food self-sufficiency is worsened, and economic inequality is exacerbated (Rich, 1994a). The bank's position has been that until the macroeconomics are right, economic development will continue to stagnate for everyone. Without policies to promote stability and growth, accelerating inflation and unfiananceable current accounts deficits will sap sustainable growth (World Bank, 1991: 110).

As the role of the World Bank evolved from postwar reconstruction to development assistance, its profile of lending activities shifted significantly. In 1960, the bank established the International Development Association (IDA) to carry out technical assistance and extend loans under terms more generous than those of the IBDR. Technical assistance to developing nations was not in the bank's original charter, but it became clear that new investment required new ways of thinking and new ways of doing business in developing contexts. Those technical activities that may be carried out in support of a loan include assistance in project identification, preparation, feasibility, and sector studies—usually carried out by foreign consultants (Mason and Asher, 1973). In addition, assistance may be provided in project design, administrative and technical aspects of projects, and the mobilization of local capital.

IBRD and IDA loans represent one of the most powerful forces in international development. The current outstanding loan portfolio is approximately $140 billion (Rich, 1994b). The bank and the IMF seek to leverage their loans with support from private investors, other multilateral banks (e.g. Asian Development Bank), cofinancing by the host government, and cost sharing with development agencies such as the United States Agency for International Development (USAID) and the Japan International Cooperation Agency (JICA). The emergence of the multilateral banking institutions such as the IMF, World Bank, Inter-American Development Bank, and the Asian Development Bank, has eclipsed the role of foreign assistance agencies (such as USAID and JICA) in economic development.

Foreign assistance agencies had an important role in economic development during the Cold War era because western democracies were intent on creating allies and economic partners throughout the developing world. The Soviet Union's express desire to export revolution to LDCs was a major challenge to Western democracy and market economics. The West responded by investing billions of dollars and providing large numbers of technical experts to generate economic growth, build national infrastructure, and prop up allied governments.

With the decline of a Cold War paradigm to provide a rationale for foreign assistance and an active internationalist position for the U.S. government, support for foreign aid has dwindled and funding has declined. Ironically, Americans think that foreign aid is the largest portion of the federal budget—greater than that of defense or social entitlements. Believing that it is around 20 percent of the total budget, they are surprised to find that it constitutes less than one half of one percent. At about $7 billion/year in 1996, U.S. foreign assistance comprises 0.46 percent of the budget—an amount lower in real dollars than at any time in the past fifty years. During the past two years, USAID has closed 24 country missions around the world and laid off 1750 staff (USAID, 1997). Japan is now the world's leading donor nation in foreign assistance. America's federal commitment to international development is all but disappearing. Should the trend continue, the result may be that the multilateral banks and nongovernmental organizations (such as Oxfam or Catholic Relief) will play a greater role than the U.S. government in shaping the direction of international development policy.

USAID, despite its declining influence in economic development, remains an important instrument of official American foreign policy. It is important to recognize that development assistance is a branch of foreign policy rather than solely a humanitarian enterprise. Foreign aid has several objectives:

- *Strategic*   Foreign assistance seeks to bolster U.S. allies in the developing world to enhance the national security and promote America's long-term interests in a nation and region. Strategic interests can include the strengthening of an ally's military capacity, controlling the production and distribution of narcotics, maintaining important seaways and air routes, environmental treaties and compacts, and other long-term national objectives.

- *Economic*   Foreign aid develops markets for U.S. products and services. With an American presence and with the direct acquisition of U.S. goods to support development projects, a nation develops a propensity to look to American technology and expertise. In addition, increased standards of living generate greater demand, thereby increasing international trade.

- *Cultural and Political*   Foreign aid exports American ideas and values and in particular promotes free trade and political democratization. Technical assistance is often aimed at institutional reform, democratization, and the development of an open society.

- *Humanitarian*   Foreign aid seeks to relieve human suffering as a result of natural disaster, famine, war, or other calamity. It also seeks to promote economic growth so as to promote sustainable development of a society's capacity to meet basic human needs.

With the declining support of American taxpayers, the United States will be less than fully capable of leading the world in resolving the many development challenges of the new millennium: the opportunity to create prosperity and democracy in Russia and the Commonwealth of Independent States; the chance to bring long-term growth to Africa; the continued inequities facing women and children in the developing world; stabilization of world population; and, the critical importance of reversing environmental degradation. These important challenges may be confronted by multilateral banks that represent no single nation and NGOs that represent a particular issue or cause.

As globalization proceeds, international markets become more integrated and the flow of money, ideas, and technology accelerates; this adds to economic development. Private foreign investment far exceeds official foreign assistance and multilateral lending. The next wave of economic development may be linked to *trade, not aid.*

The technocratic approach to development has the following themes and implications:

- High levels of technical and economic expertise are needed to implement the policies and carry out the programs requisite for economic development.

- Development requires new capital for investment in infrastructure, human capital, technology, and the management of debt.

■ Sustained growth requires responsible and supportive state policies, including a balanced domestic budget and a free and fully exchangeable currency.

■ Growth is dependent upon free trade and an export economy.

■ Governments have a responsibility to invest in human capital, infrastructure, environmental management, and basic human needs.

■ Open institutions and human development are legitimate and desirable goals in international economic investment.

■ Nations should exercise their comparative advantage in achieving market share.

■ Failure to manage state spending, large deficits, excessive borrowing, and monetary expansion threaten development by fostering inflation, overvaluation of currency, and the loss of export competitiveness.

■ Globalization will bring new foreign investment as markets integrate, thereby fueling economic growth.

■ The elimination of absolute poverty remains the central goal of international development.

# Conclusion

With a worldwide shift toward more conservative governments, the continuing integration of the global economy, and the conditional loan requirements of the multilateral banks, it is clear that, for the near future, international economic development in the LDCs will be dominated by the free market, open society perspective of the western democratic countries. The challenge for this strategy will be to assure sufficient equity so as to provide for basic human needs and to fully integrate marginalized groups into the development process. Development must also produce sufficient economic growth to compensate for the planet's burgeoning population without pushing the natural ecosystem beyond its fragile carrying capacity.

## REFERENCES

Birdsall, N., and E. James. (1993). "Efficiency and Equity in Social Spending: How and Why Governments Misbehave." In M. Lipton and J. Van Der Gaag (Eds.), *Including the Poor* (Washington DC: The World Bank), pp. 335–358.

Borlaug, N. (1987). "Making Institutions Work—A Scientist's Perspective." In W. E. Jordan (Ed.), *Water and Water Policy in World Food Supplies* (College Station: Texas A&M University Press), pp. 387–395.

Chilicote, R. C. (1984). *Theories of Development and Underdevelopment* (Boulder: Westview).

Cowan, L. G. (1987). "A Global Overview of Privatization." In S. H. Hanke (Ed.), *Privatization and Development.* (San Francisco: International Center for Economic Growth), pp. 7–16.

Daly, H. E., and J. B. Cobb. (1989). *For the Common Good: Redirecting the Economy Toward Community, the Environment, and a Sustainable Future* (Boston: Beacon Books).

de Soto, H. (1987). *El Otro Sendero: La Revolución Informal. (The Other Path: An Informal Revolution)* (Lima, Peru: Instituto Libertad y Democracia).

de Soto, H. (1996). "The Missing Ingredient: What Poor Countries Will Need to Make Their Markets Work." In T. L. Anderson and P. J. Hill (Eds.), *The Privatization Process: A World Wide Perspective.* (London: Rowman & Littlefield), pp. 19–24.

Driscoll, D. D. (1995). *What Is the International Monetary Fund?* (Washington DC: The International Monetary Fund).

Durkheim, E. (1965). *The Division of Labor in Society* (New York: The Free Press). (Original work published in 1893.)

"Emerging Market Indicators." (1997, September 20). *The Economist,* p. 116.

Fanon, F. (1963). *The Wretched of the Earth* (New York: Grove Press).

Foster, G. M. (1973). *Traditional Societies and Technological Change* (New York: Harper and Row).

Frank, A. G. (1967). *Capitalism and Underdevelopment in Latin America* (New York: Monthly Review Press).

Gallagher, M. (1991). *Rent-Seeking and Economic Growth in Africa* (Boulder: Westview Press).

George, S., and F. Sabelli. (1994). *Faith and Credit: The World Bank's Secular Empire* (Boulder: Westview Press).

Harrison, L. E. (1985). *Underdevelopment Is a State of Mind: The Latin American Case* (Lanham, MD: University Press of America).

Harrod, R. (1939). "An Essay in Dynamic Theory." *Economic Journal,* March.

Hettne, B. (1995). *Development Theory and the Three Worlds* (Essex: Longman Scientific and Technical).

Holden, P. and S. Rajapatirana. (1995). *Unshackling the Private Sector: A Latin American Story.* (Washington, DC: The World Bank).

Hunt. D. (1989). *Economic Theories of Development: An Analysis of Competing Paradigms* (Savage, MD: Barnes and Noble).

"Income Distribution." (1997, September 20). *The Economist,* p. 116.

Janicke, M. (1990). *State Failure: The Impotence of Politics in Industrial Society* (University Park: Pennsylvania State University Press).

Klitgaard, R. (1990). *Tropical Gangsters: One Man's Experience with Development and Decadence in Deepest Africa.* (New York: Basic Books).

Knott, J. H. and G. J. Miller. (1987). *Reforming Bureaucracy: The Politics of Institutional Choice* (Englewood Cliffs, NJ: Prentice-Hall).

Kuznets, S. (1955). "Economic Growth and Income Inequality," *American Economic Review* 45, 1–28.

Lieberman, I. W. and S. Rahuja. (1995). "An Overview of Privatization in Russia." In I. W. Lieberman et al., (Eds.). *Russia: Creating Private Enterprises and Efficient Markets* (Washington DC: The World Bank), pp. 7–33.

Mamen, K. J. (1990, February 8). "Toward a New Growth Strategy." *Indian Express.* Ahmedabad, India, p. 8.

Mariátegui, J. C. (1972). *Seven Interpretive Essays on Peruvian Reality* (Austin: University of Texas Press). (Original work published 1924.)

Mason, E. S., and R. E. Asher. (1973). *The World Bank Since Bretton Woods* (Washington DC: The Brookings Institution).

McClelland, D. C. (1960). *The Achieving Society* (New York: John Wiley & Sons).

McCormack, R. T. (1984). *The Bretton Woods Legacy: Its Continuing Relevance* (Washington DC: U.S. Department of State).

Memet, O. (1995). *Westernizing the Third World: The Eurocentricity of Economic Development Theories* (London: Routledge).

Poole, R. W. (1995) "Privatization for Economic Development." In T. L. Anderson & P. J. Hill (Eds.), *The Privatization Process: A Worldwide Perspective.* (London: Rowman & Littlefield), pp. 1–18.

Prebisch, R. (1984). "Five Stages in My Thinking on Development." In G. M. Meier & D. Seers (Eds.), *Pioneers in Development* (London: Oxford University Press), pp. 175–191.

Rich, B. (1994a). "World Bank/IMF: 50 Years Is Enough." In K. Danaher (Ed.). *50 Years Is Enough: The case Against The World Bank and the International Monetary Fund.* (Boston: South End Press), pp. 6–13.

Rich, B. (1994b). *Mortgaging the Earth: The World Bank, Environmental Impoverishment, and the Crisis of Development* (Boston: Beacon Press).

Rostow, W. (1960). *The Stages of Economic Growth* (London: Cambridge University Press).

Schumpeter, J. (1961). *The Theory of Economic Development* (London: Oxford University Press). (Original work published in 1911.)

Selowsky, M. (1979). *Balancing Trickle Down with Basic Needs Strategies: Income Distribution Issues in Large Middle-Income Countries with Special Reference to Latin America* (Washington, DC: The World Bank).

Solow, R. (1956). "A Contribution to the Theory of Economic Growth." *Quarterly Journal of Economics* 70, pp. 65–94.

Summers, L. (1997). "1996 Was a Year Consumed Less by Policy Than by Politics and Cardiology," *Transition* 8 (1), pp. 5–6.

Todaro, M. (1997). *Economic Development,* 5th ed. (New York: Longman).

United Nations (1996). *Human Development Report 1996.* (New York: Oxford University Press).

USAID. (1997). "About the United States Agency for International Development." [On-line], Available: www.usaid.gov/about/

"The Visible Hand." (September 20–26, 1997). *The Economist,* pp. 17–18.

"The World Economy." (September 20–26, 1997). *The Economist,* pp. 5–48.

Weber, M. (1958). *The Protestant Ethic and the Spirit of Capitalism.* (New York: Charles Scribner's Sons). (Original work published 1921.)

Webster, A. (1990). *Introduction to the Sociology of Development,* 2nd ed. (London: Macmillan).

World Bank (1991). *The Challenge of Development: World Development Report 1991* (New York: Oxford University Press).

World Bank (1995). *Social Development Indicators 1995* (Baltimore: The Johns Hopkins University Press).

World Bank (1996). *From Plan to Market: World Development Report 1996* (New York: Oxford University Press).

World Bank (1997). *The State in a Changing World: World Development Report 1997* (New York: Oxford University Press).

# 7 Community Development

> ...No theory emanating from the high-technology wo,·ld, whether capitalist or
> Marxist in bias, is going to solve the problems of the "developing world"...
> Tomorrow's "development" strategies will come not from Washington or
> Moscow...but from Africa, Asia, and Latin America. They will be
> indigenous...They will not imitate any outside model [but will provide]
> ...wholly new opportunities.

So predicted Alvin Toffler in *The Third Wave* nearly two decades ago. If his projected vision was accurate, he will have to wait a bit longer to see it come to pass. The developing world of which he wrote in 1980 was caught between the competing systems of Western-style capitalism and Soviet-style socialism, a competition that seemed destined to continue for many more years. No one anywhere imagined that the system dominated by the Soviet Union would start to crumble within less than 10 years and that the Soviet Union itself would collapse, leaving no major examples outside China. Nor could anyone have guessed that China herself soon would embrace a modified form of capitalism.

Toffler was writing at a time when the concept of development itself was undergoing extensive review and revision. There had been an explosion of literature describing and discussing "community development," beginning in the 1960s, growing into the 1970s, followed by a steady decline. It was as though the idea of "community" could not survive the powerful centripetal pressures of capitalist concentration on the one hand or socialist central planning on the other. It was just as the popularity of community development was fading that the pressures of the centrally planned economy switched from centripetal to centrifugal and the Soviet Union flew apart. One consequence of the sudden change was the renewed sense of viability for development to take place at the community level.

## Problems of Definition

The concept of "community" is very old, but not necessarily one on which there is consistent agreement. Christenson (1989) observed that the word "community" derives from the Greek word for "fellowship," indicating some sort of close bond as a necessary condition for a community to exist. However, the basis for this bond may vary widely. It may seem primarily geographical, with physical boundaries, such as a neighborhood; or political, wherein the geographical, physical boundaries denote a specific political entity such as a village. Or it may be closer to the original Greek meaning, indicating a bond of common interests, such as a discipline, familiar in the term "community of scholars." The net may reach even wider, according to Gittell (1980), who includes "ethnicity," "class," and "issue" as providing boundaries for communities. In any case, community stands for more than just "group" or a mere aggregate of individuals; it always implies a set of common interests, which may be economic, religious, political, educational, social, or any of the other characteristic concerns that distinguish human society. As Van Til (1988) observed, communities existed to deal with human needs long before governments did—indeed, before modern governments were created. It has always been the collective identity or the sharing of concerns that fuse individuals into communities in the developmental sense.

"Community development" embodies the concept that collectivities of people who share common concerns have the potential capacity to deal jointly with those concerns in ways that advance the common interest. In this sense, the term "community development" is almost the antithesis of "rugged individualism," which places the burden of advancement on the individual and also reserves the rewards of such efforts for individuals. At its root, community development is social rather than personal, collective rather than singular. However, the scale of the collectivity that forms the community may be small enough to provide for distinctive personal concerns, as well.

It is generally agreed that community development includes social development, but that they are not the same. As Chekki (1979: 8) noted, they are distinct from each other, but "there is no clear-cut division" between them. In fact, the precise nature of community development is elusive; it is a complex idea, which Chekki describes as a method, a program, a movement, a process of change, and the preparation for change.

The characteristics of community development identified by Chekki echo earlier attempts by Sanders (1970) to encompass the many nuances of community development into a comprehensive definition. He called it a process, method, program, and movement. As a process, Sanders asserted, community development (CD) moves decision making from elites to whole populations; as a method, it is a set of procedures for reaching an agreed goal; as a program, it is a specific plan through which the method operates; and as a movement, it is a moral crusade. Of these four facets of CD described by Sanders, the fourth was closest to the one adopted by the United Nations, which conceived of CD as a program of techniques.

One of the most ambitious attempts to pin down the exact nature of CD was undertaken by Christenson (1989). Reviewing the literature from the preceding two decades, he listed ten different definitions from ten different sources and then added partial definitions from several others. His review led him to the conclusion reached nearly twenty years earlier by Sanders—namely, that community development is a process, method, program, and movement. Moreover, he agreed with the Sanders interpretations in which these four elements differed. All but the fourth or "movement" sense were seen as being "neutral." "Process" seemed to suggest an essential democratization of decision making; "method" comprised process, plus particular objectives; "program" resulted from method plus content, which in the Sanders discussion referred to special types of goals, such as economic, political or social. As a "movement," community development lost its "neutrality," taking on an "emotional dynamic," becoming a philosophical rather than a scientific concept.

Perhaps it is in the attempts to distinguish between the "scientific" or "neutral" aspects of community development and those that are "emotional" or "philosophical" that disagreement, or at least confusion, is most likely to arise. The implication is that these are distinct and separate aspects of community development. However, consistent in all common definitions of CD is the idea of change, what Cary (1970) called deliberate joint activity to alter the future of the community. Sanders called it a way to bring about change. In his review of definitions, Christenson (1989) skirted around this idea, using terms such as "improvement" and "growth" rather than "change," but they are terms in which the idea of change is embedded. Even his attempts to assess the interpretations of various disciplines seemed to lead him to the same conclusion. Sociologists, he noted, saw CD as "adaptation"; anthropologists saw it as "cultural modification"; economists as "transformation"; historians as "evolution"; and so on, all of which could be termed kinds of change. Ultimately, he also seemed to end up with the idea of "change" as the essential ingredient in CD.

If it is conceded that change in an inherent part of CD, whether its basic essence is process, method, or program, it does not seem feasible to avoid the emotional or, more accurately, the subjective aspect of it. Change, after all, is never intended to be random; it always is intended to move toward and to achieve some goal, so that it would seem always to contain a subjective element.

Warren (1988) went even farther along this road. He argued that the goal of CD always had to do with resource distribution and always in the direction of adequacy, efficiency, and/or distributional equity. This seemed to represent a movement toward greater specificity than his much earlier position that "there is no simple recipe or formula for community development" (1970). While adequacy, efficiency, and equity scarcely constitute a "simple formula," they do represent a clearer formulation of purpose for CD activity than Warren's cautious claim, made at the same time as the "no simple recipe or formula" statement, that "many of the most vital problems communities face are not resolvable at the community level" (1970: 50). After all, it seemed to be precisely because of the belief that problems can be solved at the community level that people were impelled to engage in CD and to endorse it so vigorously during the 1960s and 1970s. At the beginning of this period of focus on CD as a viable enterprise, Cary (1970) argued that CD required deliberate and joint activity using identified techniques to "guide" the future.

That the fundamental element in community development is change and that the intended change is always in a consciously chosen direction would indicate that CD is not so much a "neutral" or "scientific" activity as it is a political one. As such, it might well include particular techniques, processes, and methods that themselves are neutral, but which never are used in a completely "neutral" context. In a sense, this perception of CD is similar to the celebrated Clausewitz description of war as an extension of diplomacy by other means. The methods and techniques of CD may be inherently neutral, but they have little meaning outside of their application, and their application always has political implications.

When the concept of change is seen as an essential element in community development and change is seen as essentially political in nature, discussions of models of CD make more sense than they do when it is stripped of its activist, change-related nature, as though trying to conceive of it as an abstract scientific exercise, such as observing the interaction of microbes or finding the properties of steel.

# Historical Background

As noted, the idea of "community" is ancient; "community development" is almost as old. Virtually all peasant societies created some form of institution for mutual protection and economic enhancement. They were often based, according to Fafchamps (1992), on the right to subsistence, and they employed the principle of reciprocity. These "elaborate mutual insurance networks" provided the foundation of collective activities for economic and social betterment, since they reduced the individual risk of starvation or lack of other basic human needs. They were not generally provided by law, but they represented the acceptance of mutual obligation that made survival of the community the paramount concern, and community survival provided the best assurance for the survival of the individual.

Some very early forms of community development grew out of religious activities. The kinds of religious activities that brought together Latin American and some North American Indian tribes into communities that worked together in projects of mutual assistance are discussed elsewhere. These were legitimate examples of community development with tribes in specific geographic regions. The Roman Catholic religious leaders of these activities were themselves members of "religious communities" that were identified and bonded to each other by mutual beliefs rather than geographical boundaries. Cosio (1981) described some of these early movements, including the work of Vasco de Quiroga, who organized the Tarascan Indians in 1535 for the purpose of "integral development and understanding." Cosio noted that the economic vestiges of this 450+-year-old example of successful CD are still apparent.

The church's early CD activities were also described by Zimmerman (1994), who argued that in Roman Catholic countries, the government ceded the social function of charitable activity to the church. He distinguished this environment from that in Protestant countries, where such responsibilities, particularly health and education, became secularized and were taken over by community groups. This is one reason, he asserted, why private, secular social agencies so frequently have religious origins. An especially interesting example is the creation of the United Way "prototype," which was formed in 1887 by a Protestant minister, two Roman Catholic priests, and a Jew. Additional examples of late nineteenth-century community development activities were given by Davis (1994), who described the founding of settlement houses as one such instance, but also pointed to the creation of workers' affordable housing by unions, philanthropists, and religious groups. An even broader historical interpretation was provided by Wileden (1970), who saw the history of community development as a procession of all the late nineteenth-century social betterment movements; not only settlement houses and worker housing were involved, but even playground and recreation movements, neighborhood school-centered community centers, and federations of social agencies.

Community development in the later twentieth century became a post–World War II strategy for rebuilding devastated areas, but even more, a strategy for helping "less developed" or "undeveloped" (now: "developing") countries, particularly those emerging from colonial status, to achieve self-sufficiency and political stability. The same strategy was found useful when applied to the "developing" areas within major industrial powers, including the United States. The War on Poverty of the mid-1960s included massive CD programs in Appalachia and similarly afflicted areas of the country.

By the late 1960s, CD had reached the peak of its popularity, but it already was being replaced by the idea of "national planning," and within ten years, was being redefined as "participatory development" in a variety of guises. In the United States, a combination of factors led to the decline of CD as a strategy of choice. Having provided a focus on the community as the unit for development, and having funded assorted CD initiatives, the federal government found itself faced by organizations with goals quite outside the original intent of the programs. Black leadership coalesced around the issue of civil rights for black Americans, a movement supported by large numbers of middle-class whites. The success of the civil rights movement may have provided the impetus, in turn, for the organization of various feminist groups who demanded equal rights for women. What originally had been conceived as a community-based program of self-help for economic betterment of poor Americans ballooned into a major movement for vast social and political reforms. In this transition, the assumed "objective" or "scientific" view of community development inevitably ran headlong into its "subjective" or "moral" manifestations. The civil rights movement led to numerous successes, but the economic objectives were less effectively achieved, and disappointment led to decline.

By the 1980s, there arose a new emphasis on the role of the private sector in development with a parallel loss of emphasis on community development. It was a case in which success had been achieved in unexpected areas, but not in target areas, which led to a loss of faith on the part of those who did not succeed and a loss of drive on the part of those who did. That is, the failure of community development to bring any significant improvement in the economic well-being of poor people led to a decline of interest in it as a useful approach, among both the poor and their middle-class champions; conversely, the success of community development in achieving a greater degree of parity for blacks and for women was followed by organizational atrophy. Within twenty years, a whole generation of black Americans had grown up without any firsthand experience with truly ruthless discrimination, and women had made significant legal and economic strides. Many among the new generation found little reason to undertake the risks and privations of organization and became content with the satisfactions of rhetoric.

Elsewhere in the world, communities continued trying to deal with what Warren (1970) called "the great change"—a combination of population growth; industrialization; urbanization; growth of large-scale organizations; and perhaps most important for CD, the replacement of informal associations with large formal organizations, leading to a decline of "locality" as the basis for association and organization. However, just as CD was entering a decline in the United States, it was emerging as a potent force in some socialist countries. The growth of these community-based and issue-based organizations there was largely overlooked while they proliferated in the late 1970s, especially in central/eastern Europe. By the end of the 1980s, they had become a major organizational base for the revolutions of 1989 (Starr, 1991). For example, in Hungary, two kinds of community development groups arose—one (SZETA) to seek pathways for direct action on poverty and the other (LARES) to find ways to provide services not available from the state. The first group operated underground until 1989; the other was tolerated by the government, eventually breaking the state monopoly in a vital area of human concern (Hegyesi, 1997). By the time of the political crises of 1989, it was too late for the state to take effective action against these grassroots organizations.

The political and social success of community development activities in the old Warsaw Pact countries assured CD of new opportunities there. In Asia and Africa, where oppressive political regimes proved unable to halt the hemorrhaging of their economies, development moved back to the community level as a simple matter of peoples' survival. Where the industrial countries had endorsed a vague kind of "social development" in these countries, community development began addressing economic issues of daily life, rather than more abstract issues of political equality. By the end of the 1990s, community development was beginning to experience a possible rebirth, albeit in new forms and with changed rationales. However, even in the its newer manifestations, the basic CD elements can be identified.

# Basic Elements

Although it should be clear that community-based development is basically political activity, it is nevertheless the case that it also has a moral component. The basic elements that comprise CD tend to fall into two broad categories: philosophical and structural. The philosophical category includes values, such ideas as equity, hope, will, improvement, loyalty, care, progress and social justice. The structural category includes organization, including leadership, planning, staffing, management, strategy, and resource allocation. The philosophical elements tend to be what Brandt and Lee (1981) referred to as "intangible qualities" that provide cohesion and purpose. These are qualities that impel people to act on behalf of the group or to further abstract principles and involve considerations such as a loyalty and obligation, as well as fear of censure and ostracism. Other factors that influence the conditions under which community development can proceed are recognition of status and legitimacy.

Since the heart of CD is the ability of collections of people to act in the interests of the group while forgoing their personal gain in favor of a principled gain, the philosophical aspects of the community are in certain respects more significant than the structural aspects. Without agreement on the philosophical issues, the organization, as such, is irrelevant. This agreement may exist only on a fairly abstract level, but it must exist somewhere for any CD operation to achieve long-term success. It is the philosophical issues that act as the cement molding a collection of individuals into a community and transforming an assortment of personal interests into a collective goal. If that cohesion disappears, the community ceases to be a community and reverts to being a mere collection of individuals. Doing good for others in order to give yourself pleasure is "sympathy," according to Douglas (1983), who also defined "commitment" as doing good that does no good for you and may even harm you. Both sympathy and commitment are involved in community development, but so may be self-interest. What sets CD apart from simple acquisitiveness or self-indulgence is the overriding concern for the group or of the group for a principle; a compelling feeling of mutual obligation that would appear to be more than either sympathy or commitment.

However, the philosophical aspects of community development are rarely sufficient to assure any measure of success in achieving community goals of development. While they may provide the legitimation for the intended change, there must be a mechanism that permits movement from intention to operation. That mechanism is structure. Structure is what moves the philosophical belief or goal from the realm of the abstract into the realm of the tangible, and transforms intention into action.

Structure implies organization, and organization requires leadership. Possibly the most crucial factor in developing an effective organization is able leadership, and for community development, the optimal leadership is usually considered to be local. As noted in the chapter on missionaries, it was the failure to identify, train, and promote local leadership that proved the fatal flaw in the Spanish mission system. However, local leadership can be effective only to the extent that it actually reflects the local will; as Smillie (1991) expressed it, the organization is always an extension of the values of community it represents.

Initially, the major responsibility of the leadership is to build a viable organization through which the objectives of the community can be pursued. The organization requires staffing with people who have the skills and knowledge to identify the critical issues, engage in long-range planning, guide short-term strategy, provide convenient avenues for expression of community desires, and ensure a mechanism for ongoing evaluation, correction, and renewal. Long-range planning, as Wileden (1970) observed, should ensure the diversity and innovation that flows from group involvement, and involvement of the group, in turn, increases the likelihood of subsequent support for decisions made by the leadership. A central function of the organization is to resolve disagreements and to provide for coordination of efforts. Since community development groups may grow to a large size and involve many different activities around different issues, coordination is essential in order to avoid duplication—or worse, mutual cancellation of particular actions. In fact, community development organizations may begin around specific, relatively local issues, but if successful, they tend to expand the range and scope of their interests, sometimes moving far from the original issues and objectives, as happened in the 1960s.

Leadership style is another important element in CD organization. When maximum feasible participation is encouraged, the benefits reach beyond support for subsequent decisions. The participation itself is instructive, helping the group members learn skills in political influence, planning, lobbying, debate, and other aspects of CD activity. Regular evaluation is essential in assuring that the goals of the various activities remain clear and consistent with the members' wishes and that those activities are the most effective in any particular situation, time, or place. Such a system of evaluation invites steady input from many sources. It requires strong leadership to assure the steady flow of information and opinion that can be used to advance the effectiveness and interests of the community, but also because evaluation is a device that may be used to depose any particular leader. Thus, the leadership must be alert to efforts to use supposedly objective evaluation as a device for undercutting legitimate leadership.

On the other hand, while the leadership must reflect local interests and values, it must be able to marshal community resources in ways that promote and benefit the community's overall developmental agenda rather than primarily the interests of indigenous powers. As was pointed out by Dore (1981: 31), local decisions may reflect local power structures more than they do the good of the community, so it is important to avoid the kind of collaboration that "can be a recipe for rule by local bosses." For this reason, leadership cannot merely invite local participation; it must assure that such participation is appropriate and consistent with the overall CD objectives. Where the understandings and skills for development and evaluation are not present, they need to be taught. Community development, Mushi (1981) observed, cannot progress any faster than the knowledge and skills in the community or the ability of the community members to learn them.

The leadership and structure of the CD organization also reflects the basic functions needed, and these may change with time. Christenson (1989) identified them as: facilitator/educator, advisor/consultant and organizer/advocate. More on them later.

# Models

Three models of community development were identified by Mushi (1981), comprising the liberal-incremental, revolutionary-change, and guided evolutionary. These CD models seem to fit well with Christenson's three types of leadership or CD "themes." The Mushi models reflect the general orientation of the society in which they are most likely to be found.

What he called the "liberal-incremental" model is "rooted in the basic values of Western liberal democracy" (p. 105). This kind of CD requires strong but flexible leadership in stable organizations to assure that any successes reach the general populace. It also requires a strong faith in the political system, so that innovation that sometimes leads to failure is not discouraged. However, it also requires strong faith in the group and the process rather than reliance on government intervention (although targeted government intervention may be one of the goals). A major problem in this model is its vulnerability to concentration of benefits at the top, since a primary goal may be a focus on economic growth without a parallel focus on fair distribution of the fruits of that growth.

The kinds of CD activities found in socialist countries have tended to reflect the revolutionary-change model. While liberal democracies seek change within the system, this model seeks fundamental change of the system, with the state taking leadership in bringing such change about. In this model, the leadership is less likely to emerge from the community than to be determined by central authority. It has the virtue of being able to focus on specific goals and to prevent deflection from them. A major problem with this model is that the organization created to confront the existing elites is likely to develop its own cadre of elites, who are answerable to the central authority rather than the community.

The guided evolutionary model may be something of a compromise between the other two. Rather than seeking changes whose benefits can be monopolized by the leadership of the organization, or change that is directed by only by the leadership, to the possible exclusion of the community interests, this model seeks a measured improvement at a pace consistent with the equitable distribution of the benefits of the change. It requires neither the entrepreurship of the liberal-incremental model, nor the potential for upheaval in the revolutionary-change model, but rather change is sought at a speed that permits the improvements to be shared fairly, whether they are economic, political, social, or other types of benefits.

Examples abound in cases in which economic change is the objective, but they can be found in the other types, as well. For example, community development projects that seek social justice for women may resemble any of these categories. In the first, the benefits initially may be general for all women, but with special benefits for the leadership, which then is able to exploit those with less power. Scandals, such as those involving "liberal" feminist leaders who employ immigrant women "under the table" for domestic labor without providing fair salaries or unemployment insurance and other routine benefits, illustrate a type of CD that may mitigate the oppression of women in general terms, but reserve the major benefits for the few at the top. Objections to this sort of exploitation are dismissed by the leadership as attacks on the movement itself.

The kind of control exercised by the centrally named leadership in the second model may simply replace entrepreneural exploitation with officially sanctioned exploitation. Scandals rampant in socialist countries concerning the creation of "the new class" of government bureaucrats who enjoy the benefits formerly reserved for the social elite furnish extensive documentation for the perils of this model. Moreover, even where this model is used in a democratic society, there may be prolonged tension regarding general expectations with respect to the actual implementation of the achievements of the CD action. An example is the struggle to achieve civil rights for African Americans. As the civil rights movement succeeded and community leadership was supplanted by governmental bureaucracies set up to interpret and enforce the successes of the CD actions, the lofty goals of fellowship that had originally animated the movement tended to degenerate into endless squabbles over preferences and priorities. Government rigidity in enforcement ultimately led to a substantial backlash that caused a certain amount of retreat from the original objectives.

Mushi's guided evolutionary model is described as a way in which to get the benefits of the other two while reducing their costs. It is intended to provide for a balance between state and local initiative, with compromise rather than either overthrow or complete accommodation as the expected outcome. Unfortunately, this arrangement tends not to be stable and may result in opportunism by the elites with either overt or tacit concurrence of the state. Avoiding the stateless, personalized liberalism of the first model and the state-sponsored, controlled change of the second does not assure an organization that is either more equitable or more efficient.

In summary, Mushi's models are interesting and useful, but none seems entirely satisfactory in providing an understanding of community development organization that is both efficient and fair. Perhaps the models are captives of the time that produced them, in which community development often was conceived as dramatic organization of or by the urban oppressed or the rural victims of capitalist abuse. Or perhaps, as Sanders (1979) claimed, no general theory leading to a consistent CD model is really possible; rather, certain principles of community development can eventuate as a wide range of models, sometimes unique to the community or region.

Attempts to identify some of these basic principles have taken the form of descriptions of how CD progresses (the process and method perspectives), how it is organized (the program perspective), and how it arouses strong emotional reactions (the movement perspective). Each has its eloquent spokespersons.

One of the early examples was a description of "phases" of community development, taken from observations of programs under the 1960s "War on Poverty." In this example, Weissman (1969) postulated four phases through which a CD passes. The first related to creating an organization and cementing useful affiliations; the second, identifying key issues and goals; and the third, evaluation and making necessary adjustments in goals, structure, personnel, and direction. The fourth phase was to institutionalize the gains achieved from the process of community development.

About the same time, Schler (1970) developed a similar series of steps, calling them "stages" in community development. He applied these four steps to three different CD "dimensions," namely, the "procedural," the "content," and the "human interaction" dimensions. In Schler's approach, the four stages are the same within each dimension, although its application varies from one to the other. The four stages resemble those of Weissman in several respects. They include resource organization, engagement of resources with the community, activation of the organization, and operation of the system. Hence, the "procedural dimension" passes through the four stages listed, as do the content and human interaction dimensions.

Schler also claimed that there were five "basic change tendencies" in community development. Schler's five basic change tendencies are interesting for their similarity to those identified by Sanders (1970) at about the same time. Schler called them tendencies toward goal setting, self-help, democratization, rational decision making, and "concerted decision making and action system." What Schler called "tendencies," Sanders called "principles." The principles identified by Sanders were somewhat more complex, but covered much of the same ground found in Schler, except that all of them were related to change, specifically. They included the ideas that change is necessary for survival, may be brought about in assorted ways, is tridimensional, requires special knowledge and skills, and requires some manner of imbalance to be brought about.

From these examples, it is obvious that CD has been seen as a systematic, manageable process that can be taught and learned as basic, underlying principles and applicable, predictable procedures. This perspective fits well with Christenson's three types of leadership mentioned earlier. Weissman's "phases," Schler's "tendencies," and Sanders's "principles" imply different functions for CD leadership, which Christenson called "themes." The themes he identified were "self-help," "conflict," and "technical assistance." The differences in these themes denote different requirements for leadership, already listed: educator, consultant, or advocate. What distinguishes the Christenson "themes" from the other approaches discussed is the nature of his application. Not all communities or organizations need the same kind of leadership, he held, and the kind of leadership not only was related to the goals and objectives of the activity, it also tended to vary by class. In his interpretation, self-help is seen as largely a middle-class activity, while conflict is identified with the "poor" and with "minorities". This interpretation is consistent with the time context in which it was made; CD movement activities varied, from the work of middle-class liberal efforts to help people gain the skills to advance themselves, to more confrontational tactics favored in the movements that demanded immediate changes that involved massive redistribution of society's resources. The former approach favored an incremental amelioration of living conditions, by way of self-improvement within the existing system; the latter insisted on instantaneous modification of conditions by upending the existing system.

One issue not addressed by Christenson, nor by the other discussions of leadership, was the difficulty of sustaining group participation. The popular proposition that maximum group participation strengthens cohesion and collaboration is not necessarily true. In her studies of citizen participation movements, Gittell (1980: 243) found that organizations actually do not express much faith in the idea of "internal democracy" and that "the potential for effective participation was [found to be] less real than a majority of the organizations perceived it to be." The type of leadership needed and the likelihood of effective member activity in all phases of the movement might be related to a great extent to the goals and ultimate objectives of the movement. A key factor in effective participation may be the degree to which the outcome has personal benefits for the participants. Female members of a community seeking equal job opportunities for women, and disenfranchised members of a community seeking a role for themselves in government may require different sorts of leadership and may participate with levels of commitment and passion different from those of a community development movement by middle-class people to improve child welfare services for the poor.

Since the collapse of world socialism, community development models and activities seem to have entered a new era, with CD activities centered on nongovernmental organizations (NGO) and Third Sector groups. This will require a revision in the thinking about leadership, organization, and mission of CD, as well as the relationship of such organizations and activities to the government.

As might be expected, the relationships of governments to the many different models of CD vary considerably, as do government responses to the goals and objectives of the movements and government relationships to the agencies through which CD takes place. Similarly, the impact of government on the change that is sought by the activists may range from active support to general indifference. CD movements may be suppressed by direct government intervention, defanged by tolerant detachment until the activists tire and give up, or co-opted by allowing harmless dissent and, then, recruitment of the dissenters so that they become functionaries of the institutions and organizations they initially sought to change.

## Venues of Community Development

Community development often has been construed as a movement detached from the established institutions of society, except the church. There is, of course, a long history of church involvement in CD activities, although that involvement appears to be manifest in different styles. Different missionary styles are discussed elsewhere, but they bear some semblance to the differences in community development.

At the height of the CD movement of the 1960s, Coughlin (1965) described what he saw as the differences in styles. A priest himself, he claimed that Roman Catholics preferred direct involvement in shaping both society and individuals, with government support for these efforts; Protestants sought less direct personal participation in improving society, in favor of working primarily to motivate individuals to take responsibility for themselves and for the achievement of CD objectives. In both cases, the church would have an active leadership role as the bearer of the moral standards of society. Jews could be expected to be wary of direct religious authority in community development activities, opting for social involvement as an ethical responsibility in a secular society.

The black church in America has occupied a unique position. Although overwhelmingly Protestant, it has a long and distinguished history of direct and active involvement in community development, covering virtually the full spectrum of possibilities, from the creation of church-based service agencies and secular housing projects to strong activism in human rights struggles of many kinds. In many respects, the black church in America provides the quintessential example of successful community development. One of their most effective strategies has been to work with federal government agencies around specific efforts, such as housing for the poor elderly. The former secretary of Housing and Urban Development (HUD), Henry Cisneros (1996), described effective ways in which the black church has gained experience from its housing projects and applied it in other areas of economic and social development, such as the creation of senior centers, establishment of credit unions, and the training and encouragement of minority entrepreneurs, and then moved on to affiliations with other groups that allowed greater projects to be undertaken, such as the building of shopping centers and office buildings.

The critical position of religious organizations in CD activities is sometimes overlooked. The importance of this position is assured not only through indirect activity and moral support of religious organizations, but also through their direct financial support. As recently as ten years ago, American churches and synagogues were giving more money to charitable activities "than all American foundations and corporations combined" (O'Neill, 1989: 23). Thus, religious organizations can be seen as not only providing the moral and ethical (philosophical) justification for community development, but also being significant in the financial and organizational (structural) aspects, as well.

During the last two decades of the twentieth century, the involvement of universities, often at the forefront of CD movements through the 1960s and 70s, seemed to have declined, perhaps because of the perception that they have become dominated by agendas set by government (Levy, 1996) or corporate interests (Zimmerman, 1994) in their efforts to meet their allegedly relentlessly rising operating expenses. This decline in the role of universities has been noted even in areas (such as Latin America) where universities once were the primary centers of political ferment and economic change.

## The Third Sector

Growth in the Third Sector was phenomenal during the 1980s and 1990s, as was the interest in studying that sector and trying to understand it. This growth seemed to parallel the decline of community development as it was conceived at that time.

The "Third Sector" is a term at least as imprecise as is "community development." It is similar to nongovernmental organizations (NGOs), but not quite the same. Nonprofit agencies also may be found within the Third Sector, but they are not exclusive to it. To qualify for Third Sector designation, organizations must be both nongovernmental and nonprofit. Some NGOs may not be nonprofit and some nonprofits may not have the independence from government or the sorts of social change agendas typically identified with the Third Sector.

One difficulty in trying to articulate a clear and precise definition of the Third Sector is that it seems to be much more frequently and easily defined in terms of what it is not than what it is, resulting in a conceptual fuzziness or sense that one cannot be sure about the terms used when discussing it. An additional difficulty is that other common terms are often used interchangeably with Third Sector, including "independent" and "voluntary," and while they share key features with the Third Sector, their boundaries are not exactly the same.

Salamon and Anheir (1997) are among the most respected scholars of the Third Sector who have tried to craft a workable definition. After extensive research into the usage of the term, they concluded that the applied concepts tend to be "murky and imprecise." They even proposed abandoning the effort to find an institutional definition in favor of accepting an operational definition, a recommendation reminiscent of the earlier effort by Van Til (1988) to define the Third Sector in terms of its purposes and outcomes: to do what the other two sectors are doing badly or not doing at all. Unfortunately, such a definition does not answer an important question posed by O'Leary and Takashi (1995: 319); namely, why is it that the private and government sectors are considered either inadequate or unacceptable, or both, to accomplish what must be undertaken by the Third Sector? Finding no viable response, they dealt with the troubling definitional dilemma by concluding that there simply is "no widely accepted definition of [the] third sector."

The central features of the Third Sector that distinguish it from the others are what it is not; that is, unlike the First Sector (private, for-profit business), it is not driven by a profit orientation and a market mentality; and unlike the Second Sector (government), it does not have direct access to the public purse, nor to the vast authority residing in government police power to command resources or services. Therefore, it has to rely on philosophical and moral authority and such resources as it can attract without economic exploitation. These are not necessarily shortcomings, and in fact, may result in certain strengths important to community development. For one thing, the Third Sector is generally much more trusted by the people than either government or market forces (Smith, 1989). Government often is considered incompetent or inefficient, while private industry is understood to be more interested in extracting benefits from the community than adding benefits to it. Indeed, corporate interests themselves may trust the Third Sector more than they do the government, and government may trust the Third Sector more than it does corporate interests. Smith notes that even in time of war, Third Sector agencies have been able to provide services across borders that the nations cannot cross. During peacetime efforts of industrial governments to support community development initiatives in developing countries, Third Sector agencies have been the vehicles of choice for carrying out the work simply because governments of many developing countries cannot be trusted with the funds, which often are absorbed by corrupt or inept bureaucracies, or find their way into the offshore bank accounts of loyal government officials. In addition, the trust that all parties seem to place in Third Sector organizations permits them to fulfill a "mediating" function (Douglas, 1983), a service usually considered useful and important to all sides and one that comes at minimal cost and with minimal risk to any of the contending parties. Since Third Sector organizations are committed neither to preserving the status quo nor encouraging radical change, they may be described as "transformational" (Wallis and Dollery, 1995)—that is, skilled at promoting and assisting in the pursuit of new systems and changes in social and economic arrangements within the major values of the society in which they operate.

Third Sector agencies typically include religious organizations, including those involved in community development. According to O'Neill (1989, 20: 13), they comprise "the oldest, largest, and most generously supported component" of the Third Sector in the United States. The size of the sector itself is much more massive than is comprehended by most Americans. By 1986, the Third Sector "employed more civilians than the federal and fifty state governments combined"; a more recent estimate placed the number of Third

Sector employees at nearly three times the entire federal civilian workforce (Zimmerman, 1994).

Despite the independence that is vital to their success, Third Sector agencies, in their role as nonprivate and nonpublic agencies nevertheless receive large percentages of their incomes from government sources. Given the size of their operating budgets, the support figures involved are substantial. Taken collectively, their budgets in the United States alone exceed the budgets of all but a handful of industrial countries. In the United States, about 40 percent of their budgets is received from public sources (Salamon and Anheir: 1996); only 20 percent derives from private donations. The rest is raised through quasi-commercial (but nonprofit) operations, through provision of services that may not appear to have specific marketplace values but are esteemed by the society, such as education. In other countries, where the status of the Third Sector is less well-defined but growing rapidly, the rate of government support may be much higher. In Germany, for example, the government supplies from public funds almost 70 percent of the revenue of its Third Sector agencies (Salamon and Anheir, 1996); and between 1980 and 1990, these organizations accounted for one-ninth of all the new jobs created in Germany. In some central/eastern European countries, the growth is comparably rapid.

Third Sector services correspond with the general goals of community development, such as social justice, protection of the environment, and economic development; they also deal with more specific, narrow issues that tend to be secondary CD objectives, such as education, health services, and promotion of cultural affairs. In each case, the focus of the services is on general social goods rather than personal preferences. However, marked differences are apparent in the priorities of Third Sector activities, according to the countries in which they have taken place, and demonstrating the principle that community development should reflect the general social values and cultural traditions of the places in which they are found.

## Community Development Activities: Examples

By the end of the 1990s, the growth of the Third Sector, including nongovernmental agencies, was significant, and its participation in community development activities was apparent all over the world. In developing countries, it has tended to give priority to economic issues related to improving agricultural practices or moving toward a more industrial base for the economy. In industrial countries, it has sought to improve the economic status and quality of life of the most vulnerable populations. In the formerly socialist, now transitional economies, it has had to try to provide services formerly assured by the government, but largely lost in the transition to a market economy.

An example of how Third Sector agencies work through community development in a developing country can be seen in Gambia (Schneider, 1995). As reported by OECD, workers provide technical assistance to expedite at the community level the building of participation in the national Strategy for Poverty Alleviation. The objective is to extend education and communication in order to increase access of rural people to the national planning and implementation of the project. The intention is to involve local people throughout the project, from design to evaluation. Called "participatory development," it is seen as "a political and social process as much as an economic one," involving the use of workshops, popular theater, and interviews with small groups to determine how communities can help shape and derive benefit from the national antipoverty initiative. Another example from Africa is the network of craftsmen in Ghana who opened vehicle repair centers and later expanded into making spare parts, partly with consultation from the local university (Mytelka, 1993).

Schneider reported CD activities in Sri Lanka and Brazil. In Sri Lanka, the Sarvodaya movement seeks to build local groups with the capacity to advocate for themselves. The Sarvodaya representative lives in the local community, assisting with chores and helping local groups identify needs and potential leaders. The worker then helps the leaders build an organizational structure through which the villagers set up a development plan based on the ten basic needs they consider most important. As the plan progresses, the worker provides information for securing support funding from banks and government sources. As the community begins to produce a surplus, further planning is initiated and the Sarvodaya representative gradually withdraws.

Not all CD projects succeed; not all groups within a community benefit equally; and not all successes are in the areas where improvement was anticipated. In some programs in Sri Lanka, there has been general improvement, but traditional artisans have fared better than the rest (Winslow, 1996). In that case, it had been expected that modernization would create serious problems for local craftsmen, but as communication and access to outside markets developed, the traditional pottery of the region became a much-sought-after commodity, and local potters moved from subsistence living to merchant status.

The example from Brazil given by Schneider describes a project called PRO-RENDA, through which a German-Brazilian collaboration effort seeks to help farmers organize themselves into self-help groups for the purpose of raising their general standard of living. The process is typical: A representative of PRORENDA makes contact with the local community; helps groups to identify needs and goals; aids in establishment of priorities; remains available if needed in long-range planning; and encourages movement in measured, achievable steps until the project can progress with the community alone. This kind of collaboration of an organization from a major industrial country with a region or community in a developing country has grown rapidly in the past twenty years, with Latin American countries increasingly involved. In certain areas, such as research, independent policy centers may actually be replacing universities, which are considered to be too reliant on government support to be adequately objective (Levy, 1996). These centers have thrived and multiplied under democratic conditions and curiously, have been able to survive even under military rule. However, universities are far from disappearing from the CD scene. One example of university–community collaboration that succeeded (similar to the case in Ghana) is ANPEI, a consortium of small firms created with the assistance of the University of Sao Paulo for mutual support and research (Mytelka, 1993).

Early community development activities in Tanzania outlined by Mushi (1981) are instructive because they show how such work varied under succeeding regimes, through the colonial period, the nationalist movement, and the socialist period. Although his analysis did not extend into the 1980s, Mushi showed how activities are influenced by the dominant political system. He emphasized the importance of building self-confidence in locals who had become accustomed to taking orders. The setting of priorities showed the importance of securing basic human needs before serious major planning could be undertaken. In Tanzania, that meant concentrating on access to clean water before health and education schemes could be launched. It was typical of the hierarchical approach common to CD programs, in which priorities require attention to life essentials and then to life enhancement. Moreover, effective development requires that the priorities be influenced by practical fiscal considerations; what Bullard (1995: 89) called "the ability to achieve... objectives at a reasonable cost." His strategy for dealing with this matter, through his agency called TechnoServe, has been to work with farmers in developing countries by helping their analysis of needs and priorities, assessment of possibilities, development of an organization and pilot project and, if successful in those, in planning for long-range operations (after the departure of TechnoServe personnel).

In socialist countries, community development has been a monopoly of the state; however, well before the dramatic changes of 1989, independent programs were successfully underway throughout the Warsaw Pact countries, particularly those abutting the West. Development activities faced special problems under socialism. First, they dealt with issues that were officially nonexistent in centrally planned economies: inequality, poverty, inefficient production, and so on. Since such issues were officially nonexistent, any activity to correct them was considered subversive and, therefore, personally dangerous. The second problem was that Third Sector organizations could expect no help from the state, not only because they were considered at worst subversive and at best unnecessary, but because any need officially recognized by the state could be met only through state agencies. A third problem also related to support; since the agencies could expect no state support, they had to support themselves through fees and other money-raising devices. Such fees may be considered "profit," in which case, the offense to state policy was compounded. This problem was not as straightforward as it may seem, however. The reason is that the state could, and sometimes did, choose to overlook a small community development scheme and even disregard the income it derived from its services, but if the organization was successful and its income rose or the organization expanded, the strong likelihood existed that it would be nationalized. Once it had been taken over by the government, it no longer would exist as a Third Sector operation, since control would shift to the official state bureaucracy.

Despite the pitfalls and perils of being involved in Third Sector activity, there were many instances of its taking place in the years before 1989. In one view, the growth of what were essentially "underground" organizations (albeit sometimes overt) helped lead to the collapse of the socialist governments (Starr, 1991). The countries with centrally planned economies had abolished Third Sector agencies and replaced their characteristic horizontal organizational structures with vertical structures that functioned to pass orders from the top down. The spontaneous creation of Third Sector organizations within the socialist system, but separate from its command structure, provided the opportunities for training, systematic communications, regular meetings for planning, and the reform spirit that was evident in the downfall of the socialist governments.

Hegyesi (1997: 69) has described the community development activities of SZETA, the Fund for Assisting the Poor, in Hungary, a full decade before the end of socialism there. He called it as a "grassroots civil organization…whose members were involved in direct social work, though this activity [became] increasingly political." Technically not legal, SZETA sought to deal in an organized way with the poverty that didn't exist "officially," but was clear every day to the populace, especially to those without sufficient funds to survive. The organization also arranged summer vacations for children and documented the extent of deprivation in the country. By the end of 1981, its members had become involved in the Polish Solidarity movement to the extent that it was forced underground, where it remained active until 1989. In that year, the Law of Associations made it legal, along with other such organizations, and in the late 1990s, another law allowed them to engage in contracting of certain public services. More than half their income has come from earned income, as opposed to donations. Since they became legal, over 20,000 more Third Sector organizations have appeared in Hungary (Salamon and Anheir, 1996), a phenomenon also apparent in Poland, where they have been taking up many of the social provisions that people formerly received from the state. According to Starr (1991), the single most striking outcome of the 1989 changes has been the appearance and growth of a very vigorous Third Sector.

In the case of Poland, some large industrial cities such as Nowa Huta were built around single industry complexes in which the full range of social provisions could be found, as in any socialist state monopoly. With the arrival of the market economy, these industries began to feel the pressure of competition, so they disclaimed responsibility for the aged, child care, community centers, and other social provisions, severing them from central operations and financial support. Some the services were privatized; some shrank; others disappeared altogether. But many more became projects of community groups, often with direct church support. Community development, which had been an activity under the domination of central government, increasingly devolved into local initiatives. Often, it has been a painful transition for some workers and managers who formerly had to do no more than follow orders; however, it has opened a door to new opportunities for workers and community activists who in earlier days would likely have been severely punished for independent community development.

In the industrial countries, the boom in Third Sector community development has been striking. Equally astounding has been its variety. Outside the United States and the United Kingdom, the growth is relatively new, with the exception of church-related programs. The British gave them legal sanction as long ago as 1601; the most recent growth spurt was given impetus by the Thatcher government's efforts during the 1980s and 1990s to remove social service and development activities from the public sector.

The largest nongovernmental, nonprofit community development sector is found in the United States, where it has been fueled by a tradition of individualism and self-help, coupled with a basic distrust—if not hostility—toward government. It is also in the United States that the economic orientation of community development, still its primary focus elsewhere, has been surpassed by assorted social agendas; civil rights in the 1960s, feminism in the 1970s and beyond, gay and lesbian demonstrations in the 1980s, and health-related concerns such as AIDS and breast cancer in the 1990s. Community projects related to consumer issues have been noteworthy since the early days of the settlement houses in the 1890s and continue in the struggles over such topics as alternative medicine and tobacco use.

In France and Germany, Third Sector growth has been so rapid that it has overtaken that of the U.K. in size (Salamon and Anheir, 1996), becoming one of the largest sources of new jobs in Germany between 1980 and 1990. In that country, it is more integrated with the government, from which it receives most of its revenues. Elsewhere in western Europe, there remains a certain wariness about (nonchurch) Third Sector activities. They have confined themselves largely to cultural and recreational projects in France, where there is strict government control and little independent foundation support. In their far-reaching survey, Salamon and Anheir (1996) also found slower growth in Italy, as a result of hostility from the Roman Catholic church to nonchurch Third Sector organizations, in a state that has been historically apprehensive about providing any support. Under 1990s legislation, conditions were set for legitimating voluntary organizations, and this may lead to expansion, once the movement takes hold. (Of course, the church in Italy is itself a Third Sector organization in its social service activities.)

These examples demonstrate how community development tends to reflect a national "style," or the accumulated cultural traditions of the country. These organizations are seen by O'Leary and Takashi (1995) as a compromise in power struggles among market, state, and consumer interests. In their description of a massive community development project in Japan, they try to show how the project, on the Tokyo waterfront, could not have been undertaken successfully by either the public or the private sectors; and in the search for a basis of collaborative or joint planning, consumer-oriented community development interests were able to wield extensive influence. If the project had been left to the private sector alone, the public interest would have been ignored; but the project was too expensive to be paid by public tax revenues alone. In the ensuing compromise, community development activists were able to secure increased housing, an improved public infrastructure, expanded public recreational and cultural spaces, and other social benefits.

Historically, community development in developing countries has tended to be primarily (but not exclusively) local, relatively small-scale activity involving village-level workers, sometimes with outside assistance, although with the potential, through networking, to expand into large-scale movements. By the middle of the 1960s, it was beginning to be replaced by "national planning" schemes but rebounded in the 1970s as "participatory development" (Voth and Brewster, 1989). In industrial countries, it tended to become more involved in large-scale projects, even though local and regional activities may have dominated in sheer number and continued to demonstrate extensive need, such as that found in the Appalachian region of the eastern United States or in many parts of Sicily in Italy's south. In developing countries, community development is likely to be based on citizen coalitions; in industrial countries, it is sometimes likely to be the province of huge, influential, and financially powerful Third Sector organizations. In both cases, government funding may play a significant role. During the decade from 1972 to 1981, the U.S. government funded about 100 CD major projects, and local organizations started hundreds more (Davis, 1994); most of the government funding ended during the Reagan administration. By the 1990s, there was a resurgence of private-sector foundation initiatives, and the number of CD projects in the United States reached thousands, supported by organizations such as the Council for Community-Based Development. Obviously, scope of activity, procedures and techniques vary greatly between the projects in developing countries and those in the industrial countries.

# Problems and Contradictions

Partly because of the differences between industrial and developing countries, because of ingrained cultural friction within individual countries, and also because of organizational stresses within any group, many problems and contradictions have been identified in analyses of community development around the world.

Winston Churchill allegedly remarked that the inherent weakness of capitalism is the unequal sharing of blessings, while the inherent strength of socialism is the equal sharing of misery. In a sense, he could have been describing the difference between the role of community development in the market economy countries and its role in the countries with command economies. In the democratic industrial nations, the unequal distribution of resources and benefits has been a major factor in the growth of CD initiatives; in many socialist countries, the Third Sector developed largely in response to the perception of corruption that let social problems fester but forbade any state remedies that might seem to undermine the official denial of those problems. In developing countries, the struggle may have been for an objective no higher than a basic level of survival.

Since CD inevitably reflects the social and cultural traditions of the country or region in which it grows, it is to be expected that there will be differences of scale, and there are. Although national programs of development have been found in developing countries, the norm is for village-level activity, or networks that connect numbers of villages.

Similar sorts of cultural and organizational issues appear in all three contexts, differing largely in terms of size and tradition. For example, it is generally agreed that a major early requirement for successful community development is the identification and recruitment of competent, reliable leadership. Another requirement is for maximum local participation in planning and decision making. There is always likely to be a problem of balance between these requirements. The exact qualities needed in a leader are seldom clear or consistent or permanent. As Dore (1981) expressed it, they defy "generalized prescription"; that is, there are no useful overall rules governing what is needed in a leader, nor how forcefully she or he should lead. A leader must have the capacity to mobilize the resources needed for CD to be effective, but "mobilization" may mean anything from whipping up popular enthusiasm for a cause, to creation of a viable organization for pursuit of specific concrete aims, to astute deployment of resources in strategic ways during the engagement, to seizing control of the movement. Leadership generally refers to hierarchical power rather than to equality. Similarly, local participation in planning and decision making can lead to democratic collaboration, or it can help reinforce existing power alliances. As Dore (1981: 31) warns, "the more decisions are left to the village community, the more they will reflect that community's power structure. Participation can be a recipe for rule by local bosses."

Large community development organizations, more typical of industrial countries, may become too distant from local groups to be effective in tapping their strengths. It is a danger Warren (1970) identified in his early analysis of CD; it was his experience that large organizations lose most of the people as active participants and that the global changes that fuel CD efforts may actually make communities less self-sufficient. Citing Michels, Wolfe (1985) charged that large organizations foster dependence rather than participation and usually fall under the control of oligarchies rather than resulting in the growth of democratic participation. The problem of organizational distance is a familiar one in the management of all large bureaucracies, and successful CD programs become bureaucracies. In fact, large CD programs are likely to become as bureaucratic as the government agencies they may oppose. One danger of this phenomenon is the likelihood that the line between the CD program organization and the government it tries to change may become almost indistinguishable. As was observed by Zimmerman (1994), the globalization of the economy has forced the Third Sector to respond more to market discipline, and as it has done so, it has become more market-oriented itself. This is seen distinctly in the United States, where salaries and perquisites of large agency leaders rival those of the CEOs in major industrial firms. Despite occasional scandals such as the one that rocked the United Way in the mid-1990s, this corporate trend has not shown any real sign of slowing.

Not unrelated to the problems of leadership and participation is the charge that community development ultimately rewards the elites more than it does the grassroots workers who are assumed to benefit. What in developing countries is seen as provision of bonuses for "local bosses" becomes institutionalized in industrial countries as systematic advantages for the elites.

Other critics of Third Sector activities, such as Bennett and DiLorenzo (1985), describe them as "inequitable as well as inefficient." They note that private enterprises must respond to customer demands, and (at least in democracies) government officials to voters, but Third Sector organizations can operate according to the "whims" of their managers and also compete unfairly with the other two sectors. Levy (1996) pointed out that the independence that allows them the latitude they need in order to work, free of outside interference, also leaves them relatively unchecked when they do harm or simply do no significant good, an argument supported by Zimmerman (1994), who noted that in the United States, where Third Sector activities often concentrate on education, health, and poverty issues, the nonprofit agencies ultimately do not serve those most in need. He provides many examples, ranging from the fact that few poor students are able to attend nonprofit universities, even though many wealthy families send their children to public universities; to cases in the health arena, where more and more poor patients are turned away from nonprofit hospitals.

One reason for this outcome, following Zimmerman's reasoning, is that community development activities do not reach the general populace with services and have little redistributive effect. Most of their efforts are intended only to help their own participant members, and if the assets spill over, they reach only the next rung down on the social ladder. People want to help themselves and others most like themselves, not some theoretical outside group or some vague, abstract ideological principle.

Another reason, given by Chekki (1979), is that all community development activities are subject to varying degrees of government manipulation. They may be actively suppressed, as in developing countries and socialist regimes; in democratic countries, they may be accepted by the government and converted from advocacy groups to service delivery or advisory organizations; or their leadership may be co opted or simply tolerated until they tire. In this latter strategy, the governments are able to take credit for being accepting of dissent and open to alternatives without actually having to change.

Another problem or contradiction in community development is the requirement for both an emotional and an organizational component. Striking a useful balance between these two requirements is usually difficult and may be impossible. The solidarity that is sought in CD most often results from a shared sense of injustice. People must feel committed and motivated to devote themselves to CD work on behalf of unexploitive and egalitarian results. This commitment comprises loyalty, cooperation, selflessness, and a sense of social obligation, but the organizational structure required and the strategies needed for success may not mix well with the emotional aspects. In describing CD in South Korea, Brandt and Lee (1981) noted a "tension" that they observed between CD doctrines such as cooperation and self-help and the way the development actually took place. The ideology of community development supported "utopian communalism," but they found that actual implementation had to be based on "hard-headed competition," While trying to reflect the local traditions, CD also seemed to be speeding their extinction. Local customs and desired relations are sometimes the price of CD success. "What people *want,*" Bruyn and Meehan (1987: 15) found, is much easier to influence than what people *need*." One of the most difficult and ambiguous tasks of community development may be the changing of values which, according to Chekki (1979), need not necessarily precede social change, but may follow such change as one of its consequences. The problem, of course, is that it is not possible to know with certitude the exact nature of the changes that will take place as a result of the CD program.

CD activists are not especially comfortable with the concept that the decline of the community as a viable unit, which has been underway since the beginning of the Industrial Revolution, has been accelerated by the global economy, leaving less "community" to "develop." However, without an understanding of how the community has changed, efforts to promote and initiate community development are likely to founder. Successful leadership comes not from what Skocpol (1994) called "the most consistent and innovative ideologies," but from what she described as the ability successfully to mobilize popular movements into new structures with adequately supportive bureaucracies.

This suggests another inherent problem in community development. Although seeming to support the individual, it really requires that individuals submerge their needs and desires into the communal pool. This would seem to undermine the basic idea of CD as a democratizing activity. Yet, to maintain solidarity, a community must be able to censure deviant members. Collective success depends, as Portes and Sensenbremner (1993: 1332) put it, on the individual's "disciplined compliance with group expectations," since "the predictability in the behavior of members of the group is in direct proportion to its sanctioning capacity." To the extent that individuals do not comply with group goals and decisions, the community development effort is weakened. Everyone is obliged to be loyal and to work toward group goals. This is an obligation that has been a part of all utopian proposals since Thomas More published his classic in 1516 (Roebroek, 1992). Nevertheless, preservation of community solidarity sometimes may require that people who do not work for community ends must be allowed to remain in the community and to enjoy the benefits of any success, since the public appearance of disunity could be fatal for any CD effort.

Accordingly, some of community development's inherent problems and contradictions involve conflict between the emotional and the structural, both of which are necessary; constraints on individual freedom even though greater democracy is a fundamental goal; tolerance for dissenters and freeloaders even when communal solidarity is considered essential; the continuous risk that excessive power will accrue in the leadership, whose power is necessary for both successful organization and implementation; the likelihood that any fruits of success will not be equitably distributed in any event; and finally, Warren's (1970: 50) haunting observation that, in any case, "many of the most vital problems communities face are not resolvable at the community level."

## Future Prospects

In 1981, Dore wrote that institutionalized community development "is here to stay." While that assertion may be true, the form it takes is likely to be different from what it was when the statement was written. One reason is that there have been dramatic changes in the world; and the pace of the changes has not abated. Warren (1970) described these "global changes" as including population growth, urbanization, industrialization, replacement of informal organizations with formal ones; alterations in family and gender relations; decline of proximity or "locality" as the basis for associations; and others. He felt that CD should help developing countries adapt to the changes through programs that increase literacy, good health, and collective improvement. In the industrial countries, CD should aim at ameliorating conditions that impede personal participation on a community level.

A change that was not foreseen by Warren, or by noted futurologist Toffler (1980)—who predicted a break-up of major corporations into units that could help build community—was the rapid concentration of industries and corporate power, such that communities in industrial countries found their influence over their own affairs sharply reduced. Indeed, Morss (1991) was led to conclude that even nations, as such, were declining as dominant powers, and being replaced in part by the new global corporations and their mastery of electronic media. He questioned the future authority of national leaders in controlling world events; they are likely to be replaced by corporate leaders of multinational industries.

Of course, the speed of the collapse of Communism was not anticipated, but another global change that was not anticipated was that the dramatic collapse of the Stalinist socialism would be followed by a severe retrenchment of "third-way socialism"—that is, the welfare state in the major industrial countries. Sweden was often used considered the model of third-way socialism, but major revisions were being recommended there even before 1989. Describing Sweden's economy as "white" and "black," Ingelstam (1983) defined the second as profitable illegal transactions, such as tax fraud and organized crime, and the first as including work in the "informal sector": work that is paid or substitutes for paid work, such as shopping, child care, commuting to a job, and so on. His proposal was that more paid work in the formal "white economy" should be shifted to the unpaid sector in a kind of "gray" economy, to rely more on voluntary organizations and the local communities rather than the state. In his judgment, such necessary tasks as child care did not require massive state bureaucracies and ought to be shifted to the Third Sector. Considered more curious than profound when it was proposed, Ingelstam's idea has had to be taken seriously, since employment in the Third Sector has expanded more rapidly than in the other sectors. Challenges to government as the logical provider of services have been based on sound comparisons: For example, Sweden as the premiere welfare state, has services only marginally higher than those provided by nonprofits in the Netherlands (Zimmerman, 1994).

Future community development is likely to remain anchored in two very different worlds: the developing countries and the industrial countries. Former initiatives to improve life in developing countries by helping them industrialize may well fade as they are replaced by more realistic goals. One reason is that community development has not been able to produce impressive results in creating enduring grassroots organizations or in improving national economies (Voth and Brewster: 1989). It has had some success in creating viable small-scale economies in developing countries and in advancing major projects in industrial countries, but the former have had a very modest range, and in the second, players have been secondary.

Community development can be expected to merge into the Third Sector even more than it has in the recent past, sharing its philosophy, methods, and techniques in new contexts. In developing countries, the focus will be on small-scale enterprise based on unique local conditions, products, skills, or other marketable features. Ingelstam (1983) proposed that these sorts of "mini-enterprises" be assisted, and that is where a great deal of growth has taken place. The network of mechanics in Ghana reported by Mytelka (1993) is one such example. They represent what OECD calls "niche markets" ("Better Policies," 1995) and they permit populations to capitalize on local specialties. They may involve a territorial image (such as the Cognac region in France or the Vidalia region in Georgia), and require the creation of regulatory and protective mechanisms. Impressive successes cited by OECD of this kind of local development are floriculture on northern Kyushu Island in Japan, crafts unique to the Lapps of northern Norway, and the conversion of an Austrian region from textiles to tourism when the textile industry there crashed. Other successful cases involve historic preservations or reconstructions, or the preservation of natural habitats ("Amenities," 1996). Large-scale quasi-public schemes have been created in the Third Sector to finance great numbers of small economies, the most impressive of which is the Grameen Bank, which is discussed elsewhere in this volume. In many of these initiatives, such as the Grameen Bank, women have emerged with new status and power, reversing one of the more formidable barriers to community development of past centuries. It is parenthetically interesting to note the assertion of Elizabeth Janeway (1980) in her writing on the importance of the female factor in future successful development. Quoting (exactly) from an 1866 letter by Marx, she wrote: "Great changes are impossible without the feminine ferment. Social progress can be measured exactly by the position of the fair sex (the ugly ones included)." This new involvement of women in the community development activities of developing countries is adding a new dimension that cannot yet be assessed.

One particular aspect of Third Sector growth that bears watching is the movement that calls itself "communitarianism." Attributed to the writing and ideas of Amitai Etzioni, the movement began to attract attention in the early 1990s and within a few years occupied an important position within Third Sector research and development. Communitarians oppose both unrestricted individualism and its so-called "greed principle," as well as the excessive reliance on the government and its so-called "dependency." They propose restoration of communities and families as the base of social organization.

One proponent of communitarianism (Wagner, 1991, 1992, 1995, 1997) has written extensively in seeking to identify a sound theoretical base for the movement. His reasoning recalls very traditional philosophical ideas of the public good. For example, he challenges the assumption that human interaction is based either on mutual benefit or coercion, showing how goods frequently are exchanged for nonmaterial rewards. Arguing against both organizations that exclude and those that only selectively include, he calls them "clubs" rather than communities and proposes that communities be seen as groups in which giving is not based on expectation of exchange; he proposes a principle that he calls "sharing." While there is an exchange, it is one that need not diminish the resources of the giver. He uses the example of revolutionary France, in which "liberty" and "equality" could not be considered adequate without the inclusion of "fraternity." The community model proposed is one in which identity is bestowed not by state membership (as in citizenship), but by community participation. Such communities would become "the chief source of individual and collective identity" (1997: 66). As Third Sector organizations, these communities allow for transactions that are neither oriented to the market nor determined by the state. They replace the "impossibly high costs of social transfers" (Spiegal and Wagner, 1986) in both socialist and democratic industrial countries with structures that emphasize both personal and collective responsibility. Although communitarianism has gained followers from all parts of the political spectrum, it also suffers from the problems and inherent contradictions of all Third Sector agencies (McNutt, 1997). One of its major strengths, however, is that its principles seem equally applicable in developing and industrial societies, given appropriate modifications. Rural, economic issues are likely to continue to dominate efforts in developing countries, although South Korea exemplifies a program in which conditions in rural areas were improved by first concentrating on urban industrial development and then spreading its benefits to remote parts of the country. Part of the success of this program was attributed by Dore (1981: 44) to the principle of helping people with daily quality of life issues before trying to move them toward long-range development goals. He recommended that one should "never provide information and guidance...if the provision of useful material resources is a feasible alternative." Hungry people usually prefer food to advice.

Community development in its current manifestation as part of the growth of the Third Sector throughout the world stirs both enthusiastic support and strong skepticism. Both the functioning and stability of all Third Sector organizations are still "a relatively unexplored territory" (O'Leary and Takashi, 1995), a situation being attacked vigorously by members of the International Society for Third-Sector Research. It still faces several crucial issues identified by Salamon and Anheir (1997), including its virtual invisibility as an area of serious and sustained academic inquiry; its legitimacy in many countries that have neglected or avoided giving its legal status; its ambiguous status as "agent" or "vendor" while still asserting independence; its lack of sustained, reliable funding; its lack of accountability to the public; and barriers to its globalization at a time when its must reinvent itself on a global scale.

In addition, community development activities vary by level in various venues. In an era of communication by fax and e-mail, some of its methods may seem hopelessly primitive and outmoded. Its global growth may be held back until the legal issues can be addressed regarding its status (Salamon and Anheir, 1996). National rules vary according to ancient traditions, such as the different assumptions that underlie common law and civil law. As Salamon and Anheir (1997) distinguish between them, countries whose legal codes are based on common law (such as the United States and the United Kingdom) take the general position that "if it isn't forbidden, it's all right," while those whose foundation is civil law hold that "if it isn't approved, it's forbidden." In countries based on the civil law (such as Egypt and Japan), all Third Sector activity takes place at the sufferance of the government and is considered a privilege that may be revoked at any time.

Community development has had a distinguished history in some instances and has been profoundly disappointing in others. It is without doubt that community development, as a method, program, process, and movement continues to capture the popular imagination and inspire hope among many of the world's most vulnerable populations, both in the most primitive and remote regions of some developing countries and in the ghettos of the world's richest cities. It is also without doubt that community development must undergo constant adaptation to changing world conditions if it is to succeed, both in terms of identifying, selecting, recruiting, and keeping competent leadership and organization and in terms of maintaining its capacity to create and transmit to society an image of its own transformation into a more just, caring, equitable, and sustainable enterprise.

# REFERENCES

*Amenities for Rural Development.* (1996). (Paris: OECD).

Bennett, J., and T. DiLorenzo. (1985). *Unfair Competition.* (New York: Hamilton Press).

*Better Policies for Rural Development.* (1996). (Paris: OECD).

Brandt, V., and M. Lee. (1981). "Community Development in the Republic of Korea." In R. Dore and Z. Mars (Eds.), *Community Development* (Paris: UNESCO), pp. 47–136.

Bruyn, S. (1987). "Beyond the Market and the State. In S. Bruyn and J. Meehan (Eds.), *Beyond the Market and the State* (Philadelphia: Temple University Press), pp. 3–27.

Bruyn, S., and J. Meehan (Eds.). (1987). *Beyond the Market and the State* (Philadelphia: Temple University Press).

Bullard, E. (1995). "Participatory Enterprise Development: The Experience of TechnoServe." In H. Schnieder (Ed.), *Participatory Development from Advocacy to Action* (Paris: OECD), pp. 81–90.

Cary, L. (1970). *Community Development as a Process.* (Columbia, MO: University of Missouri Press).

Chekki, D. (1979). "A Prologomena to Community Development and Planned Change." In D. Chekki (Ed.), *Community Development* (Bombay: Vikas), pp. 3–24.

Christenson, J. (1989). "Themes of Community Development." In J. Christenson & J. Robinson (Eds.), *Community Development in Perspective* (Ames: University of Iowa Press), pp. 26–47.

Christenson, J., and J. Robinson (Eds.). (1989). *Community Development in Perspective* (Ames: University of Iowa Press).

Cisneros, H. (1996). *Higher Ground: Faith Communities and Community Building* (Washington, DC: HUD).

Cosio, I. (1981). "Community Development in Mexico." In R. Dore & Z. Mars (Eds.), *Community Development* (Paris: UNESCO).

Coughlin, B. (1965). *Church and State in Social Welfare* (New York: Columbia University Press).

Davis, J. (Ed.). (1994). *The Affordable City.* (Philadelphia: Temple University Press).

Dore, R. (1981). "Introduction." In *Community Development* (Paris: UNESCO), pp. 13–46.

Dore, R., and Z. Mars (Eds.). (1981). *Community Development* (Paris: UNESCO).

Douglas, J. (1983). *Why Charity?* (Beverly Hills: Sage).

Fafchamps. M. (1992). "Solidarity Networks in Preindustrial Societies: Rational Peasants with a Moral Economy," *Economic Development and Cultural Change* 41: (1), October, pp. 147–174.

Friedman, E. (1992). Review Article: "What Do Peasants Really Want? An Exploration of Theoretical Categories and Action Consequences." *Economic Development and Cultural Change* 41 (1), October, pp. 197–205.

Gittell, M. (1980). *Limits to Citizen Participation* (Beverly Hills: Sage).

Hegyesi, G. (1997). "The First Hungarian Generic Social Worker Training Model." In *Festschrift* (Zurich: Turicum).

Ingelstam, L. (1983). "A Third Sector Approach to Sweden's Future," *Futures* 15 (2). April, pp. 137–151.

Janeway, E. (1980). *Powers of the Weak* (New York: Knopf).

Levy, D. (1996). *Building the Third Sector* (Pittsburgh: University of Pittsburgh Press).

McNutt, J. (1997). "New Communitarian Thought and the Future of Social Policy," *Journal of Sociology & Social Welfare* 24 (4), December, pp. 45–56.

Morss, E. (1991). "The New Global Players: How They Compete and Collaborate." *World Development* 19 (1), pp. 55–64.

Mushi, S. (1981). "Community Development in Tanzania." In R. Dore and Z. Mars (Eds.), *Community Development in Perspective* (Paris: UNESCO).

Mytelka, L. (1993). "Rethinking Development." *Futures* 25 (6), July/August, pp. 694–712.

*Niche Markets as Rural Development Strategy.* (1995). (Paris: OCED).

O'Leary, J., and M. Takashi. (1995). "Between State and Capital: Third Sector Organizational Development in Tokyo." *Comparative Politics* 27 (3), April, pp. 317–337.

O'Neill, M. (1989). *The Third America* (San Francisco: Jossey-Bass).

Portes, A., and J. Sensenbremner. (1993). "Embeddedness and Immigration: Notes on the Social Determinants of Economic Action." *American Journal of Sociology* 98 (6), July, pp. 1320–1350.

Roebroek, J. (1992). "The Contradictory Entity of Social Solidarity and Welfare State Evolution. *Acta Sociologica* 35 (1), pp. 63–68.

Salamon, L., and H. Anheir. (1996). *The Emerging Nonprofit Sector* (New York: Manchester University Press).

Salamon, L., and H. Anheir. (1997). *Defining the Nonprofit Sector* (New York: Manchester University Press).

Sanders, I. (1970). "The Concept of Community Development." In L. Cary (Ed.), *Community Development as a Process* (Columbia: University of Missouri Press).

Sanders, I. (1979). Foreword. In D. Chekki (Ed.), *Community Development* (Bombay: Vikas), pp. v–viii.

Schler, D. (1970). "The Community Development Process." In L. Cary (Ed.), *Community Development as a Process* (Columbia: University of Missouri Press), pp. 113–140.

Schneider, H. (Ed.). (1995). *Participatory Development from Advocacy to Action* (Paris: OECD).

Skocpol, T. (1994). *Social Revolutions in the Modern World* (New York: Cambridge University Press).

Smillie, I. (1991). *Mastering the Market* (Boulder: Westview).

Smith, B. (1989). "More Than Altruism: The Politics of European International Charities." In E. James (Ed.), *The Nonprofit Sector in International Perspective* (New York: Oxford University Press), pp. 319–338.

Spiegal, M., and A. Wagner. (1986). "Resocializing Social Policy: A Strategy for Survival of the Modern Welfare State and Its Impact on Social Work Education," *International Social Work* 29, pp. 123–134.

Starr, F. (1991). "The Third Sector in the Second World," *World Development* 19 (1), January, pp. 65–71.

Toffler, A. (1980). *The Third Wave* (New York: William Morrow & Sons).

Van Til, J. (1988). *Mapping the Third Sector* (New York: The Foundation Center).

Voth, D., and M. Brewster, (1989). "An Overview of International Community Development." In J. Christenson and J. Robinson (Eds.), *Community Development in Perspective*. (Ames: University of Iowa Press), pp. 280–306.

Wagner, A. (1991). "On Sharing: A Preface to an Economic Theory of Voluntary Action." *Nonprofit and Voluntary Sector Quarterly* 20 (4), Winter, pp. 359–370.

Wagner, A. (1995a), "Communitarianism: A New Paradigm of Socioeconomic Analysis," *Journal of Social Economics* 24 (4), pp. 593–605.

Wagner, A. (1995b). "Reassessing Welfare Capitalism: Community-Based Approaches to Social Policy in Sweden and the United States," *Journal of Community Practice* 2 (3), pp. 45–63.

Wagner, A. (1997). "Joint Review of Amitai Etzioni...," *Voluntas* 8 (1), pp. 64–70.

Wallis, J., and B. Dollery. (1995). "A Communitarian Perspective on Government Failure," *International Journal of Social Economics* 22 (4), pp. 33–48.

Warren, R. (1970). "The Context of Community Development." In L. Cary (Ed.), *Community Development as a Process* (Columbia: University of Missouri Press), pp. 32–52.

Warren, R., M. Rosentraub, and L. Wechsler. (1988). "A Community Services Budget: Public, Private and Third Sector Roles in Urban Services," *Urban Affairs Quarterly* 23 (3), March, pp. 414–431.

Weissman, H. (Ed.). (1969). *Community Development in the Mobilization for Youth Experience* (New York: Association Press).

Wileden, A. (1970). *Community Development* (Totowa, NJ: Bedminster Press).

Winslow, D. (1996). "Pottery, Progress, and Structural Adjustments in a Sri Lankan Village," *Economic Development & Cultural Change* 44 (4), July, pp. 701–733.

Wolfe, J. (1985). "A Defense of Participatory Democracy," *Review of Politics* 47 (3), July, pp. 370–389.

Zimmerman, U. (1994) "Exploring the Non-Profit Motive (or: What's in It for You?)," *Public Administration Review* 54 (4), July/August, pp. 398–402.

# 8  Sustainable Development

> *If every company on the planet were to adopt the best environmental practices of the leading companies, the world would still be moving toward sure degradation and collapse. Rather than a management problem, we have a design problem, a flaw that runs through all business.*
>
> —Paul Hawken (1993: p. xiii)

Increasing evidence suggests that systems of production and economic development that have led us to the present cannot be sustained indefinitely. As much as is owed to the ways of doing business that have produced this century's unprecedented progress in wealth and living standards, current development practices cannot carry on unchanged without undermining the basis for development itself—the natural environment. Although by no means universally accepted as fact, this dilemma has led to a new way of thinking about development.

Sustainable development stresses the longevity of production systems. It aims at maximizing the long-term return on natural resources with an eye to extending their supportive capability indefinitely and even perpetually. This stands in stark contrast with previous developmental theory and practice. International development (qualitative improvement) is based on economic growth (quantitative increase). Traditionally, growth has been defined as expanded output, usually over the short term. In simplest terms, the economic output of products and goods requires corresponding inputs of capital, labor, and raw materials. An incessant and nearly inexhaustible supply of raw inputs, such as energy and ores, is taken as a given. As materials become scarcer, new technologies emerge and alternative materials are developed, but the fundamental process remains the same. An industrial economy uses up or exhausts material inputs in order to create wealth.

The challenge of sustainable—or lasting—development is not to eliminate growth as the engine of development, but to redefine it. Sustainable development seeks also to utilize materials in such a way as to restore them to alternative use. It shifts the economic paradigm from consumption to reproduction. Sustainable development is "an economic strategy which simultaneously pursues increased food and fiber production for the immediate needs of the world's poor and the preservation of the common natural resources which will support their children and subsequent generations" (Lusk and Mason, 1991: 8).

# Limits to Growth

Sustainable development theory has its roots in the work of Thomas Malthus[1] who first presented the "limits to growth" thesis. He argued that population grows exponentially while food production grows arithmetically; therefore, with time, population outstrips the planet's capacity to feed itself. In various forms, this thesis has been presented again and again and invariably has been proved wrong. Malthus thought that Great Britain would undergo a massive famine. The U.S. Bureau of Mines said in 1914 that America would run out of coal in ten years; environmentalist Paul Erlich predicted massive famines during the 1970s and the exhaustion of world minerals; and President Carter said the world's oil reserves could be depleted by the end of the eighties ("Plenty of Gloom," 1997). Although each successive prediction of environmental collapse has proved to be unfounded, the pessimism underlying Malthusianism has gained ground as evidence of the planet's limited carrying capacity mounts. It is too soon to forecast ecological catastrophe, but not too early to begin to manage the world's resources as if they were limited.

An influential study of environmental decline was the 1972 Club of Rome report on *The Limits to Growth* (Meadows, 1972). A group of distinguished thinkers examined the interdependency of economic, social, financial, and environmental factors on a global scale and argued that their increasing level of complexity was leading to a stressed world system in which the physical exhaustion of natural resources was an inevitable outcome. Population growth, air and water pollution, use of petrochemical inputs, and energy consumption were perceived as threatening the viability of the ecosystem (Carley & Christie, 1993). Although the specific predictions by the Club of Rome all proved to be wrong, their overall thesis of natural resource limits to growth has come to be widely accepted. The decade following the report was marked by a worldwide increase of awareness in environmental issues. A plethora of studies were published documenting the damage wreaked by traditional development on forests, rivers, lakes, and wildlife species. Coupled with the recognition that economic growth had not produced prosperity for the majority of the world's population, disenchantment with growth as the primary goal of development led to new models. Instead of seeking to boost GNP/capita, a more balanced perspective emerged that also stressed balancing growth with equity and quality of life—sustainable development.

# Sustainable Development

The antigrowth implications of the Club of Rome study were discredited by the continuing success of the Green Revolution (Muschett, 1997). The no-growth perspective of steady state economies, zero population increase, and a shift to fully renewable energy sources was challenged by the continuing success of the developing nations to become food self-sufficient through the introduction of new seed varieties, improved irrigation practices, and new agricultural technologies. Predictions of famine and fossil fuels depletion were not

---

[1] See Chapter 6 for a discussion of Malthusianism.

realized. Yet it was also apparent that the world's poorest were adding disproportionately to the decline of the stock of renewable natural resources through deforestation, overgrazing, poor soil management, and unsymmetrical population growth. Moreover, the industrial world's use of fossil fuels has continued to accelerate over the past three decades, with no leveling off in sight. It has become necessary to devise an international development perspective that accounts for the very real limits of renewable resources but allows for the increased economic output necessary to improve the quality of life for the world's burgeoning population (see Table 8.1, Development Models).

The United Nations World Commission on Environment and Development published what may be the definitive statement on sustainable development in its 1987 report, *Our Common Future.* The concept of sustainable development had achieved wide usage in development circles throughout the 1980s and became a powerful influence on the policies and programs of the World Bank, U. S. Agency for International Development (USAID), and Japan International Cooperation Agency (JICA). The UN report brought some needed definition and focus to sustainable development and overcame the bias against growth that had limited much of the previous environmental writing on international development.

*Sustainable development maintains intergenerational equity.* At the core of sustainability is the need to preserve the capital stock of natural resources necessary for future generations to enjoy a standard of living that is at least as good as that of the present (Pearce, Barbier, and Markandya, 1990). It is crucial that improved welfare for the present not be made at the expense of lowered prospects for the future. Nonsustainable definitions of development stress the present value of development benefits and discount future values. Maximization of present values tends to lead toward strategies of optimal use that

**TABLE 8.1    Development Models**

| Factor | Economic Development | Social Development | Sustainable Development |
|---|---|---|---|
| Goal | Growth with equity | Basic human needs | Growth with equity for posterity |
| Method | Free Trade<br>Exports<br>Human capital<br>Technology | Infrastructure<br>Universal education<br>Access to housing<br>Health care | Input reduction<br>Renewable fuels<br>Appropriate technology<br>Alternative agriculture |
| Organization | Multilateral banks<br>Development agencies<br>Private sector | Nongovernmental organizations (NGOs)<br>Development agencies | Polycentric (banks, NGOs, government, community organizations, international treaty organizations) |
| Science | Economics | Sociology | Ecology |
| Orientation | Technocratic | Humanitarian | Naturalistic |
| Focus | Extractive | Redistributive | Reproductive |

deplete resources and degrade the natural environment. Traditional economics would argue that "environmental degradation *should* take place if the gains from the activities causing the degradation (e.g., agricultural clearing of forests, development of wetlands) are greater than the benefits of preserving the areas in their present form" (Pearce, Barbier, and Markandya, 1990: 2). Indeed, depletion of an existing resource not only produces short-term gains, it also raises the value of remaining resources. By this logic, it would make more sense to cut down a Costa Rican forest to export its tropical hardwoods and convert it to cattle ranching because of a present-oriented cost benefit analysis. The sustainable alternative goes beyond simple short-term economic efficiency and requires costing out the lost future value of the decimated forest. It also deducts the future value of the forest from the current cost benefit analysis. Environmental economics stress the constancy of natural capital stock in which the current resource base is maintained or improved. This suggests conservation of current biodiversity; a radiation-protective atmosphere; preservation of forest resources, soils, fresh water, and energy sources; and the ongoing ecological processes of dilution and purification of airborne and waterborne contaminants.

*Sustainable development requires economic growth.* If every woman of reproductive age were to choose to have only two children, population would continue to grow for at least several decades. This phenomenon of *population momentum* is due to the large size of the cohort of reproductive-aged women. Although fertility rates are declining, women are not having two children on average and population will not level off for the foreseeable future. World population grew by 1.48 percent annually from 1990 to 1995, and women had an average of 2.96 children each; unless a significant change in fertility patterns emerges, population will grow from its current 5.77 billion to 9.4 billion by 2050 (Crossette, 1996). Most of this growth will occur in the developing nations, where about 80 percent of the world's population already resides, thereby limiting the capacity of these nations to achieve an adequate standard of living even if GNP grows moderately.

A no-growth economic scenario will not allow for the increase in food, fiber, and energy production necessary to offset the growing population base. Although it can be argued that population growth must be contained, this is clearly a long-term solution. In fact, economic development is inversely correlated to population growth; as a nation's standard of living increases, its fertility rate declines. The incentives for large families (old age security, household labor, added workers) disappear in a highly developed context in which pensions support the elderly, costs of raising children are high, and labor-saving devices replace manual labor. Thus, population control strategies must be considered in light of the need to improve living standards in developing nations where fertility is disproportionately higher and the costs to the environment of added population pressure are particularly high (Table 8.2).

Population growth exerts strong adverse pressures on the natural environment in the form of diminished forest resources, degraded agricultural soils, overgrazed rangelands, water pollution, diminishing wildlife stocks, declining biodiversity, and urban pollution. This has much to do with the incentives that impinge upon the poor as their numbers grow. Those traditional means of managing common resources, such as crop rotations, forest culling, contour plowing, fallow lands maintenance, conservation tillage, and range herd rotations are untenable when the maximum yield must be generated in the shortest time

**TABLE 8.2    Population in Selected Economies, 1997**

| Nation | Total (millions) | Average Annual Growth Rate (%) | Fertility Rate* | 1995 GDP/Capita ($) |
|---|---|---|---|---|
| Bangladesh | 120 | 1.6 | 3.5 | 240 |
| Kenya | 27 | 2.7 | 4.7 | 280 |
| India | 929 | 1.8 | 3.2 | 340 |
| China | 1200 | 1.1 | 1.9 | 620 |
| Kazakstan | 17 | 1.1 | 2.3 | 1330 |
| Russia | 148 | 0.0 | 1.4 | 2240 |
| Peru | 17 | 2.0 | 3.1 | 2310 |
| Mexico | 92 | 1.9 | 3.0 | 3320 |
| Brazil | 159 | 1.5 | 2.4 | 3640 |
| Sweden | 9 | 0.6 | 1.7 | 23740 |
| United States | 263 | 1.0 | 2.1 | 26980 |
| Japan | 125 | 0.3 | 1.5 | 39640 |
| World | 5673 | 1.5 | 2.9 | 4880 |

*Fertility rate is the average number of children born per woman.

*Source:* From *World Development Report 1997* by World Bank. Copyright © 1997 The International Bank for Reconstruction and Development/The World Bank. Used by permission of Oxford University Press, Inc.

frame. Rotations change to monocropping, forests are stripped for firewood, erosion control is perceived as too expensive, and water is overapplied. The results include an increase in pesticide use, soil salinity, waterlogging, overgrazing, and a pressure to convert forestlands to crop production or animal husbandry. Long-term management for posterity is seen as an unaffordable luxury when land is scarce and food demand is high. A vicious cycle is created between population growth, poverty, and environmental degradation in which factors accelerate each other (Pearce & Warford, 1993).

The vicious cycle can be broken by a significant expansion of output through improved technologies that are more environmentally friendly and which raise living standards and educational achievement to levels at which the incentives for high fertility are absent. Improved technologies will yield higher rates of production and thereby increase net carrying capacity, but at some point—which is exceedingly difficult to identify—the capacity of resources to sustain a population is exhausted, and added growth in output becomes impossible. Beyond the carrying capacity limit, production actually falls as the resource base degrades. In some cases, as with soil erosion, the recovery time of the resource extends over such a long period that, for all practical purposes, the resource is permanently depleted. The United Nations Food and Agriculture Organization (FAO) has estimated carrying capacities for various regions under different levels of technology and found that, in some regions, such as South Asia, agricultural carrying capacity has effectively been reached. Although improved practices can produce additional yields on current croplands, related resources such as fuel wood are beyond replacement levels (FAO, 1982). Thus, continued economic growth is imperative because it raises living standards to such a level that the vicious cycle of poverty, population growth, and environmental degradation is ruptured.

*Sustainable development requires subsidy reform.* Much as the poor respond to the incentives of using resources for short-term production and discount future losses because the immediate food, fiber, and fuel needs of a family are so pressing, so do the nonpoor respond to the perverse incentives provided by their governments to strip resources at below cost for short-term gain. For example, a California farmer can buy water from the Bureau of Reclamation for $2.84 per thousand cubic meters, when it costs the government $24.84 to deliver the water and the free market price of irrigation water is about $100 (Roodman, 1997). In Kazakstan, where rainfall is a fraction of that of California, irrigation water is effectively free (Lusk & Ospanov, 1997). Similarly, governments routinely provide infrastructure at little or no cost to timber, fishing, energy, and agricultural industries. Public land-use prices and export subsidies to grow cattle may combine to lead to wide-scale conversion of forestry to range. Interestingly, these incentives are usually set up in such a way as to advantage the powerful and affluent over the poor and politically disenfranchised. Information on the environmental costs and expenses to the taxpayer are obscured so that the public believes in false trade-offs such as "owls versus loggers" or "environmental protection versus jobs."

Subsidies are government payments, exemptions, or forgone taxes and royalties that alter the risks of the market and hold down prices and costs for beneficiary groups. They are "rents" that beneficiaries spend a great deal of unproductive time and money obtaining and keeping. Such subsidies and incentives tend to reduce profit-seeking and replace it with rent-seeking, whereby the beneficiary captures a competitive advantage without paying the real market costs. Part of the dilemma is related to the way in which natural resources are valued.

The accounting of a development project or activity, such as a loan-assisted development of a new fishing fleet or a project to increase hardwood exports, has been based on procedures that do not consider the value of the resource to be exploited. It is often viewed as infinite and thereby creates a contradiction between sustainability and growth. If, for example, the market prices used in a tropical forestry harvesting program account only for labor, freight, and extraction costs, the forest resource itself is valued at zero (Boyce, 1994). In theory, sustainability requires a nondecreasing stock of natural capital over time such that if harvesting were to take place, it would be profitable only by replacing the forest stock. Such losses as are taken in a given year must be offset by future increases in supply. In addition, if logging increases soil losses through runoff, these externalities must also be included in the costing so that we obtain a social supply curve that raises the actual prices of the hardwoods produced. This provides an incentive to harvest the timber using environmentally friendly techniques so as to reduce the market price of wood while maintaining the soil resources on which its production is based.

*Sustainable development functions in a free market when policies and incentives are adjusted to promote conservationist strategies.* Contrary to logic, most current government of natural resources creates incentives to overconsume rather than conserve. Subsidies and tax expenditures for ranching, irrigated farming, dairy, forest products, mining, and energy production are the most glaring. A nation may also favor private automobile and truck transportation over public transportation by providing nearly free roads and cheap gas. It is encouraged when the social externalities of wide-scale private vehicle use (such as congestion and air pollution) are not borne by the users themselves, but are passed on to the public ("Jam Today," 1997). It is not only the statist economies of the developing world and the former Soviet Union in which we see government incentives to devalue natural resources; the wealthiest nations with the "freest" economies provide enormous breaks to polluters.

The challenge is to get government to facilitate that combination of free market and public measures that can constrain resource depletion. This defies conventional wisdom, which has it that free markets and environmentalism are incompatible and that the role of government is to provide the regulatory framework to mediate the depredations of the market. Yet, historically, government has only marginally constrained resource depletion, and those resources owned by government—such as rangelands and forests—are managed far less productively and wisely than privately held resources. Bureaucrats, who do not have a personal stake in the outcome, have little reason to follow the advice of scientists or the forces of the market, but every incentive to respond to the political will of elites. While it seems obvious that the private owner who does not have to pay any associated costs may elect to dump toxins into a river, it should also be apparent that a political appointee might allow a firm to dump wastes into a public waterway if there are no associated costs and the bureaucracy's incentives favor the development. The task is not to displace the role of government in natural resource management, but to use its policy-making authority to assist the market in optimizing resource utilization.

One mechanism that can be used to provide greater accountability in environmental management is to establish clear and transferable property rights. Such rights over land and resources must be transparently and accurately measured, monitored, and marketed. In the absence of well-defined property rights for natural resources, we run the risk of the *tragedy of the commons,* in which the incentives to overuse a resource are not counterbalanced by having to pay for the consequences. For example, irrigation water is a natural resource that can be used by multiple beneficiaries. One person's use reduces the amount available to other users. If property rights (or rights of use) are not specified in terms of cost, volume, and timing, each user's individual incentive will be to apply as much irrigation water as possible regardless of other farmers' needs. When there are appropriate costs for use and when other users have property rights that must be honored, a system of rotation and shared use can emerge. When these rights are absent or unenforced, the water will be used indiscriminately, thereby reducing system productivity and depriving some of access to the resource. The same logic can be used to describe air pollution, deforestation, overgrazing, and industrial dumping.

Another market-based technique is to cost out the adverse externalities generated by a project or industry. Rights to release pollutants such as carbon dioxide emissions or water effluents can be traded in the open market, as is done in the United States. In this way, incentives can be created to reduce emissions or other similar externalities. An oversight agency issues a limited number of pollution permits at a level that is considered environmentally sustainable. Companies can exchange the permits freely so they may increase pollution at a location where air quality is less vulnerable and reduce pollution where it is high. If a company is able to reduce its pollution below its permit authority, it can sell the difference to a less efficient firm. Overall efficiency is improved and incentives are in place to reduce net emissions or effluents (Anderson and Leal, 1991).

*Sustainable development reflects a shift in cultural values.* If the prevailing models of development at a given time tend to reflect the values of a particular era, then it is clear that sustainable development mirrors new attitudes and priorities. The environmental movement of the seventies has become mainstream, and virtually all of the major international development agencies and multilateral banks have incorporated sustainability into their policies and programs. Those environmental values that undergird the sustainable development approach are a commitment to preservation of natural capital stock, intergenerational equity, and intragenerational equity (Hoff, 1998).

The commitment to maintenance of natural capital stock cannot be taken strictly literally. The extraction of minerals, such as copper and coal, as well the continued use of petroleum is obviously a permanent and irreversible reduction of a resource. The value emphasis is on reducing the use of primary resources and, whenever possible, reusing existing materials. Therefore, a goal of sustainable development is to reduce the effects of permanent consumption of resources by recycling, factoring environmental costs into prices, and energy conservation (Myers, Vincent, and Panayotou, 1997). Natural capital stock such as fresh water and forests can be regenerated, and the use of these resources must be adjusted to the time frame for replacement. Other resources, including soils, have such long time periods for regeneration that to deplete them is equivalent to "mining"—an irreversible consumption or loss.

The commitment to intergenerational equity implies that current resource utilization for the production of wealth should not be at the expense of the ability of future generations to achieve a similar or better standard of living. Current development practices must add value or, at a minimum, maintain the basis for equivalent living standards. Because environmental degradation is partly accounted for by poverty, population growth, and indebtedness, these factors must be addressed in the present to reduce future losses (Pearce and Warford, 1993).

Finally, intragenerational equity refers to the tendency for access to resources and wealth to be maldistributed in the present. Sustainable development is concerned with equalizing the access a society offers to benefit proportionately from the collective assets of a nation—its natural resource base. Intragenerational equity is particularly aimed at the elimination of "environmental racism" wherein a cultural minority or poor nation is disproportionately exposed to toxic wastes, environmental dumping, and dangerous products (Bullard, 1990).

In addition to environmental values, sustainable development is also informed by the values of the social development perspective that stresses basic human needs and quality of life. One line of reasoning within this perspective critiques the industrial world's preoccupation with consumerism, the private accumulation of material goods, and the unending pursuit of wealth and status. These fixations of western industrial societies are seen as important causes of the nonsustainable development in which economic growth is aimed at acquisition, consumption, mass culture, and individual aggrandizement. An alternative to this preoccupation with materialist values is the "cultivation of non-material goods, such as leisure and community interaction, family and friendship, development of arts and personal skills and so forth" (Hoff, 1998). The obsession with consumption and private property is replaced by an emphasis on the quality of life as measured by access to basic services, freedom, social justice, and self-determination.

The rapid assimilation of sustainable development into the mainstream of contemporary social and economic thought reflects a change in worldview as industrial nations are confronted with the environmental and cultural losses associated with their means of pursuing progress. It mirrors a search for a new set of values to guide international development—one that respects traditional societies, acknowledges the importance of social capital, and celebrates community over consumption. As one Hauorani Indian from Ecuador observed when confronted with the oil exploitation of his tribal reserve, "We live with the spirit of the jaguar. We do not want to be civilized by your missionaries or killed by your oil companies. Must the jaguar die so that you can have more contamination and television?" (Kane, 1995: 4).

Sustainable development theory challenges many of the values and ideas that have shaped contemporary development practice. In addition to the emphasis on the environment there is a commitment to the development of sustainable institutions—public and private entities that genuinely represent the needs and aspirations of their constituencies. Sustainable development is a direct challenge to global industrialism. Several themes of sustainability counter the contemporary technocratic approach to development including grassroots development, feminism, and social capital (McMichael, 1996).

## Grassroots Development

In contrast to the macroeconomic strategies of the multilateral banks and foreign assistance agencies that stress aggregate growth, equity, and the environment, grassroots development emphasizes autonomous and local tactics of achieving higher standards of living. The perspective seeks to empower local communities to take the initiative to pursue improvements on their own, thereby avoiding the perceived paternalism of industrial nations that presumably seek to replicate themselves in the developing world. In this way, the changes induced are presumed to reflect local culture, skills, and comparative advantage.

Grassroots development occurs independently of the international banking and development agencies, which frees communities from the potential burdens of international debt. Those goods and services produced are reflective of the talents and interests of a particular community. The means by which development is generated is through self-governing, community-based agencies and nongovernmental organizations (NGOs), which assures that strategies are consonant with self interest and independence. Instead of adjusting macroeconomic strategies to meet local needs, the grassroots approach strives to create replicable examples of community success that can be scaled up to the regional and national levels (Chambers, 1992).

Grassroots development is associated with several social movements, including development feminism, environmentalism, and "base communities," which strive to shift the leadership of development back down to the constituents most affected. Base communities are a byproduct of Catholic liberation theology which, as practiced in Latin America, stresses communities of fellowship among the poor through which members forge their community's future. *Comunidades de base,* as they are known, emphasize shared leadership, family integrity, cooperative child care, and community participation in housing, sanitation, and environmental improvement. The groups also provide a contemporary context for the practice of religion in development. Discussion and worship groups stress the moral basis of society and the need for mutual support and community self-sufficiency.

## Development Feminism

Sustainable development has been significantly affected by feminism and the international Women's Movement. The sustainability concept may have its primary origin in long-term environmental viability, but gender issues have figured into the paradigm as well. Partly, this grows out of the synergy of the feminist and environmental movements; to some extent it results from the idea that for development to be sustainable, it must be inclusive.

For well over two decades, there has been widespread recognition of the fact that development is highly uneven with respect to gender. Although men work more in the official economy in which wages are paid for contracted time and effort, women, on average, work longer hours than men when all forms of labor are included—especially agricultural work and household labor. Development initially has a negative effect on women's labor. As communities make the transition from a rural agricultural economy to an urban industrial and services economy, women are more likely to be displaced in the workforce and female employment declines. In official employment, women earn a fraction of the wages paid to men. Women who are formally employed are far more likely to be involved in lowpaid service sector jobs. Women are more likely to be laid off in economic recession and are less prone to be protected by social insurance and retirement programs. In agricultural communities, women also work longer hours than men in farm work and tend to cultivate subsistence and food crops as opposed to cash crops. In addition, female labor force participation varies widely by country, indicating significant cultural forces that limit women's prospects in selected economies (World Bank, 1995a; World Bank, 1995b; United Nations, 1997; Black, 1991).

Similarly, in most countries girls get less education than boys and have higher rates of illiteracy. This is an artifact of both cultural beliefs and the differential access of women to paid employment. On average, women of a specific educational attainment, such as college graduate, earn significantly less than identically educated men. The lower educational attainment of women has an adverse impact upon infant mortality and total fertility; the health and life expectancy of children can be improved by closing the gap between female and male educational attainment (World Bank, 1991; Black, 1991).

The extent of the divide between women and men in developing nations may be narrowing, yet is still quite wide. On the positive side, female life expectancy has been rising steadily and the rate of maternal mortality continues to decline. Moreover, women's income has been increasing in real terms. Unfortunately, however, the gap between male and female income has actually been growing over the past three decades. In addition, the phenomenon of female-headed households, once rare in the developing world, is growing rapidly. These households are at far greater risk of poverty than households with two parents.

Girls in some regions of the developing world are also at far greater risk of infanticide (Nisbet, 1996; "Female Infanticide," 1993). Cultural preferences for the male child in some settings increase the risk that the female child will be killed or seriously neglected. When one examines fertility, morbidity, and mortality data, there are about 100 million "missing females" in the world, meaning that girls and women face higher risks of infanticide and medical neglect (Fathalla, 1995). Finally, girls also run the risk in selected nations of genital mutilation. This practice, also called clitoridectomy and female circumcision, is surprisingly common. Estimates are that 120 million women and girls have undergone some form of genital mutilation and that two million girls per year are affected (Dorkenoo, 1996). In some countries in Africa, 70 to 90 percent of females have been mutilated in this manner ("Circumcision," 1997).

These alarming statistics on education, employment, income, infanticide, and mutilation have finally been incorporated into the development dialogue, largely under the umbrella of sustainable development. Pressure from women's groups and development NGOs have impelled foreign assistance agencies and multilateral banks to incorporate *women in development* (WID) components into project design, implementation, and evaluation. Since the late '70s Percy Amendments to the Foreign Assistance Act, official U.S. foreign assistance policy has required that WID be a consideration in all American development assistance. The UN administers a special development fund for women and also has similar requirements (Black, 1991). Numerous projects have emerged to equalize girls' education and to eliminate medical neglect and mutilation. Current requirements in foreign aid are such that the impacts of projects from dams to rural electrification must be designed and evaluated in light of their effect upon households, women, and children. The dependent variable of foreign aid has tended to shift from aggregate economic growth to measures of average household well-being such as income, access to potable water, infant mortality, educational achievement, and related factors.

In addition to the incorporation of women's issues into international development practice, feminism has made recent contributions to development theory. One such addition has been the *Women, Environment, and Alternative Development* (WED) Model, which seeks to redirect development away from remediation toward alternative strategies for addressing environmental and feminist issues (McMichael, 1996). In addition to noting that women have been the invisible de facto economic producers of the developing world, the WED model argues that traditional development, in addition to being Eurocentric, is also male-oriented. It stresses the production of wealth and cash crops by male workers in a traditional economic paradigm that assumes that man's "dominion over nature" is a normal and desirable condition. In contrast, WED asserts that such dominion reflects a paradigm that itself is at the heart of the destruction of the planet's human and natural resources. Traditional economic development is predatory; it plunders nature and pushes women and children to the margins where they become an afterthought that must be remedied by *women in development* requirements. Furthermore, it is argued that rationalist, western development has the effect of minimizing traditional cultures and displacing local agricultural and crafts traditions.

The alternative view, it is argued, is to replace the domination of nature paradigm with a nurturing world view that values and accounts for local traditions that have successfully husbanded resources for millennia (Harcourt, 1994). A resulting goal is to incorporate "ecofeminism" into development practice, a process by which the family and the natural environment are valued above other factors that have traditionally received more emphasis. Finally, the view is that women across the divides of wealth and poverty, both north and south, have a shared interest and commitment in preserving the planet for their offspring.

## Sustainability and Social Capital

A more recent addition to sustainable development theory and practice is the idea that development is predicated on the expansion of civil society. There has been some recognition that democracy and development are synergetic. Democracies are more likely to pursue a peaceful foreign policy, support free markets, and reflect the will of the electorate, yet democracy in the developing world is often quite superficial. Although much attention has been given to the worldwide march toward democratic forms of government over the past two decades, only recently has it been recognized that many of these governments are democratic in name only. Moreover, the societies governed by ostensibly democratic governments often lack the traditions of civil society that make democracy work.

The rise of democracy during the past two decades is really quite unprecedented. By the late '70s, quite in contrast to the region's history, most Latin American governments were of the elected variety. The process of democratization accelerated to include parts of Asia and Africa, and most surprisingly, eastern Europe and the former Soviet Union. "Today, 118 of the world's 193 countries are democratic, encompassing a majority of its people (54.8 percent, to be exact), a vast increase from even a decade ago" (Zakaria, 1997: 23). Yet, as even a casual observer will recognize, most of these new democracies are not representative in any meaningful sense. In other countries such as Belarus, Kazakstan, Gambia, Central African Republic, Pakistan, and elsewhere, democratically elected governments have retrenched into authoritarianism (Carothers, 1997).

Democracy necessarily entails more than multiparty elections that withstand the scrutiny of international observers. Implicit in democracy is the division of powers by which the branches of government exert a mediating influence upon each other and balance the tendency of the executive to rule by decree. The constitutional separation of powers is evident in a fraction of the new democracies and is a major force in the retrenchment of such governments into authoritarian forms (Carothers, 1997).

Also crucial to democracy is the enforcement of constitutional rights of the individual—constitutional liberalism. While many developing nations have wordy constitutions that pay tribute to individual freedoms, the reality is inconsistent with the rhetoric. The guarantees of freedom of speech, assembly, and worship must be coupled with impartial courts, separation of church and state, and the right to own and transfer property. Finally, these factors must be grounded in the rule of law, by which the basic security of the population is ensured, contracts are enforced, and rights are protected. This more far-reaching definition of democracy clearly puts it into the minority of forms of government. As Samuel Huntington has observed, "Western ideas of individualism, liberalism, constitutionalism, human rights, equality, liberty, the rule of law, democracy, free markets, the separation of church and state, often have little resonance in Islamic, Confucian, Japanese, Hindu, Buddhist, or Orthodox cultures" (1993: 40).

If development is to be lasting, it is crucial that it not be subverted by illiberal governments that act in their own interest and hold little accountability to their constituencies. Sustainable development requires enduring institutions that are open, accountable, transparent, and representative. Borrowing from philosopher Karl Popper, noted international philanthropist George Soros describes such development as the search for an "open society." This type of society, Soros says, is "characterized by a reliance on the rule of law, the existence of democratically elected government, a diverse and vigorous civil society, and a respect for minorities and minority opinions" (1997).

A civil society is held together by *social capital*. In contrast with human capital, which is the sum of education, skills, and abilities individuals bring to the labor market, social capital refers to the connectedness of people in a society. It is the sum of informal associational networks and social trust or "the degree to which we feel we can expect strangers to do right by us" (Lappe and DuBois, 1997: 119).

Social capital is a comparatively new and important concept in international development because it describes the glue (or the lack thereof) that holds societies together. Previous development theory has given emphasis to physical capital (money and infrastructure) and human capital (skills and knowledge), both of which are required for development to occur. But as sociologist James Coleman has recognized, although social capital is less tangible, embodying as it does the relations among people that facilitate action, it too is a necessary ingredient because it indicates the level of trust between people and the degree to which they may be expected to repay obligations (1990: 304–308).

The concept of social capital implies that a more functional society has those *mediating institutions* that stand between the individual and the large governmental and corporate organizations that tend to dominate modern life (Berger and Neuhaus, 1977). In the absence of intermediary organizations at the community level (such as churches, clubs, volunteer associations, and fraternal groups), the individual has little in the way of social middle ground between the privacy and intimacy of the home and the impersonality and formality of the social system. The individual in such a society has little reason to trust those outside of the kinship group, and the result is not unlike the society we can see today in the Russian Federation—characterized by enormous anomie, minimal rule of law, utter distrust of government, and rapacious capitalism.

Francis Fukuyama has argued that social capital and trust vary widely both by country and by culture (1995). Individuals in countries with strong traditions of familism, such as China, Italy, and Mexico, have a lower propensity to trust formal and community institutions. Business and social relations tend to be structured around kinship affiliations, and the emergence of a vital civic culture is muted by the absence of mediating institutions. Social capital has a powerful effect upon economic development, Fukuyama contends, because societies with large reservoirs of social capital are more inclined to develop large-scale businesses, adopt new organizational forms, and adapt more readily as technologies and markets change. High-trust societies, such as Japan, Germany, and Canada, not only have firmly in place the rule of law and a clear and transparent system of property rights, they also have a rich bedrock of social and cultural habits that support economic development—a healthy endowment of social capital, spontaneous sociability, group cohesiveness, and dense layers of associational memberships that support the public sphere. Fukuyama thinks that this represents no small part of why these nations are able to achieve such high standards of living while enjoying domestic security and a high level of public civility.

Social capital seems to have a profound effect on the way states and markets operate. Strong voluntary associations and an active civic sector foster more effective and transparent government, and such associations and NGOs become important development actors in their own right (Babbington, 1997). The potential for building social capital into the design of development projects remains comparatively untapped, yet the importance of local self-governing networks and associations to international development is well established. The sustainable development agenda will increasingly take stock of the rich local social and cultural resources that work in support of community, trust, and cooperation as the paradigm continues to unfold.

# Conclusion

Sustainable development is the latest in a long and rich tradition of international development theory and practice. It embodies a significant counterpoint to the way in which development has been conventionally defined. Foremost among the challenges of sustainability is the call to conceive of development as a perennial process that will improve living standards for generations to come. This shifts the view of activities in the present to one in which each development endeavor is evaluated in light of its long-term future impact. The question, "Is it a sustainable practice?" is now mainstream among development workers. And when this question is asked, it refers not only to the viability of a practice with respect to the environment, but also to families, women, children, and the cultural and social traditions that sustain them.

# REFERENCES

Anderson, T. L., and D. R. Leal. (1991). *Free Market Environmentalism* (San Francisco: Pacific Research Institute for Public Policy).

Babbington, A. (1997). "Social Capital and Rural Intensification: Local Organizations and Islands of Sustainability in the Rural Andes. *The Geographic Journal, 163* (2), pp. 189–198.

Berger, P., and R. Neuhaus. (1977). *Empower People: The Role of Mediating Structures in Public Policy* (Washington, DC: American Enterprise Institute).

Black, J. K. (1991). *Development in Theory and Practice: Bridging the Gap.* (Boulder: Westview Press).

Boyce, J. K. (1994). "Toward a Political Economy of Sustainable Development," *12, Working Paper Series on Development at the Crossroads* (Madison: University of Wisconsin Global Studies Research Program).

Bullard, R. (1990). *Dumping in Dixie: Race, Class and Environmental Quality.* (Boulder: Westview Press).

Buvinic, M. (1997). Women in Poverty: A New Global Underclass. *Foreign Policy, 108,* pp. 38–53.

Carley M., and I. Christie. (1993). *Managing Sustainable Development* (Minneapolis: University of Minnesota Press).

Carothers, T. (1997). "Democracy Without Illusions." *Foreign Affairs, 76* (1), pp. 85–99.

Chambers, R. (1992). "Spreading and Self-Improving: A Strategy for Scaling-Up." In M. Edwards and D.

Hulme (Eds.), *Making a Difference: NGO's and Development in a Changing World* (pp. 40–48). London: Earthscan Publications Ltd.

"Circumcision Goes On." (1997, July 7). *Maclean's, 110* (27), p. 47.

Coleman, J. S. (1990). *Foundations of Social Theory* (Cambridge: Harvard University Press).

Crossette, B. (1996, November 12). "World Less Crowded Than Expected, the U.N. Reports." *New York Times International* (p. Y3).

Dorkenoo, E. (1996). "Combating Female Genital Mutilation: An Agenda for the Next Decade." *World Health Statistics Quarterly, 49* (2), pp. 142–147.

FAO. (1982). *Potential Population Supporting Capacities of Lands in the Developing World* (New York: United Nations Food and Agriculture Organization).

Fathalla, M. (1995, Winter). "World Report on Women's Health." *Women's International Network News, 21* (1), pp. 22–27.

"Female Infanticide Growing in India." (1993, Autumn). *Women's International Network News, 19* (4), pp. 61–66.

Fukuyama, F. (1995). *Trust: The Social Virtues and the Creation of Prosperity* (New York: The Free Press).

Harcourt, W. (1994). Introduction. In W. Harcourt (Ed.), *Feminist Perspectives on Sustainable Development* (London: Zed Books).

Hawken, P. (1993). *The Ecology of Commerce: A Declaration of Sustainability* (New York: Harper Business).

Hoff, M. D. (1998). Sustainable Community Development: Origins and Essential Elements of a New Approach. In M. D. Hoff (Ed.), *Sustainable Community Development.* (pp. 5–21) (Boston: CRC Press/Lewis Publishers).

Huntington, S. P. (1993). "The clash of civilizations?" *Foreign Affairs, 72* (3), pp. 22–49.

"Jam Today, Road Pricing Tomorrow." (1997, December 6). *The Economist* (pp. 15–16).

Kane, J. (1995). *Savages* (New York: Vintage Books).

Lappe, F. M., and D. M. DuBois. (1997). "Social Capital." *National Civic Reporter, 86* (2), pp. 119–129.

Lusk, M. W., and D. T. Mason. (1991). "Development Theory for Rural Practice." *Human Services in the Rural Environment, 16* (1), 5–10.

Lusk, M. W., and S. I. Ospanov. (1997). "Toward Sustainable Irrigated Agriculture in Kazakstan." In M. Hoff (Ed.), *Sustainable Community Development* (Boston: CRC Press/Lewis Publishers).

Meadows, D. H., et al. (1972). *The Limits to Growth* (New York: Universe Books).

McMichael, P. (1996). *Development and Social Change: A Global Perspective* (London: Sage Publications).

Muschett, F. D. (1997). An Integrated Approach to Sustainable Development. In F. D. Muschett (Ed.), *Principles of Sustainable Development* (pp. 1–45) (Delray Beach, FL: St. Lucie Press).

Myers, N., J. R. Vincent, and T. Panayotou. (1997). "Consumption: Challenge to Sustainable Development." *Science, 276* (5309), pp. 53–56.

Nisbet, D. (1996). "Female Infanticide in China." *Quadrant, 40* (5), pp. 26–30.

Pearce, D., E. Barbier, and A. Markandya. (1990). *Sustainable Development: Economics and Environment in the Third World* (London: Edward Elgar).

Pearce, D. W., and J. J. Warford. (1993). *World Without End: Economics, Environment and Sustainable Development* (New York: Oxford University Press).

"Plenty of Gloom." (1997, December 20). *The Economist.* pp. 19–20

Roodman, D. M. (1997). "Reforming Subsidies." In L. Brown (Ed.), *State of the World 1997* (pp. 132–150) (New York: W. W. Norton & Co).

Soros, G. (1997). What Is an Open Society? [On-line]. Available: www.soros.org/debate/mission.htm.

United Nations. (1997). *Human Development Report 1996* (New York: Oxford University Press).

World Bank. (1991). *The Challenge of Development: World Development Report 1991* (New York: Oxford University Press).

World Bank. (1995a). *Workers in an Integrating World: World Development Report 1995* (New York: Oxford University Press).

World Bank. (1995b). *Social Indicators of Development* (Baltimore: Johns Hopkins University Press).

World Commission on Environment and Development (1987) *Our Common Future* (New York: Oxford University Press).

Zakaria, F. (1997). "The Rise of Illiberal Democracy." *Foreign Affairs, 76* (6), pp. 22–43.

# 9 Case Study: Nowa Huta

## The Ever-present Past

Europeans each tend to think of their countries in terms of the era that represents its periods of greatest glory. The English remain largely Edwardian, or even Victorian, when "the sun never set on the British Empire." Many Austrians still identify with the days of Franz Joseph; only a few years ago, tens of thousands lined the streets of Vienna as the royal coaches, taken out of museums for the occasion, were part of the procession taking their last empress to her final rest, over 70 years after her empire had disappeared. The British may be indulged their nostalgia for their period of global domination, since it ended within the lifetime of living Britons who can remember those glory days; and the Austrians' lingering devotion to their vanished age of imperial splendor can be understood because so many trappings of empire still surround them: During a walk around Vienna's marvelous Ringstrasse—even today—it is easy to imagine that a royal ball will be held in the Palace this very evening.

The longer ago in history a country enjoyed its moment at the pinnacle—its national, historic equivalent of Andy Warhol's observation about everyone's fifteen minutes of fame—the more unrealistic the present preoccupation of its people with their perished past may seem to others. Thus, the famous French fixation on the Napoleonic Age is mildly amusing to non-Gauls, since that age ended nearly 200 years ago; at the outer extreme, Mussolini's promise to his countrymen in the 1930s that he would restore the Roman Empire was seen even then as an absurd caricature of political reality—except to large numbers of Italians of that time.

This deep sense of longing for a glorious vanished era is something most Americans have trouble understanding. The United States never had such a "golden age," now forever gone; during the slightly over two centuries of its existence, it has enjoyed almost constant geographic expansion, along with steady increase in power and world prestige. There is no imperial American past; Americans tend to be oriented toward the future, even though the typical American belief that the country will become ever better and more powerful may not be held as strongly or uniformly as it has been before. Often, Americans are seen by Europeans as shallow and impetuous; as disrespectful of tradition and lacking in culture. The idea that Americans consider their United States an "established" or perhaps even "old" country is occasion of mild amusement almost anywhere in Europe; it is not uncommon for ancient European cities to have "new" roads or suburbs that were built while primitive tribes still hunted deer on Manhattan Island.

To many Europeans, there is no real "then" and "now" for their nation (which is always an older and more important concept than "country"), with a clear line of demarcation between distant past and present. There is just "history" as time that flows from the past to the present and on to the future. There are points or periods that distinguish some developments or changes, but they are like islands in the river, points by which one may orient one's current place in relation to other places and times. Even if the river changes course, or floods, it is still the same river; it still flows relentlessly onward and people go on taking food from it or irrigating with it or plying boats upon it, while it remains oblivious of their coming and going. The pride of the people is in the times when the river was *theirs* and took care of them. Their conception of their country's past is a mystical bond that is almost religious, not very different from their bond with their God and their feelings of pride for those times when God raised them above all others. For eastern Europeans (except the Russians), those days of wonder, when things were "more normal" are part of the middle-distant past, mostly beyond individual memory but fully alive as part of their shared cultural memory.

Tadeuz Sendzimir was born to the aristocratic tradition in Lwow during a time when Poland was "a stateless nation." But his grandfather had been decorated by the great Prince Poniatowski, defender of his country against the Russians and Austrians both before and after the partitions of the 1790s. A seasoned world traveler, Sendzimir happened to be in the United States when the Nazis invaded his country, and he stayed on to assist the war effort and to become a citizen after the war. His inventions in the field of high-grade steel were extremely important: some of the processes on which he held more than 70 patents had made it possible to equip planes with radar and, later, were used to fabricate the skin of the Apollo rocket (Sendzimir, 1994). He was always something of an enigma, even to his children, whose outlook seems to have been thoroughly American: they were eager to "get on with it" and impatient with time they felt he wasted thinking about a vanished world. Sendzimir shared with lots of other naturalized Americans the sense of having one foot in the old world and one in the new. He worked prodigiously and became a successful, prosperous American entrepreneur, but he always remained interested in the possibilities of development in the land of his birth and hoped to play a part in restoring Poland to a place of honor in the company of the world's nations. He thought of development largely in American terms: bigger and better, more efficient and cheaper. He believed that development, particularly economic development, would bring comfort and happiness to all the people. As a good American (albeit one with "airs"), he seems to have conceived of development as the road to a better society, even though he also always remained a keeper of the old traditions, right up to his death in 1989.

## Krakow Feels the Steel Fist

Many people seem to think of "development" exclusively—or at least primarily—in social or economic terms, as a way to change the present state of the economy or social structure for the better. Opposition to this conception of development is considered "conservative" or "old-fashioned" or simply not realistic.

When Stalin took control of the Soviet Union after Lenin died, he saw development as the device by which he could wrench a feudal society into the present century; in effect, to convert a medieval social and economic structure into a modern industrial power within one generation or, at the most, two. To do it required absolute control, and Stalin perfected the concept of the totalitarian state that had been pioneered in Germany and Italy. He also harbored that persistent European dream of restoring his country to what it considered its normal status; that is, to the time of the farthest historic extent of its borders and the highest level of its power. But unlike other dreamers of that pervasive Eastern European dream, he was in a unique position to perfect his ideas.

Poland's eastern border had been created, not at the end of hostilities of World War I, but after the Polish invasion of Russia in 1920, while that country was torn internally by the struggle between the White Russians and the Bolsheviks, a struggle ultimately won by Stalin's Reds. The secret border agreement in the 1939 German–USSR pact had been no more, from Stalin's point of view, than a restoration of the boundary originally intended by the Versailles treaty. Moreover, it seemed clear to many people in 1945, at the end of World War II, that neither democracy nor rightist regimes had been successful in those countries of eastern Europe created at Versailles.

Between 1944 and 1949, there was what Berend (1996) called a "revolt against the West" in eastern Europe, and despite the agreements and promises of free and open elections, Communists managed to seize control of the governments of all those countries during that short time. In 1946, the Communists took over the government of Poland and held a national "election," asking for legitimation of their takeover. They received the general confirmation they sought, except for one overwhelming rejection—by Krakow. The city of Krakow has always been the academic and cultural center of the country, with the largest medieval marketplace in Europe, rich in customs and history. One example may serve to illustrate this sense of tradition: Every hour of every day, a uniformed bugler appears in the topmost tower window of the central church and plays a plaintive theme that is cut short in mid-phrase. This ceremony has been acted out for untold generations, in commemoration of an anonymous thirteenth-century bugler who sought to warn the people of an approaching Mongol army when he was killed by a Tartar arrow in the throat. In the city of Krakow, Poland's historical soul and intellectual heart, the Communists received their most stinging rebuke: Ninety percent of the votes cast said "No."

By 1948, the Polish Communist government had consolidated its power and set out to duplicate the Soviet "miracle" by converting Poland from a primarily agrarian country into a modern industrial state capable of meeting the West on its own terms. It was decided to develop centers of heavy industry that would be entirely self-contained. Having been forced by Moscow to decline aid from the Marshall Plan, the Polish leaders had to turn increasingly to the Soviets for support; after NATO was formed in 1949, the military presence of the USSR came to dominate foreign and domestic policy.

In order to achieve the maximum benefits of central planning, it was determined to build an entire city around an industrial development. This would permit total control of all aspects of the economy, as well as the social life of the workers, by providing for all their needs within the context of the industry. The decision was made to build this new city just outside the city of Krakow. Although not universal, the prevailing opinion is that the choice of location was "a punishment of sorts" (Husarka, 1991) for the humiliation of the city's earlier "No" vote. The new city would bring masses of workers into the region and "turn this cultural center and university town into a city of proletarians" (Bell, 1984), or at least balance its Catholic, academic population with a "fully developed working class."

The heavy industry that was the center of the development was steel; the planned city was called "Nowa Huta." "Nowa" means "new" in Polish, but the translation of "huta" varies—"furnace" (Husarka, 1991; Dicks, 1995), "steelworks" (Sendzimir, 1994), "foundry" (Perdue, 1995), "mill" (Kabala, 1985), "forge" (Viviano, 1993), and so on—but there is no disagreement about the meaning in naming the enterprise itself: the Lenin Steelworks.

## Master-Plan Development—Soviet Style

Modeled after the Soviet planned city and steel works at Magnitogorsk, Nowa Huta was constructed on what has been described as the richest farm land in Poland; a site that had yielded human relics from 300 B.C.—coins from Roman times and Celtic ceramic ovens (Husarka, 1991). The work was preceded and accompanied by a major campaign to inform the people of its importance and to assure their support. Children were told stories about it; extensive discussions and informational meetings were conducted; songs were played on the radio; the countryside was plastered with the motto: "The Whole Nation Builds Nowa Huta" (Husarka, 1991). Every aspect of the workers' lives and comfort was addressed. The most respected and highest-paid laborers in the country, they were housed in subsidized apartment blocks. Schools, hospitals, canteens, and cultural centers were provided; separate units prepared hot meals for the workers and their families below cost; another unit ran canteens, theaters, and recreation centers, as well as hostels and vacation hotels. There was a printing plant, a mineral water bottling plant, even pig-fattening farms ("Sendzimir Steel Mill, 1997"). Only one omission was readily apparent: In the central square, where in Poland there is usually a church, stood instead a large statue of Lenin.

Once it was fully operational, the Lenin Steelworks employed 40,000 workers in a centrally planned and managed, fully integrated operation. The execution of the project was not intended to deal with problems, but to avoid them; the concept was one of an approach to development so comprehensive and inclusive that no grounds would exist for discontent, insecurity, or even boredom. Except for the purposeful omission of the church, almost everything was provided; almost nothing was overlooked.

Almost nothing. There was one oversight that did not become apparent for several years. That was the fact that the steelworks, constructed largely as a copy of the Soviet mills of an earlier time, were not significantly more advanced than those older mills. In essence, the new steelworks at Nowa Huta began operation in 1952 at the technological level of Pittsburgh steel mills of the 1930s. Moreover, so integrated were all operations, from coke manufacturing to lime processing to finished steel, that modification was difficult. The objective had been to create a fully self-contained entity: raw materials in one end, finished steel out the other, and it had succeeded. Unfortunately for Nowa Huta, at the very time its already outdated mill was being built, rapid changes in the manufacture of steel were taking place in the West. The introduction of "basic oxygen steelmaking" in the 1950s "revolutionized" the field; by 1980, it had virtually replaced other methods of producing bulk steel. The changeover to continuous casting increased efficiency and cut costs; by 1985, more than 75 percent of all steel was made that way in the West (Hardy et al., 1996). The Lenin Steelworks at Nowa Huta were outmoded when they began operation; insulated from advances in the West, they continued to fall steadily behind, not only in modern methods of production, but in the conversion to computers and fiber optics—"the power to store, process, analyze, and retrieve knowledge" (Perdue, 1995). This was not so great a problem as long as purchase of the mill's output of inferior steel was assured by other eastern European countries and the Soviet Union, but it locked them into methods of production and quality of product that became increasingly noncompetitive with Western steel.

The antiquated processes and low-grade raw materials, many shipped in from the USSR, had another important and far-reaching consequence: pollution. The levels of pollution in the area, mostly generated by the mill, were staggering. Estimates of air pollution vary from 50,000 to 100,000 tons of toxic dust and from 440,000 to 600,000 tons of gases, principally sulfur dioxide, every year (Husaka, 1991; Trevelyan, 1990). By 1984, sulfur dioxide deposition was estimated to be 1687 tons per square kilometer. Water pollution was equally calamitous. In 1980, the Vistula River at Krakow was declared "virtually devoid of biological life" (Kabala, 1985). In one school, 61 percent of the children were

*Lenin Steel Works, producing steel, pollution, and poisonous air covering housing, child care facilities, schools, and dining halls.*

under medical treatment for ear and respiratory ailments (Sweeney, 1991) and Krakow had the highest infant mortality rate in Poland. Adults also suffered: Ninety-two percent of the workers suffered some occupational illness (Fura, 1985). These grim circumstances were well-known to the people living in the low valley in which Krakow is located. The dullness of the sun through the brown-yellow air, their scratchy throats, and the dissolving monuments reminded them daily. But openly addressing the problems was not then feasible, since reports of ecological studies were "strictly suppressed or censored" (Fura, 1985) and government regulations right through the 1970s expressly prohibited the publication of any "specific examples of air, water, or soil pollution that are an endangerment to life or health" (Sweeney, 1991).

The workers in Nowa Huta were expected to be the most contented in the country; they were among those who had brought the Communists to power. But something troubled them almost at once: the absence of a church. Despite considerable agitation, it was 1970 before they finally were able to erect a cross. A church still lay far in the future.

Worker agitation elsewhere in the country was picked up, and sometimes led, by workers at Nowa Huta. After the brutal suppression of the 1956 riots, Gomulka returned to power. He ruled with his fist, but he began to make Polish Communism national rather than an extension of Moscow. He also recognized that Polish industry needed to be modernized. One of the people who tried to help in this endeavor was Tadeusz Sendzimir. In 1961, Sendzimir's processes were being used throughout the world, and when he visited Nowa Huta, he was startled to find that the plant that was producing half of all Poland's steel was almost hopelessly antiquated and inefficient. He strongly urged modernization and was able to make some small changes, but the Cold War was under way and the U.S. government, fearful of the possible military uses that might be made of it, would not allow his more advanced technology to be sent to Poland (Sendzimir, 1994).

Gomulka's policies finally led to economic collapse, and he was succeeded by Gierek, who relied on heavy borrowing to keep things afloat. Some private property ownership was introduced and there was an underground economy. However, Poland's foreign debt soared: in 1971, it was US$1.8 billion; ten years later, it was US$23.5 billion. Since the borrowed money was not used to "facilitate any major structural changes in the country's economic mechanism" (Ekiert, 1996: 223), it only exacerbated the economic problems.

## Unrest Development

During the 1970s, the slight loosening of government control resulted in a beginning recovery of the intelligentsia, who had been ruthlessly suppressed in the aftermath of the 1956 revolt. Unrest grew, and the workers from Nowa Huta were usually involved, as in the 1977 demonstration protesting the death of a student (Bernhard, 1993). In 1978, Krakow was named a "world heritage centre" by UNESCO (Dicks, 1995), providing some moral leverage for protecting it from the depredation of the Lenin Steelworks, but the pivotal event of the year was the elevation of Cardinal Woityla to the papacy, the first non-Italian Pope since 1522. As Pope John Paul II, this former archbishop of Krakow and graduate of the city's venerable Jagiellonian University paid a return visit to the city the next year. Filled with piety and pride, the Polish people poured into the streets in great nonconfrontational gatherings that left the government perplexed but powerless. The new unity carried over into meetings around other issues, and when the government again raised prices the next summer, the workers, students, and intellectuals for the first time stood together, under the Solidarity movement (Rothschild, 1989), winning major concessions, both economic and in civil rights. The concessions permitted, among other things, the formation of civic organizations not under government control. One group, concerned with freedom of worship, was the Christian Community of Working People, founded in Nowa Huta, which began to publish its own paper, *Krzyz Nowohucki* or Cross of Nowa Huta, in honor of the cross they had succeeded in erecting ten years earlier (Bernhard, 1993). About the same time, a group of Krakow academics, workers, physicians, and journalists came together to form the country's "first independent environmental pressure group," the Polish Ecological Club (Fura, 1985) which conducted "high quality scientific analyses" and immediately began pressing for modernization of the Nowa Huta works.

As Solidarity began to reveal that the Polish Communist leaders had been providing benefits for themselves and their bureaucracies rather than for the workers, a spirit of open revolution grew and, purportedly to avoid an invasion by the USSR or the Warsaw Pact nations, the Polish Army took over of the government, led by General Jaruzelski, a much-respected member of an old Polish family. Jaruzelski moved swiftly to assert control, and in fall 1981, he closed the borders and declared martial law, banning Solidarity, arresting thousands of Solidarity leaders, and suppressing dissent.

This time, there was a response from the West. Led by the United States, the European Community reluctantly passed economic sanctions against Poland, intensifying its fiscal crisis. Investment declined at a time when competition from the Third World countries was increasing. People began leaving the country: Between 1983 and 1988, 100,000 Poles emigrated; 400,000 more took "vacations" abroad and never returned (Nagorski, 1988). Even population stagnated; by the middle of the decade, the growth rate among working age adults was actually negative (Adam, 1996). The government position deteriorated under steady pressure from labor, with the Nowa Huta steelworkers taking a central role through strikes and demonstrations. Solidarity had decentralized, making it more difficult for the government to fight its activities, which were supported from the outside with money, publications, and other goods smuggled through the closed borders. The unit of Solidarity in Nowa Huta remained one of the most active in the country. There was another wave of mass arrests in 1984, with more than 300 people receiving sentences, but the Polish government never succeeded in wiping out public opposition as the Hungarian and Czech governments had done, and in 1986, Jaruzelski broke the stalemate by issuing a general amnesty and began to ease his controls sufficiently to be admitted to the IMF and World Bank (Ekiert, 1996). However, the economy remained in a slump, leading to more strikes. Growing resistance to the government was crystallized by a major strike at the Nowa Huta steelworks, where workers remained on the premises. Only one western reporter was able to witness the raid that dislodged the workers. He later wrote that over 2000 secret police and "elite commandos" using concussion and flash grenades stormed the plant while the workers were sleeping, seriously injuring many of them (Doerner, 1988). The workers retaliated with massive absenteeism.

The unrest continued, and the next year, 1989, Solidarity was relegalized. Its worker representation among Nowa Huta steel workers was exceeded only by that of the Gdansk shipyard workers. The most privileged workers in Poland, who had formed the core of the movement to institutionalize the communist regime, now led the movement to dismantle it. In elections held later that year, Solidarity candidates took every seat but one in the Sejm, the Polish legislature.

Old laws requiring participation by "workers' councils" in major industries had been ignored by the Stalinists; now that the workers controlled the government, the councils began to take their power seriously. At Nowa Huta, the worker council members insisted on their authority to hire or fire managers, but there was no agreement on privatization because of fears over job losses and the likelihood of "sweetheart deals" in which the bureaucracies, still well-entrenched, would keep the best assets for themselves (Engelberg, 1990). One of the first acts was to honor the Polish-American who had done so much for their industry, renaming the steelworks Huta T. Sendzimira (HTS). The debate over the fate of the mill and Nowa Huta continued. During this crucial period, there was a world-wide crash in the price of steel. In addition, the guaranteed eastern European markets for Polish products evaporated and the Polish economy fell into recession. The hard-won popularity of Solidarity was short-lived. In the first fully free national elections in 1991, Solidarity candidates lost heavily, although there was no clear winning group; the 1993 elections were a total defeat for Solidarity, with former communist candidates, renamed or reconstructed, taking 63 percent of the Sejm (Berend, 1996).

## What Should We Do after the Party?

At Nowa Huta, a new phase of development had to be faced. The workers, accustomed to having all decisions made for them, found that the decisions facing them were prickly. As one manager put it: "For 40 years...I didn't have to take decisions—everything was done in Warsaw. Now, I must fight" (Trevelyan, 1990). Many of the people of Krakow simply wanted to tear down the whole complex; the managers wanted to keep it open, claiming they could make it show a profit; still others wanted to break it up into a number of smaller companies, an idea that was first strongly proposed in 1990. Initially, there was a lot of optimism about operating HTS as a private enterprise, even though the workers were warned that conversion would "take years, not months" (Fairlamb, 1990). The initial fears of the workers became realities with great frequency: Old-line communist bureaucrats retained control of key institutions needed for market conversion, sometimes simply renaming the firm or their offices.

Eager to convert to the Western market system and fearful, as one observed put it, that "staying permanently behind western Europe is [a] very real [possibility]" (Longworth, 1992), the Solidarity government introduced "shock therapy" in the form of the Balcerowicz Plan. The principal goals of the plan were to liberalize the market, hold down inflation, make the currency convertible, cut subsidies, control wage increases, and privatize all major state-owned industries. It was expected that benefits would appear quickly (Cannon, 1997; Berend, 1996). Instead, the economy slumped. Privatization of state retail enterprises progressed rapidly; by 1992, 85 percent of them had been converted. Resistance developed to privatization of the major state-owned enterprises, the heavy industry.

No one in Poland could afford them and no one outside Poland wanted them. Workers at the Sendzimir facility began to feel betrayed. They had assumed that removal of central planning and introduction of privatization would mean that they would be on the boards of directors, not that the plant would be sold and new managers would be brought in over them. The workers were very troubled about foreign ownership. It seems clear that their dream was for a restoration of a "greater Poland," the most powerful country in eastern Europe—that is, the Poland of the sixteenth century. The reality of world economics was difficult for the Nowa Huta workers to accept. Just as they seemed to have gained control over their own destinies, it was apparent that they had exchanged the economic stability but political oppression of Communism for the political freedom but economic insecurity of free market. The head of the workers' party (KPN) muttered darkly about people "selling off the nation's assets to foreigners" ("Clean Hands," 1992). The Balcerowicz Plan had begun with great enthusiasm and had some spectacular successes, such as reducing the rate of inflation from nearly 1000 percent a year to 60 percent but it was abandoned within two years largely because of widespread resistance to selling off major state-owned enterprises. That sector did not respond as expected to the changes, neither flourishing nor collapsing but resembling, as one observer noted, an apple tree that gives no fruit but will not die.

It also became clear at Nowa Huta that the workers still desired change, but were not prepared to accept the pain that would accompany it. They had retained a "firm attachment" to a system that "they hated, but which had permeated them" with its job security, cheap flats and food, and freedom from responsibility (Majman, 1992). The state did everything; the workers just had to do what they were told. However, they were not yet ready to give up. They believed that if they could make the mill profitable, they could justify keeping it open; and to do that, they would need to have it modernized. In one well-publicized episode in 1992, the HTS workers conducted a hunger strike, demanding modernization of the plant by the government. They were marginally successful in that some new production methods and equipment were introduced. The problem was that modernization of one portion of the works was not sufficient to make it competitive, and a program to fully modernize it was beyond the fiscal capacity of the government.

When a parallel action, a decision to try to sell the HTS enterprise, was explored, the workers estimated that it would bring US$400 million, but the best offer they received was from Sweden—for US$7 million, and that was for the land; the mill was considered worthless and would be torn down (Remnick, 1991). Traveling to Western countries for ideas on how to make the mill competitive, workers were reportedly astounded in Essen to see "no smoke at all" in Germany's vast steel operations. Although operations at Nowa Huta had been cut back sharply, the sky over Krakow was still thick with what a *Washington Post* reporter described as a "hideous cloud of multicolored smoke" (Remnick, 1991).

The concern over foreign control also had a more sinister subtext. The dark horse who had amazed everyone by finishing second in the 1990 election for president returned to his home in Canada telling a reporter that he didn't want to be "in a Poland which will be turned into a Jewish colony" (Wohlfarth, 1992).

In 1991, the government engaged a consortium of Canadian consultants (Hatch Associates, Ernst & Young, and Steltech) to study Poland's steel industry. Their report, issued the next year, was a blow to the HTS workers. The recommendation was to close most of Poland's steel mills and to merge HTS operations with the newer steel works at Katowice in an arrangement that was an obvious pretext for the ultimate closing of Sendzimir. Other recommendations included separation of the ancillary services into private companies and cutting manpower. The HTS works, employing 40,000 workers at its peak, was to have no more than 10,000 within ten years, and probably fewer than 8000. The scheme would put every job in jeopardy (Viviano, 1993).

The workers at Nowa Huta were caught in an economic vice. Only a few years earlier, they had been Poland's elite corps but they now had to face being obsolete by Western standards. The Soviet market was gone; in fact, eastern Europe was being flooded by steel from Russia and the Ukraine at price lower than HTS was charging (Viviano, 1993). With tariff restrictions protecting them from better Western steel due to expire by the end of 1997, they were forced to face the painful economic reality of their situation. At HTS, old-fashioned methods of steel making used large amounts of energy, were labor intensive, and poisoned the soil, the air, and the water. For example, it took 22 work hours to make a ton of steel at HTS; in the West, it took between 1.5 and 6 work hours (Sosnowska-Smogorzewska, 1993); energy use in HTS was 60 percent higher and the final product yield was 20 percent lower (Chojnacki, 1995). Most of the HTS machinery was more than 40 years old; in the West, such machinery was considered uneconomical and obsolete after 15 years. During a general upturn in the economy after 1993, the HTS mill made a profit, but by 1996, its profit figures remained unimpressive. To make matters worse, the small retail and manufacturing sector that had become almost entirely private was booming. A small heating system business virtually in the shadows of the Sendzimir chimneys had grown steadily and financed all of its expansion out of profits.

## Not Quite Market Reform

In spite of some resistance, the Polish Council of Ministers adopted the recommendations of the Canadian consortium in December 1992. However, there were some loopholes. For one, the Sendzimir and Katowice steel works happened to fall under two separate ministries, with the result that each ministry protected its major industries. By the middle of 1997, the merger still had not taken place and probably was dead. With German help, continuous casting lines were installed in the HTS mill, which cut energy use and pollution. The difference in air quality was immediately noticeable; by 1995, Krakovians were beginning to feel that their air was returning to normal. These signs were taken as positive, but it was charged that management decisions are not yet governed by market thinking. For example, although the modernization left the HTS facility with heavy debts, when the mill made a profit in 1994, the money went to worker raises rather than paying down the debt. Moreover, it is charged that operating funds came not from profits, but from loans, subsidies, sale of assets, and by delaying or ignoring payments due to social insurance programs (Lesniewski & Niewrzedowski, 1996).

The privatization of state-owned industries had received a severe setback in 1992, when the Sejm rejected a bill that would have privatized 600 major industries in one stroke.

*Clean air returns to Krakow's historic medieval marketplace.*

The bill had been the result of three years of debate and negotiation, but the decision was made to treat major industries under different rules from those successfully applied to smaller state-owned business (Darnton, 1992). Instead, a complex system was set up to assess and oversee restructuring of large enterprises. At the end of 1996, the Polish subsidiary of Dun & Bradstreet found that among the 100 top Polish enterprises, those owned by the state still predominated and that the state remained "entrenched in areas of poor competitive strength" (Chmielewski: 1996). The report further noted that the steel industry was "increasingly more outmoded."

The method adopted to privatize large state-owned firms such as the Sendzimir works was for them first to pass through a stage of "commercialization." Under this procedure, the state-owned enterprise became subject to commercial laws without being privately owned, and would then be restructured and sold. The problem with this procedure is that it tends to keep the same managers in place, with no pressure to sell or even to change, since the security of the state ownership remains, rather than the risks of competition. Moreover, no deadline was set for the final stage—selling the enterprise.

Early in 1997, HTS was moving toward privatization. As a wholly owned Treasury company since 1992, it had already begun streamlining in order to avoid bankruptcy, by spinning off fifteen of its related businesses and offering workers an early retirement package. Examples of the portions spun off were design, scrap, catering, child care, and the recreation divisions. As a result of these moves, the original 40,000 employees had been cut over time to 17,000; however, this reduction was not due to lay-offs, but to retirements and the employees joining the new quasi-independent firms (Hardy, 1996). It is necessary to call them "quasi-independent" because HTS still retained a heavy investment in most of them through stock ownership and other mechanisms. Nevertheless, by this action of spinning off units, HTS became basically just a steel mill. (Formerly, it had also been a major welfare agency!) As a result of the selective modernization during the same time, product quality had been improved significantly, although not enough to meet Western standards; a potentially important contract with General Motors could not be closed because the mill could not meet GM specifications ("Sendzimir Steel Mill," 1997).

In April 1997, under the newly passed Commercialization and Privatization Act, permission was given for HTS to incorporate as a joint-stock company, owned by the Treasury. It was decided to split it into three independent units: one for steel production, the others covering machinery and power supply. Along with the Krakow East Industrial Development Agency, these would form a holding company. The top managers at HTS would become a board of directors. Originally, workers and pensioners had been given the chance to buy up to 20 percent of the stock at a discount, but for various reasons, this was changed to a plan to distribute 15 percent of the shares gratis ("Sendzimir Steel Mill," 1997). This approach seemed to reflect a continued fear of foreign domination.

Not everyone was pleased with Poland's cautious steps toward the market economy. One observer called its economic policies "investor unfriendly" and predicted that the state holding companies would not succeed in converting state firms to private ones. Instead of such companies, it was asserted, the state should really privatize those firms it can sell, liquidate those it cannot, or "forget about joining the European Union" (Anonymous, 1997b). In mid-1997, state-owned enterprises still represented 50 percent of those in the top 500 Polish firms, and the pace of privatization had slowed. These were the firms whose "claim to prominence is their talent for wasting money" (Anonymous, 1997b). Polish economist C. Jozefiak specifically identified the HTS arrangement as unsatisfactory, actually a slowdown in the process of privatization. He noted that investors and stockholders could influence the "constituent units" but not the mother company, thereby shielding the incompetent management from pressures by the stockholders.

While the large state-owned sector continued to resist true privatization, with all the risks of competition and all the possibilities of profit, the rest of the Polish economy boomed. In November 1996, the *Wall Street Journal* referred to Poland as a "tentative tiger," an allusion to the Four Asian Tigers. The growth noted was almost entirely in the private sector; the state monopolies remained impoverished, ineffective, and intransigent (Michaels, 1996). At Nowa Huta, it was decided in July 1997 to conduct yet another study and to bring in another multinational consortium to advise on the full privatization of the Sendzimir mill (Anonymous, 1997b).

## Development: Disaster or Dilemma

The history of Nowa Huta is virtually a casebook study in problems of development. As a command economy enterprise, it was expected to showcase the best in economic and social development and to be a model for the future. The Communist Polish government intended to show that central planning of gigantic industrial centers, with loyal workers for whom all needs were provided, would outproduce and ultimately defeat capitalism. What became clear instead was that rigid ideology, job security, and guaranteed welfare benefits could not overcome problems created by overlooking cultural concerns. Contrary to official expectations, frequent indoctrination sessions did not seem adequate to replace church services, and the huge statue of Lenin proved a poor substitute for the Virgin Mary. The people of Nowa Huta were among the most loyal Party members in Poland, but they were also good Catholics and they saw no conflict in being both. When they began to organize to demand their right to religious observances, they laid the groundwork for organization that subsequently overthrew the communist government.

Once they had wrested power from the Communists, the workers at Nowa Huta fell back on traditional views. Suspicious of outsiders, they consistently objected to foreign investment. Their identification with the present took the form of naming their mill after a Pole who had left the country forty years earlier, but remained faithful to the memory of Poland's glorious fifteenth- and sixteenth-century traditions. Having resisted the unrealistic and rigid development approach of the Stalinists, they resisted with equal vigor the methods of development that had emerged in the rest of the world while they were sequestered in the Stalinist dungeon.

Nowa Huta has not yet solved its development dilemma. Even the success of the firms spun off since 1992 is not certain, since they remain tied to the HTS plant through lease arrangements, joint directorships, and so on. They have not learned how to pursue new markets and they cannot retain the old ones. They remain stuck in the central-planning thinking they thought they had rejected. Having demanded, successfully, respect for and recognition of their cultural values, they do not seem to understand that they will have to modify some of those values voluntarily or fall ever-farther behind the rest of the industrial world of which they long to be an important part.

Part of their difficulty is what one observer called "the fear factor." It is difficult to leave the familiar. For forty years—nearly ten times as long as the Nazi occupation and twice as long as the interwar national independence—government made all the major decisions and it was understood that this was just another phase in the long history of the Polish worker outwitting the government. After 1989, they *became* the government, demanding that Poland join the world economic community. Things could never be the same again, but the workers were not prepared for the basic kinds of changes in store for them. For example, child care and catered family meals had made it possible for women to be full participants in the workforce. Once these benefits or subsidies come to an end, as they are now in the process of doing, there will have to be careful consideration of the implications for women workers. It is not at all clear that such consideration has become widespread.

Development is never solely economic. Social, political, cultural, and other aspects of development, if overlooked, can doom the most well-meaning program. But it is also the case that traditions are subject to change as circumstances warrant. The price of maintaining ancient cultural traditions is to remain an historic artifact.

Tadeusz Sendzimir was a man who was entranced his whole life by the past glories of Poland, and he was true to her culture and traditions. But he also lived in the present and he brought his remarkably inventive mind to bear on the problems of modern industrial society. In so doing, he was able to become extremely wealthy and to use that wealth to help preserve the cultural life of his native land. If they are to avoid becoming redundant in present-day Western society, the devout and courageous workers of Nowa Huta will need to learn the flexibility and adaptability of the countryman after whom they named their newly independent steelworks.

# REFERENCES

Adam, J. (1996). *Why Did the Socialist System Collapse in Central & Eastern European Countries?* (London: Macmillan).

*Anonymous. (1997a). Bulletin: *Economic Review* (July 23).

*Anonymous. (1997b). Bulletin: *Economic Review* (May 17).

Bell, D. (1984). "Krakow Walks." *The New Republic, 190* (May 14), pp. 9–10.

Berend, I. (1996). *Central & Eastern Europe: 1944–1993* (New York: Cambridge University Press).

Bernhard, M. (1993). *The Origins of Democratization in Poland* (New York: Columbia University Press).

Cannon, L. (1997). "Polish Transition Strategy." In J. Zacek and I. Kim (Eds.), *Society in Change* (Gainesville: University of Florida Press), pp. 142–158.

*Chmielewski, A. (1996). Bulletin: *Economic Review* (December 10).

*Chojnacki, I. (1995). "Steel Industry: Strong in Weakness." *Economic Review* (May 7).

*Clean Hands. (1992). Interview. *The Warsaw Voice* (February 23).

Darnton, J. (1992). "Polish Parliament Rejects Bill to Privatize Industries." *New York Times* (March 19), pp. 3.

Dicks, B. (1995). "Saving Krakow's Face." *Geographical Magazine, 67* (February), 53–55.

Doerner, W. (1988). "Duel of the Deaf." *Time, 131* (May 16), p. 4.

Ekiert, G. (1996). *The State against Society* (Princeton: Princeton University Press).

Engelberg, S. (1990). "Polish Workers Wield New Power." *New York Times* (December 28), Section D, p. 1.

*Fairlamb, D. (1990). "So Far So Good." *Institutional Investor* (September), p. 72.

Fura, Z. (1985). "Institutions: The Polish Ecological Club." *Environment, 27* (9), p. 4–5, 43.

Hardy, J., A. Rainnie, J. Kot and E. Piasecka. (1996). "Restructuring Huta T. Sendzimira—From the Lenin Steelworks to Lean Production." *Communist Economies & Economic Transformation, 8* (2), pp. 237–249.

Husarka, A. (1991). "The Pearl of Poland." *Conde Nast Traveler, 26* (August), pp. 64–67, 122–129.

Kabala, S. (1985). "Poland: Facing the Hidden Costs of Development." *Environment, 27* (9), pp. 6–13, 37–42.

*Lesniewski, B., and A. Niewrzedowski. (1996), "State-Owned Bankruptcies: Life Preserver for the Chosen." *Analyses and Commentaries* (May 26).

Longworth, P. (1992). *The Making of Eastern Europe* (New York: St. Martin's).

*Majman, S. (1992). "Make Wire!" *The Warsaw Voice* (January 26).

Martin, D. (1996). "Booming Economy in Poland Brings Jobs, Wealth and Apathy." *The Wall Street Journal* (November 25), pp. 1, A12.

Michaels, D. (1996). "Booming Economy in Poland Brings Jobs, Wealth and Apathy," *The Wall Street Journal* (November 25), pp. 1, 12.

Nagorski, A. (1988). "Old Troubles, New Threats in Poland." *Newsweek, 111* (May 19), pp. 27–28.

Perdue, W. (1995). *Paradox of Change* (Westport, CT: Praeger).

Remnick, D. (1991). "Stalin's Lethal Legacy of Filth." *The Washington Post* (May 21), p. A1.

Rothschild, J. (1989). *Return to Diversity* (New York: Oxford University Press).

Sendzimir, V. (1994). *Steel Will* (New York: Hippocrene Books).

*"Sendzimir Steel Mill: Albatross of Commercialization" (1997). *Economic Review* (April 29).

*Sosnowska-Smogorzewska, L. (1993). "Polish Steel Industry Landscape: Future Shock Needed." *The Warsaw Voice* (January 24).

Sweeney, P. (1991). "Krakow at the Crossroads." *Sierra Magazine* (March/April), pp. 56–60.

Trevelyan, M. (1990). "A Relic of Stalinism in Poland Seeks Renewal in Free Market." *The Chicago Tribune* (August 27), p. 6.

Viviano, F. (1993). "Future Shock Arrives for Blue-Collar Workers in East Europe." *The San Francisco Chronicle* (April 14), p. A7.

*Wohlfarth, T. (1992). "Poland's Economic Disaster." *Canadian Dimension, 26* (3) (April), p. 31.

*Full text downloaded from Polish News Bulletin, a non-profit organization.

# 10 First Nations Development Institute

*For tribal people, who see the world as a whole, the essence of our work is in its entirety. In a society where all are related, where everybody is someone else's mother, father, brother, sister, aunt, or cousin, and where you cannot leave without eventually coming home, simple decisions require the approval of nearly everyone in that society.*

*This is the Native understanding. It is the understanding in a global sense.*

*As more and more technology shrinks our planet Earth, the commonality that emerges is our interdependence. We, our, yours, and theirs. If we see that so clearly, then just on the horizon lies the vision of humanity.*

—Rebecca Adamson (1994)

In 1979, a Cherokee activist cashed her unemployment check, took a plane to New York City, and began knocking on the doors of America's major philanthropies in search of resources to fulfill her dream: an organization that would forever rid Native Americans of their dependence on the federal government. To the shear audacity of the idea, Rebecca Adamson brought a road-savvy that was the result of years hitchhiking across the United States, a patience from being a single parent and cancer survivor, and a wisdom from years of organizing Native Americans. By the end of her trip, she clenched in her hand a check from the Ford Foundation for $25,000 to establish First Nations Development Institute. A decade and a half later, First Nations was providing $3 million in aid to support Native American self-sufficiency; in addition, First Nations was consulting with indigenous peoples as far afield as Botswana and Australia. In 1997, Rebecca Adamson was honored by *Ms. Magazine* as a "woman of the year" for her "gift not only for bringing people together, but for bringing worlds together" (Steinem, 1997: 49).

## The "Miner's Canary"

Among the paradoxes of development are indigenous populations who struggle to retain native traditions in the face of oppressive cultures. Adamson uses the metaphor of the "miner's canary" to describe the importance of first peoples, indigents who comprise four percent of the world population (Boustany, 1997). As exploitive strategies of development consume exhaustible supplies of fossil fuels in the process polluting the environment, leveling biodiversity, and skewing the distribution of wealth, the condition of first peoples becomes an indicator of global well-being, hence the metaphor of the "miner's canary." By the 1990s, traditional methods of development had failed to generate sustainable prosperity.

- The number of the world's poor continues to increase, despite rapid economic growth globally.
- The richest fifth of the world's population consumes four-fifths of the earth's resources.
- Forty-seven of the largest firms in the world are corporations that exceed the wealth of more than 130 nations, yet have no obligation for education and welfare of citizens.
- Human sustenance now consumes 40 percent of the plant matter produced by photosynthesis.
- Nonsustainable production has already degraded 35 percent of the land, contributing to deforestation and desertification.
- Human predation contributes to the extinction of 5,000 species annually (Adamson, 1994).

If conventional routes to development, which had been taken by industrial nations, were no longer tenable, then alternative routes were needed for developing nations. As they had in the industrial world, Adamson and her associates contend, the ultimate indicator of responsible development would be the condition of first peoples in the Third World.

The plight of Native Americans in the United States, Aborigines in Australia, and the Maori in New Zealand are well-documented, of course. But first peoples in developing nations, such as the Maya in Guatemala and the San bushmen of southern Africa, are similarly disadvantaged, if not more so, simply because they must fight two battles at once: one to survive, another to assert traditional customs. At first glance, native populations of the First World might seem to be at an advantage compared to those in the Third World, but not necessarily so. As several observers have come to realize, the circumstance of Native Americans in the United States is not unlike that of a developing nation. In many American reservations, unemployment exceeds 50 percent; alcoholism is rampant, contributing to a high incidence of Fetal Alcohol Syndrome; and only 12 percent earn more than $7,000 per year (Adamson, 1994). "Our resources, for the most part have already been expropriated, exploited, and depleted to fuel the engine of the U.S. economy, just as those of indigenous peoples in the poor nations of the 'South' are now being used," noted Oglala Sioux, Sherry Salway Black, a vice-president of First Nations. "Our diminishing land base and dwindling natural resources, largely remote and isolated locations, high unemployment and poverty rates, lack of adequate infrastructure, lack of access to financial and other markets make one think of a lesser developed country than the U.S." (1996: 33).

An indigenous tribe more destitute than many Native Americans is Australia's Aborigines. Having populated Australia for at least 40,000 years, Aboriginal groups evolved as small, nomadic bands that eventually spoke more than 400 languages (Farnsworth, 1997b). Journeying considerable distances through parched countryside, Aborigines recited the directions through elaborate "songs" that guided them (Chatwin, 1988). For British penal agents who claimed eastern Australia in 1788, this was so much primitive nonsense, and the colonists proceeded to expropriate lands without any regard to native rights whatsoever (Farnsworth, 1997c). Among the most horrific of government policies

*Rebecca Adamson, bringing worlds together*

was the Native Welfare Acts, which allowed Australian officials to remove Aboriginal children from their homes and place them with whites. Between 1910 and 1970 some 100,000 children were forcibly removed in an attempt by the government to depopulate Aboriginal tribes. Because lighter-complected children were more desirable to white families, Aboriginal mothers resorted to smearing their children's faces with charcoal to harbor them from acquisitive government agents. However genocidal the policy, it effectively diminished the native population; in 1879 some 60,000 Aborigines lived in western Australia, by the 1930s, the number had dropped to 20,000 (Farnsworth, 1997b). By the 1990s, the Aborigines had only a tentative hold on existence; at 400,000 to 500,000 they represented but 2 to 3 percent of the Australian population. The life expectancy of Aborigines is 15 to 20 years less than that of whites, they are 15 to 18 times more susceptible to fatal infectious disease, and the infant mortality rate is four times that of whites (Farnsworth, 1997d). It was not until 1992 that the Australian Supreme Court upheld a claim for Aboriginal land rights (Farnsworth, 1997a). While the Australian government dithered as to whether or not to issue a formal "apology" for anti-Aboriginal policies, claims for compensation inundated the courts (Farnsworth, 1997b), evidence that Australia is just beginning to address the rights of the continent's native inhabitants.

Nascent native rights movements are also evident in South America. In northern Brazil, the Macuxi tribe has mobilized to protect its native region from an invasion of prospectors who had been expelled from the region of the Yanomami. The mercury and high-pressure hoses the miners used to extract gold and diamonds polluted streams and left stagnant pools that bred mosquito-transmitted malaria. With the assistance of the Catholic Church, the Macuxi have blocked the construction of a dam, blockaded roads to prevent the transport of supplies to miners, and lobbied for a 6,500-square-mile preserve. By mid-1996, miners were moving away due to Macuxi opposition (Schemo, 1996). In Guatemala, Mayans have organized to become a national political force. For five centuries, the 21 linguistic groups descended from Mayan civilization have been dominated by a well-off minority descended from Spanish colonists. As part of the end of a protracted civil war, the government and insurgents signed an "Accord on the Identity and Rights of Indigenous Peoples," which guaranteed Mayan descendants political influence for the first time. As part of the transition, the government established the Guatemalan Fund for Indigenous Development that promises to assure Mayans of their political rights. In turn, Mayan groups have targeted indigenous land ownership, native health practices, and bicultural education as central issues. The national constitution has been published in four Mayan languages, prompting one Maya priest to prophesy the end of "a bitter history of 500 years of marginalization" (Rohter, 1996).

While such incidents of tribal self-determination are laudable, they remain relatively isolated. In the far recesses of the development literature lurks an assumption that runs counter to the interests of indigenous populations. The anthropologist Marvin Harris put it succinctly: "Civilized man was supposed to have literally thought himself out of the state of nature by steadily inventing more and more clever and reasonable institutions, customs, and subsistence processes" (1968: 39). Development perforce relegates nature and its habitants to a primitive past, one the expert seeks to eclipse as rapidly as possible; taking indigenous populations as a point of departure, the purpose of modernization is to leave them in the dustbin of history. Cast in such light, there is little of value to first peoples save a romanticism that affirms a naive reciprocity between natives and nature. This simplification diminishes the intimate relationship between indigenous groups and their environment, of course, one that has only recently begun to be appreciated. Reversing the denigration that has been heaped on native populations historically, the International Indigenous Commission (1991) has documented the many ways first peoples have evolved sophisticated practices that complement development, such as enhancing biodiversity, controlling population, balancing resource distribution, and encouraging technological innovation. Although important conceptual ground has been turned by the work of the International Indigenous Commission, an organizational void remained—the need for an institution that would transform indigenous development from theory to practice.

## The First Nations Development Paradigm

Growing up, Rebecca Adamson might not have seemed likely to develop a world-class advocacy organization. Born in Ohio in 1949 of a Swedish father and part-Cherokee mother, she was a quiet student, speaking little in school. Her powers of observation were acute, however, and they were honed by her enthusiasm for hitchhiking. Several trips to visit her Cherokee relatives in North Carolina not only acquainted her with the traditional beliefs of her grandfather, but also left her a keen judge of human character. She was struck by the "poverty and lack of opportunity of her cousins" (Ridley, 1997: 35). After stints studying philosophy, law, and economics, she dropped out of college and hitchhiked to the West Coast, a hub of the nascent Native American movement. Immersed in organizing activities, she found a job on the Nez Perce reservation in Idaho, where she butted heads with the federal government. An application to assist the Nez Perce to revive their breeding of Appaloosa horses was rejected because of a preference for building industrial parks in reservations, not nurturing tribal traditions. Adamson would later reverse this rejection by establishing an organization that would make the appropriation that the federal government would not.

At the age of twenty-three, Adamson became director of the Coalition of Indian Controlled School Boards in 1972. Historically, the education of Indian children had been controlled by the U.S. government, often with the assistance of Christian religious organizations. "Generations of Indian children had been taken from their families and sent to Indian boarding schools, where they were not allowed to speak their own language or follow their tribes' cultural and spiritual teachings" (Ridley, 1997: 35). The Coalition fought for Native American control of schools through a variety of tactics, including peaceful demonstrations that resulted in Adamson's arrest on three occasions. By the mid-1970s, her persistence was paying off. The Indian Self-Determination Act was passed; she married and gave birth to a daughter. The joy of the moment was transitory, however. The marriage dissolved, and she recognized that Indian self-determination was illusory if Native Americans did not have control of their own purse strings.

During the next few years Adamson experimented with different ideas to promote tribal economic development. She took a job at the Indian Controlled School in Bismark, North Dakota, which allowed her to refine her thinking. Nagging her was a paradox: while Native Americans were the nation's "fastest growing underclass," they possessed enormous assets. While Indians represented only one percent of the population, they controlled five percent of the land, including 15 percent of the nation's low-sulfur, surface-minable coal, 40 percent of its uranium, four percent of the oil and gas in production, and 5.3 million acres of commercial forest, to say nothing of substantial reserves of oil shale and geothermal energy (Black, 1996: 9). How, she wondered, could a people so rich in resources be so destitute? The answer came into focus as an organization that promoted culturally appropriate, sustainable development. In 1979 she left for the East Coast to found the Native American Financial Self-Sufficiency Project, which would later become the First Nations Development Institute (Ridley, 1997).

Rebecca Adamson crafted First Nations Development Institute in counterpoint to conventional ideas of development. Instead of "Euro-American values of individualism, equal opportunity, private property and accumulation" she emphasized "kinship, communal usage, sharing, cultural identity and spirituality." Four principles provided the foundation for First Nations:

- Community is "essential for survival."
- Nature is "a source of knowledge, a model to emulate, and a mentor."
- Subsistence emphasizes "the interplay of spiritual beliefs with hunting and fishing."
- Culturally, subsistence "derives its meaning from the context of the group."

The essence, as Adamson was to reveal later, was to create an alternative to traditional, consumption notions of development. The purpose was to build an organization that "is not market-based but rather [consists of] extensive intracommunity and intercommunity trade and exchange networks," she observed. "Based on reciprocity, those who receive are expected to give something to someone else. The value is sharing. People's prestige and influence within the community is based largely upon their generosity, not on their personal wealth" (1994: 4–6).

As First Nations evolved, the model for an alternative development paradigm came into clearer focus. Sherry Salway Black, an Oglala Sioux and vice-president of First Nations, identified the components that were central to constructing an alternative to the "economic growth paradigm which has driven the United States as well as most of the countries of the Northern Hemisphere": it must be "people-centered," "sustainable," and "self-reliant." These, Black argues, are in contrast with "a western economic approach [that] does not regard the world as alive but rather as a machine producing limitless resources which continue to be depleted" (1994: 4, 11). But First Nations would have to go beyond rhetoric if it were to have an effect on native development. Thus, a two-part strategy was pursued. First Nations would work with Native Americans on reservations, at the same time lobbying for policy changes that were more consistent with sustainable development. At the reservation level, six efforts would be undertaken: technical assistance, facilitating capital formation, research, local and national advocacy, marketing, and education in development. First Nations' experience with development led to the formulation of a unique model of development, as shown in Figure 10.1 on page 190.

The First Nations model has four primary vectors—assets, kinship, personal efficacy, and spirituality—the interactions among which produce more subtle outcomes as indicated in the model.

*Adamson in the American west*

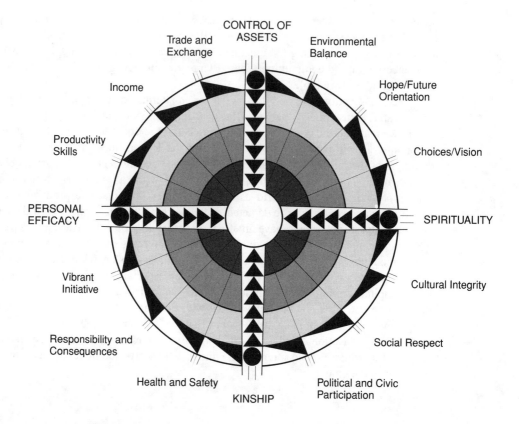

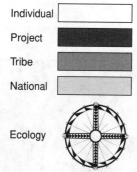

**FIGURE 10.1    Elements of Development.**

Copyright 1991 © by First Nations Development Institute

## Assets

It is significant that the First Nations model begins with control of assets. The fundamental source of assets is land, of course, an issue of particular sensitivity to Native Americans. Aside from the outright theft of land by government and settlers, the 1887 Dawes Allotment Act encouraged Indians to perceive land as private property, a conceptual transformation that led the sale of substantial native lands to whites. "The principle of control of assets is applicable to any social and economic program for disenfranchised people," contends Black, "If you do not control assets, you do not have the ability to create wealth from them, and your life is always subject to someone else's control" (1994:16).

## Kinship

According to native customs, kinship was the vehicle for transmitting assets and wealth. Instead of accumulating resources in order to become wealthy, tribal members shared them for the common good. Today, this form of distribution is evident in barter and trading that is a regular occurrence on reservations. Such sharing is contrary to the welfare mentality of governmental social programs of which Black is particularly critical: "The government welfare systems, superimposed on a complex and existing system of giving, sharing and reciprocity has facilitated the breakdown of the kinship system" (1994: 16). Thus, governmental welfare is contradictory to economic development.

## Personal Efficacy

The competence of native peoples is what allowed them to prosper across all ecosystems. In contemporary economics the knowledge, health, and capacity is recognized as human capital. Following the economic growth model, personal efficacy is valued according to the accumulation of wealth that it generates. First peoples view this differently; "in a tribal sense, individual achievements are valued in terms of their benefit to the extended family and to the tribe" (Black, 1994: 17). While children are raised to be capable and independent, upon adulthood they are expected to use their talents for the benefit of the community, not to ostentatious, individual excess.

## Spirituality

In posing spirituality as a benchmark for development, the founders of First Nations state that they do not refer to any established religious orthodoxy. Rather, "it is from spirituality that you gain your sense of yourself and your meaning within the community, and within the larger universe" (Black 1994: 17). In so doing, spirituality poses an ontological question that is often omitted from discussions of development: What is the meaning of progress, what are the choices to be made, and with what consequences? For native peoples who have had their traditional answers to such questions smothered by Christian dogma, the appeal to spirituality invites a return to old beliefs and ceremonial activities.

In interaction, these four benchmarks animate the First Nations development paradigm. Assets and personal efficacy stresses the value of a "dignified livelihood" beyond wage-labor; personal efficacy and kinship promote indigenous initiatives in entrepreneurship and innovation; kinship and spirituality encourage political participation and cultural empowerment; spirituality and assets project the future (Black, 1994: 17–19). In this respect, the First Nations paradigm of development is more vital than the mechanistic and numerically driven formulations of the economic growth model.

# First Nations Programs

In deploying programs, First Nations has striven to avoid the pitfalls of the "Indian entrepreneur model," which places individual success above interconnectedness, and the "Chamber of Commerce model," which brings in business activity from the outside, essentially denying the value of indigenous resources (Black 1994: 10), by charting a third way.

## Eagle Staff Fund

This fund pools monies that have been contributed by various granting agencies, then makes grants to specific Native American projects. By mid-1995, First Nations invested $1.5 million in projects designed to enhance self-sufficiency through culturally appropriate activities. Among Eagle Staff Fund ventures are

*The Inter Tribal Bison Cooperative*    Headquartered at the Fort Belknap Reservation in Montana, the Bison Cooperative attempts to restore the buffalo to the centrality of traditional Indian plains culture. To date, 36 member tribes have begun to work in consort toward cultivating herds of buffalo, managing slaughter and packaging operations, and marketing the sale of products to optimize profits. Exploiting a niche market that appeals to domestic, European, and Japanese consumers who prize low-fat, high-protein meat, the Bison Cooperative anticipates profiting from this traditional asset. At the same time, the objective is to manage herds in a way that is sustainable, while nurturing traditional beliefs related to the buffalo.

*Nez Perce Young Horseman*    The Nez Perce program will restore the Appaloosa to tribal culture while righting an historical wrong: the 1877 flight of the Nez Perce from Army troops in a futile attempt to reach Canada which resulted in the disbanding of their distinctive breed of horses. In order to restore the breed, Asian horses of akhal-teke stock are being bred with native Appaloosa in order to produce a new breed, the Nez Perce horse (Robbins, 1996). Beyond the breeding program, the initiative restores the role of the horse in traditional culture. The Young Horseman's program complements the breeding program by encouraging academic studies in math and history (*Biennial Report,* 1994/95).

*The Hopi Foundation*    The Hopi Foundation was established to reinforce traditional beliefs among the Hopi in the Southwest. The Hopi Foundation sought Eagle Staff Funds for projects that would improve the housing stock for stone buildings that are among the oldest continuously inhabited structures in North America. Included in the initiative are the restoration of run-down houses in the 12 Hopi pueblos, the installation of solar panels to provide electricity on a sustainable basis, and a health forum that encourages traditional healing practices (*Biennial Report,* 1994/95).

*California Indian Basketweavers Association*    Among the most distinctive native crafts are the baskets that are woven for various daily and ceremonial purposes. In addition to transmitting this ancient artistic skill to younger generations, CIBA has advocated for pesticide-free land management so that children are not exposed to harmful chemicals. "CIBA also works to increase access to gathering sites for basket weaving materials, food, and medicines, and increase their ability to plant resources by traditional methods" ("First Nation Development Institute's Success Stories...," n.d.)

*Kalalea Farmers Association*   Native Hawaiians had begun an organic gardening business, but a hurricane blew away their greenhouse. With an Eagle Staff Fund grant, the Kalalea Farmers Association increased production by expanding the greenhouse growing area. While the new greenhouses are expected to generate $18,000 in income in the first year alone, this is not the sole purpose of the project. Recalling the traditional meaning of *mahele,* or sharing, the project will encourage the exchange of other foods in order to promote self-sufficiency (*Biennial Report,* 1994/95).

*White Earth Land Recovery Project*   In Northern Minnesota, the Ojibwe Tribe's relationship to the land was deteriorating. Traditional food-gathering practices, such as wild rice cultivation, corn-planting, and sugar maple tapping, were becoming less common. Of particular concern was the loss of maple groves to clear-cutting for lumber and firewood. In reversing the habitat exploitation, the Land Recovery Project encouraged the production of maple sap for conversion into syrup. Since maple syrup was traditionally used during ceremonies, this became a route to encouraging Ojibwe beliefs. Soon the project was developing a marketing plan for its products (*Biennial Report,* 1994/95).

In addition to these ventures, Eagle Staff Funds have been allocated to develop eco-tourism at the Fort Belknap Reservation, to protect native resources held by Athabascan Tribes in Alaska, to cultivate ginseng on the Olympic Peninsula of Washington State, to support Native Action, a mobilization of Northern Cheyenne in Montana, to protect water rights for the tribes of the Mni Sose Intertribal Coalition of the Missouri River basin, to expand housing through the Northern Circle Indian Housing Authority in California, and to initiate entrepreneurial activities through the Native American Business Association among the Coeur d'Alene of Idaho (*Biennial Report,* 1994/95).

## The Oweesta Program

In Mohawk, "oweesta" translates as money, a commodity that complements a First Nations objective: asset accumulation. In establishing Oweesta, First Nations learned from demonstrations, such as the Lakota micro-credit fund, a field project that First Nations deployed in 1985. In subsequent years, First Nations refined technical assistance skills in micro-credit, eventually training 20 indigenous groups. Using micro-credit as a platform, First Nations expanded its financial service activities, encouraging tribes to establish banks and credit unions. By the mid-1990s, First Nations had invested $1 million to enhance the financial capacity of tribes in New Mexico, Nebraska, Oklahoma, Montana, South Dakota, and Minnesota (*Biennial Report,* 1994/95).

The incursion of First Nations into more affluent financial circles surely presented odd moments. Among the most amusing had to have been the November 21, 1996, hearing at the Office of the Comptroller of the Currency (OCC). After a flag song and traditional blessing by Clayton Old Elk, a Crow tribal member, the currency examiners were introduced to the capital capacity of Indian Country. Due to the opening of credit opportunities to Native Americans, loans had increased 16 percent in 1995 alone. Norwest Corporation increased its lending to Native Americans to $6 million and committed $450,000 to Indians who completed a financial management course. Mike Roberts, First Nations' Financial Officer, noted the central role that Community Development Financial Institutions would continue to play on reservations. By the end of the program, bankers of the OCC not only learned about the latent capital on reservations, but also received an introduction in Indian ceremony ("'Extra Effort'," 1996).

In many respects, the Oweesta program represents the bending of traditional economic development strategies to culturally appropriate objectives. The most important lesson is that these values are not mutually exclusive. As Adamson argues, the purpose of sustainable development is not to reject capital formation, but "toward appreciating the cumulative [economic] power of nurturing many small ones" (Ridley, 1997: 39). Toward that end, First Nations has organized self-sustaining economic ventures on reservations at the same time it has used Native American economic principles to leverage resources for all low-income communities. For example, Adamson convinced the Calvert Fund, a socially conscious mutual fund, to set aside a portion of its investment portfolio for community development loans for all low-income communities (Adamson interview, 1997).

## First Peoples Worldwide

As the First Nations development paradigm resonated through North America and its programs became more well known, requests for assistance came from abroad. Fully 10 percent of the 2,000 requests for aid from First Nations came from, or on behalf of, indigenous peoples in Africa, Australia, Russia, and Latin America. Adamson's extensive travel and economic development expertise was later complemented by the legal expertise of a Canadian Anishinabe (Ojibwe), Kristyna Bishop, a Canadian-trained lawyer. They formed the nucleus for First Nation's international arm, First Peoples Worldwide (FPW). As explicated by First Nations,

> FPW is an organization that can provide indigenous communities with the necessary financial and technical resources to build national-level indigenous development intermediaries. To assist in the institutional capacity building of these national-level organization, FPW will spearhead the gathering of culturally appropriate economic development models and legal precedents that will be made available to them and to international indigenous groups and corporations through the development of the Indigenous Network for Global Linkages, a mutual self- help network (database). ("First Peoples Worldwide," n.d.: 1)

FPW soon established demonstration projects in Botswana and Australia. In Botswana, San residents were being removed from the Central Kalahari Game Reserve, part of an area that had been the hunting grounds of the San people since time immemorial. The prohibition against hunting by nomadic tribes has been documented to destroy the social fabric of native groups (Turnbull, 1987), so the First Peoples of the Kalahari (FPK) requested assistance from First Nations to craft a transitional development program. It then became apparent that a comprehensive legal strategy was also necessary. First Nations has worked with FPK, the Working Group on Indigenous Minorities in Southern Africa, and Ditshwanelo (Botswana Center for Human Rights) to establish "a land claim precedent" for land usage by first peoples. In Australia, First Nations has advocated the organization of an Aboriginal Foundation that would promote the interest of indigenous peoples on that continent. When appropriate, First Nations programs, such as the Eagle Staff Fund, are proposed as models to facilitate sustainable development for Aborigines and other indigenous groups seeking assistance.

## The Future of First Nations

Sixteen years after its inception, First Nations has achieved high visibility in Native American development efforts. By 1997, First Nations had made 33 start-up grants, 8 working capital grants, 25 seed grants, and two development capital grants ("Eagle Staff Fund Grantees," 1997). Despite this impressive beginning, several issues appear on the horizon for First Nations. Foremost is the magnitude of the needs of indigenous peoples. If the economic and cultural rights of Native Americans are just being recognized, those of first peoples in developing nations have yet to register visibly on the radar screen. To compound matters, the legal infrastructure from which tribal advocates can leverage native claims is virtually nonexistent in much of the Third World. It bears repeating that an industrialized nation, Australia, had failed to recognize the property rights of Aborigines until a Supreme Court ruling of 1992. With the exception of United Nations declarations (Rao, 1997), which provide guidance but have no enforcement authority, the policy and program foundation that would secure and protect first peoples internationally is virtually nonexistent.

In the United States, First Nations is confronted with something of a conundrum for Native American advocates: a paradox of riches. For decades the Bureau of Indian Affairs (BIA) has overseen $2.9 billion in trust accounts, reserved for some 300,000 individuals and 280 tribes. Yet, the BIA has so mismanaged the funds that President Clinton had to appoint a bank regulator, Paul Homan, to straighten out the mess. Homan's assessment on taking the job was that "without question, this is the worst I've seen as a banker and as an auditor...Simply put, we cannot account for their money." To make matters worse, the BIA spends $33 million annually just to track trust accounts (McAllister, 1997: A19). Given First Nations propitious beginning, it is easy to speculate how productive a joint partnership between the Institute and the BIA could be if trust funds were used to capitalize development projects on reservations.

Since passage of the Indian Gaming Regulatory Act of 1988, tribes were allowed to establish commercial gambling operations as a function of their sovereignty, an option asserted by about one-third of the 554 recognized tribes in the United States. For 1996, tribal gaming revenues brought in about $7 billion, an amount sufficient to induce conservative legislators to attempt to append riders to BIA budget authority that would force tribes to waive tribal immunity from lawsuits (Campbell and McCain, 1997) or deny federal funds to tribes generating revenues above a certain level (Egan, 1997). While gaming operations are profitable for perhaps ten percent of tribes that operate casinos, most find them marginal operations (Ridley, 1997). The question that remains, however, is, how can the enormous revenues—$600 million from slot machines owned by the Pequot tribe of Connecticut, for example (Egan, 1997)—of some tribes be diverted to better the circumstances of all Native Americans. While casino gambling is a far cry from the culturally appropriate, sustainable orientation that First Nations has cultivated in its model of development, the gaming revenues generated by some tribes might warrant the inception of a tribal development fund or foundation that could be managed by First Nations to promote development initiatives on nongaming reservations.

Since the earliest history of the United States, the objective of Anglo-Americans has been to contain and subordinate the interests of Native Americans (Ambrose, 1996). The conquest of the wilderness brought with it the submission, if not the annihilation, of many tribes—all of which was justified by the desirability, if not the inevitability, of progress. Nearing the end of two centuries of domination on the part of the Anglo-industrial complex, the consequences are increasingly obvious: a polluted environment, depleted resources, a hyperconsumption culture, and a dispirited population. As the search for alternatives to the mass-consumption, metastatic industrialization model continues (Henderson, 1997), organizations such as First Nations remind us of the virtue of sustainable development, in the process serving as the "miner's canary" for the Earth.

# REFERENCES

Adamson interview at the First Nations Development Institute, August 19, 1997.

Adamson, Rebecca. (1994) "What are Sustainable Communities?" address in Oakland, California (June 2) (Fredericksburg, VA: First Nations Development Institute).

Ambrose, Stephen. (1996). *Undaunted Courage* (New York: Touchstone).

*Biennial Report.* (1994/95). (Fredericksburg, VA: First Nations Development Institute).

Black, Sherry Salway. (1996). "Indigenous Economics," *YES! A Journal of Positive Futures* (Spring/Summer).

Boustany, Nora. (1997). "Advocating Aid for Africa," *Washington Post* (February 14).

Campbell, Ben Nighthorse, and John McCain. (1997). "Keeping Our Word to the Indians," *Washington Post* (September 10).

Chatwin, Bruce. (1988). *The Songlines* (New York: Penguin).

"Eagle Staff Fund Grantees," *Indian Giver.* (Spring 1997). (Fredericksburg, VA: First Nations Development Institute).

Egan, Timothy. (1997). "Now, a White Backlash Against Rich Indians," *New York Times* (September 7).

"'Extra Effort' in Lending Is Theme of OCC Heritage Month Forum," (1997). *Business Alert* (November/December, First Nations Development Institute).

Farnsworth, Clyde. (1997a). "Blaming It All on 'Them'," *New York Times* (May 11).

Farnsworth, Clyde. (1997b). "Australians Resist Facing Up to Legacy of Parting Aborigines from Families," *New York Times* (June 8).

Farnsworth, Clyde. (1997c). "Enclave Reflects Aborigines Plight," *New York Times* (February 9).

Farnsworth, Clyde. (1997d). "In a Land of Plenty, Good Health Still Eludes the Aborigines," *New York Times* (June 1).

"First Nations Development Institute's Success Stories…" (n.d.) (Fredericksburg, VA: author).

"First Peoples Worldwide (FPW) and Indigenous Network for Global Linkages (INGL)." (September 1997). (Fredericksburg, VA: First Nations Development Institute).

Harris, Marvin. (1968). *The Rise of Anthropological Theory* (New York: Crowell).

Henderson, Hazel. (1997). *Building a Win-Win World* (San Francisco: Berret-Koehler).

International Indigenous Commission. (1991). "Indigenous People's Traditional Knowledge and Management Practices" (Fredericksburg, VA: First Nations Development Institute).

McAllister, Bill. (1997). "Indian Trust Accounts," *Washington Post* (February 27), p. A19.

Rao, Mukunda. (1997). "Global Perspectives in Social Work Education." In Lynne Healy and Yvonne Asamoah, Eds., *Global Perspectives in Social Work Education* (Alexandria, VA: Council on Social Work Education).

Ridley, Kimberly. (1997). "Indian Giver," *HOPE* (May/June).

Robbins, Jim. (1996). "Tribe Famous for Horses Sees Future in Them," *New York Times* (November 3).

Rohter, Larry. (1996). "Maya Renaissance in Guatemala Turns Political," *New York Times* (August 12).

Schemo, Diana. (1996). "In Brazil, Indians Call on Spirits to Save Land," *New York Times* (July 21).

Steinem, Gloria. (1997). "Rebecca Adamson," *Ms. Magazine* (January/February).

Turnbull, Colin. (1987). *The Mountain People* (New York: Penguin).

# C H A P T E R

# 11 Habitat for Humanity

Habitat for Humanity is a Christian nonprofit organization that builds housing for the poor. From its inception, Habitat for Humanity has been active in developing nations with two-thirds of its housing units built in the Third World. The organization relies on volunteers who commit to a three-year stint as "international partners" (IPs). With technical assistance and resources coordinated through its international headquarters in Americus, Georgia, IPs organize local, indigenous populations to build low-cost, permanent structures to replace the shacks that typify the housing of the poorest of the poor. Habitat for Humanity prides itself on its resolve to build community along with the houses it constructs. Cofounder Millard Fuller's "theology of the hammer" professes the Christian value that self-sacrifice for the poor has its ultimate expression in the provision of tangible improvement of their circumstances. Marking its twentieth anniversary in 1996, Habitat for Humanity claimed 200,000 volunteers who constructed 1,000 houses per month in the United States and 50 nations overseas. By the end of the century, Fuller expected that Habitat for Humanity would be the largest home builder in the world (Mayer, 1996).

## Malawi

A landlocked nation in East Africa, Malawi is among the poorest nations in the world. Malawi's history is more colorful than its small size might suggest, however. An appreciation of colonial and postcolonial events in Malawi not only provides benchmarks for development, but also demystifies conventional understandings of European settlement. Formerly known as Nyasaland, Malawi was a center of the slave trade during the eighteenth and nineteenth centuries. Coastal East Africa had been explored by Arabs and Portuguese navigators who worked with the Yao, a tribe actively engaged in slaving. Between 1858 and 1863, British explorer David Livingstone visited the region and later lectured at Cambridge University about the evils of the slave trade. As a result of Livingstone's appeal, the Universities' Mission to Central Africa was organized to oppose slaving there. Eventually, Scottish missionaries of the United Free Church of Scotland proved a powerful opposition to Yao slavers; the Scotch settlement in the South, Blantyre, was to become a center of economic activity (Pike, 1968: 75–77).

Unlike India, the British colonial experience in East Africa failed to generate a corporation that coordinated development of resources and exploitation of the native population. Malawi was not easily accessible by rail or boat, and the country lacked precious minerals.

Thus, what became the Nyasaland Protectorate oversaw a rural, colonial backwater that attracted few Europeans. Those colonists who migrated to Nyasaland tended to favor the highlands, a decision that avoided the diseases typical of low-lying areas and which proved ideal for the establishment of tea plantations. Rail egress to the Indian Ocean was not achieved until 1935, but this did little to accelerate development. By the Second World War, colonists had experimented with a number of crop exports, including coffee, tobacco, and cotton, but none was as profitable as tea. The indigenous population lived at the subsistence level, cultivating plots that were limited to the area that could be worked by a short-handled hoe, and primarily growing maize, tobacco, and ground nuts (Pryor, 1990: ch. 2).

With the exception of a short-lived rebellion led by John Chilembwe in 1915, Malawian independence avoided the violence characteristic of the independence movements in other African colonies (Pike, 1968: 97–102). The political base for African participation was formalized in the Nyasaland African Congress (NAC) founded in 1944, an organization that transmitted African opposition to the confederation of Nyasaland with two Rhodesias (now Zimbabwe) that lasted from 1954 to 1964. African calls for independence attracted the attention of expatriate Malawian, Dr. Hastings Kamuzu Banda, a physician educated in the United States and Britain who had an established medical practice in suburban London. After a 40-year absence, Banda returned to Malawi in 1958 and quickly assumed the leadership of the Malawi Congress Party (MCP), formerly the NAC. Banda's popularity soared as a result of a year's incarceration for anticolonial activities. When Malawi gained independence in 1964, Banda became the first prime minister (Pryor, 1990: 32–35).

Banda's actions immediately following independence ran counter to those of many African nationalists who assumed leadership of their nations. Banda did not nationalize industries, opting instead for market developmental strategies. Infuriating many in the MCP, Banda insisted that African civil servants attain the same level of skill possessed by their European predecessors prior to promotion. Then, in an ultimate expression of pragmatism, Banda maintained diplomatic relations with Rhodesia and South Africa in order to assure trade routes for exports and imports, even when the governments of those nations fought African insurgents. Such actions riled colleagues in the MCP, who became increasingly antagonistic; Banda's response was autocratic. Exploiting his charisma, Banda instituted policies that effectively outlawed political opposition and in 1971 proclaimed himself "President for Life." In his bid to eliminate political competitors, Banda made membership in the MCP compulsory and transformed the Malawi Young Pioneers from a peasant training effort to a 2,000-member paramilitary, security force (Young, 1994: 12). If Banda was successful in centralizing power and establishing himself as a "big man," it was at the expense of national development. Writing for the World Bank, observer Frederic Pryor noted that the Malawi of 1990 ranked among the poorest of the world's nations. "The level of education was low, and health conditions were appalling" (Pryor, 1990: 31).

During the early 1990s, a convergence of forces weakened Banda's grip on power. In 1992, Catholic bishops publicly criticized the government for abuses of power. Emboldened trade unionists defied government authority, leading to the trial and imprisonment of labor leader Chakufwa Chihana. Demonstrations and strikes in favor of Chihana turned into riots when the Young Pioneers appeared, resulting in forty deaths. Political turmoil abated only after Banda agreed to a referendum on multiparty elections set for 1993. The outcome of the election vindicated Banda's opposition: two-thirds of Malawians affirmed political pluralism. His authority diminishing, Banda agreed to nationwide elections, and in 1994 the 96-year-old patriarch was defeated by Bakili Muluzi, a Yao. As a former chair of the Chamber of Commerce and government minister, Muluzi was expected to endorse International Monetary Fund (IMF) austerity measures designed to invigorate the economy (Young, 1994: 13–14).

Three decades after attaining independence, Malawi had little to show for it. Even though the nation had avoided civil strife and enjoyed political stability in the transition to statehood, most Malawians survived at the subsistence level. Although Malawi's GDP had grown at an annual rate of 4.6 percent, population growth consumed all but 1.6 percent of that (Pryor, 1990: 43). Banda's departure marked the end of an era in Africa, the defeat of yet another of a rapidly diminishing number of national leaders since independence (Ransdell, 1994: 16). By the mid-1990s, the UN Human Development Index ranked Malawi 157 of 174 nations, its attributes tragically typical of sub-Saharan Africa:

| | |
|---|---|
| Life expectancy at birth | 45.6 years |
| Adult literacy rate | 53.9% |
| School enrollment | 46% |
| Per capita GNP | $230 |
| Per capita caloric supply | 1,827 |
| Children malnourished under five | 466,000 |
| Children dying before age five | 117,000 |

In the early 1990s, 88 percent of Malawians lived in rural areas, and agriculture accounted for 87 percent of the labor force (*Human Development Report,* 1995). Today, electricity and running water are virtually unknown to rural families in Malawi. Indeed, the prosperous farmer is one able to claim ownership of a bicycle.

## The Habitat Program

Although Habitat for Humanity is widely known as an American housing program, its origins have been shaped significantly by the African experience. Conceived in the Deep South, Habitat for Humanity was intended as a vehicle for personal redemption as well as racial reconciliation. Since the beginning, Habitat for Humanity has focused on the plight of the rural, minority poor in the American South. At the same time, Habitat has maintained programming in Africa, among many locales. Since its inception, Habitat for Humanity founder Millard Fuller and his wife Linda have actively promoted housing in Zaire. From its base in Americus, Georgia, Habitat for Humanity maintains a vigorous international program, fostering programs around the world. Because of its volunteer emphasis, Habitat has been able to mount programs in extraordinarily diverse locations, often as a result of the infectious enthusiasm of the Fullers' books: *No More Shacks* (1986) and *The Excitement Is Building* (1990). Of course, the conscription of former President Jimmy Carter, who has volunteered for week-long construction projects for the past several years, has provided invaluable public relations support (Jenish and MacGillivray, 1993). Indeed, the growth of Habitat for Humanity has accelerated to the point that as early as 1981 cofounder Fuller stated the organization's objective as no less than the total elimination of substandard housing (Gaillard, 1996: 138).

## History

The origins of Habitat for Humanity can be traced to the desperate attempt of a wealthy attorney to salvage a disintegrating marriage and his encounter with an irascible Georgia preacher. In 1965, Millard Fuller enjoyed the marvelous prosperity of a young and ambitious attorney: a healthy family, a thriving law practice, a farm, a place at the lake, and a Lincoln Continental. All this collapsed when Fuller's wife, Linda, threatened to leave the marriage. Shocked into recognizing the superficiality of his life, Fuller vowed to change it if Linda would return. Initially doubtful, she soon learned that Millard was serious—perhaps too serious. After tidying up his affairs, Millard Fuller sold virtually everything, gave the proceeds to charity, packed the family in the Lincoln, and headed for Florida en route to a life of Christian service. At a whim, the Fullers stopped to visit friends at Koinonia in Albany, Georgia, an interracial community that had been established by Clarence Jordan, a Baptist preacher.

Koinonia was Jordan's attempt to put Christian principles in practice by encouraging both races to live and work together. In the volatility of the Civil Rights era, Jordan's activities provoked visits and violence by the Ku Klux Klan, but Jordan persevered. The Baptist preacher's intransigence about *living* Christian values resonated with Fuller. "God calls us," Jordan explained, "to be bold and radical in applying the way of Christ to our living" (Gaillard, 1996: 14). Returning to Koinonia in 1968, Jordan and Fuller determined to realize their principles by establishing a Fund for Humanity. Adhering to the Old Testament admonition—"If you lend money to my people, to the poor among you, you shall not deal with them as a creditor; you shall not exact interest from them" (Exodus 22:25)—the fund would make no-interest loans to the poor for home construction. In October 1968, a solicitation from Koinonia generated sufficient funds for constructing a few homes; the first went to Bo and Emma Johnson, who had once lived at Koinonia. Tragically, Clarence Jordan died before the first house was completed (Gaillard, 1996).

Inspired by the logic of the project, the Fullers accepted a missionary assignment to Zaire in 1973. After language study in France, the family moved to Mbandaka and established a Fund for Humanity. The adversity was unbelievable. As Millard Fuller recounted later, "For three years Linda and I wrestled with problems and discouragements ranging from thievery, a ludicrous bureaucracy, capricious arrests, and a perpetual shortage of funds and materials, to cultural adjustments like learning to be patient in a land where time means very little." Once again, the Fullers' faith pulled them through. By the time they left Zaire, 80 families were making mortgage payments to the Mbandaka Fund for Humanity (Fuller, 1986: 31–32). Returning to Koinonia in 1976, the Fullers and two dozen confederates agreed to form a new organization: Habitat for Humanity.

### The Theology of the Hammer

Following the Biblical teaching, "it is more blessed to give than to receive" (Acts 20:35), Fuller has crafted "the theology of the hammer" to explain the philosophy of Habitat for

Humanity. Seizing on the hammer as the symbol of Jesus as carpenter, Fuller built a credo that bonded divergent religious sects. "We all take our hammers and saws and levels and other instruments of the building trade and we work together," the Fullers explained, "letting the world see that we Christians can agree on something! We can agree on a hammer and a nail, and we can and do drive nails together as a manifestation of God's love" (Fuller and Fuller, 1990: 32). Thus, Habitat not only derives volunteers who are Jewish, Muslim, and Hindu, it also builds housing for people from innumerable faiths. Habitat for Humanity is ecumenical, radically so.

Beyond religious translation, "the theology of the hammer" has important social dimensions. The most obvious of these are the Fullers themselves. Once prosperous, middle-income professionals, they divested themselves of the trappings of mass-consumption, turning their material wealth over to charity, and assuming roles as moral crusaders for the poor. In the context of the hypermaterialism of global capitalism, this may seem naive; but from the standpoint of the rise of evangelicalism, the Fullers are nothing less than disciples in a postmodern age. As much as Habitat for Humanity has provided the opportunity and structure for the moral impulses of hundreds of thousands of volunteers, it also represents what Max Weber termed, the "routinization of charisma" (Gerth and Mills, 1974). The best example of the ways that the Fuller's have exploited their moral capital has been the frequency with which they conscript high-visibility personalities, the most well known being President Carter, to work on various projects (Gaillard, 1996).

Habitat for Humanity also contributes to social development at the community level. Out of the Old Testament teaching that God is in solidarity with the poor and the New Testament portrayal of Jesus as among the poor (*Habitat for Humanity's Christian Principles*, n.d.), Habitat works to integrate the poor into the social organization of established communities. This occurs when local affiliates select for home ownership from among the poorest families, as well as the requirement that eligible families contribute "sweat equity" in order to be eligible for a home, themselves. This complements the theology of the hammer, as Rendell Day noted, "The hammer should be unifying symbol of the need for people to work together to eliminate poverty housing from the face of the earth. This is done by wording **with** those in need of housing, not simply **for** them" (n.d.: 2). In this respect, the local affiliate functions not unlike the Christian Base Communities that evolved through "liberation theology," though in this case the target population was not illiterate poor, but the morally challenged middle-class.

## Organization

The structure of Habitat for Humanity was as simple as it was expansive. Essentially, the organization was a franchise of quasi-independent, nonprofit agencies that would build housing for the poor.

> Each local Habitat project to be formed would be totally ecumenical, each would keep the overhead as low as possible and would be financed by a revolving Fund for Humanity. Money would be raised from private sources—individuals, churches, companies, etc. Volunteers would do most of the building to keep the cost down and to give people an opportunity to do "hands on" work as an expression of their faith. Houses would always be simple,

but they would be solid and of quality construction. They would be sold to needy families with no profit added and no interest charged. And the families would be involved through "sweat equity." They would be required to give several hundred hours of work toward building their own houses and houses for others. (Fuller and Fuller, 1990: 5)

Soon Habitat for Humanity units were being organized around the United States: San Antonio; Johns Island, South Carolina; New York City; Charlotte, North Carolina; Nashville; Miami; Jackson, Mississippi; Atlanta; Watts in Los Angeles; Baltimore; and rural areas in Appalachia and the Cheyenne River Sioux Indian Reservation. By 1995, Habitat for Humanity boasted 1,200 affiliates throughout the 50 states and the District of Columbia (*Building the Future,* 1995: 16).

Habitat's international efforts were no less ambitious. From the humble beginnings in Zaire, the organization established affiliates for the Maya in Guatemala, in remote areas of Uganda, on riversides in Papua New Guinea, and in the slums of Bombay. Mindful of its reconciliation potential, the Habitat for Humanity project in Belfast, Northern Ireland, brought Protestants and Catholics together in common Christian purpose. Cognizant of the momentous changes that sweep across whole nations, Habitat for Humanity established an affiliate in Hungary to mend the social fabric that had frayed during the transition from Soviet Communism to market capitalism (Gaillard, 1996). Since the early 1980s when most Habitat international affiliates began, the organization has racked up impressive numbers of new homes:

since 1982, 3,200 houses completed in Peru

since 1983, 2,600 houses built in India

since 1986, 1,400 homes constructed in the Philippines

since 1989, 6,000 houses finished in Mexico (*The Momentum Is Building,* n.p.)

Of Habitat's $18 million budget in 1995, $11.5 million was expended through international affiliates (*Building the Future,* 1995).

Table 11.1 summarizes building activities of Habitat for Humanity projects in the developing world.

## Habitat for Humanity in Malawi

The Malawi Habitat for Humanity project is one aspect of a multicountry initiative. Since the initial organizing activities in Zaire in 1973, Habitat affiliates in Africa have expanded rather dramatically. During the intervening two decades, about 2,000 houses had been constructed in Zaire, out of a total of almost 11,000 on the African continent. In addition to Malawi, Habitat reported 28 International Partners working in affiliates in Botswana, Central African Republic, Egypt, Ethiopia, Ghana, Kenya, South Africa, Tanzania, Uganda, Zaire, and Zambia. By 1994, Habitat African affiliates were constructing more than 2,400 houses annually. The cost of housing varied considerably among African nations, with Malawi being among the least expensive, as noted in Table 11.2.

**TABLE 11.1   International Housing Statistics**

| Country | Year of Habitat for Humanity Affiliation | Housing Totals, End of 1996 |
|---|---|---|
| Botswana | 1987 | 372 |
| Central African Republic | 1991 | 270 |
| Egypt | 1989 | 281 |
| Ethiopia | 1990 | 82 |
| Ghana | 1987 | 877 |
| Kenya | 1982 | 624 |
| Malawi | 1986 | 3,623 |
| South Africa | 1987 | 50 |
| Tanzania | 1986 | 804 |
| Uganda | 1984 | 1,460 |
| Zaire | 1976 | 1,999 |
| Zambia | 1982 | 497 |
| Zimbabwe | 1996 | 14 |
| **Area Total** | | **10,953** |
| Fiji | 1991 | 102 |
| India | 1983 | 2,840 |
| Indonesia | 1991 | 52 |
| **Area Total** | | **2,994** |
| Papua New Guinea | 1983 | 663 |
| Solomon Islands | 1986 | 27 |
| Sri Lanka | 1995 | 99 |
| **Area Total** | | **789** |
| Bolivia | 1985 | 1,044 |
| Brazil | 1987 | 273 |
| Colombia | 1994 | 39 |
| Costa Rica | 1987 | 64 |
| Dominican Republic | 1987 | 257 |
| El Salvador | 1987 | 498 |
| Guatemala | 1979 | 2,263 |
| Haiti | 1981 | 308 |
| Honduras | 1984 | 570 |
| Jamaica | 1992 | 16 |
| Mexico | 1989 | 7,326 |
| Nicaragua | 1983 | 1,391 |
| Peru | 1982 | 3,805 |
| **Area Total** | | **17,854** |
| **Cumulative Total 1976–1996** | | **32,590** |

*Source:* Habitat for Humanity International 1997.

The first Habitat for Humanity affiliates were established in the capital, Lilongwe (1985), and Zomba (1989). South Lunzu and Nambiti were approved in 1991; by 1994 an additional nine communities were building housing ("International Partners: Mary Rakocy", n.d.). By 1996, some 12 Habitat affiliates had constructed 3,500 units that became home for 21,000 Malawians. The average monthly repayment was 75 Kwacha or US$5.00. The model unit for which materials were produced in Kasungu was a home of 6' by 9' of kiln-baked brick with a roof of cement tile. Outbuildings included the kitchen, an enclosed latrine, and bathhouse. The kitchen is detached in order to avoid smoke resulting from burning wood that is used for cooking.

In 1996, Habitat for Humanity Malawi received the United Nations' Best Practices award. Of 900 organizations that apply, the UN selects 100 that are noteworthy. The Habitat Malawi program was cited for its extensive partnerships with other development organizations. In addition to its delegation of IPs and an indigenous board of directors, the Malawi program had collaborated with the Peace Corps, World University Service of Canada, International Executive Service Corps, Coordinating Unite to Rehabilitate the Environment, and the Presbyterian and Baptist churches, among others. In noting the honor associated with the award, Habitat International Program Coordinator Matthew Maury said staff of the project were humbled, "We will be working even harder to show we deserve this recognition" ("News from Habitat for Humanity [Malawi]," 1996: 1–2).

## Lessons from Habitat for Humanity

By the late-1990s, Habitat for Humanity was well-established in the developing world; associates in Africa and Latin America were particularly strong. Having established the viability of voluntary groups partnering with indigenous populations, Habitat for Humanity was being replicated successfully in some of the poorest regions of the globe. Millard Fuller's "theology of the hammer" had become a creed that attracted the allegiance of a

**TABLE 11.2    Average House Costs—Africa**

| | |
|---|---|
| Botswana | $1,700 |
| Central African Republic | 1,500 |
| Ethiopia | 2,000 |
| Egypt | 1,500 |
| Ghana | 850 |
| Kenya | 500 |
| Malawi | 700 |
| South Africa | 4,000 |
| Tanzania | 630 |
| Uganda | 1,000 |
| Zaire | 1,600 |
| Zambia | 700 |

*Source:* "Fact Sheet," n.d. Habitat for Humanity International 1997.

*Mary Rakocy: Habitat for Humanity International Partner*

wide range of people concerned about development—from affluent American college graduates to illiterate Third World peasants. With minimal outside assistance, Habitat for Humanity had used faith to leverage labor and housing materials to become one of the largest housing builders in the world.

Despite Habitat's success, many challenges remain. Foremost, Habitat for Humanity projects in developing nations continue to struggle to organize boards of directors that function effectively as intermediaries with the local elites. In the absence of a strong tradition of voluntarism and public service, the idea of contributing to the general welfare through service in a nonprofit and nongovernmental organization is simply foreign. This is an acute problem when much of the population lives as a subsistence level. Under such circumstances, the first priorities for a healthy, young adult are toward immediate family, extended family, and clan or tribe in that order. The needs of those social groups are dire, immediate, and supersede a nonprofit group such as Habitat unless a compelling case can be made otherwise. In such instances, faith can serve as an umbrella and rationale for such activities by the native population (Maury, 1996).

*The Habitat for Humanity materials production facility in Kasungu, Malawi*

*A completed Habitat for Humanity home*

Once established, local groups may determine different priorities than those initially instituted via Habitat International Partners. That local groups may make minor alterations in Habitat's traditional formula—substituting tin for cement shingles, reducing the size of a house, or changing the hour requirements of "sweat equity," as examples—is the inevitable consequence of empowering the indigenous population. When local control devolves to a cabal that seeks to enhance its members at the expense of the needy public, however, the consequence is corruption, an all-to-frequent possibility in countries that have little tradition of a civil society. In such cases, Habitat has to send in a trouble-shooting team to put the program back on track, or even close down the project.

There are also structural impediments to Habitat for Humanity. To be effective, non-profit organizations require the latitude to operate, the permission to do so often granted by the national government. However, in many nations the head of government is too autocratic to allow such organizations to operate freely. Dictators are usually the first to be threatened by a group, such as Habitat for Humanity, that serves as an independent source of goods and services to the destitute outside of government. Under such circumstances, nonprofits are either prohibited from setting up operations or elect to terminate projects as a result of government harassment. Another obstacle is the sheer magnitude of the problem. While the United Nations does not track the inadequacy of housing in developing nations, a casual acquaintance with Third World conditions—families living on the street, the absence of sanitary facilities, let alone electricity and running water—quickly registers the enormity of the task. This is particularly the case in urban areas that continue to swell as desperate peasants leave the countryside for the most minimal chance at prosperity. The resulting squatter neighborhoods represent a particularly difficult problem for Habitat because their residents lack the social cohesion that is much of the reason for Habitat's success (Maury, 1996).

Beyond the dynamic of faith, the most significant lesson of Habitat for Humanity is the emergent role that nongovernmental organizations (NGOs) are playing in development. Currently, some 35,000 NGOs operate in the Third World, providing more developmental assistance than the entire United Nations. Jessica Mathews, a senior fellow at the U.S. Council on Foreign Relations, contends that NGOs provide an essential bond among peoples whose interconnection has been disrupted by the competitiveness of global capitalism and the antiquation of the nation-state.

> At a time of accelerating change, NGOs are quicker than governments to respond to new demands and opportunities. Internationally, in both the poorest and richest countries, NGOs, when adequately funded, can outperform government in the delivery of many public services. Their growth, along with that of the other elements of civil society, can strengthen the fabric of many still-fragile democracies. (1997: 63)

As regional trading syndicates, such as the European Economic Community and the North Atlantic Free Trade Agreement, supersede national governments in the new world order, NGOs may provide the necessary cohesion that unites humankind.

At a more pragmatic level, networks of NGOs may serve to define much of how international development proceeds in the near future. In the following chapter, another NGO, the Grameen Development Bank, is described. The Grameen Bank capitalizes peasants by providing modest loans through peer-lending, loans that are often used to improve or build new housing. In many ways, the Grameen Bank complements Habitat for Humanity; indeed, collaboration between these NGOs could increase the developmental impact beyond what each might have independently. In this respect, NGOs may be the primary path of future development.

# REFERENCES

*Building the Future: Financial Report 1995.* (1995). (Americus, GA: Habitat for Humanity). Day, Rendell. "Christian Witness and Partnership." (n.d.) (Reprint from Habitat for Humanity Kenya).

Fuller, Millard. *No More Shacks* (1986). (Waco, Texas: Word).

Fuller, Millard, and Linda Fuller. (1990). *The Excitement Is Building* (Waco, TX: Word).

Gaillard, Frye. (1996). *If I Were a Carpenter* (Winston-Salem, N.C.: John F. Blair).

Gerth, Hans, and C. W. Mills. *From Max Weber* (1974). (New York: Oxford University Press).

*Habitat for Humanity's Christian Principles.* (n.d.). (Murfreesboro, TN: Habitat for Humanity Church Relations department).

Habitat for Humanity. (1997). "International Housing Statistics" (Americus, GA, May 12).

*Human Development Report* (1995). (New York: Oxford University Press).

Jenish, D'Arcy, and Don MacGillivray. (1993). "Carter the Carpenter," *Maclean's,* vol. 106 (August 2).

Mathews, Jessica. (1997). "The Age of Nonstate Actors," *Foreign Affairs,* vol. 76, no. 1 (January/February).

Maury, Matthew. (1996). Personal interview in Nairobi, Kenya, December 31.

Mayer, Caroline. (1996). "Carpenters on a Global Crusade," *Washington Post* (August 22), p. A-1.

*The Momentum Is Building: 1996 Yearbook* (1996). (Americus, GA: Habitat for Humanity).

"News from Habitat for Humanity (Malawi)." (1996). (P.O. Box 2436, Blantyre, Malawi, July).

Pike, John. (1968). *Malawi: A Political and Economic History* (New York: Praeger).

Pryor, Frederic. (1990). *Malawi and Madagascar* (Washington, DC: World Bank and Oxford University Press).

Ransdell, Eric. (1994). "End of the Road for a 'President for Life'," *U.S. News & World Report* (May 30).

Young, Nicholas. (1994). "Malawi: Two Cheers for Democracy," *History Today,* 44(12) December.

# CHAPTER

# 12 The Grameen Development Bank

In August 1976, a Bengladeshi economics professor loaned 50 taka to Sophia Khatoon of Jobra Village (Fuglesang and Chandler, 1994: 2). Khatoon was one of several women who eked out a living making bamboo stools. Since the women had to borrow from a money-lender at astronomical interest rates in order to purchase supplies, their effective daily wage was negligible, one-half taka or $0.02 (Counts, 1996: 39). The economics professor, Muhammad Yunus, had returned to his homeland from teaching at Vanderbilt University in the United States, deeply troubled by a famine that had decimated Bangladesh. Few would have predicted that such a modest gesture would, in two decades, mark the creation of a financial institution that would embarrass such preeminent institutions as the World Bank and the International Monetary Fund. Through the education of the poorest of peasants—most of whom were women—about the value of credit, Yunus built the Grameen ("village" or "rural" in Bangladeshi) Development Bank into an imposing international network of village-based franchises. By mid-1996, the Grameen Bank claimed 1,056 branches and 2 million members in Bangladesh and had exported the model to Bolivia, China, India, Indonesia, Lesotho, Nigeria, Nepal, Philippines, Tanzania, Vietnam, and the United States (*Grameen Dialogue*, October 1996: 16).

The philosophy that Yunus evolved to guide the Grameen Bank did not regard traditional forms of international aid highly, however. "Aid money goes to benefit the people at the top—at best, the upper half of the population. It makes the people in power more powerful, allowing them to grab more and deprive others," Yunus argued. Targeting the aid technocrats, he contended that "consultants are the creation of the aid bureaucracy" (1994: 7). Having distanced the Grameen Bank from traditional vehicles for economic development, it was not until 1995 when Yunus supported a $100 million microlending initiative through the Consultative Group to Assist the Poorest, a semiautonomous organization associated with the World Bank (Counts, 1996: 345). That same year, Yunus was sufficiently confident about the Grameen Bank to propose redesigning the institutions emerging from Bretton Woods and the United Nations in order to realize "a poverty free world by the year 2025" (Yunus, 1995b: 3). Clearly, the Grameen Bank had become one of the signal events in international development.

*Yunus reviewing the sixteen decisions with a bank member*

*Yunus visiting a village in Bangledesh*

# Bangladesh

Formerly East Pakistan, Bangladesh gained independence from Pakistan in 1971. The nation is predominantly rural, with agriculture accounting for 38 percent of the Gross National Product. Despite its rural character, Bangladesh is one of the most densely populated nations, with 111.4 million people. It is also among the poorest: the per capita GNP is US$200; the illiteracy rate is 67 percent; the infant mortality rate is high at 120 per 100,000 births; and the per capita calorie intake is 1,925, below that required for survival (Todaro, 1994: 171).

The chronic poverty of Bangladesh is exacerbated by an erratic climate that contributes to famine and a postcolonial economic system that disenfranchises peasants. Although the nation has tremendously fertile soil, as a result of its being the delta for several major rivers, unpredictable weather wreaks havoc periodically. With such a large part of the population living in marginal circumstances, the slightest disequilibrium can be catastrophic. For example, inept economic planning shortly after independence exacerbated a famine that killed 1.5 million Bangladeshis in 1974 (Jolis, 1996: 17). Much of the poverty of Bangladesh is less dramatic and more corrosive than that connoted by famine, however.

During colonial rule, the British East India Company assumed control of a quite profitable textile industry in Bangladesh. By the early 1800s, weaving was diminishing as a viable source of income for villages as contracts were channeled through *gomastas,* middlemen of the East India Company. Rapid industrialization of the textile industry in Britain effectively doomed the less competitive village weavers, and by the end of the century the textile industry was all but dead. The peasantry found livelihood providing the labor for large landowners who produced cotton and jute for export, while trying at all cost to retain possession of small plots of land in order to grow crops necessary for consumption. But this was a tenuous arrangement, particularly when famine struck, as it did in 1943, killing 3 million people (Counts, 1996: 20).

As life became increasingly perilous for peasants, they resorted to moneylenders for loans to tide them through tough times. A man faced with a poor crop would often pawn less-essential items in order to obtain a loan from a moneylender, or *mohajan,* at an annual interest rate of from 300 to 400 percent. When the crop was harvested, the peasant could pay off the loan and repossess the item. When a peasant was confronted with a starving family, however, he would pawn a part of his land for a loan. When the peasant was unable to repay, the land reverted to the moneylender, who would then share-crop it, often to the man who had formerly owned it. Because moneylenders often worked for, or in consort with, large landowners, this system proved a reliable, if gradual, method for transferring the ownership of quite substantial amounts of land from the rural poor to the wealthy. By the end of the colonial period, what had been a network of self-sufficient villages had been reduced to a landscape of punishing poverty, peasants having become indentured servants of the wealthy. As the "cycle of degradation" spiraled downward, peasants lost possessions, then land, finally the very nutrition necessary for survival (Fuglesang and Chandler, 1994: 28).

The dire straights of Bangladesh received the attention and assistance of traditional aid organizations, but little of this trickled down to the poorest of the rural poor. The dispersion of the funds was, according to Yunus (1995b), typical for foreign aid of the period:

Bangladesh has received over $26 billion in foreign aid during the last 23 years of its exist-
ence. Seventy-five percent of the aid money went back to the donor countries as payments
for commodities, equipment, services of the consultants, contractors, and experts. A major
portion of the remaining 25 percent spent locally went to the consultants, experts, contractors, and bureaucrats. (p. 8)

Consequently, foreign aid did little to bolster the economy, which grew from 2 to 4 percent
annually, barely keeping pace with population growth of 2.6 percent during the 1980s.
Since little aid benefited the rural poor, their circumstances worsened. Bangladesh became
one of the poorest nations on the globe: life expectancy was 55 years, underemployment
and unemployment exceeded 30 percent; the poverty rate was 86 percent (Todaro, 1994:
171–72).

# The Grameen Bank

To appreciate the Grameen Bank is to recognize that Yunus spent several years of trial and
error perfecting a financial institution that was apropos to the rural poor in Bangladesh.
Given the social, economic, and historical problems confronting him, this was a remarkable accomplishment. Two decades after its inception, the Grameen Bank is a novel, indigenous financial institution that generates economic *and* social development from the
bottom up.

### History

The evolution of the Grameen Bank was in response to both the persistence of Yunus and the
unwillingness of commercial banks to make loans to the landless poor without collateral. In
making the first Jobra loans in 1976, Yunus sought the services of the Janata Bank, but found
that officials would not authorize loans to the assetless poor without Yunus's guarantee.
Eventually, Yunus learned that commercial banks also denied loans to the illiterate and
women. Nonetheless, Yunus proceeded to underwrite the loans. The first loans were made to
loan groups, and repayment was on a daily basis; soon this changed to "mutual aid cells," and
payment was changed to a weekly installment. The cells eventually evolved into groups of 5
to 10 people who shared a common interest. Despite a high repayment rate, Yunus found the
Janata Bank taking four to six months to process his loan applications.

After airing these frustrations with an official of the Krishi Bank in Dhaka, Yunus
secured a commitment to deploy a branch bank in Jobra. Since the branch bank would be
focusing on agricultural loans, Krishi Bank agreed to rename it the Grameen Bank.
Although limited financial services were offered, Yunus maintained authority over operations beginning with its establishment in 1978. Despite the success of the Grameen Bank,
Yunus continued to argue with commercial bankers who insisted on traditional forms of
collateral as a condition for making loans. Yunus noted that the bank in Jobra was quite
successful without collateral, suggesting that the model be replicated. In 1979, another
Grameen Bank was established in Tangail, soon to be followed by three other districts and
Dhaka. While 98 to 99 percent of loans were repaid, the processing costs were high, so a
loan from the International Fund for Agricultural Development of the UN was secured.

At this point, Yunus requested that the Bangladesh Bank make the Grameen Bank a full-status commercial bank that would be owned by its borrowers, but commercial banks resisted the move, contending that another bank was not needed in Bangladesh. In response to questions of ownership, Yunus suggested that the landless control 60 percent and government 40 percent of the Grameen Bank. In 1983, the national government authorized the Grameen Bank, but reversed the ownership percentages, leaving peasants with minority interest. In 1986, this balance was altered, with the landless controlling 75 percent of the bank. By that time, ten years after Yunus's initial loan experiment in Jobra, the Grameen Bank had grown to 295 branches, in 5,000 villages, with 230,000 borrowers, 73 percent being women (Yunus in Gibbons, 1995: 21–26).

## Organization

The Grameen Bank is a carefully maintained system of franchises based on local banking centers that are comprised of lending groups. As a result, it is highly decentralized and labor-intensive. The foundation of the bank is a five-member loan group. In order to be eligible, prospective members must be "landless" and poor, be willing to join a group, the members of which cannot be related, and promise to honor any payment defaults of group members. The resultant solidarity, called *peer lending,* explains much of the financial success of the Grameen Bank. All members of the bank follow an indoctrination process:

> After five women have declared their intention to form a group, they undergo seven days of "group training" in which they learn the rules of the bank and memorize a social contract called the Sixteen Decisions. To became a recognized group, they must pass an oral examination administered by a senior bank official that tests their understanding of the rules and decisions. That way, no one can say they didn't understand the rules of the bank later on. After recognition, two members are allowed to submit loan proposals. A typical amount would be 1,000 to 3,000 taka ($25 to $75). After these first two women, normally the poorest in the group, receive their loans and pay their first five (of a total of fifty) weekly installments, two others become eligible to apply for loans. When those two repay for four or five weeks, the final member is allowed to submit her proposal. After making fifty installments, the borrower pays her interest [20 percent simple interest on the balance] and a small contribution into a side insurance fund. Then she is eligible to apply for a larger loan, sometimes as much as double the original amount. This cycle continues as long as she and her group members are borrowers in good standing with the bank. (Counts, 1996: xii–xiii)

Each loan group identifies a chairperson and secretary, who hold office for one year. None may be reelected until each member has had the experience of serving in office.

From the loan group, the Grameen Bank evolves centers, branches, area offices, zonal offices, and the head office in Dhaka. Six loan groups comprise a center, a meeting place determined by the groups for purposes of conducting bank business. Center meetings coincide with the weekly loan payment and involve meeting with the bank worker responsible for the center. Subjects discussed include loans, other bank business, and related concerns of the center. Center meetings are formally structured, with members of groups lined up in rows of six, saluting the bank worker upon arrival, and following the direction of the center chief who is elected for a one-year term by the group chairpersons. To the Western observer, a center meeting appears regimented, with great emphasis on discipline. This expedites the transaction of business, all of which is discussed openly, among members, few of whom are literate.

From the highly decentralized centers, the network of the Grameen Bank is articulated. The number of centers assigned to a branch office varies with the location of centers. Because the field staff are not expected to walk more than five miles to a center (hence the label "barefoot bank"), 30 square miles is the maximum area covered by a branch. As many as 30 centers may be coordinated by a branch office; 10 to 15 branch offices comprise an area; six area offices are managed by a zonal office; the five zones are administered through the central office. Because all of the banking decisions are conducted openly in the centers and because all bank workers tally accounts by hand, 90 percent of the Grameen Bank staff work out of the branches (Fuglesang and Chandler, 1994: Ch. 3).

## Financing

Foremost, the Grameen Bank is a for-profit organization; its purpose is to generate a surplus that can then be used to leverage additional loans to members. The distinction between the bank as a lending institution and a welfare agency is central to the Yunus "manifesto." Welfare, according to Yunus, does no favors for the poor:

> …we are fully convinced that every human being is endowed with enormous capacity to contribute to the economy and the society. By one's own effort one can pull himself/herself out of poverty.
>
> The poor do not need charity or a hand out. The only thing that the poor need is a supportive set of institutions and rules. Charity and handout were invented to avoid the issue of poverty alleviation. Handouts carry the message that the society is ignoring you. It is not interested in your ability. (Yunus, 1995b: 8)

World poverty, in an era of surpluses in the developed nations, is an inevitable by-product of institutions that reflect disparate power and resource allocation, according to Yunus. In the international aid community, the institutions that serve this functions are the World Bank and the IMF, although commercial banks are increasingly involved. Through loan arrangements that have been made with conditions that favor the developed nations, the social and economic conditions of the developing nations continue to deteriorate. Thus, aid and technical assistance serve to reinforce a foreign aid bureaucracy that actually depresses the opportunities of the poorest in the Third World rather than uplift them.

While Yunus finds a convenient target in the World Bank and IMF, the capital transfer *from* the developing nations *to* the developed nations has been substantiated. How this has come to pass has been documented by development economist Michael Todaro: A moderate indebtedness on the part of many developing nations was exacerbated by the spiking of oil import prices as a result of the first OPEC oil embargo in the early 1970s. In order to compensate for depleted reserves, nations borrowed from commercial banks that had excess cash on hand as a result of the money pouring into OPEC coffers. The second OPEC oil shock was to prove fatal to many developing nations when negative financial effects led to massive transfers of wealth abroad as the aristocracy of developing nations feared financial ruin. This, in turn, generated a second wave of borrowing from commercial banks that tagged high interest rates to loans, thus exacerbating an already tenuous economic condition. Between 1976 and 1985, almost $200 billion left the developing nations that were most indebted; "by 1984 the developing countries were paying back $10.2 billion *more* to the commercial banks than they were receiving in new loans" (Todaro, 1994: 459–464).

The implication of international aid organizations in the further deterioration of the world's poor made them a suspect source of aid, yet intranational assistance was little better. When intranational aid was an extension of international aid, it was massaged by technical consultants who essentially ratified the counterproductive decisions and processes of the World Bank or IMF. Nonforeign aid assistance was available through governmental or private banks, but these insisted on collateral, which the poor did not possess. "By insisting on collateral the financial institutions have created a caste system in the financial world," argued Yunus, "The poor became the 'untouchables' of this world" (1995b: 8).

In the face of such reinforced institutional adversity, the only solution was to build a noncollateral financial institution, targeted at the poor, from the ground up. This required nothing less than the invention of an institution of flawless design since the price of failure would be further pauperization of the poor. Coordination is required since the Grameen Bank is decentralized; each weekday some 6,000 bank workers oversee the accounts of 300,000 women members. To an extent, simplification of loans contributes to a streamlining of operations. Though the amounts of loans vary, averaging 3,000 taka ($75), interest is a standard 20 percent simple interest on a declining balance paid in 50 weekly installments.[1] With each weekly payment, every borrower contributes 3 taka of savings, one into an emergency fund, one into a children's fund, and another into the group fund (Counts, 1996: 72). The Grameen Bank boasts a loan repayment rate of 98 percent. The Bank does have a special program for housing: members may borrow up to 20,000 taka ($500) to construct a simple tin-roof house, the loans for which are paid back in 5- to 15-year installments (Yunus, 1995a: 15).

This financial arrangement generates two significant payoffs. Foremost, borrowers who continue to use the Grameen Bank as a source of credit gradually accumulate sufficient assets to escape poverty. In so doing, members of the bank escape the peonage associated with peasant labor, in exchange for self-employment. Early in the bank's development, Yunus recognized that self-employment was superior to wage labor, particularly for women. Loans, he argued, bring "a woman into the income stream without the usual sacrifices required under wage-employment situation. She does not have to leave her home and her children. She does not have to learn a new skill to adapt to a new job. She can do [what] she does best and earn money for it" (Yunus, 1993: 14).

An evaluation of bank borrowers revealed that 46 percent of women who had borrowed over eight or more years had escaped poverty and another 34 percent were on the verge of generating an adequate income. During the same period, only 4 percent of a comparison group were no longer poor (Counts, 1996: xiv). By mid-1996, the Grameen Bank had financed the construction of more than 340,000 homes (*Grameen Dialogue,* October

[1]More recently the interest has been reduced to 16 percent.

1996: 16). At the organizational level, the Grameen Bank has proved a profitable operation, a rather remarkable accomplishment given that borrowers must be the poorest of the poor. Since loan approvals outpace payments, particularly at new branches, the central bank must cover some losses. Regardless, in 1993, one-third of branches were profitable, in 1994 the number had increased to one-half of branches; by 1994, 65 percent of branches were expected to generate a profit (Counts, 1996: 261). The constant recycling of Bank funds yields remarkable amounts in circulation. In July 1996, over $1.8 billion had been disbursed, for that month $25 million. Over $128 million was available in Group Fund savings (*Grameen Dialogue,* October 1996: 16).

## The Sixteen Decisions

As significant as the Grameen Bank's economic performance has been its social benefits. Early in the evolution of the Bank, Yunus crafted a credo, "the sixteen decisions," that served as an ethical template for its members. In becoming members of the Bank, the poor must agree to adhere to this coda; because many are illiterate, they do so by committing it to memory. Prior to acceptance of an application, a prospective member is grilled by the Bank's local manager. Failure to demonstrate knowledge of the Sixteen Decisions results in rejection of an applicant and interrupts the formation of that applicant's lending group. As a result, the Sixteen Decisions become a moral guide to individuals as well as to lending groups.

### The Sixteen Decisions

1. The four principles of the Grameen Bank—discipline, unity, courage and hard work—we shall follow and advance in all walks of our lives.
2. Prosperity we shall bring to our families.
3. We shall not live in dilapidated houses. We shall repair our houses and work towards constructing new houses at the earliest.
4. We shall grow vegetables all the year round. We shall eat plenty of it and sell the surplus.
5. During the planting seasons, we shall plant as many seedlings as possible.
6. We shall plan to keep our families small. We shall minimize our expenditures. We shall look after our health.
7. We shall educate our children and ensure that they can earn to pay for their education.
8. We shall always keep our children and the environment clean.
9. We shall build and use pit-latrines.
10. We shall drink tubewell water. If it is not available, we shall boil water or use alum.
11. We shall not take any dowry in our sons' wedding, neither shall we give any dowry in our daughters' wedding. We shall keep the centre free from the curse of dowry. We shall not practice child marriage.
12. We shall not inflict any injustice on anyone, neither shall we allow anyone to do so.
13. For higher income we shall collectively undertake bigger investments.
14. We shall always be ready to help each other. If anyone is in difficulty, we shall always help him.

15. If we come to know of any breach of discipline in any centre, we shall all go there and help restore discipline.

16. We shall introduce physical exercise in all our centres. We shall take part in all social activities collectively.

So explicated, the Sixteen Decisions have significant social benefits. Analysts have noted that "the most striking characteristic of Grameen Bank's social development program is its enlightened concern with a long-term perspective" (Fuglesang and Chandler, 1994: 126). In this respect the Grameen Bank has empowered peasant women by enhancing their economic productivity and knowledge of their immediate environment. As a result, Bank members are less likely to be abused, more likely to be literate, more likely to provide their families with a diverse diet, more likely to drink potable water, more likely to use contraception and have fewer children, and more likely to vote. When the Grameen Bank decided that participation in the political process was essential for members' empowerment, it added about 2 million people to the number of Bangladeshi voters (Counts, 1996: 265).

## Social-Consciousness–Driven Entrepreneurs

More generally, the Sixteen Decisions reflect Yunus's idea of the "social-consciousness–driven (SCD)" organization, an integral part of his philosophy. The objective is to convert the impersonal aid bureaucracies into "dynamic pro-people organizations" (Yunus, 1995c: 11). To do so requires replacing the capitalist sense of "greed" with a social ethos emphasizing "social consciousness or social dreams." Using the Grameen Bank as an exemplar, Yunus has presented an SCD process in order to rid the world of poverty:

- The World Bank and other international aid agencies would be converted to SCDs with regional and local subsidiaries.
- Money would go to SCDs, not government agencies; nations that have yet to contribute 0.7 percent of GNP for development could meet this obligation by depositing funds in SCDs.
- New SCDs could be generated wherever and whenever necessary and funded by a revolving SCD Enterprise Fund.
- Investment companies, both national and international, could be evolved to support SCD activities.

In order to demonstrate the virtue of the SCD model, the Grameen Bank has already created the Grameen Agricultural Foundation, the Grameen Fisheries Foundation, Grameen Uddog (a textile company), and the Grameen Fund (a venture capital fund). Most recently, Grameen Telecom has been created in order to provide telephone service to poor women in Bangladesh (Yunus, 1995b: 10–11).

In order to promote the development of SCDs, the Grameen Bank has constructed an impressive headquarters in Dhaka, where it trains hundreds of delegates from the developing as well as developed nations. In February 1997, attention was diverted to Washington, D.C., which served as the site for the first international Summit on Microcredit, organized by the Grameen Bank and endorsed by First Lady Hillary Rodham Clinton. For the coming decades, Yunus foresees further expansion of the Grameen Bank and its satellite branches. Immodestly, he insists that poverty can be erased from the globe by 2025 through using the inherent capacities of the poor as collateral for credit. While veterans of international development might doubt such a prospect, few would have projected the remarkable accomplishments of the Grameen Bank either. Starting from the ground up, Yunus has nurtured a financial organization, tended its expansion, and evolved a philosophy that could at least make a substantial dent in world poverty. "If we imagine a world where every human being is a potential entrepreneur," he insists, "we'll build a system to give everybody a chance to materialize his/her potential" (1994: 11).

## Implications

As a development institution, the Grameen Bank is an anomaly compared to traditional forms of assistance. Its nickname, "barefoot bank"—a cultural oxymoron—typifies the degree of difference that the bank represents. The Grameen Bank's village origin, its decentralization, and its incorporation of social, educational, and health objectives—to say nothing of its wide replication—stand in marked contrast with previous forms of development aid. At Yunus's insistence, the philosophy of the Grameen Bank has been disseminated widely, from acceptance speeches for the numerous honors he has received to short, pulp pamphlets that originate from the headquarters in Dhaka. Within two decades of its inception, the Yunus "manifesto" of microcredit has become a signal innovation in international development. To Yunus's credit, the Grameen Bank has not degenerated into a personality cult that is mindlessly devoted to a charismatic leader.

The Grameen Bank is similar to conventional aid provided by the World Bank and IMF in that these forms promote democratic capitalism. Thereafter, any likeness ends, as Table 12.1 indicates.

The success of alternative models of development, such as the Grameen Bank, ripples beyond the immediate circles of the poor. Indeed, as more innovative development

**TABLE 12.1   Contrasting Models of Development**

| Attribute | Grameen Bank | World Bank |
|---|---|---|
| Political economy | Mercantile-populism | Representative-corporatism |
| Commercial status | For-profit | Nonprofit |
| Agency intermediary | Private sector/NGOs | National government |
| Nature of assistance | Credit | Grants (concessional loans) |
| Direction of authority | Bottom-up | Top-down |
| Dispersion of authority | Decentralized | Centralized |
| Nature of funded projects | Microenterprise | Massive public infrastructure |
| Technical dependence | Low | High |
| Indigenous participation | High | Low |

organizations, such as Habitat for Humanity, expand, the status quo of the lumbering bureaucracies that have typified international aid becomes less and less tenable. Thus, in February 1997, the new president of the World Bank, James D. Wolfensohn, announced an overhaul of the organization in order "to improve its performance in promoting the economic development of poor nations." In place of large, infrastructure projects that have characterized World Bank ventures, Wolfensohn plans to invest more in health, education, and welfare through collaborations with the private sector. The Wolfensohn plan calls for an additional $400 million for restructuring of the World Bank (Stevenson, 1997: B1). While Yunus has expressed gratitude for the $100 million collaboration between the Grameen Bank and the World Bank, one suspects he would have other designs for the $400 million than that intended by Wolfensohn!

## Replication

Twenty years after its inception, the Grameen Bank had been replicated in forty nations. In assessing the conditions necessary for successful replication, professor David Gibbons has identified two: the existence of a market economy and no significant political opposition. Beyond that, he suggests a dozen principles that have evolved with the Grameen Bank:

1. Exclusive focus on the poor
2. Priority for poor rural women
3. Suitable loan conditions/procedures and open, nonpartisan conduct of all business
4. Individual, self-chosen, income-generating loan activities
5. Collective borrower responsibility and mutual support through compulsory group savings
6. Small loans, weekly repayments, and eligibility for subsequent loans after full repayment of the current loan
7. Strict credit discipline and close supervision
8. Compassion, but no charity
9. Promotion of individual savings
10. A social development agenda
11. Rigorous, practical management/staff training
12. Protection of the loan fund from inflation

By the early 1990s, the Grameen Bank had been successfully replicated in several nations, as shown in Table 12.2. Following the success of the Grameen Bank, multiple initiatives were undertaken to extend credit to the poor in developing nations. Several institutional candidates were available other than the Grameen Bank, ranging from credit unions to rotating funds managed by branch banks of the central government. The U.S. Agency for International Development launched the GEMINI (Growth and Equity through Microenterprise Investments and Institutions) to identify variations and assess the performance of microcredit experiments, particularly those in South America and Africa.

In South America, rotating savings and credit associations (ROSCAs) had been in existence since the 1970s. ACCION International has facilitated the evolution of microcredit in South America. Generally, three to 10 borrowers agree to access credit collectively, guaranteeing loan repayment, with further loans contingent on repayment of previous

**TABLE 12.2    Ongoing Replications of the Grameen Bank Financial System**

| Project Name | Location | Date Started | Total Members | Repayment Rate (%) |
|---|---|---|---|---|
| Yachter | Malaysia | Dec. '86 | 19,000 | 99.9 percent |
| Usahamaju | Malaysia | June '88 | 3,200 | 92 percent |
| Sahel Action | Burkina Faso | July '88 | 7,000 | 99–100 percent |
| Full Circle | Chicago, U.S. | Nov. '88 | 150 | 100 percent |
| MSS | Dhaka, Bangladesh | Jan. '89 | 750 | 100 percent |
| Savcred | Sri Lanka | Mid-'89 | 900 | 100 percent |
| Ahon Sa Hirap | Philippines | Aug. '89 | 2,000 | 92 percent |
| Dungganon | Philippines | Dec. '89 | 7,000 | 92 percent |
| KUM | Indonesia | Early '90 | 450 | 95 percent |
| Mudzi Fund | Malawi | June '90 | 417 | N.A. |
| CARD | Philippines | Jan. '90 | 1,200 | 96 percent |

*Source:* Gibbons, 1995: 101–3.

loans. Many of the borrowers are women; loans are sought for small-scale commerce and manufacturing as well as for the provision of services. Groups are the product of self-selection, and banks are decentralized, often located in village markets. In urban areas, loans typically range from $50 to $250 for one to six months at interest rates that vary from 25 to 50 percent. The experience of three nations is depicted in Table 12.3.

In the mid-1990s, the World Bank sought information on the performance of microfinance organizations in Africa. Of the nine organizations examined, five were credit unions, two were village banks, and two were microcredit programs. Loans ranged widely from $100 to $1,000; interest rates varied from 16 to 54 percent; as many institutions provided credit to individuals as to solidarity groups; loans ranged from six to 12 months, with

**TABLE 12.3    Microcredit in Three South American Nations**

| Performance Indicator | Bolivia | Colombia | Guatemala |
|---|---|---|---|
| Portion who are women | 71% | 49% | 35% |
| Average beginning loan | $87 | $176 | $205 |
| Annual interest rate | 48% | 42% | 45% |
| Total active members | 19,901 | 33,871 | 9,436 |
| Annual membership growth | 52% | 62% | 40% |
| Active loan funds | $4,561,775 | $3,979,515 | $1,426,714 |
| Growth rate of loan portfolio | 87% | 37% | 55% |
| Loans in arrears 30 days | 0.2% | 4.0% | 8.0% |
| Loans in default | 0.0002% | 0.18% | 0.68% |

*Source:* Data from Berenbach and Guzman in Otero and Rhyne *The New World of Microenterprise Finance* (West Hartford, Conn.: Kumarian Press, 1994), 119–26.

full repayment usually due at the end of the period. Several of these characteristics thus diverge from the structure and process of the Grameen Bank. The performance of the West African microfinance institutions is noted in Table 12.4.

Reflecting on the West African experience, Leila Webster noted the rapid expansion of microfinancial institutions. Income generation through microenterprise is associated with several desirable outcomes, she observed:

> poor people are fully capable of making welfare-enhancing choices once they have the income with which to purchase services. Impact studies indicate that this is a valid assumption. The nutritional, educational, and housing status of participants' families improves with the increase in income associated with the use of savings and credit services. This approach empowers participants in that it affords them the choice of how they will improve their lives; it respects them in that it involves a contract between two parties rather than a handout; and it is efficient in that welfare choices are driven by demand rather than by supply. (1996: 73)

A problem unique to the region, however, is the institutional dependence on expatriates who have a more tentative attachment to microfinancial institutions than does the indigenous population, raising questions about the long-term viability of microcredit (1996: 74).

**TABLE 12.4   Microfinance in West Africa**

| Institution | Country | Total Assets | Number of Members | Average Loan Size | Percent of Interest | Full Repayment |
|---|---|---|---|---|---|---|
| PRIDE | Guinea | $907,000 | N.A. | $200 | 37 | 100% |
| Credit Rural | Guinea | $3,700,000 | 31,000 | $100 | 32 | 97% |
| Credit Mutuel de Guinee | Guinea | $5,000,000 | 45,000 | $1,000 | 22 | 80% |
| Credit Mutuel du Senegal | Senegal | $2,800,000 | 22,228 | $132 | 20 | 98% |
| Village Banks of Nganda | Senegal | $90,000 | 600 | $68 | 54 | 100% |
| Reseau des Caisses | Burkina Faso | $5,100,000 | 64,000 | $336 | 19 | 95% |
| Sahel Action | Burkina Faso | $760,000 | N.A. | $48 | 26 | 100% |
| Caisses Villageoises du Pays Dogon | Mali | $360,000 | 15,330 | $43 | 39 | 94% |
| Kafo Jiginew | Mali | $1,560,000 | 20,670 | $105 | 19 | 98% |

*Source:* Leila Webster and Peter Fidler, eds. *The Informal Sector* and *Microfinance Institutions in West Africa.* The World Bank, 1996: 43–52.

# The Future of Microcredit

Approaching a new millennium, microcredit has captured the imagination of the international aid community (Bornstein, 1995). Grassroots capitalization programs have not only spread throughout the developing world (Gargan, 1996), but have been designed for the poor in the advanced, industrial nations as well (Goodman, 1997; Hiatt, 1997). In so doing, microfinance has made impressive inroads among populations that had eluded development specialists. Highly decentralized, microenterprize has demonstrated that the poorest peasants, usually women, are capable of gradually extricating themselves from poverty. In the process, programs that have emphasized external social benefits relating to health, education, and mutual support have generated important indirect benefits with regard to diet, child development, and political participation as well. In these instances, microcredit has literally empowered the poor, often elevating women who had labored beneath the yoke of patriarchy up to parity with men.

These quite substantial accomplishments notwithstanding, it is important to recognize the modest aspirations of microeconomic strategies. Foremost, microcredit enhances the survival of the poorest of Third World peasants, yet it is, at present, an inadequate vehicle for addressing the increasing skewing of resources and opportunities that separates the developed from the developing nations. By the mid-1990s, for example, 85 percent of the world's wealth was controlled by the richest 1 billion people; the poorest 1 billion possess less than 2 percent.

If microcredit is to become an effective economic strategy, the connection between small borrowers and macro features of the international economy must be designed and constructed. This is a two-way street, however. It is essential to organize and mobilize the capital and motivation of microborrowers into corporate-scale economic units that can influence global markets; at the same time, international aid institutions must convince the agents of transnational capital of the benefits of investing in microfinance: social cohesion, political stabilization, and steady growth. Clearly, this is the next stage in the Yunus manifesto, and it is essential. In the absence of such integration, islands of microfinance will be swamped by the unpredictable, inevitable tsunamis of international capital.

# REFERENCES

Berenbach, Shari, and Diego Guzman. (1994). "The Solidarity Group Experience Worldwide," in Maria Otero and Elisabeth Rhyne, *The New World of Microenterprise Finance* (West Hartford, Kumarian).

Bornstein, David. (1995). "The Barefoot Bank with Cheek," *The Atlantic Monthly* (December).

Counts, Alex. (1996). *Give Us Credit* (New Delhi: Research Press).

Fuglesang, Andreas, and Dale Chandler. (1994). *Participation as Process* (Dhaka, Bangladesh: Grameen Bank).

Gargan, Edward. (1996). "'People's Banks' Help Rescue Poor Indonesians," *New York Times* (February 28).

Gibbons, David. *The Grameen Reader*. (1995). (Dhaka, Bangladesh: Grameen Bank).

Goodman, Ellen. (1997). "Small Loans, Support Groups: Bridge to Independence," *Richmond Times-Dispatch* (February 6), p. A19.

*Grameen Dialogue.* (1996). Number 28, October (Dhaka, Bangladesh: Grameen Bank).

Hiatt, Fred. (1997). "Penny-Wise Loan Policy," *Washington Post* (January 20), p. A27.

Jolis, Alan. (1996). "The Bank for the Down and Out," *World Press Review* (September).

Stevenson, Richard. (1997). "World Bank Chief Asks Slimmer Staffs and Better Lending," *New York Times* (February 21).

Todaro, Michael. (1994). *Economic Development, 5th ed.* (New York: Longman).

Webster, Leila. (1996). "A Profile of Selected Microfinance Institutions" and "Implications," in Leila Webster and Peter Fidler, *The Informal Sector and Microfinance Institutions in West Africa* (Washington, DC: World Bank).

Yunus, Muhammad. (1993). *The Poor as the Engine of Development* (Dhaka, Bangladesh: Grameen Bank).

Yunus, Muhammad. (1994). *Grameen Bank: Does the Capitalist System Have to be the Handmaiden of the Rich?* (Dhaka, Bangladesh: Grameen Bank).

Yunus, Muhhamad. (1995a). "Grameen Bank, the First Decade," in David Gibbons, Ed. *The Grameen Reader* (Dhaka, Bangladesh: Grameen Bank).

Yunus, Muhammad. (1995b). *New Development Options towards the 21st Century* (Dhaka, Bangladesh: Grameen Bank).

Yunus, Muhammad. (1995c). *Towards Creating a Poverty-Free World* (Dhaka, Bangladesh: Grameen Bank).

# 13 The Progress of Nations

Nations relate dynamically with one another. That certain cultures have aspired to conquest and shaped the course of human history only to decline as a result of internal corruption and external threat is a common theme of historians, of course (Kennedy, 1987). Somewhat less appreciated is the fact that this same flux is evident in contemporary events. During the fascism that preceded the Second World War, Italy sought to expand its influence by invading Ethiopia, a prosperous agricultural society at the time. By the end of the century, internecine conflict had reduced the nation to a husk; Ethiopia ranked among the ten least developed nations in the world. During the same prewar period, Argentina boasted a culture that paralleled the most affluent European nations. By the early 1990s , however, Argentina ranked behind every European nation in social development. More recently, the demise of the Soviet Union has fragmented a confederation of Communist states that once rivaled the West in its mastery of technology and as a military threat. A decade after the demise of the Soviet Union, the nations of the former USSR struggle to maintain their status as industrial nations. Thus, history and current events demonstrate that prosperity is often more tentative than the citizens of a nation might suspect. Contingent on a convergence of social, political, and economic circumstances, nations may prosper, struggle to maintain the status quo, or eventually fail. Development, in many respects, is relative.

## Three Worlds

Various schemes have evolved as shorthand explanations to depict the relation of nations to one another, and, by inference, their development. In recent times, a three-part classification has enjoyed extensive use: a First World, consisting of the industrial nations of the capitalist West; a Second World, comprised of the Communist nations that constructed political economies as an alternative to the market-dominated First World; and a Third World, those nations that were former colonies of the First World that achieved independence, often through revolutions of liberation. This tripart formulation became prevalent after the Second World War as the Cold War intensified. Many developing nations adopted the slogans of revolution, if not outright insurrection, in order to shed the influences of First World colonial nations. The Second World viewed the Third World as a theater of independence, an arena through which the exploitation of capitalism would be summarily ended, eventually bringing the colonized nations into the Communist sphere of influence. On the defensive, the First World deployed foreign aid, technical assistance, cultural exchange, and, on occasion, diplomatic subterfuge to neutralize Second World incursions into the Third World. In several instances—Central America, Southeast Asia, and sub-Saharan Africa—the First and Second Worlds recruited insurgents who acted as their surrogates, engaging the opposition in armed conflict at considerable cost in weapons and human life.

With the fall of the Berlin Wall in 1989, the Three World formulation lost utility. Foremost, the collapse of the Soviet Union and its Warsaw Pact satellites halved the scale of the Second World. The remaining Communist nations—the Peoples Republic of China, North Korea, and Cuba—posed no immediate threat to the First World and were unlikely to serve as models for Third World nations. At the same time, some nations of the Third World had been transformed substantially from their colonial-era status. Several Arab nations had prospered through oil exports, achieving levels of income that mirrored industrial nations, despite feudal forms of governance. In the absence of natural resources, a handful of nations in Southeast Asia—Hong Kong, South Korea, Taiwan, Singapore—experienced such consistently high levels of growth that they became known as the "Four Tigers."

Tragically, many Third World nations lost ground to the extent that they were less developed than when they achieved independence from the First World. By the mid-1990s, several of the nations of sub-Saharan Africa and Southeast Asia were significantly less developed than they had been a generation earlier. Nations such as Cambodia, Bangladesh, Afghanistan, Somalia, and Niger had lost so much capital, their infrastructure so deteriorated, and their polity so unstable, that development analysts began to speculate about the emergence of a Fourth World. Further confounding the prospects of Fourth World nations, the end of the Cold War resulted in the affluent, industrial nations of the First World, particularly the United States, expending relatively *less* on foreign aid than they had during the Soviet threat.

## The Gini Coefficient

As development research became increasingly sensitive to the circumstances to nations that had been assigned to the Third World, various indicators were presented to gauge the progress of nations. Among the first was the Gini Coefficient, the extent to which the distribution of income diverges from perfect equality. Gini coefficients range from a value of zero when the distribution of income is equal, to a value of 1 when the distribution is unequal. Nations with high degrees of income inequality have Gini Coefficients in the 0.50 to 0.70 range, while those with relatively equal distributions range from 0.20 to 0.35 (Todaro, 1994: 140). These values are multiplied by 100 to produce the Gini Index. A ranking of nations according to the Gini Index is provided in Table 13.1. Within the developing world, the former Soviet satellite nations tend to have less income inequality than other nations. Beyond this, the Gini Coefficient is of limited use.

Critics of the Gini Coefficient cite the limitations of a portrait of development that is based solely on income. Indicators, such as longevity, education, opportunity, and environment, should be included, they claim. While this has an obvious merit, defenders of the Gini Coefficient cite its value when the disparity between the rich and poor has become such a chasm. By way of illustration, "the assets of the world's 358 billionaires exceed the combined annual incomes of countries with 45 percent of the world's people" (*Human Development Report,* 1996: 2).

**TABLE 13.1    Gini Index for Selected Nations**

| Rank | Nation | Gini Index | Rank | Nation | Gini Index |
|------|--------|-----------|------|--------|-----------|
| 1 | Spain | 8.3 | 34 | Tunisia | 40.2 |
| 2 | Slovak Rep. | 19.5 | 35 | Philippines | 40.7 |
| 3 | Belarus | 21.6 | 35 | Uganda | 40.8 |
| 4 | Romania | 25.5 | 36 | Jamaica | 41.1 |
| 5 | Ukraine | 25.7 | 37 | China | 41.5 |
| 6 | Czech Rep. | 26.6 | 38 | Bolivia | 42.0 |
| 7 | Hungary | 27.0 | 39 | Mauritania | 42.4 |
| 8 | Latvia | 27.0 | 40 | Jordan | 43.4 |
| 9 | Poland | 27.2 | 41 | Madagascar | 43.4 |
| 10 | Slovenia | 28.2 | 42 | Peru | 44.9 |
| 11 | Bangladesh | 28.3 | 43 | Costa Rica | 46.1 |
| 12 | Rwanda | 28.9 | 44 | Thailand | 46.2 |
| 13 | Sri Lanka | 30.1 | 45 | Zambia | 46.2 |
| 14 | Laos | 30.4 | 46 | Ecuador | 46.6 |
| 15 | Bulgaria | 30.8 | 47 | Guinea | 46.8 |
| 16 | Pakistan | 31.2 | 48 | Malaysia | 48.4 |
| 17 | Indonesia | 31.7 | 49 | Russia | 49.6 |
| 18 | Egypt | 32.0 | 50 | Mexico | 50.3 |
| 19 | Kazakstan | 32.7 | 51 | Nicaragua | 50.3 |
| 20 | Lithuania | 33.6 | 52 | Dominican Rep. | 50.5 |
| 21 | India | 33.8 | 53 | Colombia | 51.3 |
| 22 | Ghana | 33.9 | 54 | Honduras | 52.7 |
| 23 | Moldavia | 34.4 | 55 | Venezuela | 53.8 |
| 24 | Vietnam | 35.7 | 56 | Sierra Leone | 54.1 |
| 25 | Turkmenistan | 35.8 | 57 | Lesotho | 56.0 |
| 26 | Niger | 36.1 | 58 | Guinea-Bissau | 56.2 |
| 27 | Nepal | 36.7 | 59 | Chile | 56.5 |
| 28 | Cote d'Ivoire | 36.9 | 60 | Panama | 56.6 |
| 29 | Nigeria | 37.5 | 61 | Zimbabwe | 56.8 |
| 30 | Tanzania | 38.1 | 62 | Kenya | 57.5 |
| 31 | Algeria | 38.7 | 63 | South Africa | 58.4 |
| 32 | Morocco | 39.2 | 64 | Guatemala | 59.6 |
| 33 | Estonia | 39.5 | 65 | Brazil | 63.4 |

*Source: World Development Indicators,* 1997: chart 2.6.

# The Human Development Index

Since 1990, the United Nations has published the human development index (HDI) as a register of the development of nations. The HDI is a composite of three variables: life expectancy, educational attainment, and income. A nation's HDI score, an average of the sum of the three variables, has a maximum possible value of 1. The HDI for nations in 1994 is indicated in Table 13.2. In constructing the HDI, researchers arbitrarily designated

**TABLE 13.2  Human Development Index**

| Rank | Nation | HDI | Life Expectancy (years) | Gross School Enrollment (percent) | Per Capita GDP ($) |
|------|--------|-----|-------------------------|-----------------------------------|--------------------|
| 1 | Canada | .960 | 79.0 | 100 | 21,495 |
| 2 | France | .946 | 78.7 | 89 | 20,510 |
| 3 | Norway | .943 | 77.5 | 92 | 21,346 |
| 4 | USA | .942 | 76.2 | 96 | 26,397 |
| 5 | Iceland | .942 | 79.1 | 83 | 20,556 |
| 6 | Netherlands | .940 | 77.3 | 91 | 19,238 |
| 7 | Japan | .940 | 79.8 | 78 | 21,581 |
| 8 | Finland | .940 | 76.3 | 97 | 17,417 |
| 9 | New Zealand | .937 | 76.4 | 94 | 16,851 |
| 10 | Sweden | .936 | 78.3 | 82 | 18,540 |
| 11 | Spain | .934 | 77.6 | 90 | 14,324 |
| 12 | Austria | .932 | 76.6 | 87 | 20,667 |
| 13 | Belgium | .932 | 76.8 | 86 | 20,985 |
| 14 | Australia | .931 | 78.1 | 79 | 19,285 |
| 15 | UK | .931 | 76.7 | 86 | 18,620 |
| 16 | Switzerland | .930 | 78.1 | 76 | 24,967 |
| 17 | Ireland | .929 | 76.3 | 88 | 16,061 |
| 18 | Denmark | .927 | 75.2 | 89 | 21,341 |
| 19 | Germany | .924 | 76.3 | 81 | 19,675 |
| 20 | Greece | .923 | 77.8 | 82 | 11,265 |
| 21 | Italy | .921 | 77.8 | 73 | 19,363 |
| 22 | Hong Kong | .914 | 79.0 | 72 | 22,310 |
| 23 | Israel | .913 | 77.5 | 75 | 16,023 |
| 24 | Cyprus | .907 | 77.1 | 75 | 13,071 |
| 25 | Barbados | .907 | 75.9 | 76 | 11,051 |
| 26 | Singapore | .900 | 77.1 | 72 | 20,987 |
| 27 | Luxembourg | .899 | 75.9 | 76 | 34,155 |
| 28 | Bahamas | .894 | 72.9 | 75 | 15,875 |
| 29 | Antigua | .892 | 74.0 | 76 | 8,977 |
| 30 | Chile | .891 | 75.1 | 72 | 9,129 |
| 31 | Portugal | .890 | 74.6 | 81 | 12,326 |
| 32 | South Korea | .890 | 71.5 | 82 | 10,656 |
| 33 | Costa Rica | .889 | 76.6 | 68 | 5,919 |
| 34 | Malta | .887 | 76.4 | 76 | 13,009 |
| 35 | Slovenia | .886 | 73.1 | 74 | 10,404 |
| 36 | Argentina | .884 | 72.4 | 77 | 8,937 |
| 37 | Uruguay | .883 | 72.6 | 75 | 6,752 |
| 38 | Brunei | .882 | 74.9 | 70 | 30,447 |
| 39 | Czech Rep. | .882 | 72.2 | 70 | 9,201 |
| 40 | Trinidad | .880 | 72.9 | 67 | 9,124 |

*(Continued)*

**TABLE 13.2**    *(Continued)*

| Rank | Nation | HDI | Life Expectancy (years) | Gross School Enrollment (percent) | Per Capita GDP ($) |
|------|--------|-----|-------------------------|-----------------------------------|---------------------|
| 41 | Dominica | .873 | 72.0 | 77 | 6,118 |
| 42 | Slovakia | .873 | 70.8 | 72 | 6,389 |
| 43 | Bahrain | .870 | 72.0 | 77 | 15,321 |
| 44 | U. Arab Em. | .866 | 74.2 | 82 | 16,000 |
| 45 | Panama | .864 | 73.2 | 70 | 6,104 |
| 46 | Fiji | .863 | 71.8 | 79 | 5,763 |
| 47 | Venezuela | .861 | 72.1 | 68 | 8,120 |
| 48 | Hungary | .857 | 68.8 | 67 | 6,437 |
| 49 | St. Kitts | .853 | 69.0 | 78 | 9,436 |
| 50 | Mexico | .853 | 72.0 | 66 | 7,384 |
| 51 | Colombia | .848 | 70.1 | 70 | 6,107 |
| 52 | Seychelles | .845 | 72.0 | 61 | 7,891 |
| 53 | Kuwait | .844 | 75.2 | 57 | 21,875 |
| 54 | Granada | .843 | 72.0 | 61 | 5,137 |
| 55 | Qatar | .840 | 70.9 | 73 | 18,403 |
| 56 | St. Lucia | .838 | 71.0 | 74 | 6,182 |
| 57 | St. Vincent | .836 | 72.0 | 78 | 5,650 |
| 58 | Poland | .834 | 71.2 | 79 | 5,002 |
| 59 | Thailand | .833 | 69.5 | 53 | 7,104 |
| 60 | Malaysia | .832 | 71.2 | 62 | 8,865 |
| 61 | Mauritius | .831 | 70.7 | 61 | 13,172 |
| 62 | Belarus | .806 | 69.2 | 80 | 4,713 |
| 63 | Belize | .806 | 74.0 | 68 | 5,590 |
| 64 | Libya | .801 | 63.8 | 91 | 6,125 |
| 65 | Lebanon | .794 | 69.0 | 75 | 4,863 |
| 66 | Suriname | .792 | 70.7 | 71 | 4,711 |
| 67 | Russia | .792 | 65.7 | 78 | 4,828 |
| 68 | Brazil | .783 | 66.4 | 72 | 5,362 |
| 69 | Bulgaria | .780 | 71.1 | 66 | 4,533 |
| 70 | Iran | .780 | 68.2 | 68 | 5,766 |
| 71 | Estonia | .776 | 69.2 | 72 | 4,294 |
| 72 | Ecuador | .775 | 69.3 | 72 | 4,626 |
| 73 | Saudi Arabia | .774 | 70.3 | 56 | 9,338 |
| 74 | Turkey | .772 | 68.2 | 63 | 5,193 |
| 75 | North Korea | .765 | 71.4 | 75 | 3,965 |
| 76 | Lithuania | .762 | 70.1 | 70 | 4,011 |
| 77 | Croatia | .760 | 71.3 | 67 | 5,319 |
| 78 | Syria | .755 | 67.8 | 64 | 5,397 |
| 79 | Romania | .755 | 69.5 | 62 | 4,037 |
| 80 | Macedonia | .748 | 71.7 | 60 | 3,965 |
| 81 | Tunisia | .748 | 68.4 | 67 | 5,319 |
| 82 | Algeria | .737 | 67.8 | 64 | 5,442 |
| 83 | Jamaica | .736 | 73.9 | 65 | 3,816 |

**TABLE 13.2**   *(Continued)*

| Rank | Nation | HDI | Life Expectancy (years) | Gross School Enrollment (percent) | Per Capita GDP ($) |
|------|--------|-----|-------------------------|-----------------------------------|--------------------|
| 84 | Jordan | .730 | 68.5 | 66 | 4,187 |
| 85 | Turkmenistan | .723 | 64.7 | 90 | 3,469 |
| 86 | Cuba | .723 | 75.6 | 63 | 3,000 |
| 87 | Dominican Rep. | .718 | 70.0 | 68 | 3,933 |
| 88 | Oman | .718 | 70.0 | 60 | 10,078 |
| 89 | Peru | .717 | 67.4 | 81 | 3,645 |
| 90 | South Africa | .716 | 63.7 | 81 | 4,291 |
| 91 | Sri Lanka | .711 | 72.2 | 66 | 3,277 |
| 92 | Latvia | .711 | 67.9 | 67 | 3,332 |
| 93 | Kazakstan | .709 | 67.5 | 73 | 3,284 |
| 94 | Paraguay | .706 | 68.8 | 62 | 3,531 |
| 95 | Ukraine | .689 | 68.4 | 76 | 2,718 |
| 96 | Samoa | .684 | 68.1 | 74 | 2,726 |
| 97 | Botswana | .673 | 52.3 | 71 | 5,367 |
| 98 | Philippines | .672 | 67.0 | 78 | 2,681 |
| 99 | Indonesia | .668 | 63.5 | 62 | 3,740 |
| 100 | Uzbekistan | .662 | 67.5 | 73 | 2,438 |
| 101 | Mongolia | .661 | 64.4 | 52 | 3,766 |
| 102 | Albania | .655 | 70.5 | 59 | 2,788 |
| 103 | Armenia | .651 | 70.8 | 78 | 1,737 |
| 104 | Guyana | .649 | 63.2 | 67 | 2,729 |
| 105 | Georgia | .637 | 73.1 | 69 | 1,585 |
| 106 | Azerbaijan | .636 | 71.0 | 72 | 1,670 |
| 107 | Kyrgyzstan | .635 | 67.8 | 73 | 1,930 |
| 108 | China | .626 | 68.9 | 58 | 2,604 |
| 109 | Egypt | .614 | 64.3 | 69 | 3,846 |
| 110 | Moldova | .612 | 67.7 | 67 | 1,576 |
| 111 | Maldives | .611 | 62.8 | 71 | 2,200 |
| 112 | El Salvador | .592 | 69.3 | 55 | 2,417 |
| 113 | Bolivia | .589 | 60.1 | 66 | 2,598 |
| 114 | Swaziland | .582 | 58.3 | 72 | 2,821 |
| 115 | Tajikistan | .580 | 66.8 | 69 | 1,117 |
| 116 | Honduras | .575 | 68.4 | 60 | 2,050 |
| 117 | Guatemala | .572 | 65.6 | 46 | 3,208 |
| 118 | Namibia | .570 | 55.9 | 84 | 4,027 |
| 119 | Morocco | .566 | 65.3 | 46 | 3,681 |
| 120 | Gabon | .562 | 54.1 | 60 | 3,641 |
| 121 | Viet Nam | .557 | 66.0 | 55 | 1,208 |
| 122 | Solomon Isl. | .556 | 70.8 | 47 | 2,118 |
| 123 | Cape Verde | .547 | 65.3 | 64 | 1,862 |
| 124 | Vanuatu | .547 | 65.9 | 52 | 2,276 |
| 125 | Sao Tome | .534 | 67.0 | 57 | 1,704 |

*(Continued)*

**TABLE 13.2** *(Continued)*

| Rank | Nation | HDI | Life Expectancy (years) | Gross School Enrollment (percent) | Per Capita GDP ($) |
|------|--------|-----|-------------------------|-----------------------------------|--------------------|
| 126 | Iraq | .531 | 57.0 | 53 | 3,159 |
| 127 | Nicaragua | .530 | 67.3 | 62 | 1,580 |
| 128 | Pap. New Guin. | .525 | 56.4 | 38 | 2,821 |
| 129 | Zimbabwe | .513 | 49.0 | 68 | 2,196 |
| 130 | Congo | .500 | 51.3 | 56 | 2,410 |
| 131 | Myanmar | .475 | 58.4 | 48 | 1,051 |
| 132 | Ghana | .468 | 56.6 | 44 | 1,960 |
| 133 | Cameroon | .468 | 55.1 | 46 | 2,120 |
| 134 | Kenya | .463 | 53.6 | 55 | 1,404 |
| 135 | Eq. Guinea | .462 | 48.6 | 64 | 1,673 |
| 136 | Laos | .459 | 51.7 | 50 | 2,484 |
| 137 | Lesotho | .457 | 57.9 | 56 | 1,109 |
| 138 | India | .446 | 61.3 | 56 | 1,348 |
| 139 | Pakistan | .445 | 62.3 | 38 | 2,154 |
| 140 | Comoros | .412 | 56.1 | 39 | 1,366 |
| 141 | Nigeria | .393 | 51.0 | 50 | 1,351 |
| 142 | Zaire (Congo) | .381 | 52.2 | 38 | 429 |
| 143 | Zambia | .369 | 42.6 | 48 | 962 |
| 144 | Bangladesh | .368 | 56.4 | 39 | 1,331 |
| 145 | Cote d'Ivoire | .368 | 52.1 | 39 | 1,668 |
| 146 | Benin | .368 | 54.2 | 35 | 1,696 |
| 147 | Togo | .365 | 50.6 | 50 | 1,109 |
| 148 | Yemen | .361 | 56.2 | 52 | 805 |
| 149 | Tanzania | .357 | 50.3 | 34 | 656 |
| 150 | Mauritania | .355 | 52.1 | 36 | 1,593 |
| 151 | Cen. Afr. Rep. | .355 | 48.3 | 37 | 1,130 |
| 152 | Madagascar | .350 | 57.2 | 33 | 694 |
| 153 | Cambodia | .348 | 52.4 | 58 | 1,084 |
| 154 | Nepal | .347 | 55.3 | 55 | 1,137 |
| 155 | Bhutan | .338 | 51.5 | 31 | 1,289 |
| 156 | Haiti | .338 | 54.4 | 29 | 896 |
| 157 | Angola | .335 | 47.2 | 31 | 1,600 |
| 158 | Sudan | .333 | 51.0 | 31 | 1,084 |
| 159 | Uganda | .328 | 40.2 | 34 | 1,370 |
| 160 | Senegal | .326 | 49.9 | 31 | 1,596 |
| 161 | Malawi | .320 | 41.1 | 67 | 694 |
| 162 | Djibouti | .319 | 48.8 | 20 | 1,270 |
| 163 | Guinea-Bissau | .291 | 43.2 | 29 | 793 |
| 164 | Chad | .288 | 47.0 | 25 | 700 |
| 165 | Gambia | .281 | 45.6 | 34 | 939 |
| 166 | Mozambique | .281 | 46.0 | 25 | 986 |
| 167 | Guinea | .271 | 45.1 | 24 | 1,103 |
| 168 | Eritrea | .269 | 50.1 | 24 | 960 |

**TABLE 13.2**   *(Continued)*

| Rank | Nation | HDI | Life Expectancy (years) | Gross School Enrollment (percent) | Per Capita GDP ($) |
|------|--------|-----|------------------------|-----------------------------------|--------------------|
| 169 | Burundi | .247 | 43.5 | 31 | 698 |
| 170 | Ethiopia | .244 | 48.2 | 18 | 427 |
| 171 | Mali | .229 | 46.6 | 17 | 543 |
| 172 | Burkina Faso | .221 | 46.4 | 20 | 796 |
| 173 | Niger | .206 | 47.1 | 15 | 787 |
| 174 | Rwanda | .187 | 22.6 | 37 | 352 |
| 175 | Sierra Leone | .176 | 33.6 | 28 | 643 |

*Source:* From *Human Development Report, 1997.* Copyright © 1997 by the United Nations Development Programme. Used by permission of Oxford University Press, Inc.

those nations with HDI scores above .800 as high in human development; there were 64 such nations. Those nations classified as medium, between .799 and .500, numbered 66. The 45 countries below .499 were identified as low in human development.

Because the HDI includes variables in addition to income, it provides more information on the social progress of nations than the Gini Coefficient. Thus, the HDI demonstrates that nations with somewhat lower incomes are nonetheless able to sustain longevity and mount educational programs. Despite a per capita GDP that is 58 percent that of Italy's, Greece claims comparable longevity and a higher percent of the population enrolled in educational programs. Similarly, Cuba's per capita GDP is one-third that of Saudi Arabia, yet Cubans enjoy greater longevity and more educational opportunity than Saudis. Still, the HDI is a less than optimal classification. An important qualification is that nations evidence significant variations internally that are not registered by the national HDI score. Ordinarily, national capitals, industrial cities, and ports elevate a nation's HDI score, while rural, remote areas have a depressive affect. While the "medium" developing nations rank higher than those ranked "low," the rural areas of the "medium" HDI–scoring nations tend to parallel those nations that rank lowest.

## The Human Poverty Index

As the lower registers of the HDI amply demonstrate, the populations of many developing nations evidence a degree of deprivation that is qualitatively different from the industrialized nations. In order to depict that level of destitution, the UN introduced the human poverty index (HPI) in 1997. The HPI consists of three basic indicators: (1) the percentage of people not expected to reach age 40, (2) the percentage of illiterate adults, and (3) the resources available in the form of health services, safe water, and the percentage of underweight children under age five. The HPI ranking of developing nations is found in Table 13.3.

As Table 13.3 indicates, a nation's developmental status may diverge from the extent to which it commits resources to address poverty. Nations with high negative numbers are

**TABLE 13.3    Human Poverty Index**

| Country | HPI Rank | HPI Index Value (percent) | HPI Minus HDI Rank | Country | HPI Rank | HPI Index Value (percent) | HPI Minus HDI Rank |
|---|---|---|---|---|---|---|---|
| Trinidad | 1 | 4.1 | −4 | Myanmar | 40 | 31.2 | −3 |
| Cuba | 2 | 5.1 | −18 | Cameroon | 41 | 31.4 | −4 |
| Chile | 3 | 5.4 | 1 | Pap. New Guin. | 42 | 32.0 | 2 |
| Singapore | 4 | 6.6 | 3 | Ghana | 43 | 32.6 | −1 |
| Costa Rica | 5 | 6.6 | −15 | Egypt | 44 | 34.8 | 14 |
| Colombia | 6 | 10.7 | −3 | Zambia | 45 | 35.1 | −8 |
| Mexico | 7 | 10.9 | −1 | Guatemala | 46 | 35.5 | 12 |
| Jordan | 8 | 10.9 | −11 | India | 47 | 36.7 | −2 |
| Panama | 9 | 11.2 | −13 | Rwanda | 48 | 37.9 | −29 |
| Uruguay | 10 | 11.7 | 6 | Togo | 49 | 39.3 | −7 |
| Thailand | 11 | 11.7 | 1 | Tanzania | 50 | 39.7 | −8 |
| Jamaica | 12 | 12.1 | −6 | Laos | 51 | 40.1 | 4 |
| Mauritius | 13 | 12.5 | 2 | Zaire | 52 | 41.2 | 0 |
| U. Arab Em. | 14 | 14.9 | 8 | Uganda | 53 | 41.3 | −13 |
| Ecuador | 15 | 15.2 | 1 | Nigeria | 54 | 41.6 | 3 |
| Mongolia | 16 | 15.7 | −12 | Morocco | 55 | 41.7 | 19 |
| Zimbabwe | 17 | 17.3 | −24 | Cen. Afr. Rep. | 56 | 41.7 | −4 |
| China | 18 | 17.5 | −11 | Sudan | 57 | 42.2 | −8 |
| Philippines | 19 | 17.7 | −7 | Guinea-Bissau | 58 | 43.6 | −11 |
| Dominican Rep. | 20 | 18.3 | −1 | Namibia | 59 | 45.1 | 24 |
| Libya | 21 | 18.8 | 9 | Malawi | 60 | 45.8 | −8 |
| Sri Lanka | 22 | 20.7 | −1 | Haiti | 61 | 46.2 | −3 |
| Indonesia | 23 | 20.8 | −4 | Bhutan | 62 | 46.3 | −1 |
| Syria | 24 | 21.7 | 9 | Cote d'Ivoire | 63 | 46.3 | 8 |
| Honduras | 25 | 22.0 | −8 | Pakistan | 64 | 46.8 | 14 |
| Bolivia | 26 | 22.5 | −6 | Mauritania | 65 | 47.1 | 6 |
| Iran | 27 | 22.6 | 14 | Yemen | 66 | 47.6 | 9 |
| Peru | 28 | 22.8 | 6 | Bangladesh | 67 | 48.3 | 13 |
| Botswana | 29 | 22.9 | 4 | Senegal | 68 | 48.7 | 1 |
| Paraguay | 30 | 23.2 | 6 | Burundi | 69 | 49.0 | −3 |
| Tunisia | 31 | 24.4 | 15 | Madagascar | 70 | 49.5 | 9 |
| Kenya | 32 | 26.1 | −14 | Guinea | 71 | 50.0 | 0 |
| Viet Nam | 33 | 26.2 | −4 | Mozambique | 72 | 50.1 | 2 |
| Nicaragua | 34 | 27.2 | −5 | Cambodia | 73 | 52.5 | 11 |
| Lesotho | 35 | 27.5 | −13 | Mali | 74 | 54.7 | 0 |
| El Salvador | 36 | 28.0 | 5 | Ethiopia | 75 | 56.2 | 2 |
| Algeria | 37 | 28.6 | 20 | Burkina Faso | 76 | 58.3 | 1 |
| Congo | 38 | 29.1 | −4 | Sierra Leone | 77 | 59.2 | −1 |
| Iraq | 39 | 30.7 | 1 | Niger | 78 | 66.0 | 2 |

*Source:* From *Human Development Report, 1997.* Copyright © 1997 by the United Nations Development Programme.
Used by permission of Oxford University Press, Inc.

those that have made significant inroads in combating poverty despite a relatively low development ranking. Conversely, nations with large positive numbers relative to development are those making less of a commitment to aiding the poor. HPI ranking also provides clues about the most distressed countries and regions. Note that many of the nations with the highest HPI ranking are in sub-Saharan Africa.

# The Gender Development Index

A major omission in the HDI is the gender-related disparity between men and women. Gender is an urgent concern in development because of the subordinate status of women. As a generalization, the less developed a nation, the greater the likelihood that women will be disadvantaged. This is not a benign consideration—as issues such as dowry, female infanticide, and female genital mutilation demonstrate. In order to highlight the disparate status of women, the indicators comprising the HDI have been adjusted for gender to construct a gender-related development index (GDI). The GDI for 146 nations is noted in Table 13.4, in addition to the difference with each nation's HDI.

As Table 13.4 demonstrates, controlling for gender shuffles the HDI rankings, sometimes to a considerable extent. Those nations in which the HDI minus GDI is positive are those that tend to favor women. On the other hand, those nations in which the HDI minus GDI yields a negative number are those in which women's achievement is lower than that of men. Several patterns are evident in the comparison of HDI and GDI rankings. Foremost, the welfare states of northern Europe rank among the highest of nations, producing a GDI higher than their HDI scores. Another group of nations yielding GDI scores higher than their HDI rankings are the former Soviet nations of Asia and Eastern Europe. Two negative patterns also emerge. Predominantly Catholic and Moslem nations produce GDI scores below their HDI scores, a reflection of patriarchal religious doctrine. Further exploration of gender-related differences that affect development is reflected in the gender empowerment measure (GEM), first computed by the United Nations in 1995. For the most part, nations with high GEM scores are also those that have higher GDI than HDI scores (*Human Development Report,* 1996: 34–36).

# The Sum of All Measures

As the data rankings indicate, economic growth is an essential precondition for development, but it is unlikely to promote human development without concern for noneconomic criteria, such as education, health, and gender equity. The United Nations has proposed five themes to guide human development: empowerment, cooperation, equity, sustainability , and security (*Human Development Report,* 1997: 55–56). Nations may vary considerably in how they elect to condition economic growth in order to promote human development, if they choose to do so at all. That many nations are able to generate positive human development indicators despite modest economic performance suggests a "human development frontier," or an optimal efficiency in adjusting economic growth to facilitate

**TABLE 13.4  Gender-Related Development Index**

| GDI Rank | Nation | HDI Rank* | HDI Rank Minus GDI Rank | GDI Rank | Nation | HDI Rank* | HDI Rank Minus GDI Rank |
|---|---|---|---|---|---|---|---|
| 1 | Canada | 1 | 0 | 43 | Venezuela | 44 | 1 |
| 2 | Norway | 3 | 1 | 44 | Chile | 29 | −15 |
| 3 | Sweden | 10 | 7 | 45 | Malaysia | 52 | 7 |
| 4 | Iceland | 5 | 1 | 46 | Russia | 57 | 11 |
| 5 | USA | 4 | −1 | 47 | Argentina | 35 | −12 |
| 6 | France | 2 | −4 | 48 | Malta | 33 | −15 |
| 7 | Finland | 8 | 1 | 49 | Bulgaria | 59 | 10 |
| 8 | New Zealand | 9 | 1 | 50 | Mexico | 46 | −4 |
| 9 | Australia | 14 | 5 | 51 | Kuwait | 48 | −3 |
| 10 | Denmark | 18 | 8 | 52 | Estonia | 60 | 8 |
| 11 | Netherlands | 6 | −5 | 53 | Fiji | 43 | −10 |
| 12 | Japan | 7 | −5 | 54 | Mauritius | 53 | −1 |
| 13 | United Kingdom | 15 | 2 | 55 | Lithuania | 64 | 9 |
| 14 | Belgium | 13 | −1 | 56 | Bahrain | 40 | −16 |
| 15 | Austria | 12 | −3 | 57 | Croatia | 65 | 8 |
| 16 | Germany | 19 | 3 | 58 | Turkey | 63 | 5 |
| 17 | Barbados | 25 | 8 | 59 | Romania | 67 | 8 |
| 18 | Bahamas | 28 | 10 | 60 | Brazil | 58 | −2 |
| 19 | Spain | 11 | −8 | 61 | U. Arab Em. | 41 | −20 |
| 20 | Switzerland | 16 | −4 | 62 | Macedonia | 68 | 6 |
| 21 | Greece | 20 | −1 | 63 | Jamaica | 71 | 8 |
| 22 | Israel | 23 | 1 | 64 | Qatar | 49 | −15 |
| 23 | Italy | 21 | −2 | 65 | Turkmenistan | 72 | 7 |
| 24 | Slovenia | 34 | 10 | 66 | Lebanon | 56 | −10 |
| 25 | Czech Rep. | 37 | 12 | 67 | Latvia | 76 | 9 |
| 26 | Slovakia | 39 | 13 | 68 | Cuba | 73 | 5 |
| 27 | Singapore | 26 | −1 | 69 | Kazakstan | 79 | 10 |
| 28 | Hong Kong | 22 | −6 | 70 | Sri Lanka | 77 | 10 |
| 29 | Ireland | 17 | −12 | 71 | South Africa | 76 | 5 |
| 30 | Portugal | 30 | 0 | 72 | Ukraine | 81 | 9 |
| 31 | Uruguay | 36 | 5 | 73 | Ecuador | 61 | −12 |
| 32 | Trinidad | 38 | 6 | 74 | Tunisia | 69 | −5 |
| 33 | Cyprus | 24 | −9 | 75 | Dominican Rep. | 74 | −1 |
| 34 | Hungary | 45 | 11 | 76 | Peru | 75 | −1 |
| 35 | South Korea | 31 | −4 | 77 | Lybia | 55 | −22 |
| 36 | Costa Rica | 32 | −4 | 78 | Uzbekistan | 85 | 7 |
| 37 | Poland | 50 | 13 | 79 | Botswana | 82 | 3 |
| 38 | Luxembourg | 27 | −11 | 80 | Mongolia | 86 | 6 |
| 39 | Thailand | 51 | 12 | 81 | Philippines | 83 | 2 |
| 40 | Colombia | 47 | 7 | 82 | Paraguay | 80 | −2 |
| 41 | Panama | 42 | 1 | 83 | Armenia | 88 | 5 |
| 42 | Belarus | 54 | 12 | 84 | Syria | 68 | −16 |

**TABLE 13.4** *Continued*

| GDI Rank | Nation | HDI Rank* | HDI Rank Minus GDI Rank | GDI Rank | Nation | HDI Rank* | HDI Rank Minus GDI Rank |
|---|---|---|---|---|---|---|---|
| 85 | Albania | 87 | 2 | 122 | Zambia | 122 | 0 |
| 86 | Indonesia | 84 | −2 | 123 | Tanzania | 127 | 4 |
| 87 | Georgia | 90 | 3 | 124 | Benin | 125 | 1 |
| 88 | Kyrgyzstan | 92 | 4 | 125 | Togo | 126 | 1 |
| 89 | Azerbaijan | 91 | 2 | 126 | Cote d'Ivoire | 124 | −2 |
| 90 | China | 93 | 3 | 127 | Mauritania | 126 | −1 |
| 91 | Guyana | 89 | −2 | 128 | Bangladesh | 123 | −5 |
| 92 | Algeria | 70 | −22 | 129 | Cen. Afr. Rep. | 129 | 0 |
| 93 | Moldova | 95 | 2 | 130 | Haiti | 131 | 1 |
| 94 | Maldives | 96 | 2 | 131 | Nepal | 130 | −1 |
| 95 | Saudi Arabia | 62 | −33 | 132 | Uganda | 133 | 1 |
| 96 | Tajikistan | 100 | 4 | 133 | Malawi | 135 | 2 |
| 97 | El Salvador | 97 | 0 | 134 | Senegal | 134 | 0 |
| 98 | Swaziland | 99 | 1 | 135 | Sudan | 132 | −3 |
| 99 | Bolivia | 98 | −1 | 136 | Guinea-Bissau | 136 | 0 |
| 100 | Egypt | 94 | −6 | 137 | Chad | 137 | 0 |
| 101 | Viet Nam | 105 | 4 | 138 | Gambia | 138 | 0 |
| 102 | Gabon | 104 | 2 | 139 | Mozambique | 139 | 0 |
| 103 | Honduras | 101 | −2 | 140 | Guinea | 140 | 0 |
| 104 | Cape Verde | 106 | 2 | 141 | Burundi | 141 | 0 |
| 105 | Morocco | 103 | −2 | 142 | Ethiopia | 142 | 0 |
| 106 | Nicaragua | 108 | −2 | 143 | Mali | 143 | 0 |
| 107 | Guatemala | 102 | −5 | 144 | Burkina Faso | 144 | 0 |
| 108 | Pap. New Guin. | 109 | 1 | 145 | Niger | 145 | 0 |
| 109 | Zimbabwe | 110 | 1 | 146 | Sierra Leone | 146 | 0 |
| 110 | Myanmar | 111 | 1 | | | | |
| 111 | Ghana | 112 | 1 | | | | |
| 112 | Kenya | 114 | 2 | | | | |
| 113 | Lesotho | 117 | 4 | | | | |
| 114 | Laos | 116 | 2 | | | | |
| 115 | Cameroon | 113 | −2 | | | | |
| 116 | Eq. Guinea | 115 | −1 | | | | |
| 117 | Iraq | 107 | −10 | | | | |
| 118 | India | 118 | 0 | | | | |
| 119 | Comoros | 120 | 1 | | | | |
| 120 | Pakistan | 119 | −1 | | | | |
| 121 | Nigeria | 121 | 0 | | | | |

*Source:* From *Human Development Report, 1997.* Copyright © 1997 by the United Nations Development Programme. Used by permission of Oxford University Press, Inc.

*The number of nations is fewer than the HDI table due to absence of data.

human development. Figure 13.1 charts a "human development efficiency frontier" for selected nations for 1993.

A rather more ambitious assessment of the progress of nations has been undertaken by Richard Estes, an American social work professor. For 1970, 1980, 1990, and 1995, Estes has ranked nations according to their performance along 46 variables that are grouped in ten subindeces: education, health, women, defense, economic, demography, geography, political participation, cultural diversity, and welfare. Containing so many variables, Estes's scheme is much more sophisticated than the three-variable HDI or GDI systems. At the same time, his formulation contains assumptions that are open to question. In classic American liberal tradition, for example, Estes assumes that military expenditures are inversely related to social progress. As another example, the welfare subindex consists of the foundations of the modern welfare state, another assumption of liberal ideology. Estes's 1995 ranking of social progress of nations is shown in Table 13.5.

Estes's analysis is as informative about international development as it is controversial. The top slots are reserved for the well-articulated welfare states of central and northern Europe. Of urgent concern are those nations at the bottom of the ranking; their

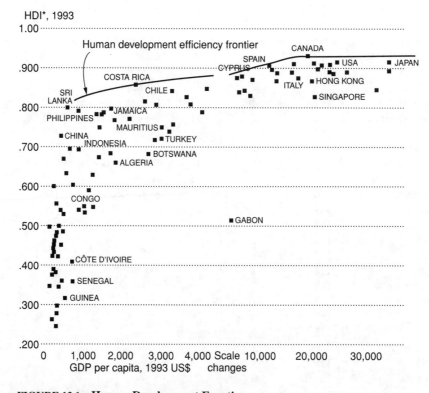

**FIGURE 13.1   Human Development Frontier**

*Source:* Human Development Report Office and World Bank 1994a. From *Human Development Report 1996* by United Nations Development Program. Copyright © 1996 by the United Nations Development Programme. Used by permission of Oxford University Press, Inc.

**TABLE 13.5   Country Scores and Ranks on the Weighted Index of Social Progress, 1995 (N=160)**

| Rank WISP95 (Base=160) | Countries | WISP 1995 (Base=160) | Rank WISP95 (Base=160) | Countries | WISP 1995 (Base=160) |
|---|---|---|---|---|---|
| 1 | Denmark | 98 | 43 | Uruguay | 71 |
| 2 | Norway | 96 | 43 | Russian Federation | 71 |
| 3 | Austria | 93 | 45 | Croatia | 69 |
| 3 | Sweden | 93 | 45 | Mauritius | 68 |
| 5 | France | 92 | 47 | Belarus | 68 |
| 6 | Luxembourg | 91 | 47 | Armenia | 67 |
| 6 | Finland | 91 | 47 | Argentina | 68 |
| 8 | Ireland | 89 | 50 | Panama | 66 |
| 9 | Poland | 88 | 51 | Singapore | 65 |
| 9 | Germany | 88 | 51 | Moldova | 66 |
| 11 | Netherlands | 88 | 53 | Thailand | 64 |
| 11 | Iceland | 88 | 54 | Cuba | 63 |
| 11 | Italy | 88 | 54 | Colombia | 63 |
| 11 | Hungary | 87 | 57 | Kyrgyz Republic | 62 |
| 15 | Slovenia | 87 | 57 | South Africa | 61 |
| 15 | Portugal | 86 | 57 | Tunisia | 62 |
| 15 | United Kingdom | 86 | 57 | Venezuela | 62 |
| 15 | Belgium | 87 | 57 | Jamaica | 61 |
| 19 | New Zealand | 85 | 61 | Brazil | 60 |
| 19 | Spain | 86 | 62 | Albania | 59 |
| 19 | Japan | 85 | 62 | Trinidad & Tobago | 59 |
| 22 | Czech Republic | 84 | 64 | Paraguay | 58 |
| 23 | Switzerland | 83 | 65 | USSR | … |
| 24 | Australia | 83 | 65 | Mexico | 58 |
| 24 | Greece | 82 | 66 | Uzbekistan | 58 |
| 24 | Bulgaria | 82 | 67 | Ecuador | 57 |
| 27 | Slovak Republic | 80 | 69 | Lebanon | 55 |
| 27 | Estonia | 80 | 69 | Macedonia | 55 |
| 27 | United States | 80 | 69 | Georgia | 55 |
| 30 | Ukraine | 78 | 69 | El Salvador | 56 |
| 31 | Canada | 78 | 69 | Jordan | 56 |
| 31 | Hong Kong | 78 | 73 | Malaysia | 55 |
| 33 | Chile | 77 | 73 | Algeria | 54 |
| 34 | Lithuania | 75 | 73 | Kuwait | 55 |
| 35 | Cyprus | 75 | 76 | Honduras | 53 |
| 35 | Yugoslav Republic | 74 | 76 | Dominican Republic | 54 |
| 35 | Romania | 75 | 78 | Philippines | 53 |
| 38 | Latvia | 74 | 78 | Azerbaijan | 52 |
| 38 | Israel | 74 | 78 | Sri Lanka | 53 |
| 40 | Taiwan | 73 | 78 | Turkey | 52 |
| 40 | Costa Rica | 72 | 82 | Peru | 52 |
| 40 | Korea, Republic | 73 | 83 | Fiji | 50 |

*(Continued)*

**TABLE 13.5** *Continued*

| Rank WISP95 (Base=160) | Countries | WISP 1995 (Base=160) | Rank WISP95 (Base=160) | Countries | WISP 1995 (Base=160) |
|---|---|---|---|---|---|
| 83 | Kazakhstan | 50 | 123 | Tanzania* | 22 |
| 83 | Libya | 51 | 123 | Haiti* | 23 |
| 86 | Bahrain | 50 | 123 | Cameroon | 22 |
| 86 | Egypt | 49 | 126 | Benin* | 22 |
| 86 | Mongolia | 49 | 126 | Malawi* | 21 |
| 89 | Guyana | 49 | 126 | Papua New Guinea | 21 |
| 89 | Saudi Arabia | 48 | 129 | Pakistan | 20 |
| 91 | Syria | 47 | 130 | Cambodia* | 19 |
| 92 | Qatar | 46 | 131 | Comoros* | 18 |
| 92 | Iran | 46 | 132 | Burundi* | 18 |
| 92 | Morocco | 45 | 132 | Nepal* | 18 |
| 95 | Botswana* | 44 | 134 | Sudan* | 16 |
| 96 | Indonesia | 43 | 134 | Mali* | 16 |
| 96 | Namibia | 43 | 136 | Central African Rep.* | 15 |
| 98 | Bolivia | 42 | 137 | Gambia* | 15 |
| 99 | Viet Nam | 41 | 138 | Mauritania* | 13 |
| 100 | Tajikistan | 40 | 139 | Bhutan* | 13 |
| 100 | Swaziland | 41 | 140 | Djibouti* | 12 |
| 100 | Lesotho* | 40 | 141 | Nigeria | 11 |
| 103 | Korea, PDR | 39 | 141 | Yemen* | 11 |
| 103 | Suriname | 40 | 143 | Zaire* | 10 |
| 105 | Turkmenistan | 38 | 143 | Lao* | 10 |
| 106 | China | 38 | 143 | Cote d'Ivoire | 10 |
| 107 | Oman | 36 | 146 | Guinea* | 8 |
| 108 | Nicaragua | 34 | 146 | Rwanda* | 9 |
| 108 | Guatemala | 34 | 148 | Uganda* | 8 |
| 110 | Iraq | 32 | 149 | Guinea Bissau* | 7 |
| 110 | Zimbabwe | 32 | 149 | Burkina Faso* | 7 |
| 112 | Myanmar* | 30 | 149 | Eritrea | 6 |
| 113 | India | 29 | 152 | Niger* | 5 |
| 113 | Bangladesh* | 30 | 153 | Ethiopia* | 1 |
| 115 | Gabon | 29 | 154 | Chad* | 1 |
| 115 | Congo | 29 | 155 | Mozambique* | –3 |
| 117 | Togo* | 28 | 156 | Liberia* | –5 |
| 118 | Madagascar* | 27 | 157 | Somalia* | –7 |
| 119 | Zambia* | 25 | 157 | Sierra Leone* | –7 |
| 120 | Kenya | 25 | 159 | Afghanistan* | –11 |
| 120 | Ghana | 25 | 160 | Angola* | –25 |
| 122 | Senegal | 24 | | | |

*Source:* Richard Estes (1998). Reprinted by permission.

*Indicates countries officially classified by the United Nations as "Least Developing" (LDC).

conditions have worsened to such a degree that they generate negative numbers, essentially indicating antidevelopment features. For the most part, these are developing nations that have experienced internal strife—armed conflict that has further detracted from an already precarious developmental status.

On the other hand, Estes's classification invites skepticism. Canada and the United States, ranking first and fourth, respectively, in the HDI schedule, fall relatively far down the scale in Estes's ranking: the U.S. is twenty-seventh and Canada thirty-first. That Bulgaria would be ranked above the United States irked a reporter from the *New York Times* who examined various development indexes. Nicholas Eberstadt of the American Enterprise Institute, a moderate-conservative policy institute in Washington, D.C., dismissed such rankings on the basis that "they pivot on arbitrary evaluations about which there is no universal consensus." In rebuttal, Estes acknowledged that "The present social situation in Bulgaria is miserable, but in terms of responding to basic human needs, Bulgaria enjoys the legacy of social provision that characterized all of the states and partners of the former Soviet Union—high literacy, high access to at least basic health care, guaranteed housing, guaranteed income support during old age and other periods of income loss, and so on" (Crossette, 1997: 4). The UN HDI ranks Bulgaria sixty-ninth, the GDI forty-ninth, suggesting a discrepancy of sufficient magnitude that rechecking the instrumentation is in order.

Since Estes has undertaken this exercise each decade, the longitudinal transformation of nations becomes evident. Between 1970 and 1992, many nations have experienced substantial change in their progress. Notably, the former satellite nations of the USSR have plummeted, primarily as a result of the removal of artificial supports of command economics and their replacement with capitalism. Of the former Warsaw Pact nations, only Hungary, the former Czechoslovakia, and Poland have been able to avoid free fall since the collapse of the Soviet Union. Another group of nations have lost ground due to revolution. By 1990, Lebanon, Kampuchea, Afghanistan, Somalia, and Ethiopia had fallen a considerable distance compared to their ranking two decades earlier. The price of ending apartheid in South Africa appears to be a dramatic drop during the past two decades.

Several developing nations have increased their ranking position by ten or more. South Korea and Singapore (and probably Taiwan and Hong Kong, had data been available in 1970) have vaulted from Third World to First World membership. Another subgroup consisting of Jordan, Indonesia, and Libya have also prospered, largely as a result of authoritarian leadership. Unfortunately, Estes's ranking in 1990 fails to capture more recent events that would pull nations downward in the rankings. Political instability, coupled with the demise of Soviet Russia, probably drops Albania into the sixth if not the seventh decile. An uncertain change in leadership compounded by famine would rank North Korea ten or twenty spaces below what it occupied in 1990. Genocide in Rwanda and Burundi could well drop these nations into the last decile, accompanying Sierra Leone, Somalia, and Ethiopia—among the most hopeless places on earth.

Finally, a regional analysis by Jeffrey Sachs and his associates provides important clues to progress among developing nations. Sachs, a scholar from Harvard University, has considerable experience with development, particularly in eastern Europe. In an attempt to predict progress in the most undeveloped regions of the world—South Asia, sub-Saharan

Africa, and Latin America—Sachs posited four crucial factors: the initial condition of the region, the impact of public decisions, basic demographic influences, and the implications of geography and natural resources. The consequences of these four factors for each region are depicted in Table 13.6.

The interaction of these variables suggest that the development prospects of South Asia are significantly greater than those of sub-Saharan Africa and South America. Indeed, Sachs and his associates suggest that the most substantial barrier to development relate to a tropical environment. High temperatures and humidity create an ideal environment for tropical infectious disease, which exacts a high cost for humans and livestock. In light of these, Sachs proposes an ambitious public health initiative for tropical regions. Until the tropics are more conducive to development, Sachs indicates that migration of tropical populations to nations with more temperate climates is inevitable. However, the willingness of developed nations to accept tropical migrants remains in question, as the xenophobia of conservatives in the United States and France attests.

**TABLE 13.6    Explaining Failure: Contribution of Selected Factors to the Difference between Growth (per person, per year) in the Regions Shown and Growth in East and Southeast Asia, 1965–90 (percent)**

|  | South Asia | sub-Saharan Africa | Latin America |
|---|---|---|---|
| Initial conditions | 0.3 | 0.7 | −1.2 |
| Initial GDP per person | 0.5 | 1.0 | −1.2 |
| Schooling | −0.2 | −0.4 | −0.1 |
| Policy variables | −2.1 | −1.7 | −1.8 |
| Government saving rate | −0.4 | −0.1 | −0.3 |
| Openness | −1.2 | −1.2 | −1.0 |
| Institutional quality | −0.5 | −0.4 | −0.5 |
| Demography | −0.9 | −1.9 | −0.2 |
| Life expectancy | −0.5 | −1.3 | 0.1 |
| Growth in working-age population | −0.3 | 0.1 | −0.2 |
| Growth in total population | −0.2 | −0.7 | −0.1 |
| Resources and geography | 0.2 | −1.0 | −0.6 |
| Natural resources | 0.1 | −0.2 | −0.2 |
| Landlocked | 0.0 | −0.3 | −0.2 |
| Tropics | 0.5 | −0.2 | 0.0 |
| Ratio of coastline distance to land area | −0.3 | −0.3 | −0.3 |
| Predicted difference in growth | −2.5 | −3.9 | −3.8 |
| Actual difference | −2.9 | −4.0 | −3.9 |

# REFERENCES

Crossette, Barbara. (1997). "Is Life Better in Bulgaria? It's a Matter of Perspective," *New York Times* (September 7).

Estes, Richard. (n.d.). "The State of Global Development" (Philadelphia: University of Pennsylvania School of Social Work).

*Human Development Report.* (1997). (New York: Oxford University Press).

Kennedy, Paul. (1987). *The Rise and Fall of the Great Powers* (New York: Vintage).

Sachs, Jeffrey. (1997). "The Limits of Convergence," *The Economist* (June 14).

Todaro, Michael. (1994). *Economic Development* (New York: Longman).

*World Development Indicators.* (1997). (Washington, D.C.: World Bank).

# 14 An Integrative Model of Development

*There are not two worlds, there is one world. We breathe the same air. We degrade the same environment. We share the same financial system. We have the same health problems. AIDS is not a problem that stops at borders. Crime does not stop at borders. Drugs do not stop at borders. Terrorism, war, and famine do not stop at borders. With a population growing at 80 million a year, instead of 3 billion living on under $2 a day, it could be as high as 5 billion. We are living with a time bomb, and unless we take action now, it could blow up in our children's faces.*

—James Wolfensohn, President, World Bank (1997)

At the cusp of the millennium, international development confronts a new set of challenges. As early as the 1980s, the utility of the post–World War II paradigm for aiding the Third World had come under scrutiny. The strategy through which international aid agencies leveraged capital to induce the elites in Third World nations to undertake developmental projects produced contradictory outcomes: Despite significant improvement in the conditions of the world's poor generally, in some regions pockets of deprivation actually deepened. Several Southeast Asian nations adopted global integration policies emphasizing export promotion, leading to the much-celebrated "miracle economies." Enthusiasm about export-led development was dampened, however, when a decade of continuous growth was interrupted by the financial collapse of Southeast Asia in the late 1990s. Meanwhile in less fortunate regions, development actually flagged—increasing urbanization while neglecting rural areas, further padding the accounts of the wealthy while encouraging capital flight, and depleting economic resources while despoiling the environment all contributed to the emergence of a Fourth World. Clearly, the historical model of development that promised economic growth, social integration, and eventually the implementation of a modern welfare state was no longer tenable. As its flaws became more evident, critics of the postwar paradigm suggested different foci—poor communities, predatory corporations, hemispheric skewing of modernization, and exhaustion of natural resources—and these in turn gave rise to competing schools of thought in development thinking. Taken together, these critical approaches signified the unraveling of conventional prescriptions for development. Rather than promising progress, international development seemed at best to generate uneven and erratic prosperity, at worst to drive many struggling nations farther backward. Of increasing urgency was the need for an integrative model of development.

# Traditional Assumptions of Development

By the 1990s, a series of events served to reshape the understanding of development. Foremost, capitalism assumed global dimensions which, abetted by information technology, diminished the regulatory capacity of national and international institutions. During the two decades prior to 1990, international trade expanded by a factor of ten, signifying the globalization of markets (Yergin & Stanislaw, 1998). Uneven and at times capricious, global markets favored the development of Third World nations during the 1980s while fluctuating with respect to the command economies of the Second World. By the 1990s, international trade was firmly controlled by the developed nations of the First World. The impact of global capitalism on various economic systems has been uneven, as depicted in Table 14.1.

Led by the exports of the Four Tigers—Taiwan, South Korea, Hong Kong, and Singapore—the Third World experienced economic growth during the 1980s, only to see that upward trajectory flatten largely as a result of the declining fortunes of sub-Saharan Africa. Meanwhile, the Communist nations struggled to become integrated with world markets.

While global capitalism favored the First World, industrialized nations actually halted the expansion of their social provisions. In the United Kingdom and the United States, conservative national leaders announced a freeze on their welfare states (Chatterjee, 1996), and subsequent neoliberal leaders actually began the process of rolling them back. Outlying New Zealand announced early cuts in social welfare (Wallace, 1995). In the early 1990s, Europe—the standardbearer of the welfare state—began to reassess its commitment to social programs (Cohen, 1993; Marshall, 1994). Even the paragon of welfare states, Sweden, began to rethink its comprehensive array of government social provisions (Sander, 1996). Foreign aid has also contracted. As a percentage of GNP, global foreign assistance plummeted from a high of 0.51 percent in 1960 to 0.35 percent in 1990 (Todaro, 1994: 539). The United States has been particularly negligent in foreign aid. Noted for its Marshall Plan to rebuild the industrial nations ravaged by World War II (Kunz, 1997; Reynolds, 1997), the United States pumped $13 billion into Western Europe between 1948 and 1951. At that time, U.S. foreign aid represented over three percent of GNP; by the 1990s, it had withered to less than one-fourth of one percent (Black, 1991). Domestically and internationally, the willingness of First World nations to transfer income to the less advan-

**TABLE 14.1   Trends in World Exports, 1970–1990***

|  | 1970 | 1975 | 1980 | 1983 | 1986 | 1990 |
|---|---|---|---|---|---|---|
| World exports | 312.0 | 872.7 | 2,002.0 | 1,813.5 | 2,113.0 | 3,187.0 |
| Share of world exports % |  |  |  |  |  |  |
| Developed countries | 71.9 | 66.1 | 66.3 | 64.1 | 69.0 | 74.6 |
| Developing countries | 17.6 | 24.2 | 27.9 | 24.9 | 20.8 | 17.8 |
| Centrally planned economies | 10.5 | 9.7 | 8.8 | 11.0 | 10.2 | 7.5 |

*Billions of 1980 dollars.

*Source:* M. Todaro, *Economic Development in the Third World,* 5th Edition. © 1994 by Michael P. Todaro.

taged has diminished despite continuing First World prosperity. Thus demolished is the prophecy of British philosopher Richard Titmuss that the welfare state would eventually become a "welfare world" (1968: 127).

The sequel to the globalization of capital is the collapse of state socialism in the form of the Soviet Union and its satellites. The fall of the Berlin Wall in 1989 following Gorbachev's failed attempt at incremental adjustments toward democratic capitalism represented the capitulation of Communism to capitalism. The results have been devastating for the former USSR. While the Soviet economy grew at relatively robust rates above 5 percent from 1955 to 1970, post-Communist economic performance has fallen to –2 percent in 1989, to –6 percent in 1990, and lower thereafter. The social dislocations associated with such a severe downturn surfaced in the form of skyrocketing unemployment and underemployment, increasing alcoholism, and a sharp drop in longevity among working-aged men (Kennedy, 1993: ch. 11). As the Russian economy imploded, financier George Soros distributed $350 million to teachers and scientists in a desperate attempt to thwart a threatened takeover by xenophobic nationalists (Boudreaux, 1994). Western nations provided substantial infusions of funds in order to prop up the economy of Russia and former Soviet allies. Between 1990 and 1994, $104 billion was injected into the former USSR (Weiss, 1997). Despite the foreign assistance, Russia and former Warsaw Pact nations stumbled toward capitalism. Abrupt privatization policies exacerbated deficits already evident in the fragile social protections of several nations, such as Poland (Sachs, 1992) and the Czech Republic (Orenstein, 1996). In many Russian cities, a voracious mafia exploited the loss of civil authority as the nation introduced privatization. In several satellite nations, particularly the former Yugoslavia and Albania, social order disintegrated into ethnic violence (Spolar, 1997).

Finally, the "bubble" economy of Southeast Asia burst late in 1997, sending a shock wave through the developing nations of the region, threatening the economic stability of the Four Tigers, and swamping financial institutions in Japan. Their difficulties attributed to a corrupt "industrial policy" in which government leaders steered contracts and financial subsidies to firms managed or owned by cronies, the economies of several Southeast Asian nations were imperiled. Much of the financial wheeling and dealing was obscured by governmental loans secured from commercial banks and Japanese holding companies glutted with currency—both beyond the oversight of regulatory agencies, such as the International Monetary Fund (IMF). Soon the quakes that had hit Indonesia and Hong Kong reached South Korea, and the world's financiers shuddered—South Korea was the eleventh-largest economy in the world. By early 1998, the damage was extensive: The currencies of Indonesia, South Korea, the Philippines, Malaysia, and Thailand plummeted, losing more than 60 percent of their previous value (Hirsh, 1998). The stock exchange of Hong Kong, still precarious since the transition from British to Chinese rule, plunged 50 percent. Quickly, the IMF acted to reassure nervous investors, crafting rescue packages for the failing economies. Indonesia received $37.5 billion in aid, Thailand $17.2 billion ("After the Meltdown," 1998). South Korea, by far the most overextended of the Southeast Asian nations, received a bailout package of $57 billion, though this was soon found to be insufficient (Blustein and Chandler, 1998). A *tsunami* of debt swept through the region, toppling financial companies and driving the stock market down as shown in Table 14.2.

As Southeast Asian nations struggled to right their unstable economies, some—such as Korea—acceded to IMF reforms as a condition for receipt of financial aid, others—such

**TABLE 14.2   The Financial Crash of Southeast Asia**

| Country | Stocks | Currency |
|---------|--------|----------|
| Taiwan | −16.6% | −14.1% |
| Indonesia | −44.7 | −69.3 |
| Hong Kong | −42.8 | NA |
| Thailand | −35.4 | −51.9 |
| South Korea | −33.3 | −44.7 |
| Malaysia | −32.9 | −37.0 |
| Singapore | −31.0 | −13.0 |
| Philippines | −25.9 | −28.4 |
| Japan | −16.7 | −10.9 |

*Source:* Bloom Financial Markets.

as Indonesia—continued the corrupt practices that had led to ruin. The imposition of reforms attached to IMF bailout packages salvaged the economies of Southeast Asia, although the consequences for their populations were yet to be known. "The spectacular growth of the Asian tigers in recent decades was not a mirage," concluded economic researchers, "It was based on combining an educated labor force, high saving and rapid capital accumulation, modern technology, and resourceful enterpreneurship—fundamentals which still bode well for the future" (Tobin & Ranis, 1998: 17).

The convergence of these events—the globalization of capitalism, the collapse of Communism, and economic turmoil in Southeast Asia—raised questions about of the possibility of achieving a commonly desired objective of development: the emergence of fully articulated welfare states. Indeed, events of the past decade present a fundamental issue: Are conventional development strategies sufficient to convert poor nations of disparate and backward markets into advanced economies? In his synthesis of varying conceptual formulations of development, Pranab Chatterjee betrays what might be called the "welfare-end-state assumption" as a formal hypothesis: "The higher the position of a state in the world system, the more likely it is that the state will have a welfare infrastructure" (1996: 48). Yet the welfare-end-state assumption has become increasingly illusory. In this respect, the retreat from social provision by industrialized nations, the collapse of command economics, and the turbulence of export-led development in Southeast Asia suggest that the national outcomes attained by the First World may simply not be replicable in the Third World, at least in the foreseeable future.

## The Consequences of Industrialization

While the objective of development may be less certain, there is little question that Third World populations have benefited during the past decades. Significant improvements have occurred in all regions with respect to the percentage of people with access to safe drinking water and of the adult population that is literate, for example. With the exception of sub-Saharan Africa, all regions have seen a reduction in the percentage of underweight children under age five (*Human Development Report,* 1997: 26). Nonetheless, development has tended to be uneven.

### Distorted Development

Sharp unevenness in development, a chronic feature of the Third World, has become more evident in the First World, as well. "Distorted development exists in societies where economic development has not been accompanied by a concomitant level of social development," writes James Midgley. "In these countries, the problem is not an absence of economic development but rather a failure to harmonize economic and social development objectives, and to ensure that the benefits of economic progress reach the population as a whole" (1995: 4).

Severe distortions in development can appear between, as well as within, countries. As shown in Figure 14.1, comparable per capita income can translate into quite different levels of human development. Similarly, significant differences exist between regions within nations (see Figure 14.2). As these figures suggest, distorted development follows patterns that have become geosocial fault lines that follow the urban versus rural, as well as southern versus northern, hemispheric dualism.

## Dualism and Development

In some respects, the consequences of globalization of the economy are reducing the distinctions between north-south and urban-rural issues to the point at which those old terms no longer adequately describe the relationships within or between regions. Until fairly recently, the almost exclusive focus worldwide on economic development was expected to fulfill social development aims, as well. The underlying assumption was that a society that became richer through economic growth would divert an appropriate portion of its excess resources to deal with pressing social problems such as education, health, housing, child welfare, and social protection. This has not happened. As a report from the United Nations Centre for Regional Development showed, economic growth in developing countries "failed to alleviate poverty, reduce interregional disparities and income inequality between various social groups" (Kumsaa : 1996). The shift of the World Bank toward a more consciously targeted social agenda is one of the more dramatic examples of the growing recognition that economic progress does not necessarily and by itself significantly advance social progress for the general population. It may actually have the opposite effect.

The temporary decline of the social sector was expected to occur at least as a phenomenon of the initial stages of economic transformation, but what was less well anticipated was the extent of that decline, in terms of both the depth of its severity and breadth of its reach. Another striking feature of the reduction of social programs has been the universality of the change, which was not limited to transitional economies. In almost all regions, the only direction for social programs has been down.

In the industrial countries, social welfare programs have been reduced with varying degrees of severity for almost two decades. In the UK, the government of Margaret

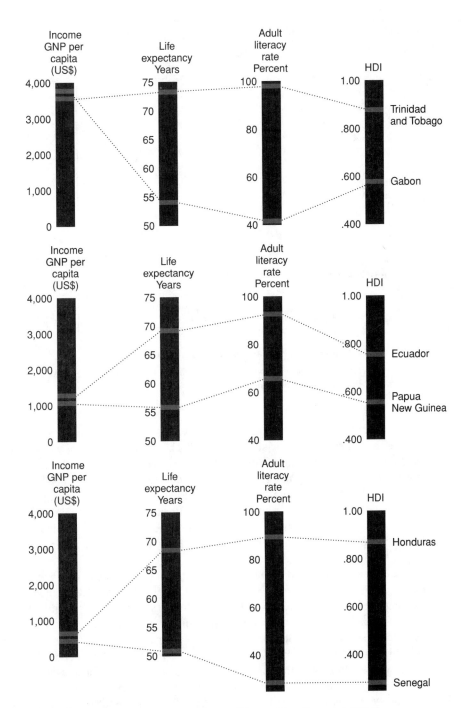

**FIGURE 14.1   Similar Income, Different Human Development, 1994**

*Source:* From *Human Development Report 1997.* Copyright © 1997 by the United Nations Development Programme. Used by permission of Oxford University Press, Inc.

Human poverty index (percent)

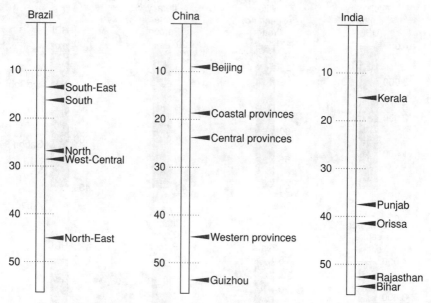

**FIGURE 14.2   Disparity in Human Poverty within Countries**

*Source:* From *Human Development Report 1997.* Copyright © 1997 by the United Nations Development Programme. Used by permission of Oxford University Press, Inc.

Thatcher conducted a focused, purposive, systematic, and highly successful campaign of reducing its tax-supported social "safety-net." The Thatcher strategy was adopted in the United States by the administration of President Ronald Reagan in the 1980s with such political success that its program became the template for additional reductions by subsequent administrations, leading to the Personal Responsibility and Work Opportunity Reconciliation Act of 1996, in partial fulfillment of President Bill Clinton's campaign promise to "end welfare as we know it." One of the provisions of this act eliminated the federal floor on benefits for poor children, reversing a policy that had been in place since the passage of the Social Security Act in 1935.

Even so-called "model welfare states," including Sweden, which is probably the most commonly cited example of social welfare program success, joined the trend of reducing social benefits and began to revise their commitment to social welfare, despite continuous national economic success. Virtually every industrial country reduced social programs to some extent. Only a few, such as Norway, appear to have resisted the trend.

In countries engaged in transforming themselves from socialist command economies to free-market economies, the loss of support from the social sector was the most dramatic, and much more severe than in the First World states. In the period of the five years after the socialist system was replaced by a market orientation, many of the major social benefits that had been part of the system since the early 1950s were severely reduced or entirely swept away. The impact fell heaviest on pensioners and others with fixed incomes in occupations depending on skills of limited marketability. By the early 1990s, new class divisions were appearing in these countries. The emerging privileged classes included craftsmen with necessary, desired, and portable skills, such as carpenters and plumbers; certain relatively indispensable technical professions, such as medicine and dentistry; and service entrepreneurs, such as taxicab operators. In the period before the final collapse of Communism, a limited amount of individual enterprise had been tolerated, and this new cadre already had begun to surface as a new economic and social force. What had been a trickle of change before 1989 quickly became a cascade afterward. Once the market approach was in favor, they were free of restrictions on what they could charge for their services and also free to select their clientele instead of having to serve those assigned by the government. The result was a sharp rise in the incomes of many ambitious artisans and professionals. They were joined in their ascent to power and privilege by those entrepreneurs who could successfully identify and provide the consumer goods and services desired by this newly wealthy elite. Most of the fixed-income professionals, such as teachers, suffered an often brutal and precipitous economic decline as their income lost purchasing power. For old-age pensioners, the change was disastrous. Inflation eroded their ability to buy even the minimum essentials of life. The pathetic sight of elderly people on the street, trying to sell whatever marketable goods they had, including old family treasures, became a familiar scene in all the major cities of countries undergoing the socialist-to-capitalist transformation. They resembled the broken men trying to sell apples on the street corners of America during the Great Depression of the 1930s.

In developing countries, even modest economic transformation sharpened the disparities between social classes and intensified religious and ethnic tensions. The sub-Saharan African nations seem to have fared the worst. One expert was cited as describing the "first three decades of African independence...an economic, political, and social disaster" (Hope, 1997). This forlorn situation was considered the result of statist economic policies, but weakening of autocratic regimes did not improve the economic and social positions of the people so much as it unleashed ancient tribal disputes that strong central governments had held in check. Even worse were problems of simple demographics: The dropping of mortality rates in developing countries placed additional stress on already overburdened systems. Real change in a positive direction is not expected for these countries until well into the twenty-first century.

Similar—although less severe—circumstances can be found in Latin American countries. Although the course of development is somewhat different in each country, Argentina illustrates some of the basic issues. The old Peronist government had provided development programs in the large cities, but it did little to advance the situation in rural areas, accentuating rural-urban dualism. Rural program development did not grow until the middle of the 1990s, when further cuts in fiscal support led to a hue and cry from the Third Sector. Some program support was restored in 1997, with expectations of more before the 1999 elections. The cuts were part of the restructuring program of President Menem, who moved swiftly to privatize a vast array of government services, from the airlines to the post office. These moves initially attracted enormous amounts of foreign capital investment. Although there was little increase from 1995 to 1997, in the first nine months of 1997, growth of the economy reached 8 percent. The excitement caused by this growth was of a somewhat different order for Argentinian workers who lost their jobs. In some cities, the charities of the

Catholic Church were overwhelmed, as in the province of Jujey, where unemployment was estimated in early 1998 at 42 percent; among agricultural workers, unemployment stayed at about 17 percent, while the beneficiaries of the economic changeover enjoyed buying luxury goods in the new, upscale shopping malls (Cohen, 1998).

In the United States, the surging economy has reduced some disparities between certain groups, particularly between black and white workers. The gap between their incomes has narrowed fairly steadily, although unevenly after 1965, according to 1990 data (Barringer, 1992). In some urban centers, the gap virtually disappeared by the mid-1990s between black and white intact two-parent families where the parents were under 50 years of age. Nevertheless, black poverty remained more extensive and more resistant to amelioration than it did for whites. Moreover, the benefits of the economic growth were not distributed equitably throughout the population. The difference between the resources and income available to the top quintile and the bottom quintile continued to grow. By 1997, the top 5 percent of Americans controlled well over half of all national assets, and the gap between the wealthy and the poor had become a chasm, yawning wider than at any time in the preceding half-century. As early as 1988, the poorest U.S. quintile, primarily rural, was described as "America's Third World," one of the largest "undeveloped" national populations on Earth (McCormack, 1988).

In some respects, the north-south discrepancies have come national, apparent within countries in the North as well as in the South. The older, more traditional societies have been replaced by societies in which a new class of business entrepreneurs has achieved an extraordinary growth in wealth while the workers, who formerly were able to make an adequate living and enjoy a reasonable standard of living with the addition of government social programs, have seen their quality of life erode.

The rural-urban dualism that began with the coming of the industrialization in the North has arrived in all the countries undergoing economic transformation to the free market, and it has intensified in the North. One 1990 study of this dualism in the United States found few families in the top income quintile living in rural areas (Barancik, 1990), and the size of the gap continued to increase after that study was reported. The introduction of industrial agriculture in developing countries greatly increased productivity, but it also displaced rural laborers. With nowhere else to go, they moved their entire families to the urban areas in the hope of finding paid work. In Latin American and Southeast Asian countries, squalid slums bloomed at the peripheries of the largest cities. Normal services such as clean water, sewerage, and transportation, already taxed beyond capacities, have not reached these outlying areas, resulting in grave problems of health, sanitation, housing, crime, and others. This created a conundrum for developers: traditional methods of agriculture cannot compete on the world market with mechanization, but to the extent that agriculture is mechanized, rural workers will be displaced and, having nowhere else to go, will continue to migrate to already overcrowded cities. Within a very few years, the largest cities in the world will not be in the North, where they have dominated world commerce for generations; their center of gravity will shift to the poorest nations—that is, those least able to address the social problems that cannot be avoided.

The dilemma of development success is that it is bringing larger, more complex problems in its wake. This is a dilemma that is familiar to development: As maternal, infant and child mortality drops, population rises, generally faster than the growth of resources in the country to support it. UNICEF reported that child mortality has fallen 50 percent in recent years; since 1980s, immunization programs alone have saved the lives of about 20 million children (*State of the World's Children,* 1996). As the applause for this stunning achievement subsides, the grim realization sets in that the children who have been saved may have lives worse than death, a purgatory of famine, war, and exploitation. During the famine in Somalia, more than half the children under five on the first day in 1992 were dead by the first day of 1993. UNICEF has reported large numbers of children under arms or brutalized by wartime measures. Rural children are sold into prostitution throughout the major cities of south Asia, where a quarter of all the children in the world live. It is estimated that there are 1 million child prostitutes in Asia alone, with many more in countries in Africa and Latin America. Brazil may have half a million. Many of these children are made available for "sex tours" that cater to men, both heterosexual and homosexual, from North America and Europe (Lewis, 1994). Even the most dedicated welfare state advocates have come to recognize that the "basic conditions for social policy have changed and will continue to change for the foreseeable future" (Morris & Hansan, 1997), and these changes will have an impact on the directions and strategies of development.

# The New World Order

While the expression "new world order" was coined, as Communist governments in Europe collapsed, to explain the end of the "cold war," the term has wider implications than those associated with saber rattling. Parallel developments of comparable magnitude, such as the spread of information technology, the rise of the theocratic state, and the limits of environmental degradation, have converged to form a world that is qualitatively different than that which evolved after the Second World War. Foremost among these developments has been global capitalism.

## Global Capitalism

The past four decades have witnessed one of the greatest transitions in economic history—the globalization of advanced capitalism. While many pockets of statism, government monopoly, and authoritarianism persist, the advance of the capitalist economies has been unrelenting. The emergence of capitalism as the dominant model of economic policy at the close of the century is linked to a broader process called globalization.

Globalization refers to the integration of markets, information, technology, and cultures. It is a by-product of international mass communications, the information revolution, and improved transportation. It is also a consequence of a closer integration of political and economic policies through multilateral and international political and banking organizations. It could be said that globalization began with the conclusion of the Second World War, at which time several forces began to work in concert. Not coincidentally, the modern international monetary system was being designed at Bretton Woods. The world soon moved off of the gold standard and currency was comparatively freely exchanged in the open market. By unshackling East Asia and Western Europe from the last vestiges of feudalism and mercantilism, the postwar period created the groundwork for an integrated system that surpassed the exchange of goods and services. With the advent of inexpensive and instantaneous information, the process of integration accelerated. As Moises Naim (1997) observes, "Globalization is not a passing phenomenon that affects only international money managers, CNN viewers, or Internet surfers. It represents a profound redefinition of roles, possibilities, and risks around the world that is altering the very nature of international relations, and, therefore, the nature of foreign policy."

Whether the advance of global capitalism is good or bad depends upon where one sits. At a minimum, it must be observed that the process remains quite uneven. Vast segments of the globe remain comparatively unaffected by the changes in international markets. Sub-Saharan Africa, rural Latin America, and segments of South Asia function much as they have for decades—cut off from the modern world by isolation, poverty, and entrenched oligarchies. Other questions remain to be answered:

- Are governments becoming obsolete as they lose their capacity to regulate the global economy?
- Is the shift in manufacturing jobs to the developing world rendering an entire social strata in the West similarly obsolete?
- As nations compete for comparative advantage, is the welfare state an anachronism that must be jettisoned in order to remain competitive?

A cursory response to these questions would indicate that yes, governments are less powerful at regulating the international market than they are at regulating their own. And international agencies such as the UN are even less effective. Burdened with its own feudal era management and hiring practices, the UN can hardly expect to rise to the challenge of easing the transition to a global economy.

With respect to the question of manufacturing jobs in the industrial world, the writing has been on the wall for at least twenty years. Capital is more mobile than labor and, like water, will seek the lowest point. Labor unions and socialist political parties in Europe and the United States will be hard-pressed to do more than slow the process of manufacturing losses abroad. The creation of regional trade syndicates, such as the EEC and NAFTA, tend to accelerate this loss of higher wage jobs.

Is the welfare state an artifact of a different era? Without question, this institution is undergoing radical change. It has been downsized and decentralized in order to cut government spending throughout the industrial world. Moreover, the culture of global capitalism does not mesh well with the entitlement concepts that undergird the welfare economy. Finally, the choice between welfare states and unemployment presents itself. It can be argued that the high rates of unemployment in Europe are an artifact of high social spending. National policies must confront the trade-off between jobs and wages.

Is the globalization debate a passing fashion among Western elites? Probably not. Globalization matters; it is more than the spread of mass culture. "Due to the increased importance of trade, the options available to national policymakers have narrowed appreciably over the last three decades" (Rodrik, 1997). International forces have a profound impact on the domestic welfare of most peoples. Yet ironically, as information explodes about the global economy and culture, civilizations have seemed to turn inward. The United States is as isolationist as ever; apart from the occasional military venture that distracts them, Americans are enormously disinterested in and ill-informed about world affairs. The distrust of modernization throughout the Islamic world is another example of the inward turn. And, as Claude Moisy (1997) has noted, throughout the world, news coverage is increasingly centered on local affairs.

The globalization of democracy, markets, and culture is significant, but must not be tainted by hubris of the West. The integration of economies has been fairly fluid, yet on the cultural and political fronts, local and regional resistance to westernization is strong. Commitment to democratic principles, especially individual freedoms, is uneven. The treatment of women and cultural minorities remains a major challenge to development in dozens of countries. Although global capitalism has done much to improve the world's standard of living, many of those attributes that thrive in a market economy—such as democracy, equality under the law, and the presence of a vital civil society—are still nascent or absent in many countries.

## The Diffusion of Postindustrial Technology

As significant a technological breakthrough as the genetic engineering that introduced the Green Revolution, computer-assisted information transmission has fundamentally altered international development. Some developing nations have capitalized on the information revolution by negotiating production and assembly plants with First World information companies, as evident in the *maquiladora* plants that line the border between the United States and Mexico. With isolated exceptions, however, the information age is bypassing the Third World. As a result, many developing nations that have yet to become industrialized are even further handicapped in exploiting the advantages of the information age.

The obstacles faced by developing nations in adopting postindustrial technology are multiple. Fundamental is the absence of infrastructure, particularly electrical power. As even the casual traveler will appreciate, erratic electrical power is a chronic problem in many developing countries. A dozen nations in the Third World report the disruption or loss of at least one-fourth of the electrical power they produce. The waiting time for installation of a new telephone line is 5 years or more in 33 nations. Some 58 Third World nations report having fewer than one fax machine per 1,000 population, compared to 26.3 for Australia and 53.9 for the United States. Twenty-two nations have fewer than 5 computers per 1,000 population, but this figure fails to depict the discrepancy between the First and Third Worlds. While Australia reports 275.8 and the United States 328.0 personal computers per 1,000 population, the computer is so rare in developing nations that 64 countries do not even have data on the number of machines within their borders. A parallel discrepancy exists with respect to Internet hosts. Australia and the U.S. claim 220.15 and 313.15 Internet hosts per 10,000 respectively; 68 developing nations report less than one host per 10,000 population, and 29 fail to record any data at all (*World Development Indicators,* 1997: tables 5.11, 5.14).

These data are inauspicious for the developing world. As noted in the previous chapter, nations are in dynamic relationships with one another. Any group of nations with a structural advantage over others stands to benefit correspondingly; any group of nations with two structural advantages over others will experience benefits that increase geometrically. That is the dilemma that the information revolution poses for the Third World.

Having already industrialized, First World nations command the physical infrastructure in power, electrical grid, and satellite transmission to accelerate into the information age, while developing nations have yet to deploy the infrastructure associated with industrialization. The consequences are substantial. Except for small islands of information technology sited at universities or in major cities, developing nations are at a competitive disadvantage with respect to the First World that is structural by nature. Given the tens of billions of dollars in international currency that is transmitted hourly via electronic networks that are globally linked, is it any wonder that the finance ministers of developing nations complain that their nations' economic future is in the hands of speculators that have no understanding of the impact of their decisions on the welfare of millions of people?

## The Rise of Ethnic and Theocratic States

As the means of doing business continues to be concentrated in fewer and fewer hands at an ever-increasing rate, apprehension in the countries that see themselves falling farther behind continues to mount and sometimes to find expression in various kinds of radical movements. These movements may have an economic, religious, ethnic, or other base; but where they are successful, the political results they produce frequently fall into one of two categories: a rigid, restrictive, autocratic regime, or a kind of anarchic chaos. An obvious example of the former was the overthrow by the Shi'ah Islamic fundamentalists of the moderate, reform government of the Pahlevi regime in Iran; an obvious example of the latter was the almost total political breakdown with the revival of religious and ethnic factionalism in the Balkans after two generations of relatively peaceable relations.

These sorts of movements may combine a number of pressing issues. For example, there may be both religious and political questions, as in Ulster; or tribal and ethnic identities, as among Uyghurs, Slavs, Russians, and Kazakhs in Kazakhstan; or political and tribal antagonisms, as between the Tutsis and Hutus in Rwanda; or cultural and religious differences, as with the Sikhs in India; or they may combine the cultural, religious, and political, as in the partition of Cyprus.

An implicit assumption often made in development planning, especially in projecting probable outcomes of development in Third World countries, is that social and economic reform that brings improvement in the standard of living and quality of life, along with loosening of restrictive central authority control, will eventuate in accord and harmony among traditionally competing factions. That is not necessarily what happens.

Any major change brought about by development may easily be interpreted by the existing politically and economically privileged groups as less a great step forward for their country than a direct and present threat to their cherished prerogatives. It is usually more attractive to a ruling elite to preserve the cultural, religious, and ethnic traditions and preferences that give shape and meaning to one's world than to alter them and have to face an unknown future, bereft of the identity and privilege of custom. After all, the goal of ethnic identification, as Lieberson (1985) put it, is "never towards greater disadvantage."

The basis for ethnic conflicts and the rise of ethnic states may rest on ancient animosities, but these are often exacerbated by more recent competition for resources. For example, the surge of hatred and armed violence in the Balkans stemmed from religious conflict between Christians and Moslems that reached back hundreds of years, but it also had ethnic and political antecedents (between Bosnians and Croats) that were even older. Meanwhile, Slovenia was able to withdraw from the disorder of its neighboring states in favor of economic development within a multicultural context that managed to establish a stable political profile and a prosperous economy.

In the case of economic reform in countries that already were industrialized, but under state socialism, the consequences of political reform and economic restructuring are likely to expose serious social problems that had existed under the former governments, but either had been denied or suppressed, or had been ameliorated through the risk-reduction strategy of an omnipresent, if somewhat limited, scope of social program benefits. The premier case is Russia, but other socialist countries illustrate the problem as well. In Poland, for example, urban poverty had "been around for a long time…[but] was scrupulously concealed and obfuscated in official reports" (Marcinkowski, 1990). Russia was not alone in punishing those, politicians or scholars alike, who sought to identify common social problems. Economic issues were another case: Problems of production and distribution, with their resultant chronic shortages and inferior goods, could not be openly addressed. Religious and ethnic tensions, crime, poor or corrupt health services, oppression of minorities, the whole spectrum of social and economic problems were made nontopics for public discussion or even for academic analysis. Indeed, the Soviet Union converted traditional, humane social institutions for the service of political/social control, such as the commitment of political dissidents to asylums for the mentally ill. Social nonconformity was met with programs of mandatory "re-education"; economic nonconformity, such as free market advocacy, was considered criminal behavior, with conviction often leading to disappearance into a Siberian gulag. All the Warsaw Pact nations of Central/Eastern Europe pursued the same repressive policies, to a greater or lesser extent, as did the Stalinist and Maoist regimes elsewhere.

Once the Soviet Union was dissolved and Russia moved toward the market economy, many social problems surfaced throughout the new society. Crime, homelessness, poverty, poor health care, racial and religious conflict, and others were some of the issues that came to dominate the national agenda. In the early stages of the transformation, huge income disparities quickly appeared, and with them, the appearance of an elite that sometimes emerged from the ranks of the workers, but more often represented the entrenched bureaucrats and apparatchiks who had been able to manipulate the system to their own benefit.

Nor was Russia alone in this development. Other issues notwithstanding, the core of conflicts in the formerly socialist states always revolve around issues of economic dominance. This is why Russian professors of Marxist ideology quickly learned to teach about free market ethics; why in Hungary, the "hidden privatization" of cooperatives left the former managers and influential members of those cooperatives as their new owners (Laki, 1994–95); why even in formerly Stalinist Mongolia, one of the least developed nations, only the "inefficient and unprofitable" enterprises were sold, while the government (and its bureaucrats) retained 50 percent ownership in the profit-making and "strategically important" industries (Kumsaa & Jones, 1997).

The struggle to create new ethnic states or at least to achieve religious domination of the state included some relatively short-term conflicts, but more often, the determined commitment to hatred demonstrated an enduring and persistent capacity. Armed conflict between Tamils and the Sinhalese in Sri Lanka has gone on for 13 years; the war in Afghanistan has been fought for 19 years; in Angola the war of more than 30 years' duration has left the majority of the population with no memory of a time without strife. Almost no part of the globe is free of ethnic or religious hostility, or even open warfare. In some cases, the objective is no less than total annihilation of the opposition, either by death or expulsion. This goal has been given the euphemistic name of "ethnic cleansing," and the struggle to achieve it takes place within existing states, or between states. Whatever the reasons used to justify brutality and killing, there always appears to be a determination to achieve or to retain economic advantage. This aim, and the likelihood of open conflict, seems more pronounced at times of political and economic change. The Romanian oppression of ethnic Hungarians in Transylvania took the form of leveling their villages and farms and replacing them with Moscow-style housing blocks; the long simmering and occasionally violent revolution of the Mayan Indians in the Chiapas province of Mexico grew out of government inaction to counteract the effects of land degradation that threatened the livelihood of this rural population; the resistance of the African National Congress in South Africa was based largely on economic inequality and the exploitation of the black majority.

There is almost no place where ethnic tensions and clashes have failed to appear since World War II ended. They have persisted into the present, often in response to economic issues. The examples are seemingly endless: the Tigray Peoples' Liberation Front of Ethiopia; the Kurdish resistance in Iraq and Turkey; the separatist movement of the Malay Moslems in Thailand, or the separatist movement of the Roman Catholic French ethnics in Protestant, English Canada; the endless clashes between the Israelis and Palestinians. All these and many more have their foundation largely on development issues, both social and economic.

The success of the Shi'ah overthrow of the Shah of Iran may have served to embolden other fundamentalist religious groups to try to establish theocratic states elsewhere in the Arab world. Although such movements have been undertaken ostensibly on religious grounds, they seem also to be responses to economic and social changes that significantly alter the traditional economic and social structures. In Iran, women were beginning to win various rights that they are not allowed to enjoy under orthodox Islamic law, including the right to paid employment outside the home. Among the first acts of the theocratic regime was to restore the religious laws and regulations that rigidly order women's lives. This drive to replace existing governments in Moslem countries with conservative theocracies has continued to grow since the Iranian Islamic State was created, with outbreaks in Egypt, Morocco, Thailand, and the Indian subcontinent.

To be sure, the aim of establishing conservative religious states has not been confined to Islam. Although less direct, sweeping or dramatic, other movements to affix religious principles to secular state police authority may be more the rule than the exception. Women, in particular, face severe economic restrictions in traditionally Catholic countries, whether Roman or Eastern. In Latin American countries, newspaper advertisements openly require female applicants to be young and attractive; women may "age out" of employment very early in their careers. Even the United States, which prides itself on its historic separation of church and state, contains many conservative Protestant groups whose agenda is to enact laws that regulate social behavior in conformity with their religious beliefs. Such laws have direct and indirect economic consequences for women, as well as more marginal groups, such as homosexuals and unwed mothers. It is no exaggeration to claim that in many countries and regions, the modern secular state is in danger of being supplanted by ethnic and religious states organized to preserve or secure economic privilege for the dominant ethnic or religious group, and in the case of theocratic states, to return to a patriarchal and restrictive social and economic orientation.

Gross economic disparity has led religious and ethnic organizations to deal with the disadvantages of the member groups. Such groups are animated by a determination to change the political system that is perceived as the heart of the problem, or at least, the most likely path to change. With the collapse of state socialism, the centrally planned economy ended, but so did the centrally planned social welfare programs and the centrally controlled political structures that kept in check the latent ethnic, racial, and religious antagonisms. Transformation of the command economy into one that responds to free market mechanisms brought inflation, massive job dislocation, and sharp decline in social welfare benefits. Although these events were expected, it was believed that they would be temporary. Nonetheless, their immediate impact was devastating to many whose fear and anger manifested itself in a desire to restore the old, hated, but at least familiar system or to secure a place of privilege for those whose ethnic or religious identity one shared. That is, the demand might have taken the form of restoration to the security, if not comfort, of the old way, or to assure an advantage in receiving the benefits of the new economy.

Dissatisfaction thus was directed toward any government that seemed to place one's ethnic or religious group at a disadvantage. Horowitz (1982) postulated that people in many countries would reject any government, whether socialist or Western democratic or military oligarchy, that was considered to treat them unfairly or which seemed incapable of providing a rational economy. He noted a growing impatience with the burden of inefficient government, inequitable access to or distribution of resources, and apparent lack of moral or ethical principles to guide official decisions. The ethnic state is seen as a way to correct the inequities, or at least to reassign them; the theocratic state is seen as a way to inspire if not transcend government.

International development has been forced to address these movements simply because long years of planning and working can be undone in a brief time. Other disciplines have expressed concern over these risks in development work: sociologists have warned of the possible peripheral consequences of development, or lack of development, or inadequately planned development, or poorly implemented development. Ferge (1997) referred to the risk of "decivilization," with increased poverty and greater isolation of the poor, with a general decline in respect for the moral authority of the political and economic leadership. Similar concerns have been expressed by Judt (1997), including the risk of neofascism's becoming attractive in many countries, as it did during the social and economic dislocations of the 1920s and 1930s. Judt recommended a reconsideration of principles as necessary to avoid the "desperation and disaffection" that can become a volatile fuel for ethnic and religious restructuring when development and economic restructuring fail.

## The Environmental Factor

One of the most important unifying themes in international development over the past three decades is the growing recognition of the environmental factor. While many still disagree on the best pathway for global development, few argue that it must not be at the expense of future generations and their ability to extract an adequate quality of life from an increasingly imperiled environment. Virtually all of the major international development agencies and multilateral development banks have incorporated an environmental agenda into project and lending activity. Large-scale environmentally suspect projects such as the stalled World Bank Narmada Dam Project in western India are becoming the white elephants of a previous development agenda.

The centrality of the environmental factor is partly a by-product of the social movements of the past few decades in which women, ethnic minorities, and environmentalists have become far more effective at raising public awareness and influencing public policy. The shared use of social change tactics to influence large, comparatively impersonal organizations such as the World Bank has had a profound impact on the way in which these entities engage in development assistance. The emergence of vocal and effective nongovernmental agencies to press the environmental agenda with private funding has also accelerated the trend toward greener development. But apart from the political forces being brought to bear on development is the compelling nature of the facts in question. Even an avid industrialist cannot help but be swayed by growing evidence of the environmental fragility of the planet. From the deforestation of the Amazon, estimated at 17,000 square kilometers a year ("Brazil," 1998), to the desiccation of the Aral Sea, the unbiased observer is confronted with the enormous human impact of economic development. Moreover, development practitioners who traverse the world on projects would have to be unseeing to ignore the depredation of resources in developing contexts. On a flight from Bangkok to Bombay, the clear skies of the Bay of Bengal become muddy as one makes landfall; the smokestacks of Hyderabad and the countless dung fires in rural villages are among the sources of the perpetual atmospheric soup that envelops the subcontinent. Further east, Madagascar from 12,000 meters looks like a bleeding scar in the south Indian Ocean. A night flight over the Persian Gulf after Saddam Hussein torched the oilfields of Kuwait stands out among our memories of environmental catastrophe. Three Mile Island and Chernobyl also remind us of the permanency of the damage humanity can wreak upon the living environment that supports it. Now, in an era when biological and chemical warfare are tools of the trade, it is impossible to contemplate a development agenda that is not linked to the environmental factor.

Far from being an unrelenting and mindless swaggering toward the unplanned future, development can be a thoughtful, humane, and Earth-friendly process. The lessons of the past few decades have not gone unheeded by the most powerful agencies and organizations in the world. And as a result, it has become anachronistic to belabor the International Monetary Fund and so called multinational firms for producing the Third World's woes. Notwithstanding the development critics' claim to the contrary, development theory and practice have evolved and been attenuated to new findings. The simplistic dualism of top-down versus bottom-up, for instance, fails to account for the sophistication of current field-level practice. One would be hard-pressed to find a current official international development project that did not give serious consideration to the environment, women, and cultural heritage, as well as to the more traditional measures of success such as economic internal rate of return.

To be sure, the developing world is replete with examples of poorly planned and implemented projects. The salinization of the Indus River Basin through poor irrigation drainage or the effect of China's "one-child" policy on female life expectancy are among a plethora of cases of unintended consequences. Simple choices can have profound implications; for example, the decision to install a deep tubewell may improve efficiencies for one group of farmers while drying up the shallow tubewells of the poor. Moreover, when a project imposes unintended consequences or costs upon the environment (negative externalities), these impacts may be long-standing and, in some cases, permanent.

The recognition of the central importance of maintaining the dynamic equilibrium of the environment is now at the core of development theory and practice. Although many exceptions will occur, we can hope that the environmental factor will increasingly guide projects toward sustainable growth and development.

## New Directions in Development

The vectors defining the New World Order present challenges as well as opportunities for international development. Consider the plight of the eastern European nations wishing to privatize their economies after the collapse of the Soviet Union, for example. An antiquated phone system made discussion and negotiation of business deals too slow. So instead of rewiring the communication network, aspiring entrepreneurs acquired battery-powered portable phones that relied on satellite relays, effectively bypassing the old wired system altogether. Thus, much of the future of international development rests with the capacity to exploit new opportunities concomitant with the New World Order.

### Microcredit

In contrast to the large-scale infrastructure projects mounted by international aid organizations that promised benefits that would "trickle-down" to the poor, microcredit has evolved as an alternative to capital formation. The microcredit "trickle-up" strategy is a grassroots initiative to use social solidarity in place of traditional property as a basis for collateral. Small peer-lending groups are offered credit on a rotating basis, and loans at below-market interest rates are repaid in installments. Incorporated in many microcredit projects are social activities that promote self-sufficiency, civic responsibility, and political empowerment. The Grameen Bank, the first large-scale microcredit project, has been widely cited as a model of social and economic development at the community level. As noted in the earlier case study, after two decades of operation, the Grameen Bank has enlisted tens of thousands of members and has become the largest bank in Bangladesh. BancoSol, a microcredit venture established in Bolivia, claims a membership of 75,000 and a loan portfolio of $47.5 million (Prescott, 1997). Similar initiatives have evolved in Latin America and Africa (Otero and Rhyne, 1994; Webster and Fidler, 1996).

Microcredit is a particularly important innovation for development because it facilitates the integration of the poor with the mainstream institutions of democratic capitalism. Instead of a charitable handout, microcredit relies on the inherent capacity of the poor to be productive, and through labor and thrift to eventually pull themselves out of poverty. Economic success easily translates into political empowerment, especially when microcredit programs are organized in a manner that encourages open participation. Microcredit has two additional virtues: Many peer-lending projects require that the poorest member of the group receive the first loan, thus accomplishing a modest degree of redistribution; many of the most successful programs target benefits to the poorest of Third World populations, peasant women. In its various forms, microcredit has become a feature of innovations in democratic governance as well as economic aid (Reilly, 1995), and has become an icon for progressive worldviews (Henderson, 1996).

Its considerable grassroots achievements notwithstanding, microcredit must transcend two barriers to become a truly global vehicle for development. First, microcredit institutions must adopt computer information systems to manage their accounts. This is no small challenge for projects that have evolved in the Third World, often in remote rural locations. Yet, the acquisition and incorporation of high technology is essential if such organizations are to exploit the opportunities that arise at the interface of finance and technology. As recently as 1996, for example, the accounts managed by the Grameen Bank in Dakka were recorded by typewriter or hand. Second, microcredit must become integrated with the network of world capitalism if it is to play a role on the world stage. One of the more jarring contrasts of recent events in international development has been the failure of the national financial institutions of nations in Southeast Asia, and the enormous bailout packages offered by the International Monetary Fund to rescue them. It is questionable how much of the tens of billions in fiscal bailout will trickle down to the poor, despite the fact that several nations do have extensive microcredit projects in place. If microcredit were more integrated with world capital markets, it could provide a direct conduit of aid to the Third World poor. In its absence, international financial institutions will continue to collude with the bankrupt economic elites of development nations.

## Currency Transaction Fees

Until grassroots, microcredit institutions become integrated with global markets, regulation of international currency exchanges is in order. Currently, approximately $1 trillion per day is transmitted by unrestricted currency exchanges, an amount equivalent to the United Kingdom's annual output ("Will It Swallow Your Job?" 1998). Unregulated, international capital markets function as the "global casino," a "giant poker game for experts" that generates billions for some investors, but their winnings are often at the expense of fragile economies of developing nations. Currently, national banks of developing nations often skirmish with international traders in a contest over currency values. As Hazel Henderson and Alan Kay note, this often places the Third World poor in the middle:

> ordinary people, first of one country, then of another, will continue to be the losers in the struggle between the currency traders and the central banks whenever such open market buying operations fail or central banks try raising interest rates and trigger domestic recessions. (1996: 7)

Billionaires, such as George Soros, have built fortunes on currency fluctuations, an accomplishment that has led to criticism from Third World finance ministers.

A free-market currency exchange established by international aid organizations would provide some oversight to currency trading (Mendez, 1995). Henderson and Kay have proposed going a step further by levying a tax on currency transactions. They note that a trivial tax of .001 percent, or 1 cent per $1,000 traded, would generate $3 billion per day in revenues; a larger tax of .01 percent would return ten times that amount (1996: 26). They suggest imbedding the tax in the software used by currency traders so that it functions as part of market transactions. Logically, a small portion of this revenue would be used to operate an international oversight agency, but most of it could be diverted to economic development activities in the Third World. Affixed to global market activity, such a tax would increase as international trade expands, adding revenue for developing nations in accordance with the expansion of global trade, noted in Table 14.1.

## Restructuring International Aid

A current paradox in international development is that, just as the needs of the "fourth world" are more conspicuous and the economic "miracle" of Southeast Asia has come into question, the international agencies best positioned to contend with them are under increasing scrutiny. The United Nations has been much criticized in the United States, resulting in an American refusal to fully fund its assessed contribution for UN activities. The conservative case for structural reform states that the UN, with 53,744 personnel, is an excessively staffed organization that promotes a "one-world" agenda choreographed by Third World elites (Helms, 1996). In January 1997, African diplomat Kofi Annan became Secretary General, and he promptly moved to dampen conservative criticism of the UN (Goshko, 1997a). In an attempt to retrieve the approximately $1 billion withheld by the United States, Annan proposed a series of structural reforms: eliminating 1,000 vacant positions; merging 12 departments into five; consolidating six aid agencies into two groups, one for development, the other for humanitarian assistance; reorganizing human rights and terrorism functions; and creating a department to deal with disarmament (Goshko, 1997b). By the end of 1997, Annan 's reforms were being "buried by a blizzard of questions and objections" from members of the General Assembly (Crossette, 1997). Facing gridlock in the General Assembly, Annan rejoiced when American Ted Turner announced his intention to contribute $1 billion to the UN over the coming decade.

Similarly, the World Bank sought new leadership under the direction of James Wolfensohn. Under Robert McNamara, the World Bank had expanded its operations more than tenfold to $12 billion by investing in large infrastructure projects in the Third World. When the debt crisis reduced many of the developing nations to insolvency, the World Bank instituted economic reforms that tended to reduce governmental expenditures, those that had become most essential to the Third World's most indigent populations. The response by critics of the World Bank was a withering condemnation of the Bank's retreat from the poorest of the poor (Blustein, 1996). Upon assuming the helm of the World Bank, Wolfensohn, a former financier and cellist, promised "sweeping reorganization" of the institution's $20 billion budget and 10,100 person bureaucracy. With respect to development projects, Wolfensohn proposed to steer the Bank away from infrastructure projects that were more likely to be underwritten by commercial capital and toward social and community ventures in the Third World. Dissatisfied with the Bank's previous success rate in two-thirds of projects, Wolfensohn proposed an increase to 75 percent (Stevenson, 1997a). Confronted with having to explain a new World Bank headquarters that featured a 28-foot waterfall and cost $314 million in Washington, D.C. (Sharoff, 1997), Wolfensohn went on the offensive, proposing "The Strategic Compact," a two-year, $250 million reorganization (Blustein, 1997).

By late 1997, Wolfensohn was slowly turning the organizational behemoth, incrementally decreasing funds committed to physical infrastructure, and increasing loans to social and environmental projects. Regardless, the Bank was losing influence in development circles as much larger reserves of commercial capital eclipsed those of the Bank (Stevenson, 1997b). Then came the economic collapse in Southeast Asia. Suddenly, debt that had been underwritten by commercial banks was on the verge of crushing the regional economies that had grown so rapidly from exports, and the World Bank played an essential role in arbitrating the rescue packages. Whether this Third World operation was consistent with Wolfensohn's new direction in favor of innovative programs for the poorest or simply saving corrupt elites from economic folly remained to be seen.

# An Integrated Model of Development

At the close of the millennium, the need for an integrative model of development has become as clear as it is urgent. Previous formulations have proved unreliable in vaulting the Third World into the modern era. The postwar formulation that featured megaprojects leveraged by international finance agencies foundered on the shoals of corruption. Instead of facilitating the emergence of nascent economies of the Third World, it precipitated crushing amounts of debt that debilitated developing nations during the 1980s. Instead of expediting prosperity throughout the Third World, import substitution became associated with the emergence of a more economically backward Fourth World. A more recent development formula has also lost credibility. The promise of industrialization through export-led policies crashed along with Southeastern Asian economic institutions that they fostered. Instead of featuring a template for developing nations, the implosion of the Tiger economies presented a conundrum for international financial institutions: Divert financial reserves to shore up the corrupt industrial policies of Third World elites as opposed to funding more responsible and effective indigenous initiatives, such as micro-credit.

The interaction of the various factors comprising an integrative model has been assembled by the UN Development Program, as noted in Figure 14.3. While the "human development–economic growth" includes the most essential components of an integrative model, there are additional factors that must be incorporated.

## Transnational Accords

The notion that groups of nations aggregate for purposes of mutual interest is not new. Self-defense pacts have an extensive history, and they continue as important institutions today, as the North Atlantic Treaty Organization (NATO) attests. More recent incarnations with broader ramifications include the European Economic Union, which has been followed by other regional syndicates, including the Association of Southeast Asian Nations (ASEAN) and the North American Free Trade Agreement (NAFTA). In response to the

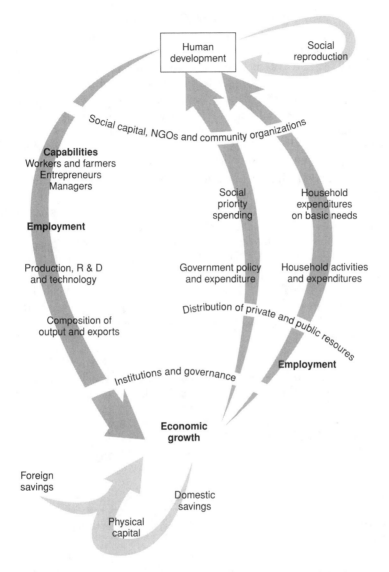

**FIGURE 14.3   From Human Development to Growth—and Back**

*Source:* From *Human Development Report 1996* by United Nations Development
Program. Copyright © 1996 by the United Nations Development Programme. Used by
permission of Oxford University Press, Inc.

predatory practices of First World nations, developing nations have created their own protective associations, though these have not been particularly successful at promoting
growth of their member nations. Regardless, development scholars, such as Michael
Todaro (1994: 512–13), believe Third World nations have little choice but to continue
experimenting with regional alliances if they are to prosper economically.

As nations evolve regional syndicates, they also develop a capacity to provide mutual development assistance. Such assistance is transnational by nature, as evident in the Social Charter that the European Economic Community (EEC) has instituted. According to the Social Charter, EEC member nations are obliged to adhere to policies and benefits for workers and dependents regardless of their national origin. The emergence of transnational accords thus becomes a mechanism for nations to facilitate development, but in a way that is quite different from the traditional model for social provision, the welfare state. Table 14.3 proposes the social compact as an alternative to the welfare state. Using the Social Charter as a template, the "social compact" may become an alternative to the welfare state for developing nations, one that draws on regional resources in order to establish benefits and opportunities that are more modest than the more extensive provisions characteristic of First World welfare states.

Adjusted for the factors previously noted, an integrative model can provide necessary direction for development in the coming millennium. Doubtlessly, further evolution of international development will bring with it more elaborate models replete with the most sophisticated statistics, giving the field a scientific facade. As appealing as this may be for those with technical inclinations, the ultimate purpose of development must be restated—to enhance the human condition in a sustainable manner, respective of individual rights and cultural practices. In the end, development is less arcane than it is a matter of simply embracing human dignity. Wislawa Szymborska said as much in accepting the 1996 Nobel Prize for Literature:

> Most of the earth's inhabitants work to get by. They work because they have to. They didn't pick this or that kind of job out of passion; the circumstances of their lives did the choosing for them. Loveless work, boring work, work valued only because others haven't even got that much—this is one of the harshest human miseries. And there's no sign that the coming centuries will produce any changes for the better as far as this goes. (1996: 28)

TABLE 14.3   Types of Organized Response to Need

| Characteristic | Welfare State | Social Compact |
|---|---|---|
| Era | Industrial | Postindustrial |
| Auspice | Nation state | Regional trade syndicate |
| Ideology | (neo)Marxist | Democratic capitalism |
| Dominant norm | Equality | Equity |
| Benefit archetype | Entitlements as right | Benefits conditioned on productivity |
| Standard of benefits | Uniform nationwide | Vary regionally |
| Role of state | Provides benefits, services | Brokers policy accords |
| Role of beneficiary | Recipient | Consumer |
| Method of finance | Compulsory taxes | Elected contributions |
| Organizational structure | Public bureaucracy | Private membership organization |

# REFERENCES

"After the Meltdown." (1998). *World Press Review* (January).

Barancik, S. (1990). *The Rural Disadvantage.* (Washington, DC: Center on Budget and Policy Priorities).

Barringer, F. (1992). "White-Black Disparity in Income Narrowed in 80s, Census Shows," *New York Times,* July 24, pp. A1, A16.

Black, Jan. (1991). *Development in Theory and Practice* (Boulder: Westview).

Blustein, Paul. (1996). "Missionary Work," *Washington Post Magazine* (November 10).

Blustein, Paul. (1997). "Wolfensohn Proposes World Bank Shakeup," *Washington Post* (February 21).

Blustein, Paul, and Clay Chandler. (1998). "Wrapping Up South Korea's Christmas Present," *Washington Post Weekly* (January 5).

Boudreaux, Richard. (1994). "U.S. Billionaire Donates Millions to Russian Causes," *Los Angeles Times* (March 17).

"Brazil: Trees and the Law." (1998). *The Economist* (February 7), p. 36.

Chatterjee, Pranab. (1996). *Approaches to the Welfare State* (Washington, DC: National Association of Social Workers).

Cohen, Roger. (1993). "Europe's Recession Prompts New Look at Welfare Costs," *New York Times* (August 9).

Cohen, Roger. (1998). "Argentine Economy Reborn but Still Ailing," *New York Times* (February 6), p. A1.

Crossette, Barbara. (1997). "Thick Maze of Objections Slows Down U.N. Reforms," *New York Times* (October 24).

Ferge, Z. (1997). "And What If the State Fades Away?" Paper delivered at the European Sociological Association Third Annual Conference, Essex University, 19 pp.

Goshko, John. (1997a). "U.N. Reform Pits U.S. and the Third World," *Washington Post* (March 10).

Goshko, John. (1997b). "U.N. Reform Falls Short, Critics Say," *Washington Post* (July 17).

Helms, Jesse. (1996). "Saving the U.N." *Foreign Affairs* (September/October).

Henderson, Hazel. (1996). *Building a Win-Win World* (San Francisco: Berrett-Koehler).

Henderson, Hazel, and Alan Kay. (1996). "Introducing Competition into the Global Capital Markets" (Washington, DC: Global Commission to Fund the United Nations).

Hirsh, Michael. (1998). "Now It's Epidemic," *Newsweek* (January).

Hope, K. (1997). "The Political Economy of Policy Reform and Change in Africa," *Regional Development Dialogue* 18(1), Spring, pp. 126–38.

Horowitz, I. (1982). "The New Fundamentalism," *Society* 20(5), November/December, pp. 40–47.

*Human Development Report.* (1996). (New York: Oxford University Press).

*Human Development Report.* (1997). (New York: Oxford University Press).

"International Partners: Mary Rakocy," (Kasungu, Malawi: Habitat for Humanity, n.d.).

Judt, T. (1997). "The Social Question Revidivus," *Foreign Affairs* 76(5), September/October, pp. 95–117.

Kennedy, Paul. (1993). *Preparing for the 21st Century* (New York: Vintage).

Kumsaa, A., (1996). "Transitional Economies and Regional Development Strategies in Developing Countries. In A. Kumsaa and H. Khan, Eds., *Lessons from Five Low-income Developing Countries* (Nagoya: United Nations Center for Regional Development), pp. 1–14.

Kumsaa, A., and J. Jones. (1997). "Mongolia's past and present transition," *Regional Development Dialogue* 19(1), Spring, pp. 110–22.

Kunz, Diane. (1997). "The Marshall Plan Reconsidered," *Foreign Affairs* (May/June).

Laki, M. (1994–95). "Opportunities for Workers' Participation in Privatization in Hungary." In M. Laki, J. Szalai, and A. Vajda, Eds., *Participation and Changes in Property Relations in Post-Communist Societies* (Budapest: Aktiv Tarsadalom Alapitvany).

Lewis, S. (1994). "They Will Not Get Away with It Forever," *The Progress of Nations* (New York: UNICEF).

Lieberson, S. (1985). "Unhyphenated White in the United States," *Ethnic and Racial Studies* 8(1), pp. 159–80.

Marcinkowski, A. (1990). "The Problems of the Polish City and Search for a Community Solution." In M. Bochenska-Seweryn and K. Frysztacki, Eds., *The Emerging Independent Nonprofit Sector in Poland* (Cracow: Jagiellonian University Press).

Marshall, Tyler. (1994). "The Welfare Costs That Are Dragging Down Europe," *Los Angeles Times* (February 15).

McCormack, J. (1988). "America's Third World," *Newsweek* (August 8), pp. 20–24.

Mead, W. (1998). "The New Global Economy Takes Over," *Mother Jones* 23(2), March/April, pp. 32–41.

Mendez, Ruben. (1995). "Paying for Peace and Development," *Foreign Policy,* No. 100 (Fall).

Midgley, James. (1995). *Social Development* (London: Sage).

Moisy, C. (1997). "Myths of the Global Information Village," *Foreign Policy, 107* (Summer), pp. 78–87.

Morris, R., and J. Hansen. (1997). "Redefining the Role of Government." In J. Hansen and R. Morris, Eds. *The National Government and Social Welfare* (Westport: Auburn House).

Naim, M. (1997). "Editor's Note," *Foreign Policy, 107* (Summer), pp. 5–10.

Orenstein, Mitchell. (1996). "The Failures of Neo-Liberal Social Policy in Central Europe," *Transition,* Vol. 28 (June).

Otero, Maria, and Elisabeth Rhyne. (1994). *The New World of Microenterprise Finance* (West Hartford, CT: Kumarian Press).

Prescott, Edward. (1997). "Group Lending and Financial Intermediation," *Federal Reserve Bank of Richmond Economic Quarterly* (Richmond, VA: Richmond Federal Reserve Bank).

Reilly, Charles. (1995). *New Paths to Democratic Development in Latin America* (Boulder, CO: Lynne Reinner).

Reynolds, David. (1997). "The European Response," *Foreign Affairs* (May/June).

Richburg, Keith. (1998). "Exploiting Asia's Crisis," *Washington Post* (January 22).

Rodrik, D. (1997). "Sense and Nonsense in the Globalization Debate," *Foreign Policy, 107* (Summer), pp. 19–37.

Sachs, Jeffrey. (1992). "Building a Market Economy in Poland," *Scientific American* (March).

Sander, Gordon. (1996). "Sweden After the Fall," *Wilson Quarterly* (Spring).

Sharoff, Robert. (1997). "World Bank: Architecture as Diplomacy," *New York Times* (March 9).

Spolar, Christine. (1997). "Albanian Leader Takes New Term as Protests, Violence Spread," *Washington Post* (March 4).

*State of the World's Children.* (1996). (New York: UNICEF).

Stevenson, Richard. (1997a). "World Bank Chief Asks Slimmer Staffs and Better Lending," *New York Times* (February 21).

Stevenson, Richard. (1997b). "The Chief Banker for the Nations at the Bottom of the Heap," *New York Times* (September 14).

Szymborska, Wislawa. (1996). "I Don't Know," *The New Republic* (December 30).

Titmuss, Richard. (1968). *Commitment to Welfare* (New York: Pantheon).

Tobin, James, and Gustav Ranis. (1998). "Flawed Fund," *The New Republic* (March 9).

Todaro, Michael. (1994). *Economic Development,* 5th ed. (New York: Longman).

Wallace, Charles. (1995). "Welfare Is No Longer on a Roll in New Zealand," *Los Angeles Times* (April 21).

Webster, Leila, and Peter Fidler. (1996). *The Informal Sector and Microfinance Institutions in West Africa* (Washington, DC: World Bank).

Weiss, Charles, Jr. (1997). "Eurasia Letter: A Marshall Plan We Can Afford," *Foreign Affairs,* Vol. 106.

"Will It Swallow Your Job?" (1998). *World Press Review* (February).

Wolfensohn, James. (1997). "The Challenge of Inclusion," Address to the Board of Governors (Washington, DC: World Bank).

*World Development Indicators.* (1997). (Washington, DC: World Bank).

Yergin, Daniel, and Joseph Stanislaw. (1998). *The Commanding Heights* (New York: Simon & Schuster).

# INDEX